Managing

FOR

DUMMIES®

Managing FOR DUMMIES®

by Richard Pettinger, Bob Nelson, and
Peter Economy

John Wiley & Sons, Ltd

Managing For Dummies®

Published by
John Wiley & Sons, Ltd
The Atrium
Southern Gate
Chichester
West Sussex
PO19 8SQ
England
E-mail (for orders and customer service enquires): cs-books@wiley.co.uk

Visit our Home Page on www.wileyeurope.com

British Library Cataloguing in Publication Data: A catalogue record for this book is available from the British Library.

ISBN: 978-0-470-05689-9

Printed and bound in Great Britain by Bell and Bain Ltd, Glasgow.

10 9 8 7 6 5 4 3 2

WILEY

About the Authors

Richard Pettinger (BA, MBA, DipMktg) has taught at University College London since 1989, where he is a lecturer in management. He teaches on the foundation courses, organisational change, and construction marketing courses. He has also taught strategic and operations management, the management of change, human resource management, and leadership to a wide range of undergraduate, postgraduate, professional, and international students. Richard is also enhancing and developing Management Studies Centre activities and courses, including the directorship of the new Information Management for Business course.

Since 2005, Richard has been a visiting professor at the Jagiellonian Business School, Krakow, teaching strategic management and developing a common UCL/Jagiellonian syllabus in strategic management and organisational change.

Richard is the author of over thirty business and management books and textbooks, and also writes journal, conference, and study papers.

Bob Nelson, PhD (San Diego, CA), is founder and president of Nelson Motivation, Inc., a management training and products firm headquartered in San Diego, California. As a practising manager, researcher, and best-selling author, Bob is an internationally recognised expert in the areas of employee motivation, recognition and rewards, productivity and performance improvement, and leadership.

Bob has published 20 books and sold more than 2.5 million books on management, which have been translated into some 20 languages. He earned his BA in communications from Macalester College, his MBA in organisational behavior from UC Berkeley, and his PhD in management from the Peter F. Drucker Graduate Management Center of the Claremont Graduate University.

Visit his Web site at www.nelson-motivation.com or contact Bob directly at BobRewards@aol.com.

Peter Economy (La Jolla, CA) is associate editor of *Leader to Leader*, the award-winning magazine of the Peter F. Drucker Foundation for Nonprofit Leadership, and author of numerous books. Peter combines his writing expertise with more than 15 years of management experience to provide his readers with solid, hands-on information and advice. He received his bachelor's degree (with majors in economics and human biology) from Stanford University and his MBA at the Edinburgh Business School. Visit Peter at his Web site: www.petereconomy.com.

Dedication

To any manager who has struggled to do the job and every employee who has had to live with the consequences.

Authors' Acknowledgements

From Richard: I acknowledge three managers who have had great influence on the ways in which things have turned out: John Taylor, who set very high standards all round, and who remains a close colleague and friend; Jack Cadogan at the Manpower Services Commission who let me do things my way; and Graham Winch who started me off at UCL. I have had wonderful support and enthusiasm all the way through from Ram Ahronov, Peter Antonioni, Roger Cartwright, Kelvin Cheatle, Frances Kelly, Paul Griseri, Jacek Klich, Robert Pringle and Andrew Scott – great colleagues all. Thanks for the great work of Rachael Chilvers and everyone at Wiley in making this project into something that we can all be proud of. Finally, I would like to dedicate this book to my wife Rebecca, without whom nothing is possible.

From Bob: Thanks to Jim Reller, a delegator par excellence in my first corporate position at Control Data Corporation, who often gave out assignments with a disclaimer such as, 'I could probably do this task faster than you, but I believe you'll learn a lot from the process'; Dr. Ken Blanchard, also known as *The One Minute Manager,* who I worked with for more than ten years, demonstrated how to get the best efforts from people by using the softer side of management and never directly telling them what to do; and Dr. Peter F. Drucker who I worked with in my PhD studies at Claremont Graduate University.

Thanks for the ongoing love and support of my father Edward, my wife Jennifer, and my children, Daniel and Michelle.

From Peter: Richard Vaaler, contracting officer for the Department of Defense, taught the benefits of upholding high ethical standards and making things happen. At Horizons Technology, Inc., CFO Debbie Fritsch demonstrated the importance of hiring and developing superior employees and challenging authority. Pat Boyce, president, taught me to look beyond the obvious to ferret out the truth and also showed me the value of becoming one with your customers. Jim Palmer, chairman, embodied the value of painting the big picture – a vision for all employees to strive for.

These people taught more than just the technical skills of assigning work, conducting a performance appraisal, or disciplining an employee. They also emphasised the people side of management: how to motivate employees by example, reward them when they exceed your expectations, and make each customer feel like he or she is your only customer – even if you have thousands of others.

Thanks to my mother Betty Economy Gritis, my wife Jan, and my children, Peter J, Skylar Park, and Jackson Warren, for their everlasting love and for putting up with my crazy life. May the circle be unbroken.

Publisher's Acknowledgements

We're proud of this book; please send us your comments through our Dummies online registration form located at www.dummies.com/register/.

Some of the people who helped bring this book to market include the following:

Acquisitions, Editorial, and Media Development

Executive Editor: Jason Dunne

Executive Project Editor: Martin Tribe

Commissioning Editor: Samantha Clapp

Project Editor: Rachael Chilvers

Development Editor: Kathleen Dobie

Content Editor: Steve Edwards

Copy Editor: Sally Lansdell

Technical Reviewer: Brenda Pugh, Achieve Greatness, Ltd.

Proofreader: Christine Lea

Special Help: Jennifer Bingham

Cover Photo: © Getty Images/Shannon Fagan

Cartoons: Ed McLachlan

Production

Project Coordinator: Jennifer Theriot

Layout and Graphics: Claudia Bell, Brooke Graczyk, Stephanie D. Jumper, Heather Ryan

Proofreader: David Faust

Indexer: Techbooks

Publishing and Editorial for Consumer Dummies

    Diane Graves Steele, Vice President and Publisher, Consumer Dummies

    Joyce Pepple, Acquisitions Director, Consumer Dummies

    Kristin A. Cocks, Product Development Director, Consumer Dummies

    Michael Spring, Vice President and Publisher, Travel

    Brice Gosnell, Associate Publisher, Travel

    Kelly Regan, Editorial Director, Travel

Publishing for Technology Dummies

    Andy Cummings, Vice President and Publisher, Dummies Technology/General User

Composition Services

    Gerry Fahey, Vice President of Production Services

    Debbie Stailey, Director of Composition Services

Contents at a Glance

Introduction *1*

Part 1: You Want to Be a Manager *7*
Chapter 1: You're a Manager – Now What? 9
Chapter 2: Delegation: Getting Things Done without Getting Done In 29
Chapter 3: Lead, Follow, or Get Out of the Way..47

Part 11: Managing People *59*
Chapter 4: Recruitment and Selection: The Million-Pound Decision........................61
Chapter 5: Inspiring Employees to Better Performance....................................79
Chapter 6: Coaching and Development 97

Part 111: Making Things Happen *107*
Chapter 7: Setting Goals and Targets..109
Chapter 8: Performance Appraisal and Management: People and Projects 125
Chapter 9: Tackling Performance Appraisals 141

Part 1V: Working with (Other) People *155*
Chapter 10: Effective Communication: Getting Your Message Across 157
Chapter 11: Working Together in Teams and Groups 179
Chapter 12: Managing Flexible Workers 197
Chapter 13: Ethics and Office Politics 207

Part V: Tough Times for Tough Managers *229*
Chapter 14: Managing Change at Work..231
Chapter 15: Employee Discipline: Setting Standards and Enforcing Them.............241
Chapter 16: Resignations, Dismissals, and Redundancies 257
Chapter 17: Managing Me: Taking Care of No. 1 273

Part V1: Tools and Techniques for Managing *285*
Chapter 18: Budgeting and Accounting 287
Chapter 19: Harnessing the Power of Technology 309
Chapter 20: Developing and Mentoring Employees...................................321
Chapter 21: Keeping Track of Management Trends 335

Part VII: The Part of Tens **343**

Chapter 22: Ten Common Management Mistakes 345

Chapter 23: The Ten Best Ways to Recognise Employees 351

Chapter 24: Ten (Plus Two) Classic Business Books You Need to Know About 357

Index **363**

Table of Contents

Introduction 1

About This Book..2
How to Use This Book 2
Conventions Used in This Book 3
Foolish Assumptions 3
How This Book Is Organised...3
    Part I: You Want to Be a Manager 3
    Part II: Managing People......................................4
    Part III: Making Things Happen 4
    Part IV: Working with (Other) People 4
    Part V: Tough Times for Tough Managers.............4
    Part VI: Tools and Techniques for Managing 4
    Part VII: The Part of Tens 5
Icons Used in This Book..5
Where Do I Go from Here?...6

Part 1: You Want to Be a Manager 7

Chapter 1: You're a Manager – Now What? 9

Identifying the Different Styles of Management 10
    Macho management 11
    Participative management 12
    The best way 12
Recognising that Quick Fixes Don't Work 13
Meeting the Management Challenge.............................15
    The old rules don't work any more.....................15
    It's a new world...17
    Trust is not a four-letter word 18
Explaining the New Functions of Management 21
    Energise 21
    Empower...22
    Support 23
    Communicate 24
Taking the First Steps towards Becoming a Manager....25
    Look and listen 25
    Do and learn 26

Chapter 2: Delegation: Getting Things Done without Getting Done In 29

Delegating: The Manager's No. 1 Tool 30
Explaining the Myths about Delegation 32
Myth No. 1: You can't trust your employees to be responsible 32
Myth No. 2: When you delegate, you lose control of a task and its outcome 33
Myth No. 3: You're the only one who has the answers.................33
Myth No. 4: You can do the work faster by yourself.....................34
Myth No. 5: Delegation dilutes your authority 34
Myth No. 6: Your employees get recognition for doing a good job, not you...................................35
Myth No. 7: Delegation decreases your flexibility.......................35
Myth No. 8: Your employees are too busy 36
Myth No. 9: Your workers don't see the big picture 36
Trusting Your Employees 37
Taking the Seven Steps to Delegate 37
Looking at the Good and the Bad of Delegation...........................38
Always delegate these things..39
Avoid delegating these things...41
Checking Up, Not Checking Out 43

Chapter 3: Lead, Follow, or Get Out of the Way 47

Understanding the Differences between Management and Leadership 48
Looking at What Leaders Do..49
Inspire action 49
Communicate...50
Support and facilitate 51
Surveying Leading Leadership Traits...52
Optimism 53
Confidence 54
Integrity 54
Decisiveness...55
Fostering Collaborative Leadership 56

Part II: Managing People 59

Chapter 4: Recruitment and Selection: The Million-Pound Decision 61

Asking for the Right Stuff 62
Defining the Job and the Person 64
Finding Good People..65
Being the Greatest Interviewer in the World 67
Asking the right questions 68
Interviewing do's 69
Interviewing don'ts 70

Evaluating Your Candidates 72
    Checking references 72
    Reviewing your notes 74
    Conducting second (or third) interviews............................74
Engaging the Best (and Leaving the Rest) 75
    Being objective 75
    Trusting your gut..76
    Adjusting after the offer 77

Chapter 5: Inspiring Employees to Better Performance **79**
The Greatest Management Principle in the World......................80
    Recognition isn't as simple as it looks................................80
    Biscuit motivation 81
Discovering What Employees Want 83
    Creating a supportive environment 85
    Having a good game plan 87
Deciding What to Reward..87
Starting with the Positive..89
Making a Big Deal about Something Little 91
Money and Motivation 92
    Compensating with wages and salaries...............................92
    Realising when incentives become entitlements 92
    Working out what motivates your staff 93
    Realising that you hold the key to your employees' motivation ...95

Chapter 6: Coaching and Development **97**
Playing a Coach's Role...98
Coaching: A Rough Guide..100
Coaching Metaphors for Success in Business.............................101
Confronting Turning Points 102
    Making turning points into big successes...........................102
    Making coaching special 103
Tapping into the Coach's Expertise 104

Part III: Making Things Happen *107*

Chapter 7: Setting Goals and Targets **109**
If You Don't Know Where You're Going, How
    Do You Know When You Get There? 110
Identifying SMART Goals..113
Setting Goals: Less Is More 115
Communicating Your Goals to Your Team....................................117
Juggling Priorities 119
Using Your Power for Good: Making Your Goals Happen 122

Chapter 8: Performance Appraisal and Management: People and Projects **125**

  Taking the First Steps 126
  Developing a System for Providing Immediate
    Performance Feedback 128
      Setting your checkpoints: The milestones.....................128
      Reaching your checkpoints: The actions 129
      Acting in sequence: The relationships 129
      Establishing your timeframe: The schedules 130
  Putting Performance Measuring and Monitoring into Practice 131
      Studying Sheerness Steel..131
      Reducing shrinkage..134
  Using Gantts, PERTs, and Other Yardsticks..............................136
      Stacking up the Gantt or bar chart 136
      Following flow charts...138
      Inserting software...139
  Reading the Results 140

Chapter 9: Tackling Performance Appraisals **141**

  Appraising Performance: Why it Matters................................142
  Spelling Out the Performance Appraisal Process 143
  Avoiding Common Traps..147
  Sorting Out Why Appraisals Go Bad......................................149
  Preparing for the No-Surprises Appraisal...............................151

Part IV: Working with (Other) People *155*

Chapter 10: Effective Communication: Getting Your Message Across **157**

  Understanding Communication: The Cornerstone of Business.............158
  The Cutting Edge of Communication and Information Technology 160
      Speed and flexibility 161
      Gadgets and gizmos 162
      Videoconferencing and electronic meetings................162
  Badmouthing Bad Communication...163
      Poisoning the well of communications........................165
  Hear, Hear! The Art of Listening 166
  Harnessing the Power of the Written Word 169
  Making Presentations 171
      Preparing presentations 171
      A picture is worth a thousand words 173
      Making your presentation 177

Chapter 11: Working Together in Teams and Groups **179**

Phasing Out the Old Hierarchy 180
    Downsizing organisations 180
    Moving towards co-operation 182
Empowering Your Teams 183
    Recognising the value of an empowered workforce 183
    Managing your teams 184
Identifying the Advantages of Teams 185
    Smaller and nimbler 185
    Innovative and adaptable 186
Setting Up and Supporting Your Teams 186
    Formal teams 187
    Informal teams 188
    Self-managed teams 189
    The real world 190
    New technology and teams 192
Meetings: Putting Teams to Work 193
    The trouble with meetings 193
    The eight keys to great meetings 195

Chapter 12: Managing Flexible Workers **197**

Making Room for a New Kind of Employee 198
    Preparing to be flexible 198
    Anticipating changes to the organisation's culture 200
Managing from a Distance 201
Managing Different Shifts and Patterns of Work 202
Telecommuting and Homeworking 203

Chapter 13: Ethics and Office Politics **207**

Doing the Right Thing: Ethics and You 208
    Defining ethics 208
    Creating a code of ethics 209
    Living ethics 212
Evaluating Your Political Environment 213
    Assessing your organisation's political environment 213
    Identifying key players 215
    Redrawing your organisation chart 216
Scrutinising Communication: What's Real and What's Not? 218
    Believing actions, not words 218
    Reading between the lines 219
    Probing for information 220
Uncovering the Unwritten Rules of Organisational Politics 220
    Be friendly with all 221
    Help others get what they want 222

Don't party at company parties 223
Manage your manager 224
Move ahead with your mentors 224
Be trustworthy...225
Protecting Yourself 225
Document for protection..226
Don't make promises you can't keep...226
Be visible 227

Part V: Tough Times for Tough Managers 229

Chapter 14: Managing Change at Work 231
Keeping Pace 232
Choosing between legitimate urgency
    and crisis management 232
Recognising and dealing with crises..233
Embracing Change 234
Identifying the four stages of change...234
Figuring out if you're fighting change 235
Aiding Your Employees through Change 237
Encouraging Employee Initiative 238
Making Changes within Yourself 240

Chapter 15: Employee Discipline: Setting
Standards and Enforcing Them 241
Understanding the Need for Employee Discipline.................................242
Following Procedures 243
Focusing on Performance, Not Personalities 245
Identifying the Two Tracks of Discipline...246
Dealing with performance problems: The first track....................247
Dealing with misconduct: The second track 248
Disciplining Employees: A Suite in Five Parts 250
Describing the unacceptable behaviour 251
Expressing the impact to the work unit 251
Specifying the required changes 252
Outlining the consequences 252
Providing emotional support 253
Putting it all together 253
Making a Plan for Improvement 254
Implementing the Improvement Plan 255

Chapter 16: Resignations, Dismissals, and Redundancies **257**

Accepting Resignations 257
Dealing with Dismissals..258
   Making employees redundant 259
   Processing the types of dismissal 261
   Gathering good reasons for firing 263
Easing into Dismissal..264
   Trying to avoid the inevitable 265
   Working up to dismissal 266
Heeding the Warning Before You Fire an Employee 267
Firing an Employee Fairly in Three Steps 268
Determining the Best Time to Dismiss...271

Chapter 17: Managing Me: Taking Care of No. 1 . . . .**273**

Weighing the Work–Life Dilemma 273
   Reaping the benefits of a balanced work life and personal life....274
   Managing balance..275
Avoiding Becoming a Workaholic 276
Knowing the Symptoms of Stress...277
Managing Your Stress 279
   Changing the things you can...279
   Accepting the things that you can't change 281
   Trying out some specific stress-reduction exercises 283

Part VI: Tools and Techniques for Managing *285*

Chapter 18: Budgeting and Accounting **287**

Exploring the Wonderful World of Budgets 287
Making a Budget..289
Budgeting and the Real World 291
   Producing real budgets...293
   Staying on budget..294
Understanding the Basics of Accounting......................................295
   Working out the accounting equation 296
   Knowing double-entry bookkeeping.....................................299
Identifying the Most Common Types of Financial Statements.............300
   The balance sheet 300
   The profit and loss account 300
   The cash-flow statement 304
Analysing Business Health...304
   Using financial ratios 304
   Using other measures 306

Chapter 19: Harnessing the Power of Technology **309**

Using Technology to Your Advantage 310
Know your business...310
Create a technology-competitive advantage 310
Develop a plan 311
Get some help 312
Evaluating the Benefits and Drawbacks of Technology 312
Improving Efficiency and Productivity......................................314
Getting the Most Out of Information Technology 317
Planning and Implementation..318

Chapter 20: Developing and Mentoring Employees **321**

Explaining How Employee Development Helps 322
Creating Career Development Plans..325
Helping Employees to Develop..328
Finding a Mentor, Being a Mentor 330
Balancing Development and Downsizing 332

Chapter 21: Keeping Track of Management Trends **335**

Beginning with the Basics...336
Creating a Learning Organisation 337
Making a Flat Organisation 338
Unlocking Open-Book Management..339
Understanding Six Sigma..340

Part VII: The Part of Tens.................................*343*

Chapter 22: Ten Common Management Mistakes **345**

Not Making the Transition from Worker to Manager.............................345
Not Setting Clear Goals and Expectations 346
Failing to Delegate..346
Failing to Communicate..347
Not Making Time for Employees..347
Not Recognising Employee Achievements 348
Failing to Develop..348
Resisting Change...349
Going for the Quick Fix over the Lasting Solution 349
Taking It All Too Seriously 349

Chapter 23: The Ten Best Ways to Recognise Employees **351**
Support and Involvement...352
Personal Praise..352
Autonomy and Authority 352
Flexible Working Hours 353
Training and Development...353
Your Time 354
Written Praise 354
Electronic Praise 354
Public Praise 355
And So to Money 355

**Chapter 24: Ten (Plus Two) Classic Business
Books You Need to Know About** **357**
In Search of Excellence 357
Managing for Results 358
The Human Side of Enterprise..358
The Peter Principle 359
Competitive Strategy 359
The One Minute Manager...360
Management Stripped Bare 360
In Search of European Excellence...360
The Fifth Discipline: The Art and Practice
  of the Learning Organisation 361
Understanding Organisations..361
Body and Soul: The Body Shop Story..361
Maverick!...362

Index..*363*

Introduction

∙ ∙

*C*ongratulations! As a result of your astute choice of material, you're about to read a completely fresh approach to the topic of management. If you've already read other books about management, you have surely noticed that most of them fall into one of four categories: (1) textbooks; (2) deadly boring tomes that make great paperweights; (3) 'I did it my way' – the war stories of successful and/or high-profile individuals (some of these are admittedly excellent, while others are little more than cynical attempts to cash in on transient fame/notoriety), or (4) recycled platitudes glazed with a thin sugar-coating of pop psychobabble, which sounds great on paper, but fails abysmally in the real world, and is as superficial as a coat of paint.

Managing For Dummies is different. First, this book is fun. Our approach reflects our strong belief and experience that management can be fun, too. You can get the job done and have fun in the process. We even help you to maintain a sense of humour in the face of the seemingly insurmountable challenges that all managers have to deal with from time to time. On some days, you'll face challenges – perhaps to your limit or beyond. However, on many more days, the joys of managing (showing a new skill to an employee, helping land a new customer, accomplishing an important assignment, and so on) can bring you a sense of fulfilment that you never imagined possible.

Second, popular business books seem to be here today and gone tomorrow. Like it or not, many managers (and the companies they work for) seem to be ruled by the business fad of the month. In *Managing For Dummies*, we get away from this by concentrating on tried and tested solutions to the most common situations that real supervisors and managers face: solutions that stand up over time and can be used in turbulent times. You won't find any mumbo-jumbo here – just practical solutions to everyday problems.

Managing For Dummies breaks the rules. It provides a comprehensive overview of the fundamentals of effective management presented in a fun and interesting format. It neither puts you to sleep nor is so glib or syrupy that it rots your teeth. We know from personal experience that managing can be an intimidating job. New managers – especially ones promoted into the position for their technical expertise – are often at a loss as to what they need to do. Don't worry. Relax. Help is at your fingertips.

About This Book

Managing For Dummies is perfect for all levels of managers. New managers and managers-to-be can find everything you need to know to be successful. Experienced managers are challenged to shift your perspectives and to take a fresh look at your management philosophies and techniques. Despite the popular saying about teaching old dogs new tricks, you can always make changes that ease your job – and the jobs of your employees – and make them more fun and a lot more effective.

But, even the most experienced manager can feel overwhelmed from time to time – new tricks or not. For Bob, it was when he was giving an important business presentation before a group of international executives – only to be told by one of the executives that his flies were undone. Although Bob did score bonus points for getting his audience's attention with this novel fashion statement, he could've done so in a more conventional way.

For Peter, it was when he reprimanded an employee for arriving late to work and later discovered that the employee was late because she had stopped at a bakery on the way to work to buy Peter a cake in celebration of Boss's Day. Needless to say, the event wasn't quite as festive as it could've been!

For Richard, it was when he turned up to give a presentation to a group of managers and executives from the central banking sector. Just before he was due to go one, he was told that he had been given the wrong brief – and that please could he speak on a different subject altogether. He survived – but it was the longest two hours of his life!

Whether you're new to the job or are faced with a new task in an old job, all managers feel overwhelmed sometimes. The secret to dealing with such feelings is to discover what you can do better (or differently) to obtain the results you want. When you do make a mistake, pick yourself up, laugh it off, and learn from it.

How to Use This Book

Despite the obvious resemblance of this book to one of the yellow bricks on Dorothy's road to Oz, the proper way to use this book is not as a doorstop or a makeshift paperweight. You can use this book in one of two ways:

- ✔ If you want to find out about a specific topic, such as delegating tasks or recruiting employees, you can flick to that section and get your answers quickly. Faster than you can say, 'Where's that report I asked for last week?' you'll have your answer.

✔ If you want a crash course in management, read this book from cover to cover. Forget going back to college to get your MBA – you can save your money and take a trip to the South of France instead.

This book is unique because you can read each chapter without having to read what comes before. Or you can read each chapter without reading what comes after. Or you can read the book backwards. Or you can just carry it around with you to make an impact.

Conventions Used in This Book

For Dummies books avoid jargon, dense reams of text, and fiddly footnotes. To make your reading experience even easier, we use a couple of simple conventions. *Italics* introduce new terms, which are always followed by a definition. Monofont text is used for Web addresses. We tend to alternate between using male and female pronouns in alternating chapters to be fair to both genders.

Foolish Assumptions

As we wrote this book, we made a few assumptions about you, our readers. For example, we assumed that you're already a manager – or a manager-to-be – and that you're truly motivated to discover some new approaches to managing organisations and to leading people. We also assumed that you're ready, willing, and able to commit yourself to becoming a better manager.

How This Book Is Organised

Managing For Dummies is organised into seven parts. Each part covers a major area of management practice. The chapters within each part cover specific topics in detail. Following is a summary of what you'll find in each part.

Part 1: You Want to Be a Manager

Successful managers master several basic skills. This part begins with a discussion of what managers are and what they do, and then looks at the most basic management skills: organisation, delegation, and leadership.

Part II: Managing People

The heart of management boils down to getting tasks done through others. This process starts with attracting, recruiting, and keeping talented workers and extends to motivating and coaching them to go above and beyond expectations.

Part III: Making Things Happen

Making things happen is another important aspect of managing that starts with knowing where you're going and how to tell when you've arrived. In this part, we consider goal setting, measuring and monitoring employee performance, and conducting performance appraisals.

Part IV: Working with (Other) People

Successful managers have discovered that building bridges to other workers and managers – both inside and outside the organisation – is important. This part covers communicating, making presentations, building high-performance teams, and dealing with office politics.

Part V: Tough Times for Tough Managers

As any manager can testify, management is not all fun and games. In fact, managing can be downright difficult at times. In this part, we consider some of the toughest tasks of managing: managing change, disciplining and firing employees, and managing yourself.

Part VI: Tools and Techniques for Managing

Being a manager requires that you acquire and apply certain technical tools and skills. This part discusses guidelines for accounting and budgeting and working with today's technologies.

The most successful managers know that standing still in business is the same as falling behind. Good managers always look to the future and make plans accordingly. Developing and training employees and creating a learning organisation are also covered in this part.

Part VII: The Part of Tens

Finally, we include the Part of Tens: a quick-and-easy collection of chapters, each of which gives you ten (or so) pieces of information that every manager needs to know. Look to these chapters when you need a quick refresher on managing strategies and techniques.

Icons Used in This Book

To guide you along the way and draw your attention to particular bits of information, this book uses icons along its left margins. You'll see the following icons in this book:

The pearl points out wise sayings and other kernels of wisdom that you can take with you on your journey to becoming a better manager.

Remember these important points of information, and you'll be a much better manager.

This icon highlights tips and tricks that make managing easier.

These anecdotes from Bob, Peter, Richard, and other real-life managers show you the right – and sometimes wrong – way to be a manager.

If you don't heed the advice next to these icons, the situation may blow up in your face. Watch out!

Where Do I Go from Here?

If you're a new or aspiring manager, you may want to start at the beginning (isn't that a novel concept?) and work your way through to the end. Simply turn the page and take your first step into the world of management.

If you're already a manager and are short of time (and what manager isn't short of time?), you may want to turn to a particular topic to address a specific need or question. The Table of Contents gives a chapter-by-chapter description of the topics in this book. You can also find specific topics in the index.

Enjoy your journey!

Part I
You Want to Be a Manager

'I'm getting worried about the boss.'

In this part . . .

*B*efore you can become an effective manager, you need to master some basic skills. In this part, we find out what management is, and we cover some of the most important managing skills, including delegating tasks to employees and becoming a leader.

Chapter 1

You're a Manager – Now What?

In This Chapter

▶ Working out what management *is*

▶ Moving from being a doer to becoming a manager of doers

▶ Understanding the changing workforce

▶ Defining the key functions of management

▶ Taking the first steps towards becoming a manager

Congratulations! You're reading this book, so you're probably

✔ A manager

✔ A manager-to-be

✔ An individual who's uncontrollably attracted to books with bright yellow and black covers (not that there's anything wrong with that!)

Of course, if you're simply curious and want to discover the intimate details about the kinds of management techniques that can help you get the best from your employees every day of the week, you're equally welcome!

Managing is truly a calling – one that, as managers, the authors of this book are proud to have answered. *We're the few. The proud. The managers.* In the world of business, no other position allows you to have such a direct, dramatic, and positive impact on the lives of others and on the ultimate success of your enterprise. (Except, of course, for the person who fixes the coffee machine.)

Identifying the Different Styles of Management

Managing is about:

- ✔ Getting things done through others
- ✔ Using scarce resources to best advantage
- ✔ Coping with change and uncertainty
- ✔ Achieving and delivering results

Seems simple enough. But why do so many bright, industrious people have trouble managing well? And why do so many companies today seem to offer flavour-of-the-month training programmes? How often have you been introduced to some hot new management concept – guaranteed to turn your organisation around in no time flat – only to watch it fade away within a few months, if not sooner? Of course, as soon as one management fad disappears, another is waiting in the wings to replace it.

> 'What? You didn't catch onto that concept of Six Sigma? That's okay – we decided that it doesn't really work anyway. Now, we want you to pay close attention to this video on Armadillo Management (hard on the outside, soft on the inside!) – this is the latest thing. The managing director read an article about it in the *Financial Times* and wants us to implement it throughout our United Kingdom operations right away!'

 Unfortunately, good management is a scarce commodity – at once precious and fleeting. Despite years of evolution in management theory and the comings and goings of countless management fads, many workers – and managers, for that matter – have developed a distorted view of management and its practice, with managers often not knowing the right approach to take, or exactly what to do. 'And, if managers don't know what to do, employees certainly won't either.

Do you ever hear any of the following statements at your office or place of work?

- ✔ We don't have the authority to make that decision.
- ✔ She's in charge of the department – fixing the problem is her responsibility, not ours.
- ✔ Why do they keep asking us what we think when they never use anything we say?

✔ I'm sorry, but that's our policy. We're not allowed to make exceptions.

✔ If my manager doesn't care, I don't either.

✔ It doesn't matter how hard you work; no one's going to notice in any case.

✔ You can't trust employees anyway.

When you hear statements like these at work, red lights should be flashing before your eyes, and alarm bells should be ringing in your ears. Statements like these indicate that managers and employees aren't communicating effectively – that managers don't trust their employees, and that employees lack confidence in their managers. If you're lucky, you can find out about these kinds of problems while you still have a chance to do something about them. If you're not so lucky and you miss the clues, you may be stuck making the same mistakes again and again.

The expectations and commitments that employees carry with them on the job are in large part a product of the way in which their managers treat them. Following are the most commonly adopted styles of management. Do you recognise your management style?

Macho management

Okay. Here's the $64,000 question: What is the best way to make something you've planned happen? Everyone seems to have a different answer to this question. Some people see management as something you do *to* people, not *with* them. Does this type of manager sound familiar? 'We're going to do it my way. Understand?' Or perhaps the ever-popular threat: 'It had better be on my desk by the end of the day – or else!' If the worst comes to the worst, a manager can unveil the ultimate weapon: 'Mess up one more time, and you're sacked!'

This type of management is often known as *Theory X management*, which assumes that people are inherently lazy and you need to drive them to per-form. Managing by fear and intimidation is always guaranteed to get a response. The question is: Do you get the kind of response that you really want? When you closely monitor your employees' work, you usually end up with only short-term compliance. In other words, you never get the best from others by building a fire under them – you have to find a way to build a fire within them.

Sometimes managers have to take command of the situation. If you have to deliver a proposal in an hour and your customer just sent you some important changes, take charge of the situation to ensure that the right people are on the task – that is, if you're serious about keeping your customer. When you have to act quickly with perhaps not as much discussion as you would like, however, it's important to apologise in advance and let people know why you're doing things the way you are.

Participative management

At the other end of the spectrum, some people see management as participative. *Theory Y management* assumes that people basically want to do a good job. In the extreme interpretation of this theory, managers are supposed to be sensitive to their employees' feelings and be careful not to do anything that may disturb their employees' tranquillity and sense of self-worth.

> 'I found a problem with your report because none of the numbers are correct. We therefore need to consider our alternatives for taking a more careful look at these figures in the future.'

Again, managers may get a response with this approach (or they may choose to do the work themselves!), but are they likely to get the best possible response? Sometimes, yes; not always, however. In many cases, employees can, and do, take advantage of their managers. But you do get a better response if you are at least supportive at first.

The best way

Good managers realise that they don't have to be tough all the time – and that participation does work if you really mean it. If your employees are diligently performing their assigned tasks and no business emergency requires your immediate intervention, you can step back and let them do their jobs. Not only do your employees become more responsible, but you also can concentrate your efforts on what is most important to the bottom-line success of your organisation.

A manager's main job is to inspire employees to do their best and establish a working environment that allows them to reach their goals. The best managers make every possible effort to remove the organisational obstacles that prevent employees from doing their jobs and to obtain the resources and training that employees need to do their jobs effectively. All other goals – no matter how lofty or pressing – must take a back seat.

Bad systems, bad policies, bad procedures, and poor treatment of other people are organisational weaknesses that managers must be skilled at identifying and repairing or replacing.

Build a strong organisational foundation for your employees. Support your people, and you find they support you. Time and time again, when given the opportunity to achieve, workers in all kinds of businesses, from factories to venture capital firms, have proved this rule to be true. If you haven't seen it at your place of business, you may be mistaking your employees for problems. Stop squeezing them and start squeezing your organisation. The result is employees who want to succeed and a business that flourishes right along with them. Who knows, your employees may even stop hiding when they see you coming their way!

Squeezing employees may be easier than fighting the convoluted systems and cutting through the bureaucratic barnacles that have grown on your organisation. You may be tempted to yell, 'It's your fault that our department didn't achieve its goals!' Yes, it may be tempting to blame your employees for the organisation's problems, but doing so isn't going to solve the problems. Of course, you may get a quick, short-lived response when you push your people, but ultimately, you're failing to deal with the organisation's real problems.

We all want to 'win'. The challenge of management is to define winning in such a way that it feels like winning for everyone in the organisation. This, of course, is extremely difficult. People are often competing with colleagues for a 'piece of the pie' rather than trying to make the pie bigger. Your job is to help make a bigger pie.

Recognising that Quick Fixes Don't Work

Despite what many people want you to believe, management is not prone to simple solutions or quick fixes. Being a manager is not simple. Yes, the best management solutions tend to be common sense; however, turning common sense into common practice is sometimes difficult.

Management is an attitude – a way of life. Management is a very real desire to work with people and help them succeed, as well as a desire to help your organisation succeed. Management is a life-long learning process that doesn't end when you walk out of a one-hour seminar or finish viewing a 25-minute video. Management is like the old story about the happy homeowner who was shocked to receive a bill for £100 to fix a leaking pipe. When asked to explain the basis for this seemingly high charge, the plumber said, 'Tightening the nut cost you £5. Knowing which nut to tighten cost you £95!'

Building a tasty, but useless, manager

Once, Peter went to one of those touchy-feely off-site management meetings meant to build teamwork and communication among the members of the group. Picture this: Just after lunch, a big tray of leftover veggies, bagels, fruit, and such was sitting on a table at the side of the room. The course leader rose from his chair, faced the group, and said, 'Your next task is to split yourselves into four groups and construct a model of the perfect manager by using only the items on that tray of leftovers.' A collective groan filled the room. 'I don't want to hear any complaints,' the trainer said. 'I just want to see happy people doing happy things for the next half-hour.'

The teams feverishly went about their task of building the perfect manager. With some managers barely throttling the temptation to engage each other in a massive food fight, the little figures began to take shape. A banana here, a carrot stick there . . . and voilà! After a brief competition for dominance, the winners got their crowns. The result follows.

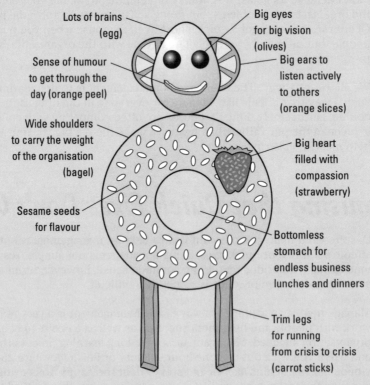

Lots of brains (egg)

Big eyes for big vision (olives)

Sense of humour to get through the day (orange peel)

Big ears to listen actively to others (orange slices)

Wide shoulders to carry the weight of the organisation (bagel)

Big heart filled with compassion (strawberry)

Sesame seeds for flavour

Bottomless stomach for endless business lunches and dinners

Trim legs for running from crisis to crisis (carrot sticks)

We have to admit that the result was kind of cute (and kind of tasty, too), but did it really make a difference in the way these managers managed their employees when they returned to the office the next day? No. Was the seminar a nice break from the day-to-day office routine? Yes. Was it a meaningful teaching tool with lasting impact? No.

Management is a people job. If you're not up to the task of working with people – helping them, listening to them, encouraging them, and guiding them – then you shouldn't be a manager.

Because management is such a challenge, an entire management training industry has sprung up, ready to help managers find out how to solve their problems. Unfortunately, trainers often focus on creating instant gratification among course attendees, many of whom have spent hundreds and even thousands of pounds to be there. 'Let's give them so much stuff to use that it's their fault if they never use any of it!'

Meeting the Management Challenge

When you're assigned a task in a non-management position, completing it by yourself is fairly simple and straightforward. Your immediate results are in direct response to your effort. To accomplish your task, you first review the task, you decide how best to accomplish it, and then you set schedules and milestones for its successful completion. Assuming that you have access to the tools and resources necessary to accomplish your task, you can probably do it yourself quickly and easily. You're an expert doer – a bright, get-things-done type of person.

However, if you hold a management position, you probably got that job because you proved yourself to be very skilled in the areas that you're now responsible for managing.

When you want to get a task done through someone else, you employ a different set of skills to when you do the task yourself. All of a sudden, because of this simple decision to pass the responsibility for completion of a task on to someone else, you introduce an interpersonal element into your equation. 'Oh, no! You mean I have to actually work with people?' Being technically good at your job is not enough – no matter how good your technical skills are. Now you must have good planning, organisational, leadership, and follow-up skills.

In other words, in addition to being a good doer, you have to be a good leader, director, and organiser of doers.

The old rules don't work any more

If this challenge isn't already enough, managers today face yet another challenge – one that has shaken the foundations of modern business. The new reality is that managers and workers have a partnership in the workplace.

Moving up and away

Peter's friend John was a member of a team of software programmers developing a complex application for portable computers. When he was a team member, everything was fine. He came to work in a T-shirt and jeans – just like the rest of his teammates – and often spent time with his programmer friends after hours. The bond that the team shared changed, however, when John was selected to manage the team.

In his new role of manager, John first shifted offices. Instead of sharing an open bay with the other programmers, he moved into his very own office – one with four walls and a window looking out over the parking lot. A secretary was assigned to guard his door. Of course, the jeans and T-shirt had to go – he replaced them with a business suit and tie. Instead of having fun programming, John was now concerned about more serious topics such as cost overruns, schedule delays, and returns on investments.

As John's role changed, so did he. And as John changed, so did his relationship with his people. He was no longer one of the crew; he was The Boss. To achieve his goals, John quickly had to make the transition from a doer to a manager of doers.

Originally, management was about dividing the company's work into discrete tasks, assigning the work to individual workers, and then closely monitoring the workers' performance and steering them towards accomplishing their tasks on time and within budget. The old reality of management often relied on fear, intimidation, and power over people to accomplish goals. If things weren't going according to management's plan, then management commanded its way out of the problem: 'I don't care what you have to do to get it done – just get it done. Now!' The line between managers and workers was drawn clearly and drawn often.

In the new business environment, what's going on inside the organisation is a reflection of what's going on outside the organisation. The following factors are creating rapid and constant change in today's new business environment:

- A surge of global competition and activity
- New technology and innovation
- The flattening of organisational hierarchies
- Widespread downsizing, re-engineering, and lay-offs
- The rise of small businesses
- The changing values of today's workers
- The increasing demands for better customer service

Watch out! Technology explosion ahead!

In the new world of information technology, the old ways of doing business are being turned on their head. With the presence of computer networks, e-mail, and voice-mail, the walls that divide individuals, departments, and organisational units have come crashing down. In the words of Frederick Kovac, vice-president of planning for the Goodyear Tire and Rubber Company, 'It used to be, if you wanted information, you had to go up, over, and down through the organisation. Now you just tap in. Everybody can know as much about the company as the chairman of the board.'

Of course, managers still have to divide and assign work, but workers are taking on more of that responsibility. Most importantly, managers are finding out that to get the best work, they can't command their employees – they have to create an environment that fosters their employees' desire to do their best work. This is the partnership between managers and workers in the workplace.

The landscape of business worldwide has changed dramatically during the past couple of decades. If you don't change with it, you're going to be left far behind your competitors. You may think that you can get away with treating your employees like 'human assets' or even like children, but you can't. You can't because your competitors are discovering how to unleash the hidden power of their employees. They're no longer just talking about it; they're doing it!

It's a new world

A few years ago, Bob made a presentation to a group of high-tech managers. As he was wrapping up his presentation, he opened the floor to questions. A hand shot up and the manager said, 'With all the downsizing and lay-offs that we've endured, people are lucky to get a salary, much less anything else. Why do we have to bother to empower and reward employees?' Before Bob had a chance to respond, another manager in the audience shot back, 'Because it's a new world.'

This response really sums it all up. In business, times are changing. Now that employees have tasted the sweet nectar of empowerment, you can't turn back. Companies that stick with the old way of doing business – the hierarchical, highly centralised model – are losing employees and customers to those companies that use the new ways of doing business and make them a part of their corporate culture. The best employees are leaving the old-model companies in droves, seeking employers who treat them with respect and who are willing to grant them greater autonomy and responsibility.

If you don't change, that leaves you with the employees who don't want to take risks or rock the boat. You get the yes-men and yes-women. No one challenges your ideas because they're afraid to. No one suggests better or more efficient ways to do business because they know that you don't listen or care anyway. Your employees don't bother to go out of their way to help a customer because you don't trust them to make the most basic decisions – the ones that can make the biggest difference to the satisfaction of your precious customers – or their lack of satisfaction.

Imagine the difference between an employee who tells your key customer, 'Sorry, my hands are tied. I am not allowed to make any exceptions to our policies,' and the employee who tells that customer, 'I'll do everything in my power to get you your order by your deadline.' With whom do you think your customers prefer to do business? With whom would you prefer to do business? (**Hint:** Don't even think about the first alternative!)

Managers used to try to buy behaviour, commitment, and loyalty; and some workers were even called 'hired hands'. Today, hiring their hands is not good enough on its own. You must find a way to engage their souls and get them to bring their best efforts to the workplace each and every day.

Trust is not a four-letter word

Companies that provide exceptional customer service unleash their employees from the constraints of an overly controlling hierarchy and allow front-line workers to serve their customers directly and efficiently. For example, while many companies devote forests of paper to employee manuals, Nordstrom, an American department store chain, devotes exactly one page to its manual.

Figure 1-1 shows you what is on that page.

You may think that a small company with five or ten employees can get away with a policy like that, but certainly not a big company like yours. However, Nordstrom is not a small business by any stretch of the imagination – unless you consider a company with 50,000 or so employees and more than $5 billion in annual sales small.

How does management at a large business like Nordstrom get away with such a policy? They do it through trust.

First, Nordstrom hires good people. Secondly, the company gives them the training and tools to do their jobs well. Then management gets out of the way and lets the employees do their work. Nordstrom knows that it can trust its employees to make the right decisions because the company knows that it has hired the right people for the job and has trained them well.

Figure 1-1:
Nordstrom's employee manual shows an exceptional amount of trust in employees.

> **We're glad to have you with our Company. Our number one goal is to provide outstanding customer service.**
>
> **Set both your personal and professional goals high.**
>
> **Nordstrom Rules:**
>
> **Rule #1: Use your good judgement in all situations.**
>
> **There will be no additional rules. Please feel free to ask your department manager, store manager, or division general manager any question at any time.**

(Source: *Business and Society Review*, Spring 1993, n85)

We're not saying that Nordstrom doesn't have problems – every company does. But Nordstrom has taken a proactive stance in creating the environment that employees most need and want.

Can you say the same for your organisation?

When you trust your employees, they respond by being trustworthy. When you recognise them for being independent and responsive to your customers, they continue to be independent and responsive to your customers. And when you give them the freedom to make their own decisions, they make their own decisions. With a little training and a lot of support, these decisions are in the best interests of the company because the right people at the right level of the organisation are making them.

The ultimate employee letter

In his book *Please Don't Just Do What I Tell You! Do What Needs to Be Done* (Hyperion, 2002), Bob talks about the 'Ultimate Expectation' of every employer – for employees to do what needs to be done. In the following letter from manager to employee, Bob clearly outlines this expectation.

Dear Employee:

You've been hired to handle some pressing needs we have. If we could have managed by not hiring you, we would have. But we've determined that we needed someone with your skills and experience and that you were the best person to help us with our needs. We have offered you the position and you've accepted. Thanks!

During the course of your employment, you will be asked to do many things: general responsibilities, specific assignments, group and individual projects. You will have many chances to excel and to confirm that we made a good choice in hiring you.

However, there is one foremost responsibility that may never be specifically requested of you but that you need to always keep in mind through the duration of your employment. This is the Ultimate Expectation, and it is as follows:

ALWAYS DO WHAT MOST NEEDS TO BE DONE WITHOUT WAITING TO BE ASKED.

We've hired you to do a job, yes, but more important, we've hired you to think, to use your judgement and to act in the best interest of the organisation at all times.

If we never say this again, don't take it as an indication that it's no longer important or that we've changed our priorities. We are likely to get caught up in the daily press of business, the never-ending changes of the operation, and the ongoing rush of activities. Our day-to-day practices make it look like this principle no longer applies. Don't be deceived by this.

Please don't ever forget the Ultimate Expectation. Strive to have it always be a guiding principle in your employment with us, a philosophy that is always with you, one that is constantly driving your thoughts and actions.

As long as you are employed with us, you have our permission to act in our mutual best interests.

If at any time you do not feel we are doing the right thing – the thing you most believe would help us all – please say so. You have our permission to speak up when necessary to state what is unstated, to make a suggestion, or to question an action or decision.

This doesn't mean we will always agree with you, or that we will necessarily change what we are doing; but we always want to hear what you most believe would help us better achieve our goals and purpose and to create a mutually successful experience in the process.

You will need to seek to understand how (and why) things are done the way they are done before you seek to change existing work processes. Try to work with the systems that are in place first, but tell us if you think those systems need to be changed.

Discuss what is presented here with me, and others, in the organisation so that we might all become better at applying the Ultimate Expectation.

Sincerely,

Your Manager

Explaining the New Functions of Management

Remember the four 'classic' functions of management – plan, organise, lead, and control – that you learned at college? These management functions form the foundation from which every manager works. Although these basic functions are fine for taking care of most of your day-to-day management duties, they fail to reflect the new reality of the workplace and the new partnership of managers and workers. We need a new set of management functions that builds on the four classic functions of management. And you're in luck, we have them. The following sections describe the functions of the new manager in the 21st-century workplace.

Energise

Think of the best managers you know. What one quality sets them apart from the rest? Is it their organisational skills, their fairness, or their technical ability? Perhaps their ability to delegate or the long hours they keep sets them apart.

Although all these traits may be important to a manager's success, we haven't yet named the unique quality that makes a good manager great. The most important management function is to get people excited and inspired – to *energise* them. You can't expect your people to be inspired, ambitious, enthusiastic, or dedicated if you yourself are not. Adopt the mantra: 'If it's to be, it's to begin with me.'

You can be the best analyst in the world, the most highly organised executive on the planet, or fair beyond reproach, but if people can liken the level of excitement you generate more to a dishcloth than a spark plug, it handicaps your efforts to create a truly great organisation.

Great managers create far more energy than they consume. The best managers are organisational catalysts. Instead of taking energy from an organisation, they channel and amplify it. In every interaction, effective managers take the natural energy of their employees, add to it, and leave the employees in a higher energy state than when they began. Management becomes a process of transmitting the excitement that you feel about your organisation and its goals to your employees in terms that they can understand and appreciate. Before you know it, your employees are as excited about the organisation as you are, and you can simply allow their energy to carry you forward.

A picture is worth a thousand words. This statement is as true for the pictures you paint in the minds of others as for the pictures people paint on canvas or print in magazines and books. Imagine taking a vacation with your family or friends. As the big day draws near, you keep the goal exciting and fresh in the minds of your family or friends by creating a vision of the journey that awaits you. Vivid descriptions of white sandy beaches, towering redwoods, glittering skylines, secluded lakes, hot food, and indoor plumbing paint pictures in the minds of each of your fellow travellers. With this vision in mind, everyone works towards a common goal of having a successful vacation.

Successful managers bring everything to life. They create compelling visions – pictures of a future organisation that inspire and compel employees to bring out their best performance.

Empower

Have you ever worked for someone who didn't let you do your job without questioning your every decision? Maybe you spent all weekend working on a special project only to have it casually discarded by your boss. 'What were you thinking when you did this, Elizabeth? Our customers will never buy into that approach!' Or maybe you went out of your way to help a customer, accepting a return shipment of an item against company policy. 'Why do you think we have policies – because we enjoy killing trees for the paper to print them on? If we made exceptions for everyone, we'd go out of business!' How did it feel to have your sincere efforts at doing a great job disparaged? What was your reaction? Simple – you didn't bother making the extra effort again.

Despite rumours to the contrary, when you empower your employees, you don't stop managing. What changes is the way you manage. Managers still provide vision, establish organisational goals, and determine shared values. However, they also have to establish a corporate infrastructure – skills training, teams, and so on – that supports empowerment. And although all your employees may not want to be empowered, you still have to provide an environment that supports those employees who are eager for a taste of the freedom to apply their personal creativity and expertise to your organisation.

Great managers allow their employees to do great work. This role is the real and vital function of management, for even the greatest managers in the world can't succeed all by themselves.

To achieve the organisation's goals, managers depend on their employees' skills. Effective managers combine the efforts of every member of a work unit towards a common purpose. If you're constantly doing your employees' work for them, not only have you lost the advantage of the effectiveness that your employees can provide for you, but you're also putting yourself on the path to stress, ulcers, and worse.

When you don't empower employees, not only do you lose out, everyone in your organisation loses too. Your employees lose because you aren't allowing them to stretch themselves or to show creativity or initiative. Your organisation loses the insights that its creative workforce brings with it. Finally, your customers lose because your employees are afraid to provide them with exceptional service. Why should they if they're constantly worried about you punishing them for taking the initiative or for pushing the limits of the organisation to serve your customers better?

As William McKnight, former CEO of manufacturing giant 3M, put it, 'The mistakes people make are of much less importance than the mistakes management makes if it tells people exactly what to do.'

And as Phil McGovern, former General Manager of Panasonic UK, commented, 'Make mistakes? Of course we do. We make thousands of mistakes every day. I myself make mistakes. The important thing is that we learn from them. And we have to learn from them if we are to remain competitive.'

Support

A manager's job is no longer that of a watchdog, police officer, or executioner. Increasingly, managers must be coaches, colleagues, cheerleaders, and advocates for their staff. The main concern of today's managers needs to be shaping a more supportive work environment that enables each employee to feel valued and be more productive.

When the going gets tough, managers support their employees. This doesn't mean that you do everything for your employees or make their decisions for them. It does mean that you give your employees the training, resources, and authority to do their jobs, and then you get out of the way. You're always there for your employees to help pick up the pieces if they fall, but fall they must if they're going to learn. The idea is the same as learning to skate: If you're not falling, you're not learning.

The key to creating a supportive environment is establishing trust or openness throughout an organisation. In an open environment, employees can bring up questions and concerns. In fact, they're encouraged to do so. When the environment is truly open, an individual can express concerns without fear of retribution. Hidden agendas don't exist, and people feel free to say the same things in business meetings that they'd say after work. When employees see that their managers are receptive to new ideas, they're more likely to feel invested in the organisation, and to think of more and better ways to improve systems, to solve problems, to save money, and to serve customers.

Managers also support each other. Personal fiefdoms, fighting between departments, and withholding information have no place in the modern organisation; companies cannot afford to support these dysfunctional behaviours. All members of the organisation – from the top to the bottom – must realise that they play on the same team. To win, team members support each other and keep their people up to date with the latest information. Which team are you on?

Communicate

Without a doubt, communication is the lifeblood of any organisation, and managers are the common element that connects different levels of employees with one another. We have seen at first hand the positive effects on a business and its employees of managers who communicate, and the negative effects on a business and its employees of managers who don't.

Managers who don't communicate effectively are missing out on a vital role of management.

Communication is a key function for managers today. Information is power, and as the speed of business accelerates, employees must get the information they need faster than ever. Continual change and increasing turbulence in the business environment necessitate more communication, not less. Who's going to be around in five years? The manager who has mastered this function or the one who has not?

With the proliferation of e-mail, voice-mail, and all the other new means of communication, managers simply have no excuse not to communicate with their employees. You can even use the telephone or try a little old-fashioned face-to-face talk with your employees if you like!

To meet the expectations that you set for them, your employees have to be aware of those expectations. A goal is great on paper, but if you don't communicate it to employees and don't keep them up to date on their progress towards achieving that goal, how can you expect them to reach it? Simply, you can't. It would be like training for the Olympics but never being given feedback on how you're doing versus the competition.

Employees often appreciate the little things – an invitation to an upcoming meeting, praise for a job well done, or an insight into the organisation's finances. Not only does sharing this kind of information make a business run better, it also creates tremendous goodwill and cements the trust that bonds your employees to the organisation and to the successful completion of its goals.

Taking the First Steps towards Becoming a Manager

Believe it or not, many managers never receive formal training in management (though thankfully this is changing). In many cases management is just something that's added to your job description. One day you may be a computer programmer working on a hot new Web browser, and the next day you may be in charge of the new development team. Before, you were expected only to show up to work and create a product. Now, you're expected to lead and motivate a group of workers towards a common goal. You may get paid more to do the job, but the only training you may get for the task is in the school of hard knocks.

Managers (or managers-to-be) can easily discover how to become good managers by following the recommendations in the sections that follow. No one way is absolutely right or absolutely wrong; each has its pluses and minuses.

Look and listen

If you're fortunate enough to have had a skilled teacher or mentor during the course of your career, you're treated to an education in management that's equal to or better than any Master of Business Administration (MBA) programme. You get to know at first hand the right and wrong ways to manage people. You discover what it takes to get things done in your organisation, and you realise that customer satisfaction involves more than simply giving your customers lip service.

Unfortunately, any organisation with good management also has living, breathing examples of the wrong way to manage employees. You know the ones we're talking about: The manager who refuses to make decisions, leaving employees and customers hanging. Or the boss who refuses to delegate even the simplest decision to employees. Or the supervisor who insists on managing every single aspect of a department – no matter how small or inconsequential: 'No, no, no! The stamp goes on the envelope first, and then the address label, not the other way around!' Examples of the right way to manage employees are, regrettably, still few and far between.

You can benefit from the behaviours that poor managers model. When you find a manager who refuses to make decisions, for example, carefully note the impact their management style has on workers, other managers, and customers. You can feel your own frustration. Make a mental note: 'I'll never, ever demotivate another person like that.' Indecision at the top inevitably leads to indecision at all ranks of an organisation – especially when people are punished for filling the vacuum that indecisive managers leave. Employees become confused, and customers become concerned as the organisation drifts aimlessly.

Observe the manager who depends on fear and intimidation to get results. What are the real results of this style of management? Do employees look forward to coming to the office every day? Are they all pulling for a common vision and goal? Are they extending themselves to bring innovation to work processes and procedures? Or are they more concerned with just getting through the day without being yelled at? Think about what you would do differently to get the results you want.

You can always pick up something from other managers – whether they're good managers or bad ones.

Do and learn

Perhaps you're familiar with this old saying (attributed to Lao Tze):

Give a man a fish, and he eats for a day,

Teach a man to fish, and he eats for a lifetime.

A world-class teacher

By many measures, Jack Welch is considered to be one of the United States' top business leaders. Welch, who until recently was chairman of General Electric, radically transformed his company's culture while dramatically improving its performance – and in the process created some $57 billion in value.

Although Welch did many different things to make the transformation a reality, one of the most telling was his take over of GE's training facility in Ossining, New York. As he realised, designing a new culture is one thing, but getting the word out to employees and making it stick is another thing altogether. By directing the class curricula for all levels of workers, and by personally dropping into the training centre every two weeks or so to meet with students, Welch was able not only to determine what message would be communicated to GE employees, but also to ensure that they received the message loudly and clearly. If the employees were confused, they had ample opportunity to ask him for clarification.

In a gesture that was at once symbolic and real, Welch directed the ceremonial burning of the old-school General Electric 'Blue Books'. The Blue Books were a series of management training manuals that prescribed how GE managers were to get tasks done in the organisation. Despite the fact that the use of these books for training had been mothballed for some 15 years, they still exerted tremendous influence over the actions of GE managers. Citing the need for managers to write their own answers to day-to-day management challenges, Welch swept away the old order by removing the Blue Books from the organisation's culture once and for all. Now, GE managers are taught to find their own solutions rather than to look them up in a dusty old book.

Such is the nature of managing employees. If you make all the decisions, do the work that your employees are able to do given the chance, and try to carry the entire organisation on your own shoulders, you're harming your employees and your organisation far more than you can imagine. Your employees never find out how to succeed on their own, and after a while, they stop trying. In your sincere efforts to bring success to your organisation, you stunt the growth of your employees and make the organisation less effective and vital.

Simply reading a book (even this one) or watching someone else manage – or fail to manage – is not enough. To take advantage of the lessons that you learn, you have to put them into practice. Keep these key steps in mind:

1. **Take the time to assess your organisation's problems.** Which parts of your organisation work, and which don't? Why or why not? You can't focus on all your problems at one time. Concentrate on a few problems that are the most important, and solve them before you move on to the rest.

Top five management Web sites

Wondering where to find the best information about the topics addressed in this chapter? Try some of our favourites:

- Chartered Management Institute: www.cmi.org.uk

- Chartered Institute of Personnel and Development: www.cipd.co.uk

- ManagementFirst: www.managementfirst.com

- London Business School: www.lbs.ac.uk

- Learning and Skills Council: www.lsc.org.uk

2. **Take a close look at yourself.** What do you do to help or hinder your employees when they try to do their jobs? Do you give them the authority to make decisions? Just as important, do you support them when they go out on a limb for the organisation? Study your personal interactions throughout your business day. Do they result in positive or negative outcomes?

3. **Try out the techniques that you learn from your reading or from observing other managers at work.** Go ahead! Nothing changes if you don't change first. 'If it's to be, it's to begin with me.'

4. **Step back and watch what happens.** We promise that you can see a difference in the way you get tasks done and in the way your customers and employees respond to your organisation's needs and goals.

Chapter 2

Delegation: Getting Things Done without Getting Done In

In This Chapter

▶ Managing through delegation

▶ Killing the myths about delegation

▶ Putting delegation to work

▶ Choosing which tasks to delegate

▶ Checking up on your employees

*T*he power of effective management comes not from your efforts alone (sorry to burst your bubble) but from the sum of all the efforts of your work group. If you're responsible for only a few employees, with extraordinary effort you perhaps can do the work of your entire group if you so desire (if you want to be a complete stranger to your friends and family).

However, when you're responsible for a much larger team or organisation, you simply can't be an effective manager by trying to do all your group's work. In the best case, the group probably views you as a *micromanager* – a manager who gets too involved in the petty details of running an organisation – with more time for other people's work than for your own. In the worst case, your employees may take less responsibility for their work because you're always there to do it (or check it) for them. Why should they bother trying to do their best job if you're just going to take the assignment back anyway?

Managers assign the responsibility for completing tasks through *delegation*. But as we explain in this chapter, simply assigning tasks and then walking away is not enough. For delegation to be effective, managers must also give authority to their employees and ensure that those employees have the resources necessary to complete tasks effectively. Managers who delegate like experts can monitor the progress of their employees towards meeting their assigned goals.

Delegating: The Manager's No. 1 Tool

Now that you're a manager, you have to develop skills in many different areas. Not only do you need good technical, analytical, and organisational skills, but most importantly, you also must have good people skills.

Of all the people skills, the one skill that can make the greatest difference in your effectiveness as a manager is the ability to delegate well. Delegating is a manager's No.1 management tool, and the inability to delegate well is the leading cause of management failure.

So why do managers have such a hard time delegating? A variety of reasons exist:

✔ You're too busy and just don't have enough time.

✔ You think you're going to lose control of the work – or, worse, the employees.

✔ You don't trust your employees to complete their assignments correctly or on time.

✔ You don't know how to delegate effectively.

Or perhaps you're still not convinced that managers need to delegate at all. If you're a member of this large group of reluctant managers, be honest with yourself! The following list is why you must let go of your preconceptions, inhibitions, and prejudices and start delegating today:

✔ **Your success as a manager depends on it.** Managers who can success-fully manage team members – each of whom has specific responsibilities for a different aspect of the team's performance – prove that they're ready for bigger and better challenges. Taking on bigger and better challenges is the stuff of ambition, advancement, recognition, and contribution. Taking on bigger and better challenges additionally delivers those things that are important to many people – status, seniority, enhanced prospects – as well as fulfilling personal goals.

✔ **You can't do it all.** No matter how great a manager you are, carrying the entire burden of achieving your organisation's goals by yourself isn't in your interest unless you want to work yourself into an early grave. Besides, wouldn't it be nice to see what life is like outside the four walls of your office? The United Kingdom has a notorious long-hours working culture, and the attendant problems of stress, heart disease, and family breakdown that come with this – and you don't want to be a part of this.

✔ **Your job is to concentrate your efforts on the things that you can do and your staff can't.** Your organisation pays you to be a manager – not a super programmer, accounting clerk, or customer service representative. Do your job, and let your employees do theirs.

✔ **Delegation gets workers more involved.** When you give responsibility and authority to employees to carry out tasks – whether individually or in teams – they respond by becoming more involved in day-to-day operations. Instead of being drones with no responsibility or authority, they are vital to the success of the work unit and the entire organisation. And if your employees succeed, so do you!

✔ **Delegation gives you the chance to develop your employees.** If you make all the decisions and come up with all the ideas, your employees never discover how to take initiative and be responsible for seeing tasks through to successful completion. And if they don't get to know this, guess who's going to get stuck doing everything forever? (*Hint:* Take a look in the mirror.) In addition, keep in mind that development opportunities are increasingly reported as one of the top motivators for today's employees. Expert, committed, and ambitious people are not going to remain with any organisation that does not give them the opportunity to progress.

As a manager, you're ultimately responsible for all your department's responsibilities. However, for most managers, personally executing all the tasks necessary for your department to fulfil its responsibilities and for you to achieve your organisational goals is neither practical nor desirable.

Say that you're the manager of the accounting department for a software development firm. When the firm had only five employees and sales of £500,000 a year, it was no problem for you to personally invoice all your customers, send cheques out to vendors, run the payroll, and take care of the company's tax bill. However, now that the company has grown to 150 employees and sales are at £50 million a year, you can't even pretend to do it all – in any case, you haven't got enough hours in the day. So you have specialised employees who take care of accounts, transport, supplies, and information systems; and you probably contract out functions like payroll and the financial accounts.

Each employee that you assign to a specific work function has specialised knowledge and skills in their area of expertise. Of course, you could do the payroll if you had to, but if you've hired someone to do that job, why would you want to? And in any case, your payroll person is probably a lot better and quicker at it than you are.

On the other hand, you're uniquely qualified to perform numerous responsibilities in your organisation. These responsibilities are likely to include developing and monitoring your operations budget; conducting performance appraisals; monitoring the progress of products and services; and helping to plan, develop, and implement the company's strategy and direction. You also have to make sure that the staff have everything they need to carry out their work – and that includes tea and coffee. Later in this chapter – in the section 'Looking at the Good and the Bad of Delegation' – we tell you which tasks to delegate to your employees and which ones to retain. First, however, consider some of the popular misconceptions about delegation.

Explaining the Myths about Delegation

Admit it: You may have many different reasons to rationalise to yourself why you can't delegate work to your employees. Unfortunately, these reasons are guaranteed to get in the way of your ability to be an effective manager. Do any of the following myths sound familiar to you?

Myth No. 1: You can't trust your employees to be responsible

If you can't trust your employees, whom can you trust? Assume that you're responsible for hiring at least a portion of your staff. Now, forgetting for the moment the ones you didn't personally hire, you probably went through quite an involved process to recruit your employees. Remember the mountain of applications you had to sift through and then divide into winners, potential winners, and losers? After hours of sorting and then hours of interviews, you selected the best candidates – the ones with the best skills, qualifications, character, expertise, and experience for the job.

You selected your employees because you thought that they were talented people deserving of your trust. Now your job is to give them your trust without any strings attached.

You usually reap what you sow. Your staff members are ready, willing, and able to be responsible employees; you just have to give them a chance. Of course, not every employee is going to be able to handle every task you assign to them. If that's the case, find out why. Do they need more training? More time? More practice? Maybe you need to find a task that is better suited to their experience or disposition. Or perhaps you simply hired the wrong person for the job. If that's the case, then face up to the fact and sort the problem out before you lose even more time and money. To get responsible employees, you have to give them responsibility.

Myth No. 2: When you delegate, you lose control of a task and its outcome

If you delegate correctly, you don't lose control of the task or its outcome. What you lose control of is the way in which the outcome is reached. Picture a map of the world. How many different ways can a person get from San Francisco to Paris? One? One million? Some ways are quicker than others. Some are more scenic, and others require a substantial commitment of resources. Do the differences in these ways make any of them inherently wrong? No.

In business, you have countless ways to get a task done. Even for tasks that are spelt out in highly defined steps – 'We've always done it that way' – you can leave room for new ways to make a process better. Why should your way be the only way to get the task done? 'Because I'm the boss!' Sorry, wrong answer. Your job is to describe to your employees the outcomes that you want and then to let them decide how to accomplish the tasks. Of course, you need to be available to coach and counsel them so that they can learn from your past experience if they want, but you need to let go of controlling the how and instead focus on the what and the when.

Myth No. 3: You're the only one who has the answers

You must be joking! If you think that you alone have all the answers, you should not be a manager. As talented as you may be, unless you're the company's only employee, you can't possibly have the only answer to every question in your organisation.

On the other hand, a certain group of people deal with an amazing array of situations every day. Those in the group talk to your customers, your suppliers, and one another – day in and day out. Many members of the group have been working for the company far longer than you, and many of them will be there long after you're gone. Who are these people? They are your employees.

Your employees have a wealth of experience and knowledge about your business contacts and the intimate, day-to-day workings of the organisation. They are often closer to the customers and problems of the company than you are. To ignore their suggestions and advice is not only disrespectful but also short-sighted and foolish. Don't ignore this resource – you're paying for it anyway, whether or not you use it.

Myth No. 4: You can do the work faster by yourself

You may think that you're completing tasks faster when you do them than when you assign them to others, but this belief is merely an illusion. Yes, discussing and assigning a task to one of your employees may require slightly more time when you first delegate that task. However, if you delegate well, things quickly improve. This frees you up to be doing the things that you should be doing anyway.

Not only does doing a specific task yourself actually cost you more time, but also you're robbing your employees of a golden opportunity to develop their work skills.

And what happens when you do something yourself instead of delegating it? When you do a task, you're forever doomed to doing it – again and again and again. But when you teach someone else to do the task and then assign them responsibility for completing it, you may never have to do it again. Not only that, your employees may come to do it faster than you can. Who knows, they may even improve the way that you've always done it.

Myth No. 5: Delegation dilutes your authority

Actually, delegation does exactly the opposite – it *extends* your authority. You're only one person, and you can do only so much. Imagine all 10, 20, or 100 members of your team working towards your common goals. You still set the goals and the timetables for reaching them, but each employee chooses their own way of getting there.

Do you have less authority because you delegate a task and transfer authority to an employee to carry out the task? Clearly, the answer is no. What do you lose in this transaction? Nothing. Your authority is extended, not diminished. The more authority you give to employees, the more authority your entire work unit has, and the better able your employees are to do the jobs you hired them to do.

As you grant others authority, you gain an efficient and effective workforce – employees who are truly empowered, excited by their jobs, and working as team players – and you gain the ability to concentrate on the issues that deserve your undivided attention.

Myth No. 6: Your employees get recognition for doing a good job, not you

Letting go of this belief is one of the biggest difficulties in the transition from being a doer to being a manager of doers. When you're a doer, the organisation rewards you for writing a great report, developing an incredible market analysis, or programming an amazing piece of computer code. When you're a manager, the focus of your job shifts from your performance in completing individual tasks to your performance in reaching an overall organisational or project goal through the efforts of others. You may have been the best marketing assistant in the world, but that is no longer important. Now you are expected to develop and lead the best marketing team in the world. The skills required are quite different and your success is because of both the efforts of others and also your organisation's support – and' your skills in delegation.

Wise managers know that when their employees shine, they shine too. The more you delegate, the more opportunities you offer your employees to shine. Give your workers the opportunity to do important work and to do it well. And when they do well, make sure that you tell everyone about it. Give your employees credit for their successes publicly and often, and they will be more likely to want to do a good job for you on future assignments. Don't forget: When you're a manager, you're primarily being measured on your team's performance – not so much on what you're personally able to accomplish. Chapter 5 covers everything you ever wanted to know about employee motivation and rewards – and even a few things you maybe didn't want to know!

Myth No. 7: Delegation decreases your flexibility

When you do everything yourself, you have complete control over the progress and completion of tasks, right? How wrong that is! How can you possibly be flexible when you are balancing multiple priorities, dealing with crises, and trying to do your own job – all at the same time! Being flexible is pretty tough when you're doing everything yourself. Concentrating on more than one task at a time is impossible. While you're concentrating on that one task, you put all your other tasks on hold. That isn't flexibility.

The more people you delegate to, the more flexible you can be. As your employees take care of the day-to-day tasks necessary to keep your business running, you're free to deal with those surprise problems and opportunities that are always coming along and to make sure that lurching from crisis to crisis is kept to an absolute minimum.

Myth No. 8: Your employees are too busy

If that belief isn't a cop-out, we don't know what is. What exactly are your employees doing that means they don't have the time to learn something new – something that can make your job easier *and* boost the performance of your work unit?

Think about yourself for a moment. What about your job makes you want to return day after day? The salary? The perks and privileges? Partly maybe – but we're willing to bet that the main reason is the satisfaction you feel when you take on a new challenge, rise to it, and succeed.

Now consider your employees – their job satisfaction is no different from yours. They want to test themselves against new challenges and succeed, too. But how can they if you don't delegate new tasks to them? Too many managers have lost good employees because they failed to meet those employees' needs to stretch and to grow in their jobs. And too many employees have become bored rigid because their managers refuse to encourage their creativity and natural yearning to develop. Don't learn this lesson the hard way!

Myth No. 9: Your workers don't see the big picture

Actually this myth may be true, but only because you make it so. How can your employees see the big picture if you don't share it with them? They are often specialists in their jobs or fields of expertise. They naturally develop severe cases of tunnel vision as they pursue the answers to their assignments or process their routine transactions. As we discuss in Chapter 1, your job is to provide your employees with a vision of where you want to go and the priorities of what needs to be achieved, and then allow them to find the best way to attain those goals.

Unfortunately, many managers withhold vital information from their employees – information that can make them much more effective in their jobs – in the hope that by doing so, managers can maintain a close rein on their behaviour and stay 'in control'. By keeping their employees in the dark, these managers don't create the better outcomes that they hope for. Instead, they cripple their organisation and their employees' ability to learn, grow, and become a real part of the organisation.

Trusting Your Employees

Myths aside, delegation can be scary, at least at first. But like anything else, the more you do it, the less scary it gets. When you delegate, you're putting your trust in another individual. If that individual fails, then you're ultimately responsible and accountable – regardless of who you give the task to. A line like this probably won't go very far with your boss: 'Yes, I know that we were supposed to get that proposal to the customer today, but Joe fluffed it.' When you delegate tasks, you don't automatically abdicate your responsibility or accountability for their successful completion.

Beginning to delegate tasks to your employees is like bungee jumping for the first time: You jump off that little platform hundreds of feet above the ground and hope that the cord doesn't break. And don't forget that your employees may be a little nervous, too. The thought of taking on a new task may cause some hesitance on their part. This hesitance requires more support from you as your employees discover how to become comfortable with their new roles.

As a part of this process, you also need to understand each of your employees' strengths and weaknesses. You probably aren't, for example, going to delegate a huge task to someone who has been in a job for only a few months.

Taking the Seven Steps to Delegate

Delegation doesn't just happen. Just like any other task that you perform as a manager, you have to work at it. The seven steps to effective delegation are as follows:

1. **Communicate the task.** Describe exactly what you want done, when you want it done, and what results you expect. Ask if the employee has any questions.

2. **Set the task in context.** Explain why the task needs to be done, its importance in the overall scheme of things, and possible complications that may arise during its performance.

3. **Determine standards.** Agree on the standards that you plan to use to measure the success of a task's completion. Make these standards realistic and attainable.

4. **Grant authority.** You must grant employees the authority necessary to complete the task without constant roadblocks or stand-offs with other employees.

5. **Provide support.** Determine the resources necessary for your employee to complete the task and then provide them. Successfully completing a task may require money, training, or the ability to check with you about progress or obstacles as they arise.

6. **Get commitment.** Make sure that your employee has accepted the assignment. Confirm your expectations and your employee's understanding of and commitment to completing the task.

7. **Keep in touch.** Make sure that your employees can get hold of you whenever they need. This does not mean that you are nannying them, though! It does mean that you're available for the sake of a quick e-mail or phone call, to address and resolve any simple but important questions that crop up.

Clearly, delegation benefits both workers and managers alike when you do it correctly. So why aren't you delegating more work to your employees? It's not too late to start!

Looking at the Good and the Bad of Delegation

Theoretically, you can delegate anything to your employees. Of course, if you delegate all your duties, then why is your company bothering to pay you? Obviously, you have tasks that you make an effort to delegate to your employees and tasks that you retain for yourself. Remember, you're the manager, not your employees.

When you delegate, begin with simple tasks that don't substantially affect the firm if they aren't completed on time or within budget. As your employees gain confidence and experience, delegate higher-level tasks. Carefully assess the level of their expertise, and assign tasks that meet or slightly exceed that level. Set schedules for completion and then monitor your employees' performance against them. This is a good opportunity to see if an employee isn't being challenged or is bored. After you get the hang of it, you find that you really have nothing to be afraid of when you delegate.

Always delegate these things

Certain tasks naturally lend themselves to being delegated. As a manager, you can take every possible opportunity to delegate the following kinds of work to your employees.

Detailed work

Truly in many cases, the devil is in the detail. As a manager, the last thing you want or need to get bogged down in is unnecessary detail – double and triple checking technical issues and data, staff expenses, or time sheets.

This is simply a waste of your time. You are there to see that things are done, not to do them yourself. So delegate – and if things are then done wrong anyway, find out why and put it right. You need to be able to leave the detail to your employees. Hold them accountable for results; and make sure your door is open and that they can always get hold of you if they do have questions or problems to address.

Information gathering

Browsing the Web for information about your competitors, spending hours poring over issues of the *Economist* magazine, or moving into your local library's reference stacks for weeks on end is not an effective use of your time. Despite that fact, most managers get sucked into the trap. Not only is reading through newspapers, reports, books, magazines, and the like fun, but it also provides managers with an easy way to postpone the more difficult tasks of management. Your organisation is paying you to look at the big picture – to gather a variety of inputs and make sense of them. You can work so much more efficiently when someone else gathers the necessary information, which frees you to take the time you need to analyse the inputs and devise solutions to your problems.

Repeat assignments

Always farm out repeat and predictable work to employees. Many of the jobs in your organisation occur again and again – jobs such as drafting your weekly production report, reviewing your bi-weekly report of expenditure versus budget, and approving your monthly phone bill. Your time is both expensive and valuable, and you should spend it on managerial priorities. Don't use repeat and predictable assignments as an easy way of postponing more complex tasks.

If you find yourself involved in repetitive assignments, first take a close look at their particulars. How often do the assignments recur? Can you anticipate the assignments in sufficient time to allow an employee to be successful in completing it? What do you have to do to train your employees in completing the tasks? When you have worked all this out, develop schedules and hand these matters over to your employees.

Surrogate roles

Not only can't you be everywhere all the time, you shouldn't be everywhere all the time. Every day, your employees have numerous opportunities to fill in for you. Presentations, conference calls, client visits, and meetings are just a few examples. In some cases, such as in budget presentations to top management, you may be required to attend. However, in many other cases, whether you attend personally or send someone to take your place really doesn't matter.

So long as the corporate culture allows, the next time someone calls a meeting and requests your attendance, do your best to send one of your employees to attend in your stead. This simple act benefits you in several different ways. Not only do you have an extra hour or two in your schedule, but also your employee can present you with only the important outcomes of the meeting. In any case, your employee has the opportunity to take on some new responsibilities, and you have the opportunity to spend the time you need on your most important tasks. Not only that, but your employee may discover something new in the process.

Future duties

As a manager, you can always be on the lookout for opportunities to train your staff in their future job responsibilities. For example, one of your key duties may be to develop your department's annual budget. By allowing one or more of your employees to assist you – perhaps in gathering basic market or research data – you can give your employees a taste of what goes into putting together a budget.

Don't fall into the trap of believing that the only way to train your employees is to sign them up for expensive classes that you may have discovered by chance on flyers that dropped out of professional journals. Opportunities to train your employees abound within your own business. An estimated 90 per cent of all development occurs on the job. Not only is this training free, but also by assigning your employees to progressively more important tasks, you build their self-confidence and help to pave their way to progress in the organisation.

Avoid delegating these things

Some tasks are part and parcel of the job of being a manager. By delegating the following work, you fail to perform your basic management duties.

Long-term vision and goals

As a manager, you're in a unique position. Your position at the top provides you with a unique perspective on the organisation's needs – the higher up you are in an organisation, the broader your perspective. As we discuss in Chapter 1, one of the key functions of management is vision. Although employees at any level of a company can provide you with input and make suggestions that help to shape your perspectives, developing the organisation's long-term vision and goals is up to you. Simply put, every employee can't decide what direction the organisation should move in.

Positive performance feedback

Rewarding and recognising employees when they do good work is an important job for every manager. If this task is delegated to lower-level employees, however, the workers who receive it won't value the recognition as much as if it came from their manager. The impact of the recognition is therefore significantly lessened (assuming it gets done at all!).

Performance appraisals, discipline, and counselling

You need a strong, professional and positive relationship with your employees; and yet in the modern workplace, strong relationships between managers and employees are often hard to come by. Most managers are probably lucky to get a brief 'hello' and 'goodbye' between the hustle and bustle of a typical working day. Given everyone's hectic schedules, you may have times when you don't talk to one or more of your employees for days at a time.

However, sometimes you absolutely have to set time aside for your employees. Whether appraising someone's performance, conducting a disciplinary matter, counselling your employees, or hearing a grievance, you're giving them the kind of input that only you can provide. You set the goals for your employees, and you set the standards by which you measure their progress. Inevitably, you decide whether your employees have reached the marks you've set or whether they have fallen short. You can't delegate away these matters – they are your direct responsibility; and they are your priority when they arise.

When delegation goes wrong

Delegation can, and does, go wrong, and so you have to identify the danger signs before it is too late and you have a crisis on your hands. You need to monitor the performance of your staff in several ways:

✔ **Personal follow-up:** Supplement your formal tracking system with an informal system of visiting your workers and checking their progress on a regular basis.

✔ **Sampling:** Take periodic samples of your employees' work and check to make sure that the work meets the standards you agreed to.

✔ **Progress reports:** Regular progress reporting from employees to you can give you advance notice of problems and successes.

✔ **A formalised tracking system:** Use a formal system to track assignments and due dates. Many organisations have these systems on computer. Progress charts pinned to the wall are highly visible, very public – and extremely useful!

If you discover that your employees are in trouble, you have several options for getting everything back on track:

✔ **Increased monitoring:** Spend more time monitoring employees who are in trouble, keeping closer track of their performance.

✔ **Counselling and support:** Discuss the problems with your employees and agree on a plan to correct them.

✔ **Taking back authority:** If problems continue despite your efforts to resolve them through counselling and support, you can overrule your employees' authority to complete the tasks independently. (They still work on the task, but under closer guidance and supervision.)

✔ **Reassigning activities:** The ultimate solution when delegation goes wrong. If your employees can't do their assigned tasks, give the tasks to workers who are better suited to perform them successfully.

Politically sensitive situations

Some situations are just too politically sensitive to assign to your employees. Say that you're in charge of auditing the travel expenses for your organisation. The results of your review show that a member of the corporation's top management team has made several personal trips on company expenses. Do you assign the responsibility for reporting this tricky situation to one of your staff, or do you do it yourself? You shouldn't even think of the question!

Not only do such sticky situations demand your utmost attention and expertise, but placing your employee in the line of fire in a potentially explosive situation is also unfair. Being a manager may be tough sometimes, but you're paid to make the difficult decisions and to take the political heat that your work generates.

Personal assignments

Occasionally, your boss assigns a specific task to you with the intention that you can personally perform it. They may have very good reasons for doing so: You may have a unique perspective that no one else in your organisation has, or you may have a unique skill that needs to be brought to bear to complete the assignment quickly and accurately. Whatever the situation, if a task is assigned to you with the expectation that you, and only you, carry it out, then you can't delegate it to your staff. You may decide to involve your staff in gathering input, but you must retain the ultimate responsibility for the final execution of the task.

Confidential or sensitive circumstances

As a manager, you know things, such as wage and salary information, personal data, and performance appraisals, that your staff doesn't know about. If this information gets into the wrong hands, it can be very damaging to an organisation. Salary information should be kept confidential, and people's personal and personnel files should never be released. Similarly, if your competitors get their hands on new products and services that your organisation has spent hours and resources developing, the impact on your organisation and employees can be devastating. It is therefore absolutely essential to evaluate the full sensitivity of any such information before you let employees look at it.

Checking Up, Not Checking Out

In practice, of course, delegation can be tough. Assume that you've already worked through the initial hurdles of delegation – you assigned a task to your employee, and you're anxiously waiting to see how he performs. You defined the scope of the task and gave your employee the adequate training and resources to get it done. Not only that, but also you told him what results you expect and exactly when you expect to see them. What do you do next?

Here's one option: An hour or two after you make the assignment, you check on its progress. In a couple more hours, you check again. As the deadline rapidly approaches, you increase the frequency of your checking until finally, your employee spends more time answering your questions about the progress he has made than he spends actually completing the task. Not only that, but every time you press him for details about his progress, he gets a little more distracted from his task. He becomes flustered with your continuing interruptions and frustrated with your seeming lack of confidence in his abilities. When the appointed hour arrives, he submits the result on time, but the report is inaccurate and incomplete.

Here's another option: After you make the assignment to your employee, you do nothing. Yes, you heard right. You do nothing. Instead of checking on your employee's progress and offering your support, you assign the task and move on to other concerns. When the appointed hour arrives, you're surprised to discover that the task is not completed. When you ask your employee why he didn't meet the goal that you had mutually agreed, he tells you that he had trouble obtaining some information and, rather than bother you with this problem, he decided to try to construct it for himself. Unfortunately, this slight diversion required an additional two days of research before he found the correct set of numbers.

Clearly, neither extreme is productive. However, this example does illustrate some of the difficulties involved, and the amount of knowledge, understanding, and expertise required if delegation is to be effective. In practice, and depending on the situation, you may ask for daily or weekly progress reports from your employee. And again, you are only going to make matters worse if your employees cannot get hold of you when they need to.

Each employee is unique. One style of monitoring may work with one employee but not with another. New or inexperienced employees naturally require more attention and handholding than employees who are seasoned at their jobs – whether they realise it or not. Experienced and expert employees don't need the kind of day-to-day attention that less experienced employees require. In fact, they may resent your attempts to closely manage the way in which they carry out their duties.

Effective monitoring of delegation requires the following:

- ✔ **Tailor your approach to the employee.** If your employees performs their job with minimal supervision on your part, then establish a system of monitoring with only a few, critical checkpoints along the way. If your employees need more attention, create a system (formal, in writing, or informal) that incorporates several checkpoints along the way to goal completion.

- ✔ **Rigorously use a written or computer-based system to keep a track on progress.** Use a daily planner, personal digital assistant, or project management software program to keep track of the what, who, and when of task assignments. Making a commitment to get organised is important – for your employees and for yourself. Do it!

- ✔ **Keep the lines of communication open.** Make sure that your employees are aware that you want them to let you know if they can't surmount a problem. This, of course, means making time for your employees when they come by to ask you for help. Find out whether they need more training or better resources. Finding out too early – when you can still do something about it – is better than finding out too late.

Top five delegation Web sites

The best information on the Web about the topics addressed in this chapter is at:

✔ Wise Women Network: `www.wise women.org.nz/words/fiona/ delegate.htm`

✔ Centre for Service and Leadership: `www.gmu.edu/student/csl/ delegation.html`

✔ Chartered Institute of Personnel and Development: `www.cipd.co.uk/ flexibleworking`

✔ Trades Union Congress: `www.tuc.org. uk/workingpractices`

✔ Advisory, Conciliation and Arbitration Service (ACAS): `www.acas.org.uk/ working practices`

✔ **Follow through on the agreements that you make with your employees.** If a report is late, then hold your employees accountable. Despite the temptation to let these failures slip ('Yes, it was a poor performance, but he has domestic problems at the moment'), ignoring them does both you and your employees a disservice. Make sure that your employees understand the importance of taking personal responsibility for their work and that the ability of your group to achieve its goals depends on their meeting commitments. Be compassionate if your employee has indeed gone through a tough personal challenge (mother died, spouse diagnosed with cancer, and so on) – you may need to assign someone else to cover his duties for a short period. If, however, an employee consistently misses goals and shows no hope of improvement, then perhaps he is in the wrong job.

✔ **Reward performance that meets or exceeds your expectations, and review performance that falls below your expectations.** If you don't let your employees know when they fail to meet your expectations, then they may continue to fail to meet your expectations. Do your employees, your organisation, and yourself a big favour and bring attention to both the good things and the bad things that your employees do. Remember the old saying (which happens to be an accurate one), praise in public and criticise in private. You can find many more details about counselling employees in Chapters 6 and 9.

Chapter 3

Lead, Follow, or Get Out of the Way

In This Chapter

▶ Comparing leadership and management

▶ Becoming a leader

▶ Zeroing in on key leadership traits

▶ Leading collaboratively

*W*hat makes a leader? Experts have written countless books, produced endless videos, and taught innumerable seminars on the topic of leadership. But leadership is still a quality that eludes many who seek it.

Studies show that the two primary traits that all effective leaders have in common are a positive outlook and forward thinking. Effective managers are sure of themselves and their ability to inspire and influence others and to shape the future.

Everyone in an organisation wants to work for great leaders. Employees want the men and women they work for to exhibit leadership. 'I wish that my boss would just make a decision – I'm just marking time until she does. So I just wait until she lets me know what she does want me to do.' And wait employees do – until the boss finally notices that the project is two months behind. Top executives want the men and women who work for them to exhibit leadership. 'You need to take responsibility for your department and pull the numbers into the black before the end of the financial year!' And employees want their peers to show leadership. 'If she's not going to straighten out that invoicing process, then I'm just going to have to work around it myself!'

A leader is many things to many people. In this chapter, we discuss the key skills and attributes that make good managers into great leaders. As the chapter explains, leadership requires the application of a wide variety of skills. No single trait, even when you've mastered it, suddenly makes you an effective leader. 'You mean that I can't become a great leader just from watching that video?' However, you may notice that some leadership skills described in this chapter are also key functions of management – ones that we outline in Chapter 1. This similarity is no coincidence. And, for an in-depth look at leadership, refer to *Leadership For Dummies* by Marshall Loeb (Wiley).

Understanding the Differences between Management and Leadership

Although similar, leadership and management are different: Leadership goes above and beyond management. A manager can be organised and efficient at getting tasks done without being a leader – without being someone who inspires others to achieve their best. In short, managers *manage* processes and resources, whilst leaders *lead* people. According to management visionary Peter Drucker, leadership is the most basic and scarcest resource in any business enterprise. We concur wholeheartedly.

Being a good manager is quite an accomplishment. Management is by no means an easy task, and mastering the wide range of varied skills required can take many years. The best managers get their jobs done efficiently and effectively – with a minimum of fuss and bother. Like the people behind the scenes of a great performance in sports or the theatre, the best managers are often those you notice the least.

Great managers are experts at taking their current organisations and optimising them to accomplish their goals and get their jobs done. By necessity, they focus on the here and now – not on the tremendous potential of what the future can bring. Organisations expect managers to make things happen now – not at some hazy point in the future. 'Don't tell me what you're going to do for me next year or the year after that! I want results, and I want them now!' Having good managers in an organisation, however, isn't enough on its own.

Great organisations need great management. However, great management doesn't necessarily make a great organisation. For an organisation to be great, it must also have great leadership.

Leaders have vision. They look beyond the here and now to see the vast potential of their organisations. And although great leaders are also effective at getting things done in their organisations, they accomplish their goals in a different way from managers.

How is the leader's way different? Managers use values, policies, procedures, schedules, milestones, incentives, discipline, and other mechanisms to push their employees to achieve the goals of the organisation.

Leaders, on the other hand, challenge their employees to achieve the organisation's goals by creating a compelling vision of the future and then unlocking their employees' potential.

Think about some great leaders:

- ✔ In the darkest hours of the Second World War, Winston Churchill challenged the British people to stand alone and to fight for what was right. They did.

- ✔ Anita Roddick challenged the management and staff of The Body Shop to inspire and excite customers, not just to sell cosmetics to them. They did.

- ✔ Michael O'Leary of Ryanair challenged – and continues to challenge – his staff to improve everything they can, including turn around times, speed of service, cleaning the aircraft cabins, and keeping to schedule. They did – and they still do.

All these leaders share a common trait. They all painted compelling visions that grabbed the imagination of their followers and then challenged them to achieve these visions. Without the vision that leaders provide and without the contributions of their followers' hard work, energy, and innovation, Great Britain would have fallen to the Nazis, The Body Shop would be just another company, and Ryanair would not be the largest airline by passenger numbers carried in the European Union.

Looking at What Leaders Do

The skills required to be a leader are no secret. Some managers have worked out how to use the skills and others haven't. And although some people seem to be born leaders, anyone can discover what leaders do and how to apply these skills themselves.

Inspire action

Despite what some managers believe, most workers want to feel pride for their organisation and, when given the chance, would give their all to a cause they believe in. A tremendous well of creativity and energy is just waiting to be tapped in every organisation. Leaders use this knowledge to inspire their employees to take action and to achieve great things.

Leaders know the value of employees and their critical place in achieving the company's goals. Do the managers in your company know the importance of their employees? Have a look at what these managers had to say in Bob Nelson's *1001 Ways to Reward Employees:*

✔ Former chairman and CEO of the Ford Motor Company Harold A. Poling said, 'One of the stepping stones to a world-class operation is to tap into the creative and intellectual power of each and every employee.'

✔ Richard Branson, founder and CEO of the Virgin Group, states: 'The staff come first. Only by having expert, highly committed, and well rewarded staff can the Virgin Organisation hope to succeed through creating and delivering top quality products and services, and the best possible customer satisfaction.'

✔ Michael Marks, former chief executive of Marks and Spencer, used to say: 'Everyone who works for Marks and Spencer wants to do a good job. Without them we have no company. They are proud to work for this company; and I am very proud to have them working for me.'

Unfortunately, few managers reward their employees for being creative or for going beyond the boundaries set by their job descriptions. Too many managers search for workers who do exactly what they are told – and little else. This practice is a tremendous waste of workers' creativity, ideas, talent, and commitment.

Use your influence as a manager to help your employees create energy in their jobs instead of draining it from them with bureaucracy, red tape, policies, and an emphasis on avoiding mistakes.

Leaders are different. Instead of draining energy from their employees, leaders unleash the natural energy within all employees. They do so by clearing the roadblocks to creativity and pride from the paths of their workers and by creating a compelling vision for their employees to strive for. Leaders help employees to tap into energy and initiative that the employees didn't know they had.

Create a compelling vision for your employees and then clear away the roadblocks to creativity and pride. Your vision must be a stretch to achieve, but not so much of a stretch that the vision is impossible to achieve.

Communicate

Leadership takes place *among* people. Leaders therefore make a commitment to communicate with their employees and to keep them fully informed about every aspect of the organisation. Employees want to be an integral part of the organisation and want their opinions and suggestions to be heard and valued. Great leaders earn the commitment of their workers by building communication links throughout the organisation – from the top to the bottom, from the bottom to the top, and from side to side.

So how do you build communication links in your organisation? Consider the experiences of the following business leaders, as listed in Bob's *1001 Ways to Reward Employees:*

✔ According to Donald Petersen, former president and CEO of Ford Motor Company, 'When I started visiting the plants and meeting with employees, what was reassuring was the tremendous, positive energy in our conversations. One man said he'd been with Ford for 25 years and hated every minute of it – until he was asked for his opinion. He said that question transformed his job.'

✔ Andrea Nieman, administrative assistant with the Rolm Corporation, a computer company now part of the IBM Corporation, summarised her company's commitment to communication like this: 'Rolm recognises that people are the greatest asset. There is no "us" and "them" attitude here; everyone is important. Upper management is visible and accessible. There is always time to talk, to find solutions, and to implement changes.'

✔ Said Robert Hauptfuhrer, former chairman and CEO of Oryx Energy, 'Give people a chance not just to do a job but to have some impact, and they'll really respond, get on their roller skates, and race around to make sure it happens.'

When Bob became a department manager at Blanchard Training and Development, he made a commitment to his team of employees to communicate with them. To make his commitment real, Bob added a specific promise: He promised that he would report the results of every executive team meeting within 24 hours. Bob's department valued his team briefings, because through this communication, he treated all individuals as colleagues – not as underlings.

Great leaders know that leadership isn't a one-way street. Leadership today is a two-way interchange of ideas where leaders create a vision and workers throughout an organisation develop and communicate ideas of how best to reach the vision. The old one-way, command-and-control model of management doesn't work any more. Ordering people about may have worked satisfactorily once. As a daily means of managing a company today, it does not work well at all. Most employees aren't willing simply to take orders and be directed all day long; if treated this way, expert and otherwise committed employees merely take their talents elsewhere. And if you think your employees want to be ordered around, you're only fooling yourself.

Support and facilitate

Great leaders create environments in which employees are safe to speak up, to tell the truth, and to take risks. An incredible number of managers punish their employees for pointing out problems that they encounter, for disagreeing with the conventional wisdom of management, or for merely saying what is on their minds. Even more incredibly, many managers punish their employees for taking risks and losing, instead of helping their employees win the next time around.

Great leaders support their employees and facilitate those employees' abilities to reach their goals. The head of an organisation where Peter once worked did just the opposite. Instead of leading his employees with vision and inspiration, he pushed them with the twin cattle prods (120 volts!) of fear and intimidation. The management team members lived in constant fear of his temper, which could explode without warning and seemingly without reason. More than a few managers wore the psychological bruises and scars of his often-public outbursts. Instead of contributing to the good of the organisation, some managers simply withdrew into their shells and said as little as possible in this leader's presence. Consider these managers' statements in *1001 Ways to Reward Employees:*

- ✔ Catherine Meek, president of compensation consulting firm Meek and Associates, says, 'In the 20 years I have been doing this and the thousands of employees I have interviewed in hundreds of companies, if I had to pick one thing that comes through loud and clear it is that organisations do a lousy job of recognising people's contributions. That is the number one thing employees say to us. "We don't even care about the money; if my boss would just acknowledge that I exist. The only time I ever hear anything is when I screw up. I never hear when I do a good job."'

- ✔ According to Lonnie Blittle, an assembly-line worker for Nissan Motor Manufacturing Corporation USA, 'There was none of the hush-hush atmosphere with management behind closed doors and everybody else waiting until they drop the boom on us. They are right down pitching in, not standing around with their hands on their hips.'

- ✔ James Berdahl, vice-president of marketing for Business Incentives, says, 'People want to feel empowered to find better ways to do things and to take responsibility for their own environment. Allowing them to do this has had a big impact on how they do their jobs, as well as on their satisfaction with the company.'

Instead of abandoning their employees to the sharks, great leaders throw their followers life-jackets when the going gets particularly rough. Although leaders allow their employees free rein in how they achieve the organisation's goals, leaders are always there in the background – ready to assist and support workers whenever necessary. With the added security of this safety net, employees are more willing to stretch themselves and to take chances that can create enormous rewards for their organisations.

Surveying Leading Leadership Traits

Today's new business environment is unrelenting change. About the only constant you can be sure of any more is that everything will change. And after it changes, it changes again and again.

Key business trends to watch out for

According to Stanley Bing, an incredibly insightful columnist for *Fortune* magazine, many trends are sweeping the business landscape. One major trend is the necessity for managers to *talk the talk* and *walk the walk.* While talking the talk means sounding like you know what you're doing, walking the walk takes this idea a step farther and requires that you also look like you know what you're doing – whether you do know or not.

The percentage of executives who can talk the talk and those executives who can walk the walk has been increasing since 1970. However, the ability of managers to talk the talk and walk the walk at the same time has steadily declined from its peak some 20 years ago. Here is some advice from Bing regarding these critical leadership skills:

✔ 'First, always talk the talk, even when others don't seem to understand what you're saying. It's all about consistency and perception – so keep it up!

✔ Second, if you're not in a position to talk the talk, either because someone superior is doing so or because you've got your mouth full, default to walking the walk exclusively, thereby projecting the necessary executive qualities in dignity and silence.

✔ Third, don't try doing both together until you're very good at it. There's nothing more pathetic than somebody attempting to walk/talk concurrently and getting his ankles all bollixed up while irreverent employees stand around chortling. So practice!'

Get used to it now, because business will continue to transform in the foreseeable future. Although so much in business is shifting, great leadership remains steadfast – like a sturdy rock standing up to the storms of change. Numerous traits of great leaders have remained the same over the years and are still highly valued today. The following sections discuss the leading leadership traits.

Optimism

Great leaders always see the future as a wonderful place. Although they may find much adversity and hard work on the way to achieving their goals, leaders always look forward to the future with great promise and optimism. This optimism becomes a glow that radiates from all great leaders and touches all those employees who come into contact with them.

People want to feel good about themselves and their futures, and they want to work for winners. Workers are therefore naturally attracted to people who are optimistic rather than pessimistic. Who wants to work for someone who enjoys nothing more than spouting doom and gloom about the future of a business? Negative managers only demotivate their employees and colleagues, which leads everyone to spend more time polishing up their CVs than concentrating on doing their work to the best of their ability and improving their organisations.

Optimism is infectious. Before long, a great leader can turn an organisation full of doom merchants into one that's overflowing with positive excitement for the future. This excitement results in greater worker productivity and an improved organisational environment. Morale increases, and so does the organisation's bottom line.

Be an optimist. Let your excitement rub off on those people around you.

Confidence

Great leaders have no doubt – at least not in public – that they can accomplish any task that they set their minds to.

'What? A 10,000 foot-high mountain is in the way? No problem – we'll climb it. You say that a vast ocean is separating us from our goal? No sweat – we'll swim it. Hmmm . . . a bottomless crevasse is blocking our path? Fine – we'll leap it. Whatever the challenge may be, we'll find a way to surmount it.'

Confident leaders make for confident followers, which is why organisations led by confident leaders are unstoppable. An organisation's employees mirror the behaviour of their leaders. When leaders are negative, tentative, and unsure of themselves, so are workers (and the bottom-line results of the organisation). When leaders display self-confidence, workers follow suit, and the results can be astounding.

Be a confident leader. You inspire the best performance from your employees at the same time as you help them to become more confident in their abilities.

Integrity

One trait that sets great leaders apart from the rest of the pack is *integrity*: ethical behaviour, values, and a sense of fair play. Honest people want to follow honest leaders. *Integrity* means establishing the standards by which you're determined to operate, and then never compromising on them. You make an absolute commitment to work on the basis of fairness, equality, honesty, and trust, and then you deliver – always! You never succumb to pressure, you never compromise on fairness, you never tell lies – whatever the circumstances or adversity with which you're faced. And you can learn all this; you can choose to do things in these ways, or you can choose not to. Which are you going to choose?

In a recent survey, integrity was the trait employees most wanted from their leaders. When an organisation's leaders conduct themselves with integrity, the organisation can make a very real and positive difference in the lives of its employees, its customers, and others who come in contact with it. This, in turn, results in positive feelings from employees about the organisation.

People working in the United Kingdom devote up to a third (or more) of their waking hours to their jobs. Whether the organisation makes light fittings, disposes of toxic waste, develops virtual reality software, or delivers pizzas, people want to be part of an organisation that makes a positive difference in the lives of others. Of course money is important – people have to pay their bills and buy clothes for their children – but unless wages are very low, few people count *external* rewards as a primary consideration over the *internal* rewards that they themselves derive from their work.

Decisiveness

The best leaders are decisive. All employees' main complaint is that their bosses won't make decisions – and they say this over and over again. Despite the fact that making decisions is one of the key reasons that people are hired to be managers, too few are willing to risk the possibility of making a wrong decision. So instead of making wrong decisions – and having to face the consequences – many so-called leaders prefer to postpone making a decision indefinitely, instead continually seeking more information, alternatives, and opinions from others. They hope that, eventually, events may overtake the need to make the decision, or perhaps that someone else takes the platform and makes the decision for them.

Great leaders make decisions. Now, this statement doesn't mean that great leaders make decisions in a shoot-from-the-hip, cavalier, guess-at-the-right-answer fashion. No, great leaders take whatever time is necessary to gather whatever information, people, or resources they need to make an informed decision within a reasonable time frame. If the data is immediately available, so be it. If not, then a leader carefully weighs the available data versus the relative need for the decision and acts accordingly.

Be decisive. Don't wait for the course of events to make decisions for you. Sometimes making a decision – even if you make the wrong decision – is better than making no decision at all.

Fostering Collaborative Leadership

A new kind of leadership is gaining strength in an increasing number of organisations: *collaborative leadership.* When leaders lead collaboratively, they share leadership with others in the organisation. And not just with other managers and supervisors, but with employees at all levels – from the shop floor to the front line and everywhere else.

So, what exactly does collaborative leadership look like in the workplace? Here are a few examples:

- ✔ To encourage collaborative leadership, banking powerhouse J.P. Morgan Chase maintains a flat organisation with only four levels of employees worldwide – managing director, vice-president, associate, and analyst. With fewer lines of reporting, every employee has the opportunity – and the responsibility – to play a much greater role in leading and in making decisions.

- ✔ Harvester, the pub/restaurant chain, did away with three levels of management – restaurant manager, office manager, and head waiter. Chefs now became responsible for planning the menus and ordering the food. Waiting staff collectively became responsible for taking and accepting bookings, showing guests to their tables, and cashing up at the end of each working day. This is truly collaborative: The staff are responsible and accountable only to a regional manager.

- ✔ Colman's Foods makes mustards, sauces, herbs, and spices for the retail grocery sector. While off duty, one employee had occasion to visit his local supermarket. To his horror, he saw that the whole stack of Colman's mustard had been badly labelled – the labels were either not straight or they were scuffed or dirty. Accordingly, he bought the whole stock, took it back to the factory and presented it to his manager. And the company even refunded him his money!

- ✔ Dutton Engineering makes steel and aluminium furniture for industrial, commercial, and office premises. In order to tackle the problem of ever-rising costs, Ken Lewis, the company's chief executive, organised everyone into self-managing teams. These teams recruit and select employees; set their own performance schedules (subject only to customer deadlines); and establish their own pay, reward, and bonus levels. Ken Lewis has one assistant, but all the work is now carried out by teams themselves. Ken Lewis no longer has an office – the employees decided collectively that this space can be better used in a directly productive capacity.

In his book *Leadership Ensemble: Lessons in Collaborative Management from the World's Only Conductorless Orchestra,* Peter (one of your authors) takes a very close look at the unique brand of collaborative leadership practised by New

York City's Orpheus Chamber Orchestra. Orpheus is one of the world's truly great orchestras, and it is one of very few to perform without a conductor. The vast majority of orchestras are noted not because of the musicians who play the music, but because of their conductors, who are often visionary, charismatic (and autocratic) leaders. The conductor calls all the shots when it comes to the notes that an orchestra's musicians play, and how and when they play them.

By forgoing the traditional model of a conducted orchestra – with one leader and many followers – Orpheus fosters a culture of collaboration where every musician can be a leader, and all are expected to play an active role in shaping the group's final product – its music. Does this system work? Yes. Orpheus's performances have been acclaimed throughout the world, and the group has numerous Grammy-winning albums and other awards to its credit.

At the heart of the Orpheus process – the system of collaborative leadership that has brought the group great success over its three-decade history – are eight principles. These principles are:

- ✔ **Put power in the hands of the people doing the work.** Those employees closest to the customers are in the best position to know the customers' needs, and they're in the best position to make decisions that directly affect their customers.

- ✔ **Encourage individual responsibility for product and quality.** The flip side of putting power in the hands of the people doing the work is requiring employees to take responsibility for the quality of their work. When employees are trusted to play an active role in their organisation's leadership, they naturally respond by taking a personal interest in the quality of their work.

- ✔ **Create clarity of roles.** Before employees can be comfortable and effectively share leadership duties with others, they first have to have clearly defined roles so that they know exactly what they are responsible for, as well as what others are responsible for.

- ✔ **Foster horizontal teamwork.** Because no one person has all the answers to every question, effective organisations rely on horizontal teams – both formal and informal – that reach across departmental and other organisational boundaries. These teams obtain input, solve problems, act on opportunities, and make decisions.

- ✔ **Share and rotate leadership.** By moving people in and out of positions of leadership – depending on an individual's particular talents and interests – organisations can tap the leadership potential that resides within every employee, even those employees who aren't part of the formal leadership hierarchy.

Top five leadership Web sites

Wondering where to find the best information on the Web about the topics addressed in this chapter? Well, you've come to the right place! Here are our top five favourites:

✔ *Management Today* magazine: www.managementtoday.com

✔ London Business School Centre for Leadership and Executive Management: www.lbs.ac.uk/leadership

✔ The Judge Institute, University of Cambridge: www.judge.ac.uk/leadership

✔ Wafic Said Business School, University of Oxford: www.said.ac.uk/leadership

✔ Institute of Directors: www.iod.org.uk/executivedevelopment

✔ **Discover how to listen, discover how to talk.** Effective leaders don't just listen: Effective leaders talk – and they know the right times (and the wrong times) to make their views known. Effective organisations encourage employees to speak their minds and to contribute their ideas and opinions – whether or not others agree with what they have to say.

✔ **Seek consensus (and build creative systems that favour consensus).** One of the best ways to involve others in the leadership process is to invite them to play a real and important role in the discussions and debates that lead to making important organisational decisions. Seeking consensus requires a high level of participation and trust, and it results in more democratic organisations.

✔ **Dedicate passionately to your mission.** When people feel passion for the organisations in which they work, they care more about them and about their performance. This caring is expressed in the form of increased employee participation and leadership.

Collaborative leadership is growing in popularity in all kinds of organisations in all kinds of places. Why? Collaborative leadership is growing because organisations today can't afford to limit leadership to just a few individuals at the top. To survive and prosper, today's organisations need to get the most out of every employee. Every employee needs to take a leadership role in her organisation, to make decisions, to serve customers, to support colleagues, and to improve systems and procedures. Employees – and leaders – who can't meet this challenge may soon find that they're left behind by others who can.

Part II
Managing People

'Well, for a start, it's your spelling . . . .'

In this part . . .

If nothing else, managing is a people job. The best managers work well with all people. In this part, we show you how to hire great employees, inspire employees to achieve their best performance, and to coach employees.

Chapter 4

Recruitment and Selection: The Million-Pound Decision

In This Chapter

▶ Determining your needs

▶ Recruiting new employees

▶ Interviewing do's and don'ts

▶ Evaluating your candidates

▶ Making the big decision

*G*ood employees are hard to find. If you've had the recent privilege of advertising for a job opening, you know that good employees aren't easy to come by. Here's the scenario: You place the advertisement and then wait for the applications to come flooding in. In just a day or two, you're pleased beyond your wildest dreams as you see the stack of applications awaiting your attention. How many are there – 100? 200? Well done indeed, what a response!

Your glee quickly turns to disappointment, however, as you begin your review. 'Why did this guy apply? He doesn't have half the required experience!' 'What? She's never even done this kind of work before.' 'Is this man joking? He must have responded to the wrong advertisement!'

Finding and hiring the best candidates for a job has never been easy. Unfortunately, with all the streamlining, downsizing, and rightsizing going on in business nowadays, a lot of people are looking for work – and the chances are that very few of them have the exact qualifications that you're looking for. Your challenge is to work out how to pluck the best candidates out of the sea strewn with the wreckage of corporate cast-offs. The lifetime earnings of the average British worker can be as high as £1,000,000. Recruitment and selection really is therefore a million-pound decision!

Asking for the Right Stuff

Your mission is to locate the most highly qualified suitable candidates for your job opening. When you locate your candidates, your task is to narrow your selection down to one person and to ensure that recruitment leads to his successful entry into the organisation. This is not always as easy or as straightforward as it sounds.

Some years ago, the Ministry of Defence (MOD) advertised for a civilian quartermaster and stores manager. The post was to be based at a large army barracks in south-east England, and would additionally require work at other barracks nearby.

The MOD advertised the post, received numerous applications, and drew up a shortlist. Finally, the organisation took on a candidate. The new employee, a man in his early 40s, was pleasant, cheerful, and polite. He made a good start to his work, and everybody liked him. At the end of his first week, his manager asked him to go off to one of the other barracks to collect some things. The conversation went like this:

'How do I get there?' asked the new employee.

'Take your car and claim the mileage – that is usual and that will be fine,' came the reply.

'But I don't drive.'

Because the MOD had not specified the need for a driving licence, and because this is something that 'everybody has', nobody had thought to check up on this small, but vital factor. The consequence was that the MOD found itself forking out for a driver whenever the new employee had to go elsewhere as part of his duties. The MOD additionally paid for driving lessons; and when the new person had passed his test, they provided a loan at favourable rates for him to buy a car.

Employers look for many qualities in candidates. What do you look for when you interview? The following list gives you an idea of the qualities that employers consider most important when hiring new employees. Other characteristics may be particularly important to you.

✔ **Hard working:** Hard work can often overcome a lack of experience or training. You want to take on people who are willing to do whatever it takes to get the job done. Conversely, no amount of skill can make up for a lack of initiative or work ethic. Although you don't know for sure until you make your choice, careful questioning of candidates can give you some idea of their work ethic (or, at least, what they want you to believe about their work ethic).

✔ **Good attitude:** Although what constitutes a 'good' attitude is different for different people, a positive, friendly, willing-to-help perspective makes life at work much more enjoyable and makes everyone's job easier. When you interview candidates, consider what they'll be like to work with for the next five or ten years. Skills are important, but attitude is even more important. This is the 'mantra' for the success of Southwest Airlines, the American equivalent of low-cost airlines Ryanair and easyJet: 'Hire for attitude, train for success.'

✔ **Experienced:** If you're asking for experience, be specific. In many cases, someone with 20 years' experience has in fact only had one year's experience – 20 times. So specify the things that you want the person to have done; and if you ask for '5/10/15 years' experience', make it clear what you expect the candidate to have done during that period of employment. Make it clear that you are not seeking people of a particular age – age discrimination is now illegal, and you can be prosecuted for unlawful discrimination. So be careful!

✔ **Initiative:** Everyone prefers somebody who takes the initiative to get work done. You are not going to get anything – from the new employee or from existing staff – if you take people on who are going to sit around waiting until you allocate tasks to them.

✔ **Team player:** Teamwork is critical to the success of today's organisations, which must do far more with far fewer resources than their predecessors. The ability to work with others effectively is a definite must for employees today.

✔ **Smart:** Smart people can often find better and quicker solutions to the problems that confront them. You need people who are going to do things for you, not say things to you.

✔ **Responsible:** You want to recruit people who are willing to take on the responsibilities of their positions. Questions about the kinds of projects that your candidates have been responsible for, and the exact roles they played in their success, can help you determine this important quality. Little factors, like showing up for the interview and remembering the name of the company they're applying to, can also be key indicators of your candidates' sense of responsibility.

✔ **Stable:** You don't want to hire someone today and then find out that he is already looking for his next position tomorrow. You can get some indication of a person's potential stability (or lack of) by asking how long he worked with his previous employer and why he left. Not only that, but you can also enjoy listening to your candidates explain, in intimate detail, how they've finished sowing their wild oats and are now ready to settle down.

Hiring the right people is one of the most important tasks that managers face. You can't have a great organisation without great people. Unfortunately, managers traditionally give short shrift to this task – devoting as little time as possible to preparation and to the actual interview process. As in much of the rest of your life, the results that you get from the hiring process are usually in direct proportion to the amount of time that you devote to it. If you commit yourself to finding the best candidates for a position, you're much more likely to find them. If you rely on chance to bring them to you, you may be disappointed by what and whom you find.

Defining the Job and the Person

Whether the position is new, or you're filling an existing post, before you start the recruiting process you need to know exactly what standards you're going to use to measure your candidates. The clearer you are about what you need, the easier and less arbitrary your selection process becomes.

Draft a job description and person specification that fully describes all the tasks, responsibilities, and characteristics of the position, and the minimum necessary qualifications and experience. And if the job requires a driving licence, for example, then say so! Otherwise, you start making mistakes right from the start.

If you're filling an existing position, review the current job description closely and make changes where necessary. This is a good opportunity to rearrange workloads and make changes if you need to. Again, make the job description reflect exactly the tasks and requirements of the position. When you hire someone new to fill an existing position, you start with a clean slate. For example, you may have had a difficult time getting a former employee to accept certain new tasks – say, taking minutes at staff meetings or filing travel vouchers. By adding these new duties to the job description before you begin recruitment, you make the expectations clear, and you don't have to struggle to get your new employee to do the job.

Finally, before you start recruiting, get the desired qualities and characteristics into a priority order. If necessary, consult with colleagues to make sure that you give yourself the best possible chance of getting the right candidate for the job.

Additionally, when you come to interviewing, by law you have to give everybody the same chance. So use the characteristics in their priority order as the basis for your interviewing and selection methods. If you fail to do this, unsuccessful candidates can question the basis on which you turned them down for the job, and if any doubt at all exists that they were given fair treatment, they can (and in many cases, do) make representations to employment tribunals. So get this right – now!

Finding Good People

People are the heart of every business. The better the people running your business, the better your business.

Some people are just meant to be in their jobs. You may know such individuals – someone who thrives as a receptionist or someone who lives to sell. Think about how great your organisation would be if you staffed every position with people who lived for their jobs.

Likewise, bad staff can make working for an organisation an incredibly miserable experience. The negative impacts of hiring the wrong candidate can reverberate throughout an organisation for years. If you, as a manager, ignore the problem, you put yourself in danger of losing your good employees. We can't overemphasise the importance of recruiting and retaining the right people. Do you want to spend a few extra hours up front to find the best candidates, or do you want to devote countless hours later trying to straighten out a problem employee? And if you still need convincing, a recent survey by the Chartered Institute of Personnel and Development estimates that it costs up to twice the annual salary to replace an employee.

Of course, as important as the interview process is to selecting the best candidates for your jobs, you don't have anyone to interview if you don't have a good system for finding good candidates. So where can you find the best candidates for your jobs?

The simple answer is everywhere. Certainly, some places are better than others – you probably won't find someone to run your lab's fusion reactor project by advertising on the backs of matchboxes – but you never know where you can find your next star programmer or award-winning advertising copywriter. Who knows, he may be working for your competitors right now!

As you maximise your chances of success, you also minimise your chances of failure. The most effective recruitment and selection processes take place when you have plenty of time to evaluate all the candidates; and when you're not pressed to take on someone if you have not so far attracted anyone of the calibre you want.

Ideally, you can involve other employees in the recruitment and selection process as well, especially if they're going to be working with the new candidate. So do at least consider any particular demands that other employees may have before you finalise your candidate list.

The following list presents some of the best ways to find candidates for your positions. Your job is to develop a recruitment campaign that can find the kinds of people that you want to take on. Don't rely solely on your human resources (HR) department to develop this campaign for you; you probably have a better understanding of where to find the people you need than they do, so work with HR to best advantage. And make sure that your contribution is noted.

✔ **Taking a close look within:** In most organisations, the first place to look for candidates is within the organisation. If you do your job in training and developing employees, then you probably have plenty of candidates to consider for your job openings. Only after you exhaust your internal candidates should you look outside your organisation. Not only is taking on people in this way less expensive and easier, but you also get happier employees, improved morale, and a steady stream of people who are already familiar with your organisation.

✔ **Personal referrals:** Whether from existing work groups, professional colleagues, friends, relatives, or neighbours, you can find great candidates by referrals. Who better to present a candidate than someone whose opinion you already value and trust? You get far more insight about the candidates' strengths and weaknesses from the people who refer them than you ever get from applications alone. Not only that, but research shows that people hired through current employees tend to work better, stay with the company longer, and are happier. When you're getting ready to fill a position, make sure that you let people know about it.

✔ **Temporary agencies:** Taking on *temps,* or temporary employees, has become routine for many companies. When you simply have to fill a critical position for a short period of time, temporary agencies are the way to go. And the best part is that when you hire temps, you get the opportunity to try out employees before you take them on. If you don't like the temps you get, no problem. Simply call the agency, and they send replacements before you know it. But if you like your temps, most agencies allow you to employ them at a nominal fee or after a minimum time commitment. Either way, you win.

✔ **Professional associations:** Most professions have their accompanying associations that look out for their interests. Whether you're a doctor (and belong to the British Medical Association), or a lorry driver (and belong to the Transport and General Workers Union), you can probably find an affiliated association for whatever you do for a living. Association newsletters, journals, and magazines are great places to advertise your openings when you're looking for specific expertise, because your audience is already pre-screened for you.

✔ **Employment agencies:** If you're filling a particularly specialised position, are recruiting in a small market, or simply prefer to have someone else take care of recruiting and screening your applicants, employment agencies are a good, albeit pricey alternative (with a cost of up to one-third of the employee's first-year salary, or more). Although employment agencies can usually locate qualified candidates in lower-level or administrative positions, you may need help from an executive search firm or *headhunter* (someone who specialises in recruiting key employees away from one firm to place in a client's firm) for your higher-level positions.

✔ **The Internet:** Every day, more and more companies discover the benefits of using the Internet as a hiring tool. Although academics and scientists have long used Internet newsgroups to advertise and seek positions within their fields, corporations are now following suit. The proliferation of corporate Web pages and online employment agencies and job banks has brought about an entirely new dimension in recruiting. Web pages let you present almost unlimited amounts and kinds of information about your firm and about your job openings – in text, audio, graphic, and video formats. Your pages work for you 24 hours a day, 7 days a week.

For an example of a particularly effective recruiting Web site, point your browser to www.qualcomm.com and click on the Careers button.

✔ **Recruitment advertising:** Recruitment advertising can be relatively expensive, but it's an easy way to get your message across. You can choose to advertise in your local paper or in nationally distributed publications such as the *Financial Times*. On the downside, you may find yourself sorting through hundreds or even thousands of unqualified candidates to find a few great ones. But that's what your human resources department is for, right?

You have to consider whether or not you proceed if you don't find the right candidate. It's a real testament to your values and preliminary work to stick with your plan and extend the candidate recruiting period to allow for additional candidates, or delay the recruitment for another time.

Being the Greatest Interviewer in the World

After you narrow the field down to the top three or five applicants, you need to start interviewing. What kind of interviewer are you? Do you spend several hours preparing for interviews – reviewing applications, looking over job descriptions, writing and rewriting questions until each one is as finely honed as a razor blade? Or are you the kind of interviewer who, busy as you already are, starts preparing for the interview when you get the call from your receptionist that your candidate has arrived?

The secret to becoming the Greatest Interviewer in the World is to spend some serious time preparing for your interviews. Remember how much time you spent preparing to be interviewed for your current job? You didn't just walk in the door, sit down, and get offered the job, did you? You probably spent hours researching the company, its products and services, its financial position, its market, and other business information. You probably brushed up on your interviewing skills and may have even done some role-playing with a friend or in front of a mirror. Don't you think that you should spend at least as much time getting ready for the interview as the people do whom you're going to interview?

Asking the right questions

More than anything else, the heart of the interview process is the questions that you ask and the answers that you receive in response. You get the best answers when you ask the best questions and actively listen to the answers. Lousy questions often result in lousy answers – answers that don't really tell you whether the candidate is going to be right for the job.

A great interviewer asks great questions. 'How do I ask great questions?' you may want to know. According to Richard Nelson Bolles, author of the perennially popular job-hunting guide *What Colour Is Your Parachute?*, you can categorise all interview questions under one of the following four headings:

- ✔ **Why are you here?** Really. Why is the person sitting across from you going to the trouble of interviewing with you today? You have just one way to find out – ask. You may assume that the answer is because he wants a job with your firm, but you may be surprised at what you discover.

  One of the candidates on the documentary *The Apprentice*, who had reached the later stages and was clearly well in contention for the final, destroyed his chances simply because he had not bothered to find out the exact nature of products made by Amstrad, the company that he'd be working for.

- ✔ **What can you do for us?** Always an important consideration. Of course, your candidates are all going to dazzle you with their incredible personality, experience, work ethic, and love of teamwork – that almost goes without saying. However, despite what many job seekers seem to believe, the question is not 'What can your firm do for me?' – at least not from your perspective. The question that you want an answer to is 'What can you do for us?'

  One manager tells a story about the job applicant who slammed his hand on her desk and demanded a signing bonus. And this was before the interview had even started! We're not surprised that this particular candidate didn't land the job or the bonus.

- ✔ **What kind of person are you?** Few of your candidates are going to be absolute angels or demons, but don't forget that you spend a lot of time with the person you hire. You want to take on someone you enjoy being with during the many work hours, weeks, and years that stretch before you. (Okay, at least someone you can tolerate being with for a few hours every once in a while.) You also want to confirm a few other issues: Are your candidates honest and ethical? Do they share your views in regard to work hours, responsibility, and so forth? Are they responsible and dependable employees? Of course, all your candidates answer in the affirmative to bland questions like these. So, how do you find the real answers?

  When Bob used to recruit, he would try to 'project' the applicant into a typical, real-life scenario and then see how they thought it through. This way, there is no 'right' answer and they're forced to expose their thinking process, for example the questions they would ask, strategies they would consider, people they would involve, and so forth. Ask open-ended questions and let your candidates do most of the talking. Your candidate should talk for at least 70 per cent of the interview.

✔ **Can we afford you?** It does you no good if you find the perfect candidate, but at the end of the interview, you bring up the topic of pay and find out that you're so far apart that you're actually in a different country. Keep in mind that the actual wage you pay to workers is only part of an overall compensation package. Although you may not be able to pull together more money for wages for particularly good candidates, you may be able to offer them better benefits, longer holidays, more development opportunities, or, ultimately, a faster career track.

Interviewing do's

So what can you do to prepare for your interviews? The following handy checklist gives you ideas on where to start:

✔ **Review the applications of each interviewee the morning before interviews start.** Not only is it extremely poor form to wait to read your interviewees' applications during the interview, but also you miss out on the opportunity to tailor your questions to those little surprises that you invariably discover (such as gaps in employment).

✔ **Become completely familiar with the job description.** Are you familiar with all the duties and requirements of the job? Really? Telling interviewees that the position requires duties that it really doesn't is poor form. Surprising new staff with duties that you didn't tell them about – especially when they are major duties – is definitely not good practice.

✔ **Draft your questions before the interview.** Make a checklist of the key experience, skills, and qualities that you seek in your candidates and use it to guide your questions. Of course, one of your questions may trigger other questions that you didn't anticipate. Go ahead with such questions as long as they provide you with additional insights regarding your candidate and help to illuminate the information that you've outlined on your checklist. And remember, equality of treatment and employment law demand that you give all candidates the same opportunities to shine at interview.

✔ **Select a comfortable environment for both of you.** Your interviewee is likely to be uncomfortable regardless of what you do. You don't need to be uncomfortable, too. Make sure that the interview environment is well ventilated, private, and protected from interruptions. You definitely don't want your phone ringing or employees barging in during your interviews. You get the best performance from your interviewees when they aren't thrown off track by distractions.

✔ **Avoid playing power trips during the course of the interview.** Forget the old games of asking trick questions, turning up the heat, or cutting the legs off their chairs (yes, some managers still do this game playing) to gain an artificial advantage over your candidates. Get real – we're in the twenty-first century, for heaven's sake!

✔ **Take lots of notes.** Write down the key points of your candidates' responses and their reactions to your questions. For example, if you ask why your candidate left his previous job, and he starts getting really nervous, make a note about this reaction. Finally, note your own impressions of the candidates:

- 'Top-notch performer – the star of her class.'

- 'Fantastic experience with developing applications in a client-server environment. The best candidate yet.'

- 'Not right for this job.' Remember that if you write anything disparaging or overtly disrespectful about a candidate, you *have* to be able to say why. If an unsuccessful candidates decides to take you to an employment tribunal, you don't want your notes coming back to haunt you. So avoid one-word statements such as 'Hopeless'; if someone isn't right for the job, briefly note why and move on. Your candidates have the right to see any notes that you may have made, so always write them as if you were going to share them anyway.

✔ **Don't rely on your memory when it comes to interviewing candidates.** If you interview more than a couple of people, you can easily forget who said exactly what and what your impressions were of their performances. Not only are your written notes a great way to remember who's who, but also they're an important tool to have when you're evaluating your candidates. And, if there is any comeback (as above), you have your notes to refer to.

As you have no doubt gathered by now, interview questions are one of your best tools for determining whether a candidate is right for your company. Although some amount of small talk is appropriate to help relax your candidates (as sweat poured down the candidate's face, the interviewer asked the opening question with razor-like sharpness: 'Hot enough for you?'), the heart of your interviews should focus on answering the questions just listed. Above all, don't give up. Keep asking questions until you're satisfied that you have all the information you need to make your decision.

Interviewing don'ts

The topic of interviewing don'ts is probably worth a chapter of its own. If you've been a manager for any time at all, you know that you can run into tricky situations during an interview and that certain questions can land you in major hot water if you make the mistake of asking them.

Some interviewing don'ts are merely good business practice. For example, accepting an applicant's invitation for a date is probably not a good idea. After a particularly drawn-out interview at a well-known high-tech manufacturer, a male candidate asked out a female interviewer. The interviewer considered her options and declined the date; she also declined to make Prince Charming a job offer.

Then you have the blunders of the major legal type – the kind that can land you and your firm in court. Interviewing is one area of particular concern in the hiring process as it pertains to the possibility of discrimination. For example, although you can ask applicants whether they are able to fulfil job functions, you can't ask them whether they are disabled.

Always ask if any adjustments or provisions need to be made in order for a candidate to gain an equal opportunity in their application. This includes access to your place of work; application forms and directions in Braille; and any other specific issues.

Because of the critical nature of the interview process, you must know the questions that you should absolutely never ask a job candidate. Here's a brief summary of the kinds of topics that may, depending on the exact circumstances, get you and your firm into trouble:

- Applicant's race or skin colour
- Applicant's national origin
- Applicant's sex
- Applicant's sexual orientation
- Applicant's marital status
- Applicant's religion (or lack of)
- Applicant's arrest and conviction record
- Applicant's height and weight
- Applicant's debts
- Applicant's disability
- Applicant's age

Legal or illegal, the point is that none of the preceding topics is necessary to determine the applicants' ability to perform their jobs. Therefore, ask questions that directly relate to the candidates' ability to perform the tasks required. To do otherwise puts you at risk. In other words, what *do* count are job-related criteria; that is, information that's directly pertinent to the candidate's ability to do the job (you clearly need to decide this *prior* to interviewing).

Five steps to better interviewing

Every interview consists of five key steps. They are

1. **Welcome the applicant.** Greet your candidates warmly and chat with them informally to help loosen them up. Questions about the weather, the difficulty of finding your offices, or how they found out about your position are old stand-bys.

2. **Summarise the position.** Briefly describe the job, the kind of person you're looking for, and the interview process that you use.

3. **Ask your questions (and then listen!).** Questions should be relevant to the position and should cover the applicant's work experience, education, and other related topics. Limit the amount of talking you do as an interviewer. Many interviewers end up trying to sell the job to an applicant instead of probing whether or not he is a good fit.

4. **Probe experience and find out the candidate's strengths and weaknesses.** The best predictor of future behaviour is past behaviour, which is why exploring an applicant's past experience can be so helpful to see what they did and how they did it. And although asking your candidates to name their strengths and weaknesses may seem clichéd, the answers can be very revealing. So ask them – and then listen carefully to the answers.

5. **Conclude the interview.** Allow your candidates the opportunity to offer any further information that they feel is necessary for you to make a decision, and to ask questions about your firm or about the job. Thank them for their interest and let them know when they can expect your firm to contact them.

Evaluating Your Candidates

Now comes the tricky part of the recruitment process – evaluating your candidates. If you have done your homework, then you already have a good selection of candidates to choose from, you've narrowed your search down to the ones showing the best potential to excel in your position, and you've interviewed them to see whether they can live up to the promises that they've made in their applications. Before you make your final decision, you need a little bit more information.

Checking references

So – you have just interviewed the best candidate on the planet. What an application! What an interview! What a candidate! Now – would you be surprised to find that this shining employee-to-be didn't really go to Oxford? Or that he really wasn't the account manager on that nationwide marketing campaign? Or that his last supervisor wasn't particularly impressed with his analytical skills?

Applications, curricula vitae, and interviews are great tools, but you do need references. However, getting references can be tricky – for although you are entitled to ask previous employers specific questions about the candidate's performance, the previous employer may choose whether or not to answer them.

The primary purpose of checking references is to verify the information your candidates provide. If you want further insights into how your candidates really performed in their previous jobs, then you need to ask specific questions about absence records, achievements, and jobs or positions held.

When you contact a candidate's referees, limit your questions to those related to the work to be done. As in the interview process, asking questions that can be considered discriminatory to your candidates is not appropriate.

Here are some of the best places to do your reference checking:

- ✔ **Check academic references.** A surprising number of people exaggerate or tell outright lies when reporting their educational experience. Start your reference check here. If your candidates didn't tell the truth about their education, you can bet that the rest of their experience is suspect, too, and you can toss the candidate into the discard pile before you proceed.

- ✔ **Call current and former supervisors.** Getting information from employers is getting harder. Many business people are rightfully concerned that they may be sued for libel or defamation of character if they say anything negative about current or former employees. Still, it doesn't hurt to try. You get a much better picture of your candidates if you speak directly to their current and former supervisors instead of to their firms' human resources department – especially if the supervisors you speak to have left their firms. The most you are likely to get from human resources is a confirmation that the candidate worked at the firm during a specific period of time.

- ✔ **Check your network of associates.** If you belong to a professional association, union, or similar group of like-minded careerists, you have the opportunity to tap into the rest of the membership to get the word on your candidates. For example, if you're a member of the Chartered Institute of Personnel and Development (MCIPD) and want to find out about a few candidates for a position in human resources, you can check with the members of your professional association to see whether anyone knows anything about them.

- ✔ **Surf the Web.** Especially for top, senior, and specialist positions, plug your candidate's name into a search engine such as Google (www. google.com), perhaps along with the name of the company where he last worked or the city in which he lives. You never know what can turn up!

Reviewing your notes

You did take interview notes, didn't you? Now's the time to drag them back out and look them over. Review the information package for each candidate – one by one – and compare your findings against your pre-determined criteria. Take a look at the candidates' applications, your notes, and the results of your reference checks, such as they are. How do the candidates stack up against the standards that you set for the position? Do you see any clear winners at this point? Any clear losers? Organise your candidate packages into the following piles:

- ✔ **Winners:** These candidates are clearly the best choices for the position. You have no hesitation in hiring any one of them.

- ✔ **Potential winners:** These candidates are questionable for one reason or another. Maybe their experience isn't as strong as that of other candidates, or perhaps you weren't impressed with their presentation skills. Neither clear winners nor clear losers, you hire these candidates only after further investigation, or if you can't hire anyone from your pool of winners.

- ✔ **Losers:** These candidates are clearly unacceptable for the position. You simply don't consider hiring any of them.

Make sure that you can justify your choice for each pile on the basis of capability, willingness, and availability to do the job alone.

Conducting second (or third) interviews

When you're a busy manager, you have pressure to get things done as quickly as possible, and you're tempted to take shortcuts to achieving your goals. It seems that everything has to be done yesterday – or maybe the day before. When do you have the opportunity to really spend as much time as you want to complete a task or project? Time is precious when you have ten other projects crying for your attention. Time is even more valuable when you're hiring for a vacant position that's critical to your organisation and needs to be filled right now.

Recruitment is one area of business where you can't take shortcuts. Finding the best candidates for your vacancies requires a very real investment of time and resources to be successful. Your company's future depends on it.

Depending on your organisation's policies or culture, or because you're undecided as to the best candidate, you may decide to bring candidates in for several rounds of interviews. In this kind of system, lower-level supervisors, managers, or interview panels conduct initial screening interviews. Candidates who pass this round are invited back for another interview with a higher-level manager. Finally, the best two or three candidates interview with the organisation's top manager.

But keep in mind that the timescale for an offer is very different depending on the job you're interviewing for. Lower-level job hunters cannot afford to be unemployed (if they are) for long, and they often get and accept job offers quickly. A higher-level position – say, a general manager – gives you more time.

The ultimate decision on how many rounds and levels of interviews to conduct depends on the nature of the job itself, the size of your company, and your policies and procedures. If the job is simple or at a relatively low level in the company, a single phone interview may be sufficient to determine the best candidate for a job. However, you may need several rounds of testing and personal interviews if the job is complex or at a relatively high level in the organisation.

Engaging the Best (and Leaving the Rest)

The first step in making a recruitment decision is to rank your candidates within the groups of winners and potential winners that you established during the evaluation phase of the process. You don't need to bother ranking the losers because you wouldn't take them on anyway – no matter what. The best candidate in your group of winners is first, the next best is second, and so on. If you have done your job thoroughly and well, the best candidates for the job should be readily apparent at this point.

The next step is to get on the phone and offer your first choice the job. Don't waste any time – you never know whether your candidate has had interviews with other employers. Investing all this time in the recruitment process is wasted if you find out that he just accepted a job with one of your competitors. If you can't get an agreement with your first choice in a reasonable amount of time, then go on to your second choice. Keep going through your pool of winners until you take someone on, or exhaust the list of candidates.

The following sections give you a few tips to keep in mind as you rank your candidates and make your final decision.

Being objective

In some cases, you may prefer certain candidates because of their personality or personal charisma – regardless of their ability or work experience. Sometimes the desire to like these candidates can obscure their shortcomings, while a better qualified, albeit less socially adept, candidate may fade in your estimation.

Be objective. Consider the job to be done and consider the skills and qualifications that being successful requires. Do your candidates have these skills and qualifications? What would it take for your candidates to be considered fully qualified for the position?

Don't allow yourself to be unduly influenced by your candidates' looks, champagne-like personalities, high-priced hairstyles, or dangerously named colognes. None of these characteristics can tell you how well your candidates can perform the job. The facts are present for you to see in your candidates' applications, interview notes, and reference checks. If you stick to the facts, you can still go wrong, but the chances are diminished.

And one more thing: Diversity in all staffing practices is positive for any organisation – both for the business and for society in general. Leave your bias at the door!

Trusting your gut

Sometimes you're faced with a decision between two equally qualified candidates, or with a decision about a candidate who is marginal but shows promise. In such cases, you have weighed all the objective data, and you have given the analytical side of your being free rein, but you still have no clear winner. What do you do in this kind of situation?

Listen to yourself. Unlock your heart, your feelings, and your intuition. What do you feel in your gut? What do your instincts tell you? Although two candidates may seem equal in skills and abilities, do you have a feeling that one is better suited to the job than the other? If so, go with it. As much as you may want your hiring decision to be as objective as possible, whenever you introduce the human element into the decision-making process, a certain amount of subjectivity is naturally present.

In reality, rarely are two candidates equally qualified, although often one or more people seem to have more to bring to the job than anticipated (for example, industry focus, fresh ideas, previous contacts, and so forth). This is again where your preliminary work can be so valuable in keeping you focused. Can they both do the job? If so, the bonus traits can tip the scale.

Other options:

- ✔ Take one or the other (or both) on for a trial period.
- ✔ Have them both back for a round of interviews (and if this seems expensive, remember the consequences of a bad decision).

A further review of two more or less equally qualified candidates may draw you to the conclusion that, in fact, neither is good enough; in that case, advertise again.

Top five hiring Web sites

Here are our top five favourite recruitment advice Web sites:

✔ Financial Times: `www.ft.com/recruitment`

✔ The Times: `www.thetimes.co.uk/careers`

✔ The Daily Telegraph: `www.telegraph.co.uk/management and executive focus`

✔ Advisory, Conciliation and Arbitration Service (ACAS): `www.acas.org.uk/employmentpractice`

✔ Chartered Institute of Personnel and Development (CIPD): `www.cipd.co.uk/recruitmentandselection`

A civil engineering company based in Central London was having great difficulty attracting and retaining reception desk staff. Employment agencies throughout the West End of London were constantly being asked to send candidates. Each person taken on was capable and competent to do the work; however, they always moved on within six months. When asked why they were moving on, the standard response was: 'Not very glamorous, civil engineering, is it?' The company solved the problem by hiring as a receptionist a man in his early 40s. An ex-soldier, this man had broken his back on a mountaineering expedition and was confined to a wheelchair. The man has now been in the post for nearly nine years; and, to date, has never had a day off sick.

One more thing: Be sure to keep in touch with other top candidates as additional needs arise in case your first choice doesn't work out.

Adjusting after the offer

What do you do if, heaven forbid, you can't hire anyone from your group of winners? This does happen; but no one said that management is an easy task. Take a look at your stack of potential winners. What would it take to make your top potential winners into winners? If the answer is as simple as a training course or two, then give these candidates serious consideration – with the agreement that they take the necessary training soon after engagement. Perhaps they just need a little more experience before you can put them in the ranks of the winners. You can make a judgement call as to whether you feel that their current experience is sufficient to carry them through until they gain the experience you are looking for. If not, you may want to keep looking for the right candidate. After all, this person may be working with you for a long time – waiting for the best candidate only makes sense.

If you're forced to go to your group of almost winners, and no candidate really seems up to the task, then don't hire someone simply to fill the position. If you do, you're probably making a big mistake. Taking people on is far easier than getting rid of them. The damage a bad choice can cause – for colleagues, customers, and your organisation (not to mention the person you hire) – can take years and a considerable amount of money to undo. Such a situation is also extremely stressful. You can also consider whether to redefine the job, re-evaluate other current employees, or give someone a temporary contract to see whether a potentially risky candidate really works out.

Chapter 5

Inspiring Employees to Better Performance

In This Chapter

▶ Introducing the Greatest Management Principle in the World
▶ Finding out what motivates employees
▶ Deciding what behaviours to reward
▶ Starting with the positive
▶ Rewarding the little things
▶ Using non-monetary rewards

*T*he question of how to motivate employees has loomed large over managers ever since management was first invented. Most of management comes down to mastering skills and techniques for motivating people – to make them better, more productive employees who love their jobs more than anything else in the world. Well, perhaps not quite that much; but you do want them to turn up and be as happy, effective, and productive as possible.

You have two ways to motivate employees – rewards and punishments. If employees do what you want them to do, reward them with incentives that they desire – awards, recognition, important titles, money, and so on. We often call these *positive consequences*. Alternatively, if employees don't do what you want, punish them with what they don't desire – warnings, reprimands, demotions, firings, and so on – often known as *negative consequences*. By nature, employees are drawn towards positive consequences and shy away from negative consequences.

Increasingly, however, with today's employees, to be an effective manager you have to work harder at providing a greater number of positive consequences on an ongoing basis when employees perform well (they expect it). And you have to be *much* more selective as to when and how you use negative consequences. It is much harder to fire people than in previous times, and wrongful and unfair dismissals get you into trouble with the law.

This chapter deals with the positive side of employee motivation – positive consequences, especially recognition and rewards. (We're sorry if you're eager to read about the punishment side, but we cover that in Chapter 15.) Besides, 100 years of research in behavioural science and continuing extensive studies at all of the world's major business schools show that you have a much greater impact on getting the performance you want from your employees when you use positive consequences rather than negative ones.

We aren't saying that negative consequences don't have a place; sometimes you have no choice but to punish, reprimand, or even dismiss employees. However, first give your employees the benefit of the doubt that they do want to do a good job and acknowledge them when they do so. Make every effort to use positive recognition, praise, and rewards to encourage the behaviours you seek, and catch people doing things right. If you do this, your employees are more motivated to want to excel in their jobs, performance and morale improve, and your company is considered a much better place to work.

By leading with positive reinforcements, not only can you inspire your employees to do what you want, but you can also develop happier, more productive employees in the process – and that combination is tough to beat.

The Greatest Management Principle in the World

We're about to let you in on the Greatest Management Principle in the World. This simple rule can save you countless hours of frustration and extra work, and it can save your company many thousands or perhaps even millions of pounds. Sounds pretty awe inspiring, doesn't it? Are you ready? Okay, the statement is:

You get what you reward.

Don't let the seeming simplicity of the statement fool you – read on to explore it.

Recognition isn't as simple as it looks

You may think that you're rewarding your employees to do what you want them to do, but are you really?

Consider the following example. You have two employees: Employee A is incredibly talented and Employee B is a marginal performer. You give similar assignments to both employees. Employee A completes the assignment before the due date and hands it in with no errors. Because Employee A is already done, you give her two additional assignments. Meanwhile, Employee B is not only late, but when she finally hands in the report you requested, it is full of errors. Because you're now under a time crunch, you accept Employee B's report and then correct it yourself.

What's wrong with this picture? Who's actually being rewarded: Employee A or Employee B?

If you answered Employee B, you're right. This employee has discovered that submitting work that is substandard and late is okay. Furthermore, she also sees that you personally fix it. That's quite a nice reward for an employee who clearly doesn't deserve one. (Another way to put it is that Employee B certainly has you well trained!)

On the other hand, by giving Employee A more work for being a diligent, out-standing worker, you're actually punishing her. Even though you may think nothing of assigning more work to Employee A, she knows the score. When Employee A sees that all she gets for being an outstanding performer is more work (while you let Employee B get away with doing less work), she's not going to like it one little bit. And if you end up giving both employees basi-cally the same pay rise (and don't think that they won't find out), you make the problem even worse. You lose Employee A, either literally, as she takes another job, or in spirit, as she stops working so hard.

If you let the situation continue, all your top performers eventually realise that doing their best work is not in their best interest. As a result, they leave their position to find an organisation that values their contribution, or they simply sit back and forget about doing their best work. Why bother? No one (that means you, the manager) seems to care anyway.

Biscuit motivation

Giving everyone the same incentive – the same salary increase, equal recog-nition, or even equal amounts of your time – we call *biscuit motivation*. Although this treatment may initially sound fair, it isn't.

Nothing is as unfair at work as the equal treatment of unequal performers. You need to assess the performance of everyone. You then make clear to each person why they have received rewards and bonuses, or why they have not. These rewards must be evenly and honestly distributed. And if everyone meets the standards demanded, then reward them all as you have promised.

Thinking through your rewards

Richard tells the story of the City of London branch of an international bank that was having problems with sickness absence. Staff were phoning in sick for all kinds of reasons, and collective absenteeism was in the order of 7 per cent (it was taking 107 people to do the work of 100 at any given time).

Being a concerned employer, the bank decided to reward positive behaviour rather than punishing bad or negative behaviour. Consequently, a note went round to all staff informing them that anyone who had not had any time off on self-certificated absence or ringing in sick was entitled to an extra week's holiday the following year.

Needless to say, the plan misfired. Genuine hardworking employees who had had a day or two off with real illnesses and injuries now found themselves slighted, tarred with the same brush as malingerers. Having had a day or two off with genuine ailments, good staff were now taking extra time off so as not to miss out on the additional week's holiday that they had been promised.

The bank's human resources department met to review the policy. Acknowledging the weaknesses, another note went round to everyone to say that staff would still get their extra week's holiday provided that all absences were covered by doctor's certificates. In a very short space of time, human resources became swamped with doctor's certificates, and had to take on another member of staff just to deal with them. Again, additional complaints came from those with genuine illnesses and injuries – that they were having to go to the doctor, and very often pay for a doctor's certificate, just in order to prove that their illness was genuine. For the malingerers, payment for a doctor's certificate simply validated a false position.

The bank reviewed the policy again. The suggestion was raised (seriously) that all those who had had fewer than five days self-certificated absence should be entitled to an extra two weeks' holiday the following year. Only at this point did the human resources director take matters into her own hands; at last, she cancelled the policy, and concentrated efforts on the malingerers rather than the genuine, committed, and hardworking staff.

If people are not performing up to standard, then take the particular individuals aside and tell them why. Tell them what they need to do to make the grade, and how they can go about it. This is a much better way of going about things than letting people go about things without your active involvement and interest. You want everyone working as well as possible, and your job is to sort out those who aren't up to scratch.

Don't forget the Greatest Management Principle in the World – you get what you reward.

Before you set up a system to reward your employees, make sure that you know exactly what behaviours you want to reward and then align the rewards with those behaviours.

After you put your employee reward system in place, check periodically to see that the system is getting the results that you want. Check with those you're trying to motivate and see if the programme is still working. If it isn't, change it!

Discovering What Employees Want

In today's tight, stressful, changing times, what things are most important to employees? Bob conducted a survey of about 1,500 employees from across seven industries to answer that question. We list the top ten items that employees said were most important, along with some thoughts on how you can better provide each of these elements to your own employees:

- ✔ **A learning activity (No. 1) and choice of assignment (No. 9):** Today's employees most value opportunities in which they gain skills that can enhance their worth and marketability in their current job as well as future positions. Discover what your employees want to find out, how they want to grow and develop, and where they want to be in five years. Give them opportunities as they arise and the ability to choose work assignments whenever possible. When you give employees the choice, more often than not they rise to meet or exceed your expectations.

- ✔ **Flexible working hours (No. 2) and time off from work (No. 7):** Today's employees value their time – and their time off. Be sensitive to their needs outside work, whether these needs involve family or friends, charity or church, education or hobbies. Provide flexibility whenever you can so that employees can meet their obligations. Time off may range from an occasional afternoon to attend a child's play at school or the ability to start the workday an hour early so the employee can leave an hour early. By allowing work to fit best with an employee's life schedule, you increase the chances that they're motivated to work harder while they are at work, and do their best to make their schedule work. And from a managerial standpoint, as long as the job gets done, what difference does it matter what hours someone works? And in any case, employees now have a legal right to request flexible working hours, and you have a legal obligation to consider their request.

- ✔ **Personal praise – verbal (No. 3), public (No. 8), or written (No. 10):** Although you can thank someone in 10 to 15 seconds, most employees report that they're never thanked for the job they do – especially not by their manager. Systematically start to thank your employees when they do good work, in person, in the hallway, in a group meeting, on voice-mail, in a written thank-you note, on e-mail, or at the end of each day at work. Better yet, go out of your way to act on and share and amplify good news when it occurs – even if it means interrupting someone to thank her for a great job she's done. By taking the time to say you noticed and appreciate her efforts, you help those efforts – and results – to continue. And bring her efforts to your manager's attention – this reinforces your own integrity, as well as making sure that full credit goes where it's due.

- ✔ **Increased autonomy (No. 5) and authority (No. 4) in their job:** The ultimate form of recognition for many employees is to have increased autonomy and authority to get their job done, including the ability to spend or allocate resources, make decisions, or manage others. Greater autonomy and authority says, 'I trust you to act in the best interests of the company, to do so independently and without approval of myself or others.' Increased autonomy and authority should be awarded to employees as a form of recognition itself for the past results they achieved. Autonomy and authority are privileges, not rights, which should be granted to those employees who have most earned them, based on past performance, and not based on tenure or seniority.

- ✔ **Time with their manager (No. 6):** In today's fast-paced world of work in which everyone is expected to get more done faster, personal time with your manager is in itself also a form of recognition. As managers are busier, taking time with employees is even more important. The action says, 'Of all the things I have to do, one of the most important is to take time to be with you, the person or people I most depend on for us to be successful.' Especially for younger employees, time spent with a manager is a valued form of validation and inspiration, as well as serving a practical purpose of learning and communication, answering questions, discussing possibilities, or just listening to an employee's ideas, concerns, and opinions.

By the way, you may wonder where money ranked in importance in this survey. A 'cash reward' ranked thirteenth in importance to employees. (We say more about the topic of money as a motivator later in this chapter.) Everyone needs money to live, but work today involves more than what anyone gets paid.

Employees report that the most important aspects at work today are primarily the intangible aspects of the job that any manager can easily provide – if she makes it a priority to do so. Now we're going to tell you a big secret. This secret is the key to motivating your employees. You don't need to attend an all-day seminar or join the management-video-of-the-week club to discover this secret: We are letting you in on it right here and right now at no extra charge:

Ask your employees what they want.

This statement may sound silly, but you can take a lot of the guesswork out of your job by simply being clear about what your employees most value in their jobs. It may be one or more of the items mentioned earlier in this section, or it may be something entirely different. The simplest way to find out how to motivate your employees is to ask them. Often managers assume that their employees want only money. These same managers are surprised when their employees tell them that other things – such as being recognised for doing a good job, being allowed greater autonomy in decision making, or having a more flexible work schedule – may be much more motivating than cash. Regardless of what preferences your employees have, you're much better off knowing those preferences explicitly rather than guessing or ignoring them. So:

> ✔ **Plan to provide employees with more of what they value.** Look for opportunities to recognise employees for having done good work and act on those opportunities as they arise, realising that what motivates some employees doesn't motivate others.

> ✔ **Stick with it over time.** Motivation is a moving target and you need to constantly be looking to meet your employees' needs in order to keep them motivated to help you meet your needs.

Consider the following as you begin setting the stage for your efforts:

1. **Create a supportive environment for your employees by first finding out what they most value.**

2. **Design ways to implement recognition to thank and acknowledge employees when they do good work.**

3. **Be prepared to make changes to your plan, based on what works and what doesn't.**

Creating a supportive environment

The new business realities of the present day bring a need to find different ways to motivate employees. Motivation is no longer an absolute, my-way-or-the-highway proposition. The incredible acceleration of change in business and technology today is coupled with greatly expanded global competitive forces. With these forces pressing in from all sides, managers can have difficulty keeping up with what employees need to do, much less figure out what to tell them to do. In fact, a growing trend is for managers to manage individuals who are doing work that the managers themselves have never done. (Fortunately, given a little time and a little trust, most employees can work out what needs to be done by themselves.)

Inspiring managers must embrace these changing business forces and management trends. Instead of using the power of their position to motivate workers, managers must use the power of their ideas. Instead of using threats and intimidation to get things done, managers must create environments that support their employees and allow creativity to flourish.

You, as a manager, can create a supportive workplace in the following ways:

- **Build and maintain trust and respect.** Employees whose managers trust and respect them are motivated to perform at their best. By including employees in the decision-making process, today's managers get better ideas (that are easier to implement) and, at the same time, they improve employees' morale, loyalty, and commitment.

- **Removing the barriers of getting to work.** If you ask your employees what are the biggest hurdles they face in coming to work, you get a huge range of answers – rush-hour traffic, getting the kids to school, having to use public transport, and so on. By allowing them to choose their hours of work, you give them the opportunity to work around these barriers. You are also entitled to expect that, having chosen their hours of work, they then show up and do a good job. You cannot do this for every eventuality, and crises always happen. However, as long as the employee is prepared to give you a reasonable and regular pattern of hours, you should at least consider being flexible.

- **Open the channels of communication.** The ability of all your employees to communicate openly and honestly with one another is critical to the ultimate success of your organisation and plays a major role in employee motivation. Today, quick and efficient communication of information throughout your organisation can be what differentiates you from your competition. Encourage your employees to speak up, to make suggestions, and to break down the organisational barriers – the rampant departmentalisation, turf protection, and similar roadblocks – that separate them from one another, where and whenever they find them.

- **Make your employees feel safe.** Are your employees as comfortable telling you the bad news as they are telling you the good news? If the answer is no, you haven't created a safe environment for your employees. Everyone makes mistakes; people discover valuable lessons from their mistakes. If you want employees who are motivated, make it safe for them to take chances and to let you know the bad along with the good. And use mistakes and errors as opportunities for growth and development; never ever punish mistakes and errors except those generated as the result of negligence or incompetence.

- **Develop your greatest asset – your employees.** By meeting your employees' needs, you also achieve your organisation's needs. Challenge your employees to improve their skills and knowledge and provide them with the support and training that they need to do so. Concentrate on the positive progress they make and recognise and reward such success whenever possible.

Having a good game plan

Motivated employees don't happen by accident. You must have a plan to reinforce the behaviour you want. In general, employees are more strongly motivated by the potential to earn rewards than they are by the fear of punishment. Clearly, a well thought out and planned motivation, incentive, and rewards system is important to creating a committed, effective workforce. Here are some simple guidelines for setting up a system of low-cost rewards in your organisation:

- ✔ **Link rewards to organisational goals.** To be effective, rewards need to reinforce the behaviour that leads to achieving an organisation's goals. Use rewards to increase the frequency of desired behaviour and decrease the frequency of undesired behaviour.

- ✔ **Define parameters and mechanics.** After you identify the behaviours you want to reinforce, develop the specifics of your reward system. Create rules that are clear and easily understood by all employees. Make sure that goals are attainable and that all employees have a chance to obtain rewards, whatever their job and occupation.

- ✔ **Obtain commitment and support.** Of course, communicate your new rewards programme to your employees. Many organisations publicise their programmes at group meetings. They present the programmes as positive and fun activities that benefit both the employees and the company. To get the best results, plan and implement your rewards programme with your employees' direct involvement.

- ✔ **Monitor effectiveness.** Is your rewards system getting the results you want? If not, take another look at the behaviours you want to reinforce and make sure that your rewards are closely linked to the behaviours. Even the most successful reward programmes tend to lose their effectiveness over time as employees begin to take them for granted. Keep your programme fresh by discontinuing rewards that have lost their lustre and bringing in new ones from time to time.

Deciding What to Reward

Most organisations and managers reward the wrong things, if they reward their employees at all. This tendency has led to a crisis of epic proportions in the traditional system of incentives and motivation in business. For example:

- ✔ A major London commodity market gave bonuses of 6 per cent of salary to outstanding employees; and it gave bonuses of 3 per cent of salary to everyone else. Average and adequate performers were therefore receiving exactly the same reward except for the extra three per cent of salary delivered to top performers.

✔ A top professional footballer on many thousands of pounds a week joined one of the very top football clubs, only to find himself playing in the reserve team at exactly the time when he was trying to develop his career and reputation through playing regularly. He was therefore receiving a very good reward, but not the one that he wanted.

✔ A council employee rated 'exceptional' was told by her manager that she had to be downgraded to 'average' because the County Council Social Services Department had no money to pay her bonus.

If workers aren't being rewarded for doing outstanding work, what are they being rewarded for? As we point out in the 'Biscuit motivation' section earlier in the chapter, organisations often reward employees just for showing up for work.

For an incentive programme to have meaningful and lasting effects, it must be contingent; that is, it must focus on performance – nothing less and nothing more.

'But wait a second,' you may say, 'that isn't fair to the employees who aren't as talented as my top performers.' If that's what you think, we can straighten out that particular misunderstanding right now. Everyone, regardless of how smart, talented, or productive they are, has the potential to be a top performer.

Suppose that Employee A produces 100 widgets an hour and stays at that level of performance day in and day out. On the other hand, Employee B produces 75 widgets an hour but improves output to 85 widgets an hour. Who should you reward? Employee B! This example embodies what you want to reward: The efforts that your employees make to improve their performance, not just to maintain a certain level (no matter how good that level is).

The following are examples of *performance-based measures* that any manager must recognise and reward. Consider what measures you should be monitoring, measuring, and rewarding in your organisation. Don't forget, just showing up for work doesn't count.

✔ Defects decrease from 25 per 1,000 to 10 per 1,000.

✔ Annual sales increase by 20 per cent.

✔ The department records system is reorganised and colour-coded to make filing and retrieval more efficient.

✔ Administrative expenses are held to 90 per cent of the authorised budget.

✔ The organisation's mail is distributed in 1 hour instead of 1½ hours.

Praising guidelines

A basic foundation for a positive relationship is the ability to praise well. Bob uses ASAP-cubed to give a good praise, which means:

✔ **As soon:** Timing is very important when using positive reinforcement. Give praise as soon as the desired behaviour is displayed.

✔ **As sincere:** Words alone can fall flat if you're not sincere in why you're praising someone. Praise someone because you are truly appreciative and excited about the other person's success. Otherwise, it may come across as a manipulative tactic or simply patronising.

✔ **As specific:** Avoid generalities in favour of details of the achievement. For example, 'You really turned that angry customer around by focusing on what you could do for him, not on what you could not do for him.'

✔ **As personal:** A key to conveying your message is praising in person, face to face. This shows that the activity is important enough to you to put aside everything else you have to do and just focus on the other person.

✔ **As positive:** Too many managers undercut praise with a concluding note of criticism. When you say something like 'You did a great job on this report, but there were quite a few typos', the 'but' becomes a verbal erasure of all that came before.

✔ **As proactive:** Lead with praise and catch people doing things right. Otherwise, you tend to be reactive – typically about mistakes – in your interactions with others.

You can give praise directly to the employee, in front of another person (in public), or when the person isn't around (via letter, e-mail, voice-mail, and so forth). Praising employees only takes a moment, but the benefits – to your employees and to your organisation – last for years.

Some managers break incentives into two categories – 'results measures', where measures are linked to the bottom line, and 'process measures', where the link to the bottom line isn't as clear. You need to recognise achievement in both categories.

Starting with the Positive

You're more likely to lead your employees to great results by focusing on their positive accomplishments rather than by finding fault with and punishing their negative outcomes. Despite this fact, many managers' primary mode of operation is correcting their employees' mistakes instead of complimenting their successes.

In a recent study, 58 per cent of employees reported that they seldom received a personal 'thank you' from their manager for doing a good job even though they ranked such recognition as their most motivating incentive. They ranked a written thank you for doing a good job as motivating incentive No. 2, while 76 per cent said that they seldom received thanks from their managers. Perhaps these statistics show why a lack of praise and recognition is one of the leading reasons people leave their jobs.

Years of psychological research clearly show that positive reinforcement works better than negative reinforcement for several reasons. Without getting too technical, the reasons are that positive reinforcement:

- ✔ Increases the frequency of the desired behaviour
- ✔ Creates good feelings within employees

On the other hand, negative reinforcement may decrease the frequency of undesired behaviour, but doesn't necessarily result in the expression of desired behaviour. Instead of being motivated to do better, employees who receive only criticism from their managers eventually come to avoid their managers whenever possible. Furthermore, negative reinforcement (particularly when manifested in ways that degrade employees and their sense of self-worth) can create tremendously bad feelings in employees. And employees who are unhappy with their employers have a much more difficult time doing a good job than the employees who are happy with their employers.

The following ideas can help you seek out the positive in your employees and reinforce the behaviours you want:

- ✔ **Have high expectations for your employees' abilities.** If you believe that your employees can be outstanding, soon they believe it, too. When Peter was growing up, his parents rarely needed to punish him when he did something wrong. He needed only the words 'we know that you can do better' to get him back on course.

- ✔ **Recognise that your employees are doing their best.** If a shortfall in performance occurs, then support and encourage; punishing people for things that they cannot do in any case has little point.

- ✔ **Give your employees the benefit of the doubt.** Do you really think that your employees want to do a bad job? No one wants to do a bad job; so your job is to work out everything you can do to help employees do a good job. Additional training, encouragement, and support should be among your first choices – not reprimands and punishment.

- ✔ **Catch your employees doing things right.** Most employees do a good job in most of their work, so instead of constantly catching your employees doing things wrong, catch them doing things right. Not only can you reinforce the behaviours that you want, but you can also make your employees feel good about working for you and for your organisation.

Making a Big Deal about Something Little

Okay, here's a question for you: Should you reward your employees for their little day-to-day successes, or should you save up rewards for when they accomplish something really major? The answer to this question lies in the way that most people get their work done on a daily basis.

The simple fact is that for most people in business, work is not a string of dazzling successes that come one after another without fail. Instead, the majority of work consists of routine, daily activities; employees perform most of these duties quietly and with little fanfare. A manager's typical workday, for example, may consist of an hour or two reading memos and e-mail messages, listening to voice-mail messages, and talking to other people on the phone. The manager spends another couple of hours in meetings and perhaps another hour in one-on-one discussions with staff members and colleagues, much of which involves dealing with problems as they occur. With additional time spent on preparing reports or filling out forms, the manager actually devotes precious little time to decision making – the activity that has the greatest impact on an organisation.

For a line worker, this dearth of opportunities for dazzling success is even more pronounced. If the employee's job is assembling lawnmower engines all day (and she does a good, steady job), when does she have an opportunity to be outstanding in the eyes of her supervisor?

We've taken the long way around to say that major accomplishments are usually few and far between, regardless of your place in the organisational chart. Work is a series of small accomplishments that eventually add up to big ones. If you wait to reward your employees for their big successes, you may be waiting a long time.

Saga Holidays recognises – everyone!

Saga, a specialist holiday, travel, and financial services company, had just completed the best year of its existence. Profits rose by 25 per cent; turnover by 40 per cent. The company was set to be listed on the London Stock Exchange.

Sydney De Haan, the company's founder, considered how best to reward everyone involved in this success. He instituted a scheme of annual bonuses, based on both individual and also collective performance. At the end of the bumper year, he also paid for a holiday for all staff and their families.

Therefore, reward your employees for their small successes as well as for their big successes. You may set a lofty goal for your employees to achieve – one that stretches their abilities and tests their resolve – but remember that praising your employees' progress towards the goal is perhaps even more important than praising them when they finally reach it.

Money and Motivation

You may think that money is the ultimate incentive for your employees. After all, who isn't excited when they receive a cash bonus or pay rise? *As visions of riches beyond her wildest dreams danced through her head, she pledged her eternal devotion to the firm.* The problem is that money really isn't the top motivator for employees – at least not in the way that most managers think. And it can be a huge demotivator if you manage it badly.

Compensating with wages and salaries

Money is clearly important to your employees. They need money to pay bills, buy food and clothes, put petrol in their cars, and afford the other necessities of life.

Most employees consider the money they receive to be a fair exchange for the work they put in. Payment for work carried out is a legal right. Recognition, on the other hand, is a gift. Using recognition, however, helps you get the best effort from each employee.

Realising when incentives become entitlements

In particular, employees who receive annual bonuses and other periodic, money-based rewards quickly come to consider them part of their basic pay.

The problem arises when achieving bonuses and incentives is easy or straightforward. Productivity and output begin to flatten out; and the incentive effect of the payments themselves begins to diminish. People work on the basis that the incentives and bonuses are forthcoming anyway.

Incentives work best when they're related to direct goals or targets and short-term performance. In particular, incentives do not make a bad or boring job more interesting – they make it more bearable, and that only in the short term.

So the issue becomes again: What are you rewarding? You need to work out what the goals and priorities are, what rewards people expect for achieving them, and the best way of delivering these rewards. Consolidating incentives into standard pay and reward packages simply puts up the payroll costs without any tangible returns.

Management expert Peter Drucker hit the nail on the head when he pointed out in his book *Management: Tasks, Responsibilities, Practices,* 'Economic incentives are becoming rights rather than rewards. Merit raises are always introduced as rewards for exceptional performance. In no time at all, they become a right. To deny a merit raise or to grant only a small one becomes punishment. The increasing demand for material rewards is rapidly destroying their usefulness as incentives and managerial tools.' In other words, money becomes an expectation, then an entitlement, for many if not most workers.

The ineffectiveness of money as a motivator for employees is a good news/bad news kind of thing. We start with the bad news first. Many managers have thrown lots of money into cash-reward programmes, and for the most part these programmes really didn't have the positive effect on motivation that the managers expected. Although we don't want to say that you waste your money on these programmes, you can use it more effectively.

Now you get the good news: Because you know that money is not the most effective motivation tool, you can focus on using tools that are more effective – and the best forms of recognition cost little or no money!

Working out what motivates your staff

If you're a busy manager, cash rewards are convenient because you simply fill out a single request to take care of all your motivation for the year. By contrast, the manager-initiated, based-on-performance stuff seems like a lot of work. To be frank, running an effective rewards programme does take more work on your part than running a simple but ineffective one. But as we show you, the best rewards can be quite simple. After you get the hang of using them, you can easily integrate them into your daily routine. Doing so is part of managing today.

Ten ways to motivate employees

Here are some easy, no-cost things you can do to create a motivating workplace:

1. Personally thank employees for doing a good job – one-on-one, in writing, or both. Do it timely, often, and sincerely.

2. Take the time to meet with and listen to employees – as much as they need or want.

3. Provide employees with specific and frequent feedback about their performance. Support them in improving performance.

4. Recognise, reward, and promote high performers; deal with low and marginal performers so that they improve.

5. Provide information on how the company makes and loses money, upcoming products, and services and strategies for competing. Explain the employee's role in the overall plan.

6. Involve employees in decisions, especially those decisions that affect them. Involvement equals commitment.

7. Give employees a chance to grow and develop new skills; encourage them to be their best. Show them how you can help them meet their goals while achieving the organisation's goals. Create a partnership with each employee.

8. Provide employees with a sense of ownership in their work and their work environment. This ownership can be symbolic, (for example business cards for all employees, whether they need them to do their jobs or not).

9. Strive to create a work environment that is open, trusting, and fun. Encourage new ideas, suggestions, and initiative. Learn from, rather than punish for, mistakes.

10. Celebrate successes – of the company, of the department, and of individuals. Take time for team- and morale-building meetings and activities. Be creative and fresh.

To achieve the best results:

- Concentrate on what the employees need, want, and expect. The only way to be absolutely sure is to ask them.

- Concentrate rewards on the things you really want done. And keep in mind that what gets rewarded gets done.

Don't save up recognition for special occasions only – and don't just use them with the top performers. You need to recognise every employee when they do good work in their job. Your employees are doing good things – things that you want them to do – every day. Catch them doing something right and recognise their successes regularly and often.

The following incentives are simple to execute, take little time, and are the most motivating for employees:

- ✔ Personal or written congratulations from you for a job well done
- ✔ Public recognition, given visibly by you for good job performance
- ✔ Morale-building meetings to celebrate successes
- ✔ Time off or flexibility in one's working hours
- ✔ Asking employees their opinions and involving them in decision making

For unbelievably comprehensive listings of incentive ideas that really work, check out Bob's best-selling books *1001 Ways to Reward Employees*, *1001 Ways to Energize Employees*, and *The 1001 Rewards & Recognition Fieldbook;* and Richard's *Managing the Flexible Workforce*.

Realising that you hold the key to your employees' motivation

In our experience, most managers believe that their employees determine how motivated they choose to be. Managers tend to think that some employees naturally have good attitudes, that others naturally have bad attitudes, and that managers can't do much to change these attitudes. 'If only we could unleash the same passion and energy people have for their families and hobbies,' these managers think, 'then we could really get something done around here.'

As convenient as blaming your employees for their bad attitudes may be, looking in a mirror may be a more honest approach. Managers need to:

- ✔ Recognise their employees for doing a good job
- ✔ Provide a pleasant and supportive working environment
- ✔ Create a sense of joint mission and teamwork in the organisation
- ✔ Treat their employees as equals
- ✔ Avoid favouritism
- ✔ Make time to listen when employees need to talk

For the most part, you determine how motivated (and demotivated) your employees are. Managers create a motivating environment that makes it easier for employees to be motivated. When the time comes, recognise and reward them fairly and equitably for the work they do well.

Top five motivation Web sites

Wondering where to find the best information on the Web about the topics addressed in this chapter? Well, you've come to the right place! Here are our top five favourites:

✔ Trades Union Congress: `www.tuc.org.uk/workplacerelations`

✔ Confederation of British Industry: `www.cbi.org.uk/recognition`

✔ Templeton College, Oxford: `www.templeton.ac.uk/employment relations`

✔ Chartered Institute of Personnel and Development (CIPD): `www.cipd.co.uk/recognition`

✔ Tesco: `www.tesco.com/careers`

When you give out rewards, keep in mind that employees don't want handouts, and they hate favouritism. Provide rewards for the performance that helps you be mutually successful. Don't give recognition when none is warranted. Don't give it just to be nice, or with the hope that people will like you better. Doing so not only cheapens the value of the incentive with the employee who received it, but makes you lose credibility in the eyes of your other employees. Trust and credibility are two of the most important qualities that you can build in your relationship with your employees; if you lose these qualities, you risk losing the employee.

Chapter 6

Coaching and Development

. . . .

In This Chapter

▶ Understanding what a coach is

▶ Developing basic coaching skills

▶ Considering the links between sports and business

▶ Identifying turning points in coaching

. . . .

*O*ne recurring theme throughout this book is the role of managers as people who support and encourage their employees, instead of telling them what to do (or worse, simply expecting them to perform). The best managers are *coaches* – that is, individuals who guide, talk with, and encourage others on their journey. With the help of coaches, employees can achieve outstanding results, organisations can perform better than ever, and you can sleep well at night, knowing that everything is just fine.

Coaching plays a critical part in the learning process for employees who are developing their skills, knowledge, and self-confidence. Your employees don't learn effectively when you simply tell them what to do. In fact, they usually don't learn at all.

As the maxim goes:

> Tell me . . . I forget.
>
> Show me . . . I remember.
>
> Involve me . . . I learn.

Nor do your employees learn effectively when you throw a new task at them with no instruction or support whatsoever. Of course, good employees can, and do, eventually work things out for themselves, but they waste a lot of time and energy in the process. 'What on earth am I supposed to be doing? Let's have a go anyway and see what happens!'

Between these two extremes – being told what to do and being given no support whatsoever – is a happy medium where employees can thrive and the organisation can prosper. This is the happy land where everyone lives in peace, harmony, prosperity, and achievement – and this happy medium starts and finishes with coaching.

Playing a Coach's Role

Even if you have a pretty good sense of what it means to be a manager, do you really know what it means to be a coach? A coach is a colleague, counsellor, and cheerleader, all rolled into one. Based on that definition, are you a coach? How about your boss? Or your boss's boss? Why or why not?

We bet that you're familiar with the role of coaches in other non-business activities. A drama coach, for example, is almost always an accomplished actor. The drama coach's job is to conduct auditions for parts, assign roles, schedule rehearsals, train and direct cast members throughout rehearsals, and support and encourage the actors during the final stage production. These roles aren't all that different from the roles that managers perform in a business, are they?

Coaching a team of individuals isn't easy, and certain characteristics make some coaches better than others. Fortunately, as with most other business skills, you can discover, practise, and improve your grasp of the traits of good coaches. You can always find room for improvement, a fact that good coaches are the first to admit. The list that follows highlights some important characteristics of coaching:

- ✔ **Coaches set goals.** Whether an organisation's vision is to become the leading provider of wireless telephones in the world, to increase revenues by 20 per cent a year, or simply to get the break room walls painted this year, coaches work with their employees to set goals and deadlines for completion. Coaches then withdraw, to allow their employees time to work out how to achieve the goals.

- ✔ **Coaches support and encourage.** Employees – even the best and most experienced – can easily become discouraged from time to time. When employees are learning new tasks, when a long-term account is lost, or when business is down, coaches are there, ready to step in and help the team members through the worst of it. 'That's OK, Kim. You've learned from your mistake, and I know that you can get it right next time!'

✔ **Coaches emphasise both team success and individual success.** The team's overall performance, not the stellar abilities of a particular team member, is the most important concern. Of course, you need everyone's contribution; but coaches know that no one person can carry an entire team to success. Winning takes the combined efforts of everyone. The development of teamwork skills is a vital step in an employee's progress in an organisation.

✔ **Coaches can quickly assess the talents and shortfalls of team members.** The most successful coaches can quickly determine their team members' strengths and weaknesses and, as a result, tailor their approach accordingly. For example, if one team member has strong analytical skills but poor presentation skills, a coach can concentrate on providing support to help the employee develop better presentation skills. 'You know, Mark, I want to spend some time with you to work on making your sales' presentations more effective.'

✔ **Coaches inspire their team members.** Through their support and guidance, coaches are skilled at inspiring their team members to the highest levels of human performance. Teams of inspired individuals are willing to do whatever it takes to achieve their organisation's goals.

✔ **Coaches create environments that allow individuals to be successful.** Great coaches ensure that their workplaces are structured to let team members take risks and stretch their limits without fear of retribution if they fail.

✔ **Coaches provide feedback.** Communication and feedback between coach and employee form a critical element of the coaching process. Employees must know where they stand in the organisation – what they're doing right, and what they're doing wrong. Equally important, employees must let their coaches know when they need help or assistance. And this must be a continuous process for both parties. Otherwise problems get raised only at performance reviews and appraisals, or, worse still, get lost altogether.

Coaches are available to advise their employees or just to listen to their problems if need be, whether the issue is work related or personal.

Firing someone doesn't constitute effective feedback. Unless an employee has engaged in some sort of intolerable offence (such as physical violence, theft, or intoxication on the job; see Chapter 16 for more details), a manager needs to give the employee plenty of verbal and written feedback before even considering termination. With employees who simply cannot see what they are doing wrong, your coaching either makes or breaks. If you simply fire someone, you never know whether the problem was theirs – or yours.

Coaching: A Rough Guide

Besides the obvious coaching roles of supporting and encouraging employees in their quest to achieve an organisation's goals, coaches also teach their employees *how* to achieve those goals. Drawing from their experience, coaches lead their workers step by step through work processes, or procedures. After the workers discover how to perform a task, the coach delegates full authority and responsibility for its performance to them.

For the transfer of specific skills, you can find no better way of teaching, and no better way of learning, than the *show-and-tell* method. If you need to get people up to speed on workplace skills, knowledge, and understanding, then do it on the job. There is simply no better place. And – if you need to – you can get people working fully productively very quickly.

Show-and-tell or on-the-job coaching has three steps:

1. *You do, you say.* **Sit down with your employees and explain the procedure in general terms while you perform the task.** Most businesses today use computers as a critical tool for getting work done. If you are coaching a new employee in the use of an obscure word processing or spreadsheet technique, the first thing you need to do is to explain the technique to the employee while you demonstrate it. 'I click my left mouse button on the Insert command on the toolbar and pull down the menu. Then I point the arrow to Symbol and click again. I choose the symbol I want from the menu, point my arrow to it, and click to select it. I then point my arrow to Insert and click to place the symbol in the document; then I point my arrow to Close and click again to finish the job.'

2. *They do, you say.* **Now, have the employee do the same procedure as you explain each step in the procedure.** 'Click your left mouse button on the Insert command on the toolbar and pull down the menu. OK, good. Now point your arrow to Symbol and click again. Excellent! Choose the symbol you want from the menu and point your arrow to it. Now click to select it. All right – point your arrow to Insert and click to place the symbol in the document. OK, you're almost done now. Point your arrow to Close and click again to finish the job. There you are!'

3. *They do, they say.* **Finally, as you observe, have your employees perform the task again as they explain to you what they are doing.** 'Okay, Miles, now it's your turn. I want you to insert a symbol in your document and tell me what you're doing.'

   'All right, Senti. First, I click my left mouse button on the Insert command on the toolbar and pull down the menu. Then I point the arrow to Symbol and click again. I decide the symbol I want from the menu, point my arrow to it, and click to select it. Next, I point the arrow to Insert and click to place the symbol in the document. Finally, I point my arrow to Close and click again to finish the job. I did it!'

It never hurts to have employees create a 'crib sheet' of the new steps to refer to until they become habit.

Coaching Metaphors for Success in Business

In business, we're constantly reminded that, when it comes to coaching and teamwork, the metaphor of a company as a winning sports team is strong. In many organisations, chief executives hire professional athletes and coaches to lecture their employees on the importance of team play and winning; managers are given the label of *coaches* or *team leaders;* and workers are given the labels of *players* or *team members.*

This being the case, ignoring the obvious parallels between coaching in sports and in business is difficult. So we're going to get this out of our system once and for all and refrain from linking coaching in sports and business anywhere else in this book after the following list of examples:

- ✔ Terry Venables, legendary football coach, on his appointment to Barcelona FC: 'The first thing that I had to do was to get this group of highly talented individuals playing as a team.'

- ✔ Clive Woodward, England world cup-winning rugby coach: 'To build a team, you have to coach people as a team. Of course, you work on individual strengths and weaknesses; in the end however, it is how they perform together, not how they perform individually, that determines your success.'

- ✔ Arsene Wenger, manager and head coach at Arsenal FC: 'One of the most important things that I have to do is to maintain the players' belief in themselves. This is easy when you are winning – sometimes you have to rein them in. But when you are losing – this is the most important part of the job. And if you simply shout at people or threaten them – you will always fail.'

- ✔ Duncan Fletcher, coach of the England Ashes winning cricket team in 2005: 'You have got to be consistent; and players have got to have confidence in you. If they think they are going to be left out of the team after one bad performance, they will be too worried to perform. So, once you pick someone – whoever it is – they need to know that they have your full confidence, backing and support.'

- ✔ Alf Ramsey, world cup-winning England football manager and coach: 'The best teams are not necessarily made up of the best individuals. The best teams are made up of talented individuals who can gel together for the good of each other and the team itself.'

One last point: In sports as in business, *everybody* needs a coach. Who's the greatest golfer of all time? Tiger Woods? Probably. But most people don't realise that even Tiger Woods has a coach to help him stay sharp and to improve.

Confronting Turning Points

Despite popular impressions to the contrary, 90 per cent of management isn't the big event – the blinding flash of brilliance that creates markets where none previously existed, the magnificent negotiation that results in unheard-of levels of union – management cooperation, or the masterful stroke that catapults the firm into the big league. No, 90 per cent of a manager's daily job consists of chipping away at problems and shaping talents.

The best coaches are constantly on the lookout for *turning points* – the daily opportunities to succeed that are available to all employees.

Making turning points into big successes

The big successes – the victories against competitors, the dramatic surges in revenues or profits, the astounding new products – are typically the result of building a foundation of countless small successes along the way. Making a voice-mail system more responsive to your customers' needs, sending an employee to a seminar on time management, writing a great sales agreement, conducting a meaningful performance appraisal with an employee, meeting a prospective client for lunch – all these are turning points in the average business day. Although each event may not be particularly spectacular on its own, when aggregated over time, they're what add up to the big things.

This is the job of a coach. Instead of using dynamite to transform the organisation in one fell swoop (and taking the chance of destroying the organisation, the employees, or themselves in the process), coaches are like the ancient stonemasons who built the great pyramids of Egypt. The movement and placement of each individual stone may not have seemed like a big deal when considered as separate activities. However, each was an important step in the achievement of the ultimate result – the construction of awe-inspiring structures that have withstood thousands of years of war, weather, and tourists.

Making coaching special

Coaches focus every day on spending time with employees to help them succeed – to assess employees' progress and to find out what they can do to help the employees capitalise on the turning points that present themselves every day. Coaches complement and supplement the abilities and experience of their employees by bringing their own abilities and experience to the table. They reward positive performance and they help their employees learn important lessons from making mistakes – lessons that, in turn, help the employees to improve their future performance.

For example, suppose that you have a young and inexperienced, but bright and energetic, sales trainee on your staff. Your employee has done a great job contacting customers and making sales calls, but he has yet to close his first deal. When you talk to him about this, he confesses that he is very nervous about his own personal turning point: He's worried that he may become confused in front of the customer and blow the deal at the last minute. He needs your coaching.

The following guidelines can help you, the coach, handle any employee's concerns:

- ✔ **Meet with your employee.** Make an appointment with your employee as soon as possible for a relaxed discussion of the concerns. Find a place that is quiet and free of distractions and put your phone on hold or forward it to voice-mail.

- ✔ **Listen!** One of the most motivating things one person can do for another is to listen to them. Avoid instant solutions or lectures. Before you say a word, ask your employee to bring you up to date with the situation, his concerns, and any possible approaches or solutions that he's considered. Let him do the talking while you do the listening. If you don't listen, you may never know what the problem actually is! And that means you can't possibly help the employee to solve it.

- ✔ **Reinforce the positive.** Begin by pointing out the things that your employee did right in the particular situation. Let your employee know when he is on the right track. Give him positive feedback on his performance.

- ✔ **Highlight areas for improvement.** Point out the things that your employee needs to do to improve and tell him what you can do to help. Agree on the assistance that you can provide, whether your employee needs further training, an increased budget, more time, or whatever else is required. Be enthusiastic about your confidence in the employee's ability to do a great job.

Everyone needs a coach

Alan Sugar, founder, chairman, and chief executive of electrical goods manufacturer Amstrad, has grown the company into one of the United Kingdom's most high-profile organisations. In his own words, Alan Sugar started off with £500, which he used to buy wholesale fresh fruit. He took the fruit to the old Spitalfields market in East London, where he sold it on to the public, aiming each day to double his money.

Alan Sugar went on to create the Amstrad company in the 1970s, first making satellite television dishes and aerials; and then subsequently moving into computer hardware, software, and other products such as smart cards. One of Amstrad's latest ventures is to recycle old and obsolete computer hardware and electronic machinery.

Alan Sugar has been phenomenally successful. He has always had two long-term associates, colleagues and friends to whom he turns for advice on every occasion. Margaret Leavy, a qualified lawyer, and Peter Watson, who worked for 20 years as Amstrad's marketing and public relations director, are always available on any matter, or subject. Their role is to act as sounding boards, critics, evaluators of ideas, and, above all, to ensure that Alan Sugar continues to run the Amstrad company to the same standards of absolute quality and professionalism that have always been required.

✔ **Follow through.** After you determine what you can do to support your employee, do it! Notice when he improves! Periodically check up on the progress that your employee is making and offer your support as necessary.

Above all, be patient. Coaching is something that you can't accomplish on your terms alone. At the outset, understand that everyone is different. Some employees catch on sooner than others, and some employees need more time to develop. Differences in ability don't make certain employees any better or worse than others – they just make them different. Just as you need time to build relationships and trust in business, your employees need time to develop skills and experience.

Tapping into the Coach's Expertise

Coaching is not a one-dimensional activity. Because every person is different, the best coaches tailor their approach to their team members' specific, individualised needs. If one team member is independent and needs only occasional guidance, recognise where the employee stands and provide that level of support. This support may consist of an occasional, informal progress check while making the rounds of the office. If, on the other hand, another team member is insecure and needs more guidance, the coach recognises this employee's position and assists as required. In this case, support may consist of frequent, formal meetings with the employee to assess progress and to provide advice and direction as needed.

Although every coach has an individual style, the best coaches employ certain techniques to elicit the greatest performance from their team members:

- **Make time for team members.** Managing is primarily a people job. Part of being a good manager and coach is being available to your employees when they need your help. If you're not available, your employees may seek out other avenues to meet their needs – or simply stop trying to work with you. Always keep your door open to your employees and remember that they are your Number 1 priority. Manage by walking around. Regularly get out of your office and visit your employees at their workstations. 'Do I have a minute, Elaine? Of course, I always have time for you and the other members of my staff.'

- **Provide context and vision.** Instead of simply telling employees what to do, effective coaches explain *why*. Coaches provide their employees with context and a big-picture perspective. Instead of spouting long lists of do's and don'ts, they explain how a system or procedure works and then define their employees' parts in the scheme of things. 'Sanjeev, you have a very important part in the financial health and vitality of our company. By ensuring that our customers pay their invoices within 30 days after we ship their products, we're able to keep our cash flow on the plus side, and we can pay our obligations such as rent, electricity, and your salary on time.'

- **Transfer knowledge and perspective.** A great benefit of having a good coach is the opportunity to discover information and know-how from someone who has more experience than you do. In response to the unique needs of each team member, coaches transfer their personal knowledge and perspective. 'We faced the exact situation about five years ago, Hayden. I'm going to tell you what we did then, and I want you to tell me whether you think that it still makes sense today, or you may have a better idea that we could try.'

- **Be a sounding board.** Coaches talk through new ideas and approaches to solving problems with their employees. Coaches and employees can consider the implications of different approaches to solving a problem and role-play customer or client reactions before trying them out for real. By using active listening skills, coaches can often help their employees work through issues and come up with the best solutions themselves. 'Okay, David, you've told me that you don't think your customer will buy from us if we put the prices up by 20 per cent. What options do we have with price increases, and are some better than others?'

Top five coaching Web sites

If you want to find out more about coaching and development, check out these Web sites:

- ✔ The Coaching and Mentoring Network: www.coachingnetwork.org.uk/

- ✔ Your Big Picture: www.yourbig picture.net

- ✔ People Management and Development: www.pmd.org.uk/coaching

- ✔ Executive Coaching at the Institute of Directors: www.iod.org.uk/coaching

- ✔ Chartered Management Institute: www.cmi.org.uk/executivecoaching

---

✔ **Obtain necessary resources.** Sometimes, coaches can help their employees make the jump from marginal to outstanding performance simply by providing the resources that their employees need. These resources can take many forms – money, time, staff, equipment, or other tangible assets. 'So, Kathleen, you're confident that we can improve our cash flow if we put two more staff on to invoicing? OK, let's give it a try.'

✔ **Offer a helping hand.** For an employee who is learning a new job and is still responsible for performing his current job, the total workload can be overwhelming. Coaches can help workers through this transitional phase by reassigning current duties to other employees, authorising overtime, or taking other measures to relieve the pressure. 'John, while you're learning how to de-bug the new software, I'm going to assign the rest of your workload to Rachel. We can get back together at the end of the week to see how you're doing.'

Part III
Making Things Happen

'I like a young man who knows where he's going.
If you'll just go through that door while
my directors & I discuss your promotion
application . . .'

In this part . . .

Employees without goals are employees without direction. And after you set goals with employees, you have to measure employee progress to their goals. In this part, we address setting goals with employees, measuring employee performance, and conducting performance evaluations the right way.

Chapter 7

Setting Goals and Targets

. . . .

In This Chapter

▶ Linking goals to your vision

▶ Creating SMART goals

▶ Concentrating on fewer goals

▶ Publicising your goals

▶ Following through with your employees

▶ Determining sources of power

. . . .

Ask any group of workers, 'What is the primary duty of management?' The answer 'setting goals' is likely to be near the top of the list. If setting goals appears near the bottom of the list, you know you've got a problem! In most companies, top management sets the overall purpose – the vision – of the organisation. Middle managers then have the job of developing goals and plans for achieving the vision that top management has established. Managers and employees work together to set goals and develop schedules for attaining them.

As a manager, you're probably immersed in goals – not only for yourself but also for your employees, your department, and your organisation. This flood of goals can overwhelm you as you try to balance the relative importance of each one.

Should I tackle my department's goal of improving turnaround time first, or should I get to work on my boss's goal of finishing the budget? Or maybe the company's goal of improving customer service is more important. Well, I think I may just try to achieve my own personal goal of setting aside some time to eat lunch today.

So when you're faced with this kind of confusion, you first need to be absolutely sure where your priorities truly lie. And, while you need goals in order to prioritise – as you discover in this chapter, having too many goals and too many divergent demands can be as bad as not having any goals at all.

Goals provide direction and purpose. Don't forget: If you can see it, you can achieve it. Goals help you see where you're going and how you can get there. And the *way* that you set goals can influence how motivating they are to others.

If You Don't Know Where You're Going, How Do You Know When You Get There?

Did you realise that Lewis Carroll's classic book *Alice in Wonderland* offers lessons that can enhance your business life? Consider the following passage from Carroll's book, in which Alice asks the Cheshire Cat for advice on which direction to go.

> 'Would you tell me please, which way I ought to go from here?'
>
> 'That depends a good deal on where you want to go,' said the Cat.
>
> 'I don't much care where . . .' said Alice.
>
> 'Then it doesn't matter which way you go,' said the Cat.
>
> '. . . so long as I get *somewhere*,' Alice added as an explanation.
>
> 'Oh, you're sure to do that,' said the Cat, 'if you only walk long enough.'

It takes no effort at all to get *somewhere*. Just do nothing, and you're there. (In fact, everywhere you go, there you are!) However, if you want to get somewhere meaningful, you first have to know where you want to go. And after you decide where you want to go, you need to make plans on how to get there. This practice is as true in business as in your everyday life.

For example, suppose you have a vision of starting up a new sales office in Prague so that you can better service your Eastern European accounts. How do you go about achieving this vision? You have four choices:

- ✔ An unplanned, non-goal-oriented approach
- ✔ A set of bland statements masquerading as goals
- ✔ A planned, goal-oriented approach
- ✔ A hope and a prayer

The choice is yours! Do note, however, the difference between setting real goals and making statements that pretend to be goals. For example:

- When asked what his goal was, Sir John French, the allied military commander on the Western Front during the First World War, stated: 'Why, to advance and win the war.'

- When asked what they intended to achieve by opening up a large call centre facility in Bombay, India, a large financial services company replied: 'We do not know, but we are confident of success anyway.'

Make up your mind now to choose the planned, goal-oriented approach. Following are the main reasons to set goals whenever you want to accomplish something valuable or worthwhile.

- **Goals provide direction.** In the example of starting up a new sales office in Prague, you can probably find a million different ways to service your Eastern European business accounts more effectively. However, to get something done, you have to set a definite vision – a target to aim for and to guide your and your organisation's efforts. You can then translate this vision into goals that take you where you want to go. Without goals, you're doomed to waste countless hours going nowhere. With goals, you can focus your efforts and your staff's efforts specifically on the activities that move you towards where you're going – in this case, opening a new sales office.

- **Goals tell you how far you've travelled.** Goals provide milestones along the road to accomplishing your vision. If you determine that you must accomplish several specific milestones to reach your final destination and complete a few of them, you know exactly how many remain. That is, you know exactly where you stand and how far you have yet to go.

- **Goals help to make your overall vision attainable.** You can't reach your vision in one big step – you need many small steps to get there. If, again, your vision is to open a new sales office in Prague, you can't expect to proclaim your vision on Friday and walk into a fully staffed and functioning office on Monday. You must accomplish many goals – from shopping for office space, to hiring and relocating staff, to printing stationery and business cards – before you can attain your vision. Goals enable you to achieve your overall vision by dividing your efforts into smaller pieces that, when accomplished individually, add up to big results.

- **Goals clarify everyone's role.** When you discuss your vision with your employees, they may have some idea of where you want to go but no idea of how to approach the process of getting there. As your well-intentioned employees head off to help you achieve your vision, some employees may duplicate the efforts of others, some employees may ignore some tasks, and some employees may simply do something else altogether (and hope that you don't notice the difference). Setting goals with employees clarifies what the tasks are, who does which tasks, and what is expected from each employee.

✔ **Goals give people something to strive for.** People are typically more motivated when you challenge them to attain a goal that's beyond their normal level of performance – this is what's known as a *stretch goal*. Not only do goals give people a sense of purpose, but they also relieve the boredom that can come from performing a routine job day after day. Be sure to discuss the goal with your employees and gain their commitment.

✔ **Goals move everyone and everything on.** Achieving one set of goals provides the foundation for establishing and determining the next set of goals.

For goals to be useful, they have to link directly to the final vision. To stay ahead of the competition, or simply to remain in business, organisations create compelling visions, then management and employees work together to set and achieve the goals to reach those visions. Look over these examples of compelling visions that drive the development of goals at several successful enterprises.

✔ Swatch, the company created by Nicolas Hayek to revitalise the declining Swiss watch industry, set the goal of creating the best component-manufacturing processes in the world. And not only were they to be the best, they were to be the most cost effective. This meant creating factory, manufacturing, and production facilities in Switzerland more cost effective than those in China and Japan.

✔ Motorola, long known for its obsession with quality, has set a truly incredible vision for where it wants to be. Motorola has set a target of no more than two manufacturing defects per billion units.

✔ Anita Roddick set out to create the Body Shop as an ethical company in terms of the ways in which it dealt with its suppliers and customers. She did this at exactly the time that Western economies were moving into recession; therefore, the last thing that the commercial world needed was a new cosmetics company; and anyone creating companies at that time sought to minimise, rather than optimise, start-up costs. However, by setting distinctive standards and reinforcing these with a commitment to dedicating the business 'to the pursuit of social and environmental change', she was able to establish clear goals and direction for the company in spite of the otherwise adverse trading conditions.

When it comes to goals, the best ones

✔ Are few in number, specific in purpose

✔ Are stretch goals – not too easy, not too hard

✔ Involve people – when you involve others, you get involvement so it becomes their goal, not just yours

Identifying SMART Goals

You can find all kinds of goals in all types of organisations. Some goals are short-term and specific ('starting next month, we will increase production by two units per employee per hour'), and others are long-term and nebulous ('within the next five years, we will become a learning organisation'). Employees easily understand some goals ('line employees will have no more than 20 rejects per month'), but others can be difficult to fathom and subject to much interpretation ('all employees are expected to show more respect to each other in the next financial year'). Still others can be accomplished relatively easily ('reception staff will always answer the phone by the third ring'), but others are virtually impossible to attain ('all employees will master the five languages that our customers speak before the end of the financial year').

How do you know what kind of goals to set? The whole point of setting goals, after all, is to achieve them. It does you no good to go to the trouble of calling meetings, hacking through the needs of your organisation, and burning up precious time, only to end up with goals that employees don't act on or complete. Unfortunately, this scenario describes what far too many managers do with their time.

The best goals are SMART. SMART refers to a handy checklist for the five characteristics of well-designed goals.

- ✔ **Specific:** Goals must be clear and unambiguous; broad and fuzzy thinking has no place in goal setting. When goals are specific, they tell employees exactly what you expect, when, and how much. Because the goals are specific, you can easily measure your employees' progress towards their completion.

- ✔ **Measurable:** What good is a goal that you can't measure? If your goals aren't measurable, you never know whether your employees are making progress towards their successful completion. Not only that, but your employees may have a tough time staying motivated to complete their goals if they have no milestones to indicate their progress. Ultimately, you can only measure anything against what you set out to achieve.

- ✔ **Attainable:** Goals must be realistic and attainable by average employees. The best goals require employees to stretch a bit to achieve them, but they aren't extreme. That is, the goals are neither out of reach nor below standard performance. Goals that are set too high or too low become meaningless, and employees naturally come to ignore them.

- ✔ **Relevant:** Goals must be an important tool in the grand scheme of reaching your company's vision and mission. The Pareto principle when applied to productivity states that 80 per cent of workers' productivity comes from only 20 per cent of their activities. Relevant goals address the 20 per cent of workers' activities that have such a great impact on performance and bring your organisation closer to its vision; as well as trying to make better use of the 80 per cent of time that is otherwise unproductive.

✔ **Time-bound:** Goals must have starting points, ending points, and fixed durations. Commitment to deadlines helps employees to focus their efforts on completion of the goal on or before the due date. Goals without deadlines or schedules for completion tend to be overtaken by the day-to-day crises that invariably arise in an organisation.

SMART goals make for smart organisations. In our experience, many supervisors and managers don't work with their employees to set goals together. And even in the organisations where they do work in that way, goals are often unclear, ambiguous, unrealistic, unmeasurable, demotivating, and unrelated to the organisation's vision. By developing SMART goals with your employees, you can avoid these traps while ensuring the progress of your organisation and its employees.

Although the SMART system of goal setting provides guidelines to help you frame effective goals, you have additional considerations to keep in mind. These considerations (explained in the following list) help you ensure that the goals that you and your employees agree to can be easily understood and acted on by anyone in your organisation.

✔ **Ensure that goals are related to your employees' role in the organisation.** Pursuing an organisation's goals is far easier for employees when those goals are a regular part of their jobs. For example, suppose you set a goal for employees who solder circuit boards to 'Raise production by 2 per cent per quarter.' These employees spend almost every working moment pursuing this goal, because the goal is an integral part of their job. If, however, you give the same employees a goal of 'Improving the diversity of the organisation', they wonder exactly what that has to do with their role. Nothing. The goal may sound lofty and may be important to your organisation, but because your line employees don't make the hiring decisions, you're wasting your time and their time with that particular goal.

✔ **Whenever possible, use values to guide behaviour.** What is the most important value in your organisation? Honesty? Fairness? Respect? These values translate into specific goals as follows:

- To be honest in all our dealings with customers and suppliers

- To be fair in all staff management practices

- To be respectful to the environment and everything that we do that affects it

In this way you're stating a direct relationship between what you do and how you do it – and both are vital.

✔ **Simple goals are better goals.** The easier your goals are to understand, the more likely the employees are to work to achieve them. Goals should be no longer than one sentence; make them concise, compelling, and easy to read and understand.

Goals that take more than a sentence to describe are actually multiple goals. When you find multiple-goal statements, break them into single, one-sentence goals. Goals that take a page or more to describe aren't really goals; they're books. File them away and try again.

Setting Goals: Less Is More

Years ago, Richard worked for an industrial training board. This organisation was a subdivision of a much larger government department, the Manpower Services Commission (MSC). The purpose of this board was to provide facilities, resources, expertise, and development for the building materials, pottery, and glass industries.

Because the organisation was a government department, everything was planned, right down to the last detail. The organisation employed a planning director, together with expert economists, statisticians, and manpower experts. The job of the planning director and his people was to give absolute assurances, both to the government and also to the industries served, on the following issues.

✔ Why the board existed.

✔ What services it provided.

✔ How the industries acquired and used these services.

✔ The number of training and development activities to be carried out.

✔ The nature of training and development activities to be carried out.

✔ The number of research activities to be carried out.

✔ The nature of research activities to be carried out.

The board employed training officers, training advisers, and researchers. When companies in the relevant industries called in training officers and training advisers to help them, they first had to check whether or not these activities had been planned for and scheduled. When researchers (such as Richard) were asked to conduct analyses for particular companies, they had to make sure that the activities had indeed been planned for, and that sufficient resources were allocated to enable the work to be done fully and effectively.

The result was that the board spent all of its time planning, and not enough time doing. On an individual basis, staff gained a reputation for being cheerful and knowledgeable, but totally unresponsive. The fact that the planning processes and the board's constitution tied staff's hands was of no concern to the industries – all they wanted was to get the work done.

Following government reforms, the MSC and most of the training boards were disbanded in 1982. This did not prevent the board's planning division from producing a strategic and operational plan until 1985 – as required by the board's constitution and MSC regulations.

Don't let all your hard work end in nothing. When you go through the trouble of setting goals, keep them to a manageable number that you can realistically follow up. And when you finish one goal, move on to the next.

When it comes to goal setting, less is more. So prioritise!

The following guidelines can help you select the right goals – and the right number of goals – for your organisation:

- ✔ **Pick two to three goals to focus on.** You can't do everything at once, and you can't expect your employees to either. A few goals are the most you should attempt to conquer at any one time. Picking too many goals dilutes the efforts of you and your staff and can result in a complete breakdown in the goal-setting process.

- ✔ **Pick the goals with the greatest relevance.** Certain goals take you a lot further down the road to attaining your vision than do other goals. Because you have only so many hours in your work day, it clearly makes sense to concentrate your efforts on a few goals that have the biggest pay-off – rather than on a boatload of goals with a relatively lower pay-off.

- ✔ **Focus on the goals that tie most closely to your organisation's mission.** You can be tempted to take on goals that are challenging, interesting, and fun to accomplish but that are far removed from your organisation's mission. Don't.

- ✔ **Periodically revisit the goals and update them as necessary.** Business is anything but static, and periodically assessing your goals is important to making sure that they're still relevant to the vision you want to achieve. If so, great – carry on. If not, meet with your employees to revise the goals and the schedules for attaining them.

Avoid taking on too many goals in your zeal to get as many things done as quickly as you can. Too many goals can overwhelm you, and they can over-whelm your employees, too. You're far better off if you set a few, significant goals and then concentrate your efforts on attaining them. Don't forget that management isn't a game of huge success after huge success. Instead, it's a game of meeting challenges and opportunities every day – gradually, but inevitably, improving the organisation in the process.

Communicating Your Goals to Your Team

Having goals is great, but how do you get the word out to your employees? As you know, goals grow out of an organisation's vision. Establishing goals helps you ensure that employees focus on achieving the vision in the desired time frame. You have many possible ways to communicate goals to your employees, but some ways are better than others. In every case, you must communicate goals clearly, the receiver must understand the goals, and the goals must be followed through by everyone involved.

Communicating your organisation's vision is as important as communicating specific goals. You can communicate the vision in every way possible, as often as possible, throughout your organisation and to significant others such as clients, customers, suppliers, and so forth. And you need to be aware of possible obstacles: Often an organisation's vision is pounded out in a series of gruelling management meetings that leave the participants (you, the managers) beaten and tired. By the time the managers reach their final goal of developing a company's vision, they are sick of the process and ready to go on to the next challenge.

Many organisations and managers like the idea of 'cascading' the vision, goals, and targets down through different layers of management. It looks neat and tidy; and the 'cascade' of pouring champagne into a stack of glasses and watching it cascade down from the top to the bottom is additionally glamorous. Unfortunately, by the time the champagne reaches the glasses at the bottom, it is warm, flat, and lifeless. Communication cascades have exactly the same effect – so don't use them unless you have to!

When you communicate vision and goals, do it with energy and with a sense of urgency and importance. You're talking about the future of your organisation and your employees – not about chopped liver. If your employees think that you don't care about the vision, why should they care? Simply put, they won't.

Companies usually announce their visions with much pomp and fanfare. The following are different ways in which companies commonly announce and communicate their vision:

- ✔ By conducting huge employee rallies where the vision is unveiled in inspirational presentations

- ✔ By printing their vision on anything possible – business cards, letterheads, massive posters hung in the office, newsletters, employee name badges, and more

- ✔ By encouraging managers to 'talk up' the vision in staff meetings and when they're having discussions with employees

Goals in the NHS

At present, the British National Health Service is (allegedly) going through a period of radical reform. Mantras such as the 'agenda for change', 'patient choice', and 'purchasing options' abound. Waiting lists are allegedly now structured so that everyone is seen within a certain period of time, subject only to medical need; targets for the treatment of high-profile diseases, especially cancer, are clearly established. At the top of the organisation, and in political circles and directorates, 'transformation' is the goal, the target – the absolute priority.

Or not. The problem is translating all of this into specific goals with which those who work in the service can identify. To many people, no relevant goal setting seems to be taking place. The basic proposal of 'We have to change' is not then followed up with a clear statement of 'Change from what? To what? When? Where? How? and Why?'

The result is that the staff don't know what they need, want, or have to do. 'Goals' therefore become simply meeting today's problems. This means:

✔ For managers: Responding to the latest edict; providing data on request; closing wards and laying off staff to save money

✔ For medical staff: Treating the patients in front of them; and where this is not possible, doing their best to make appointments to see the patients again at some indeterminate time in the future, without (hopefully) breaking the waiting list and waiting time targets

The clear, predictable, and assured results are as follows – and they apply to any organisation that does not set clear targets, goals and priorities:

✔ There is a division bordering on conflict between management and medical staff whose 'goals', such as they are, rarely coincide in practice.

✔ Anything that gets done is being achieved more slowly, for fewer people, more expensively, and with greater margins for error.

And yet the remit – the goal or target – of any hospital, doctor's surgery, or other medical facility ought to be clear and simple: To provide the necessary analysis, diagnosis, and treatment for all patients on request.

To avoid a cynical 'fad' reaction from employees suspicious of management's motives when unveiling a new initiative, make consistent, casual references to the vision, as this approach is much more effective than a huge, impersonal event. Again, in this case, less is often better.

Goals, on the other hand, are much more personal, and the methods you use to communicate them must be much more formal and direct. The following guidelines can help you out:

- ✔ **Make sure that the goals are written down**.

- ✔ **Always conduct one-to-one, face-to-face meetings** with your employees to introduce, discuss, and assign individual goals.

  If physical distance or any other reason prevents you from conducting a face-to-face meeting, have your meeting over the phone. The point is to make sure that your employees receive the goals, understand them, and have the opportunity to ask for clarification.

- ✔ **Call your team together to introduce team-related goals**.

  You can assign goals to teams instead of to individuals. If this is the case, get the team together and explain the role of the team and each individual in the successful completion of the goal. Make sure that all team members understand exactly what they are to do. Get them fired up and then let them loose. We discuss the function of teams in more detail in Chapter 11.

- ✔ **Gain the commitment of your employees**, whether individually or in teams, to the successful accomplishment of their goals.

  Ask your employees to prepare and present plans and milestone schedules explaining how they can accomplish the assigned goals by the deadlines that you agreed. After your employees begin working towards their goals, regularly monitor their progress to ensure that they're on track and meet with them to help them overcome any problems.

Juggling Priorities

After you've decided the goals that are important to you and to your organisation, you come to the difficult part. How do you maintain the focus of your employees – and your own focus, for that matter – on achieving the goals that you've set?

The process of goal setting often generates a lot of excitement and energy within employees – whether the goals are set in large group meetings or in one-to-one encounters. This excitement and energy can quickly dissipate as soon as everyone gets back to their desk. You, the manager, must take steps to ensure that the organisation's focus remains centred on the goals and not on other matters (which are less important but momentarily more pressing). Of course, this task is much easier said than done.

Implementing goals at Pret a Manger

Up-market sandwich retailer Pret a Manger produces good-quality snacks and sandwiches at premium prices. The company buys all the ingredients it uses fresh on the day it uses them. Each of the products – sandwiches, bagels, pasta mixes, croissants, and doughnuts – is made up, cooked, and baked on the premises for immediate consumption. Anything not consumed by the end of the day is given to charity.

In order to deliver this level of quality and service, the company has specific goals and targets that it communicates regularly to all staff, and displays on the walls of the retail and also the staff areas. These are as follows.

✔ Customers must not have to wait for more than three minutes before being served; longer than that and they begin to feel slighted, and this will lead to loss of reputation.

✔ Customers are not to wait for more than 90 seconds while they are being served; longer than that and they begin to feel unvalued, and again this will lead to loss of reputation.

✔ Customers do not expect to have to queue for more than 30 seconds to pay for their products if they have picked them off the shelf themselves.

Managing the overarching goals of quality, value, service, and convenience has meant that the company has had to pay attention to these specific details in order to ensure that it maximises business opportunities whenever customers come in through the door.

In order to fulfil these goals, Pret a Manger and its managers have additionally to undertake the following priorities:

✔ Assessing the peaks and troughs of demand throughout the day and scheduling staff accordingly

✔ Ensuring that all staff who are working (even during busy periods) have access to tea- and coffee-making facilities and tills

✔ Ensuring that all staff can recognise each of the products on offer

✔ Ensuring that all staff are friendly, pleasant, and polite

A lack of attention to any of these goals and targets reduces the real and perceived distinctive quality and style of Pret a Manger. This would result in customers seeing the company as a largely unbranded, undifferentiated, standard convenience food chain. So that this does not happen, the staff know and understand clearly what they have to do, why, and how, and what the results are.

Staying focused on goals can be extremely difficult – particularly when you're a busy person and the goals are on top of your regular responsibilities. Think about situations that fight for your attention during a typical day at work:

✔ How often do you sit down at your desk in the morning to plot out your priorities for the day, only to have them pushed aside five minutes later when you get a call from your boss?

Maria, I need you to drop everything and get to work on a report for the general manager right away! She has to have it on her desk by 3 p.m. today.

✔ How many times has an employee come to you with a problem?

Sorry, Maria, but I think you had better hear about this problem before it gets any worse. Jenny and Tony just had a fight and Jenny says she's leaving. We can't afford to lose Jenny – especially not right now. She's the key to the development project. What are we going to do?

✔ Do you remember getting caught in a 15-minute meeting that drags on for several hours?

Are there any questions on steps 1 through 14 of the new recruitment process? Fine, now let's get started on steps 15 through 35.

In unlimited ways, anyone can lose sight of what they need to be doing in order to get the organisation's goals accomplished. One of the biggest problems employees face is confusing activity with results. Do you know anyone who works incredibly long hours – late into the night and on weekends – but never seems to get anything done? Although this employee always seems to be busy, the problem is that she is working on the wrong things. This is called *presenteeism* or the *activity trap*, and it's very easy for anyone to fall into if they are not careful.

We mentioned the general rule that says that 80 per cent of workers' productivity comes from 20 per cent of their activity. The flip side of this rule is that only 20 per cent of workers' productivity comes from 80 per cent of their activity. This statistic illustrates the activity trap at work. What do you do in an average day? More important, what do you do with the 80 per cent of your time that produces so few results? You can get out of the activity trap and take control of your schedules and priorities. However, you have to be tough, and you have to be single-minded in pursuit of your goals. And you have to take your employees with you.

Achieving your goals is all up to you. No one, not even your boss (perhaps especially not your boss) can make it any easier for you to concentrate on achieving your goals. You have to take charge, and you have to take charge now! If you aren't controlling your own schedule, you're simply letting everyone else control your schedule for you.

Following are some tips to help you and your employees get out of the activity trap:

✔ **Do your Number 1 priority first!** With all the distractions that compete for your attention, with the constant temptation to work on the easy stuff first and save the tough stuff for last, and with people dropping into your office just to chat or to unload their problems on you, concentrating on your Number 1 priority is always a challenge. However, if you don't do your Number 1 priority first, you're almost guaranteed to find yourself in the activity trap. That is, you're almost guaranteed to find the same priorities on your list of tasks to do day after day, week after week, and month after month. If your Number 1 priority is too big, divide it into smaller chunks and focus on the most important one of those.

✔ **Do your Number 2 priority second!** This has the advantage of: keeping you concentrated on what is truly important, making sure that you don't get sidetracked by the hustle and bustle of daily life, and that you return to what's important. Additionally, priority Number 2 needs doing until it is done – the same as everything else.

✔ **Get organised!** Getting organised and managing your time effectively are incredibly important pursuits for anyone in business. If you're organised, you can spend less time trying to figure out what you should be doing and more time *doing* what you should be doing.

✔ **Just say no!** If someone tries to make her problems your problems, just say no. If you're a manager, you probably like nothing more than taking on new challenges and solving problems. The conflict arises when solving somebody else's problems interferes with solving your own. You have to constantly be on guard and fight the temptation to fritter your day away with meaningless activities. Always ask yourself, 'How does this help me achieve my goals?' Focus on your own goals and refuse to let others make their problems your own.

Using Your Power for Good: Making Your Goals Happen

After you create a wonderful set of goals with your employees, how do you make sure that the goals happen? How do you turn your priorities into your employees' priorities? The best goals in the world mean nothing if they aren't achieved. You can choose to leave this critical step in the process to chance, or you can choose to get involved.

You have the power to make your goals happen.

Power is not inherently wrong provided you use it responsibly. Everyone has many sources of power within them. Not only do you have power, but you also exercise power to control or influence people and events around you on a daily basis. So power is a positive thing; it's only negative when abused. Bullying, victimisation, manipulation, exploitation, and coercion have no place in the modern workplace. You can use the positive power within you to your advantage – and to the advantage of the people around you – by tapping into this power to help achieve your organisation's goals. People and systems often fall into ruts or into non-productive patterns of behaviour that are hard to break. Power properly applied can kick-start these people and systems and move them in the right direction – the direction that leads to the accomplishment of their goals.

Everyone has five primary sources of power, and everyone has specific strengths and weaknesses related to these sources. Recognise your own strengths and weaknesses and use them to your advantage. As you review the five sources of power that follow, consider your own personal strengths and weaknesses.

- ✔ **Personal power:** This is the power that comes from within your character. Your passion for greatness, the strength of your convictions, your ability to communicate and inspire, your personal charisma, and your leadership skills all add up to personal power.

- ✔ **Relationship power:** Everyone has relationships with others at work. These interactions contribute to the relationship power that you wield in your workplace. Sources of relationship power include close friendships with top executives, partners, or owners, people who owe you favours, and colleagues who provide you with information and insights that you normally don't get through your formal business relationships.

- ✔ **Knowledge power:** To see knowledge power in action, just watch what happens the next time your organisation's computer network goes down! Then you see who really has the power in an organisation (in this case, your computer network administrator). Knowledge power comes from the special expertise and knowledge that you have gained during the course of your career. Knowledge power also comes from obtaining academic degrees (think MBA) or special training.

- ✔ **Task power:** Task power is the power that comes from the job or process you perform at work. As you have undoubtedly witnessed on many occasions, people can facilitate or impede the efforts of their colleagues and others through the application of task power. For example, when you submit a claim for payment to your insurance company and months pass with no action ('We don't seem to have your claim in our computer – are you sure you submitted one? Maybe you should send us another one just to be sure'), you are on the receiving end of task power.

- ✔ **Position power:** This kind of power derives strictly from your rank or title in the organisation and is a function of the authority that you wield to command human and financial resources. Although the position power of the receptionist in your organisation is probably quite low, the position power of the president or owner is at the top of the chart. The best leaders seldom rely on position power to get things done.

Top five goal Web sites

Wondering where to find the best information on the Web about the topics addressed in this chapter? Well, you've come to the right place! Here are our top five favourites:

✔ Personal goal setting: `www.mindtools.com/page6.html`

✔ Learning and Skills Council: `www.lsc.org.uk/strategy`

✔ The awesome power of goal setting: `www.humanresources.about.com/library/weekly/aa121000a.htm`

✔ Appraisals and goal setting: `www.cipd.co.uk/performanceappraisalandmanagement`

✔ myGoals.com: `www.mygoals.com`

If you're weak in certain sources of power, you can work on increasing your power in those areas. For example, work on your weakness in relationship power by making a concerted effort to know your colleagues better and to cultivate relationships with higher-ranking managers or executives. Instead of declining invitations to get together with your colleagues after work, join them – have fun and strengthen your relationship power at the same time.

Be aware of the sources of your power and use it in a positive way to help you and your employees accomplish the goals of your organisation. In getting things done, a little power can go a long way.

Chapter 8

Performance Appraisal and Management: People and Projects

In This Chapter

▶ Quantifying your goals

▶ Developing a performance management system

▶ Putting your system into practice

▶ Charting your results graphically

▶ Making the most of your data

Setting goals – for individuals, for teams, and for the overall organisation – is extremely important. (Chapter 7 addresses the whys and wherefores of setting goals.) However, ensuring that the organisation is making progress towards the successful completion of its goals (in the manner and timeframes agreed to) is equally important. The organisation's performance depends on each individual who works within it. Achieving goals is what this chapter is all about.

Measuring and monitoring the performance of individuals in your organisation is like walking a tightrope: You don't want to over-measure or over-monitor your employees. Doing so only leads to needless bureaucracy and red tape, which can negatively affect your employees' ability to perform their tasks. Neither do you want to under-measure or under-monitor your employees. Such a lack of watchfulness can lead to nasty surprises when a task is completed late, over budget, or not at all. 'What? The customer database conversion isn't completed yet? I promised the sales director that we would have that job done two weeks ago!'

Please keep in mind that, as a manager, your primary goal in measuring and monitoring your employees' performance is not to punish them for making a mistake or missing a milestone. Instead, you help your employees stay on track and find out whether they need additional assistance or resources to do so. Few employees like to admit that they need help getting an assignment done – whatever the reason. Because of their reluctance, you must systematically check on the progress of your employees and regularly give them feedback on how they're doing.

If you don't monitor desired performance, you won't achieve desired performance. Don't leave achieving your goals to chance; develop systems to monitor progress and ensure that your goals are achieved. And you can't measure anything except against what you set out to achieve.

Taking the First Steps

The first step in checking your employees' progress is to determine the key indicators of a goal's success. If you follow the advice in Chapter 7, you set goals with your employees that are few in number and *SMART* (specific, measurable, attainable, relevant, and time bound).

When you quantify a goal in precise numerical terms, your employees have no confusion over how their performance is measured and when their job performance is adequate (or less than adequate). For example, if the goal is to produce 100 sprockets per hour, with a reject rate of 1 or lower, your employees clearly understand that producing only 75 sprockets per hour with 10 rejects is unacceptable performance. You leave nothing to the imagination, and the goals aren't subject to individual interpretation or to the whims of individual supervisors or managers.

How you measure and monitor the progress of your employees towards completion of their goals depends on the nature of the goals. You can measure some goals, for example, in terms of time, others in terms of units of production, and others in terms of delivery of a particular work product (such as a report or a sales proposal).

Table 8-1 offers examples of different goals and ways to measure them.

Table 8-1	Sample Goals and Measurements
Goal	*Measurement*
Plan and implement a company newsletter before the end of the second quarter of the current fiscal year.	The specific date (for example June 30) that the newsletter is sent out (*time*).
Increase the number of mountain bike frames produced by each employee from 20 to 25 per day.	The exact number of mountain bike frames produced by the employee each day (*quantity*).
Increase profit on the project by 20 per cent in financial year 2009.	The total percentage increase in profit in the year to 31 December 2009 (*percentage increase*).

Although noting when your employees attain their goals is obviously important, recognising your employees' *incremental* progress towards attaining their goals is just as important. For example:

- The goal for your drivers is to maintain an accident-free record. This goal is continuous – there is no deadline. To encourage drivers in their efforts, you can prominently post a huge banner in the middle of the garage that reads '153 Accident-Free Days'. Increase the number for each day of accident-free driving.

- The goal of your accounts clerks is to increase the average number of transactions from 150 per day to 175 per day. To track their progress, you can publicly post a summary of the daily production count at the end of each week. As production increases, praise the progress of your employees towards the final goal.

- The goal set for your production staff is to turn customer orders around within 24 hours, without errors. You can publicly post the results for all to see; and in this case, when orders are either not turned around within 24 hours or when there are errors, you have a very quick, public, and agreed point for investigation.

The secret to performance measuring and monitoring is the power of positive feedback. When you give positive feedback (increased number of units produced, percentage increase in sales, and so on), you encourage the behaviour that you want. However, when you give negative feedback (number of errors, number of work days lost, and so on), you aren't encouraging the behaviour you want; you're only discouraging the behaviour that you don't want. Consider the following examples:

- **Instead of measuring this:** Number of defective cartridges

- **Measure this:** Number of correctly assembled cartridges

- **Instead of measuring this:** Number of days late

- **Measure this:** Number of days on time

- **Instead of measuring this:** Quantity of late transactions

- **Measure this:** Quantity of completed transactions

From our experience as managers, we find that you're much more likely to get the results you want when you put group performance measures (total revenues, average days sick, and so on) out in the open for everyone to see, but keep individual performance measures (sales performance by employee, absence rankings by employee, and so on) private. The intent is to get a team to work *together* to improve its performance – tracking and publicising group measures and then rewarding improvement in them can lead to dramatic advances in the performance you seek. What you do *not* want to do is to embarrass your employees or subject them to ridicule by other employees when their individual performance is not up to par. Instead, deal with these employees privately, and coach them (and provide additional training and support, as necessary) to improve performance.

Developing a System for Providing Immediate Performance Feedback

You can measure an infinite number of behaviours or performance characteristics. What you measure and the values you measure against are up to you and your employees. In any case, keep certain points in mind when you design a system for measuring and monitoring your employees' performance. Build your system on the *MARS* system. MARS is an acronym for *milestones, actions, relationships,* and *schedules.* We describe each element of the MARS system in the following sections.

Application of each characteristic – milestones, actions, relationships, and schedules – results in goals that you can measure and monitor. If you can't measure and monitor your goals, chances are that your employees never achieve them and you don't know the difference. And wouldn't that be a shame?

Setting your checkpoints: The milestones

Every goal needs a starting point, an ending point, and points in between to measure progress along the way. *Milestones* are the checkpoints, events, and markers that tell you and your employees how far along you are on the road to reaching the goals you've set together.

For example, suppose that you establish a goal of finalising corporate budgets in three months' time. The third milestone along the way to your ultimate goal is that draft department budgets are submitted to division managers no later than June 1. If you check with the division managers on June 1 and your employees haven't submitted the draft budgets, you quickly and unambiguously know that the project is behind schedule. If, however, all the budgets are in on May 15, you know that the project is ahead of schedule and that you may reach the final goal of completing the corporate budgets sooner than you originally estimated.

Reaching your checkpoints: The actions

Actions are the individual activities your employees perform to get from one milestone to the next. To reach the third milestone in your budgeting project – submitting draft department budgets to division managers by June 1 – your employees must undertake and complete several actions after they reach the second milestone in the project. In this example, these actions may include the following:

- ✔ Review prior-year expenditure reports and determine the relationship, if any, to current activities.
- ✔ Review current-year expenditure reports and project and forecast final results.
- ✔ Meet with department staff to determine their training, travel, and capital equipment requirements for the new financial year.
- ✔ Review the possibilities of new staff, lay-offs and redundancies, and pay rises to determine the impact on payroll costs.
- ✔ Put everything on to a computerised draft budget spreadsheet using the figures from the actions already taken.
- ✔ Print off the draft budget and double-check the results, correcting them if necessary.
- ✔ Submit the draft budget to your own manager before forwarding it to the division manager.

Each action gets your employees a little farther along the way towards reaching the third milestone in the project and is therefore a critical element in your employees' performance.

When developing a plan for completion of a project, note each action in writing. By taking notes, you make concentration easier for your employees because they know exactly what they must do to reach a milestone, how far they have gone, and how much farther they have to go.

Acting in sequence: The relationships

Relationships are how milestones and actions interact with one another. Relationships shape the proper sequencing of activities that lead you to the successful, effective accomplishment of your goals. Although sequences don't always matter, it is often more effective to perform certain actions before others and to attain certain milestones before others.

Measuring instead of counting

According to management guru Peter Drucker, most business people spend too much time counting and too little time actually measuring the performance of their organisations. What does Drucker mean by this? Drucker is talking about the tendency of managers to be short-sighted in their application of management controls such as budgets. For example, most budgets are meant to ensure that company funds are spent only where authorised. They are control mechanisms that prevent spending from going out of control unnoticed by counting the amount of money spent for a particular activity. However, Drucker suggests that, instead of using budgets only to count, managers can use them to measure things that are even more important to the future of the business. Managers can relate proposed expenditures to future results, for example, and provide follow-up information to show whether the desired results were achieved, and whether or not they were cost effective.

Drucker likens counting to a doctor using an X-ray machine to diagnose an ill patient. Although some ailments – broken bones, pneumonia, and so on – do show up on an X-ray, other, more life-threatening illnesses such as leukaemia, hypertension, and AIDS don't. Similarly, most managers use accounting systems to X-ray their organisation's financial performance. However, accounting systems don't measure a catastrophic loss of market share or a failure of the firm to innovate until the problem has already gone on too long and the 'patient' is damaged – perhaps irretrievably.

For example, in the list of actions needed to achieve the third project milestone, enumerated in the preceding section, trying to perform the fifth action before the first, second, third, or fourth is not going to work! If you don't work out the right numbers to put into your spreadsheet before you fill in the blanks, your results are meaningless.

Keep in mind that you may have more than one way to reach a milestone and give your employees the scope to find their own ways to reach their goals. Doing so empowers your employees to take responsibility for their work and to benefit from both their mistakes and their successes. The results are successful performance and happy, productive employees.

Establishing your timeframe: The schedules

How do you determine how far apart your milestones should be and how long project completion should take? You can plan better by estimating the *schedule* of each individual action in your project plan.

A project's six phases

Some management techniques are so popular that they're photocopied and passed from employee to employee and from company to company in an informal system of communication that outperforms the formal communication system of many organisations. These tongue-in-cheek lists, diagrams, and cartoons help many employees find humour in their own workplaces and brighten up their days. The following list of six phases of a project has been floating around for years – our copy looks like it's at least the fifth generation:

1. Enthusiasm

2. Disillusionment

3. Panic

4. Search for the guilty

5. Punishment of the innocent

6. Praise and honours for the non-participants

Using your experience and training to develop schedules that are realistic and useful is important. For example, you may know that if everything goes perfectly, meeting with all your employees takes exactly four days. However, you also know that if you run into problems, the process can take as long as six days. Therefore, for planning purposes, you decide that five days is an appropriate schedule to apply to this particular action. This schedule allows for some variability while ensuring that you meet the milestone on time.

Putting Performance Measuring and Monitoring into Practice

Theory is nice, but practice is better. So far we've discussed the theory of measuring and monitoring employee performance, but how does measuring and monitoring really happen? Following are a couple of real-life cases for your reading pleasure. Each case takes a different path to achieve the same end – successful employee performance.

Studying Sheerness Steel

Sheerness Steel was a giant independent steelworks producing top-quality steel stock for the construction, civil engineering, aircraft, and railway industries. Additionally, the company produced specialist steel products for the luxury and exclusive motor car industries; and very fine steels for industrial cleaning and fibre optics.

Located at Sheerness on the Isle of Sheppey in north Kent, Sheerness Steel defied all the axioms of industrial and commercial location. The company wasn't close to supplies of raw materials or to its markets. Only a small country lane and a swing bridge connected the Isle of Sheppey to the mainland, so supplies had to come in by sea, and finished products had to go out by sea. The oil, gas, and coal required to fire the furnaces also had to come in by sea. And yet for nearly 20 years, Sheerness Steel was the most profitable steelworks in the European Union, and the most productive in terms of output per member of staff. How was this achieved?

Setting goals with employees

Because of its location and the squeeze on the steel industry, Sheerness Steel found itself with declining production and turnover volumes; and for three years only assured government contracts kept it in existence. This was clearly not sustainable, so Sheerness Steel hired a human resources director, Hugh Billot, and gave him absolute authority to arrange matters as he saw fit.

Hugh Billot opened consultations with all staff and with the recognised trade union, the Iron and Steel Trades Confederation (ISTC). The problem was quite simple, he said, 'We have to change or die.' With the full support of the ISTC, the following targets were set:

- All orders would be met in full and sent on or before their deadline; any order that was late would be fully investigated and followed up.

- All shipments would go out on time; everyone knew the ferry schedules, and so there was no excuse for not meeting them.

- All accidents, however small, would be investigated and followed up.

- All industrial injuries, however small, would be investigated and followed up.

- All spillages of molten material (a major cause of stoppages) would be investigated and followed up.

Addressing all staff at a mass meeting on a warm sunny day, Hugh Billot outlined his plans. He shared a platform with the local official of the ISTC. The ISTC endorsed everything he said. The meeting was followed up with detailed meetings; the production of schedules for all production and shift supervisors; and monthly meetings with all production crews.

Specific goals were translated from the targets as follows:

- All orders would go out on time.

- There would be no spillages, accidents, or injuries.

- All deliveries would meet the ferry service on which they were scheduled.

Changing the performance measuring system

The result of Hugh Billot's efforts was to change the whole approach to productivity and production schedules. Instead of concentrating purely on output volumes, the priority now was meeting deadlines. Performance bonuses were tied to meeting deadlines – again, with the full agreement of the union. Pay rises were directly linked to turnover and productivity, and were disentangled from the national agreement held between the ISTC and the United Kingdom steel industry at the time.

There were other positive effects, as follows:

- Absenteeism was lower. At one stage absenteeism had been at about 15 per cent; now it was barely measurable.
- The number of accidents was 95 per cent lower.
- Spillages of molten material reduced to the point that, over one 10-year period, only two spillages occurred.

In addition, no strikes, collective stoppages, or collective disputes happened over the entire period of Hugh Billot's tenure as human resources director. Because of the productivity increases, and of the fact that earnings were related to turnover and meeting deadlines, staff wages and salaries rose to become nearly 30 per cent higher than for the rest of the British steel industry.

The result was to transform a moribund and lifeless organisation, riddled with strikes and disputes, into the most profitable and productive steelworks in the European Union.

Further developments

Maybe the transformation would have continued if the company had remained independent. However, Sheerness Steel was sold on to a venture capital consortium. The new owners started to impose goals and volume-based output targets. Hugh Billot left; and everyone involved – company and employees – reverted to traditional targets. Productivity quickly declined, and the company was sold on again to a Canadian multinational, ASW Inc. ASW had clearly heard of the 'miracle' that Sheerness Steel and High Billot had performed. However, it too adopted a punitive and adversarial approach; and eventually the company closed down.

The clear lesson is that if you establish targets in agreement with the employees, they can work in the most extreme of circumstances. The additional – and essential – lesson is that once you set targets in these ways and establish the standards you're determined to meet, you must carry on: Any change or deviation is likely to have the direst consequences for everyone involved.

Reducing shrinkage

The problem of *shrinkage* is defined as the amount of products, equipment, and supplies lost through wastage, theft, damage, or breakage. Shrinkage is therefore a euphemism for sloppiness, lack of attention, and, above all, an inability to set standards of performance that stick.

Many organisations are complacent about this issue. Lawrence King is managing director of the ORIS Group, a consultancy that monitors the efficiency and effectiveness of resource utilisation for its customers. Lawrence King states: 'Some retailers especially do not even know what their shrinkage numbers are. I know of two major businesses, one in pharmaceuticals and the other in fashion, neither of which want to know how bad the problem is, because they know that they would have to do something about it if they did know. They have therefore put this problem into the "too hard to cope with" basket. The trouble is, it does cost money to find out what the losses are. And then once you know what the losses are, you clearly have to do something about it.'

In the past, organisations thought that shoplifting and petty pilfering were the only real sources and causes of shrinkage, and so considered they had little to worry about. Shrinkage, however, occurs through staff dishonesty and information systems failure as well as through theft by customers.

Part of the problem is a result of changing patterns of employment. Lawrence King states: 'Not that long ago, most retail staff were full-time. It was a career, and they worked until they drew their pensions. Now, retailers have cut their costs, there are far more part-time staff, so the manager in a typical retail outlet may be the only full-time member of staff. That may not be quite true in bigger stores of course; but the general trend is the same. There is consequently a lot less loyalty and a lot less commitment than there used to be. In addition, the pay is almost invariably lower. Retail has never been the best pay in the world, so maybe people feel that there is an opportunity to supplement low rates of pay by helping themselves a bit.'

Creating programmes based on desired behaviours

Any organisation faced with a serious shrinkage problem has to be able to establish absolute standards – standards below which it does not slip, nor allow employees to slip. Shrinkage problems can only be addressed under the following conditions:

- ✔ **Recognition at all levels.** Recognition must be underpinned by a determination at board level to deal fully and effectively with the problem.

- ✔ **Zero tolerance for theft or fraud among staff.** No matter how senior, experienced, or valued the colleague is, they must be dismissed if they're caught stealing from the business. This is the *only* way to deal with pilfering.

✔ **Making shrinkage culturally unacceptable.** Make it clear that shrinkage is an enemy of the business. Relate shrinkage rates to turnover and profitability in all staff briefings.

✔ **Rewarding the desired behaviour.** The desired behaviour is established through a combination of policies and practice. The policies state what's required, and also state very clearly how people are to behave and how not to behave. In particular, you need to focus on the conduct of everyone from the point of view of ensuring that:

- Everyone knows and understands that stealing, lying, and cheating are an affront to everyone.

- You monitor all aspects of shrinkage that concern you, and make sure that you also involve all of the staff.

- Shrinkage is treated from the point of view that by stealing or lying, individuals affect not just themselves but also everyone else.

The key is to make sure that you reward honest employees adequately for their work, so that you remove their temptation to steal. An open and honest culture needs to underpin the organisation; it is impossible to ensure that employees are honest if those further up the organisation are not. Paying attention to matters such as punctuality, commitment, and enthusiasm help to generate loyalty and engagement; and the more loyal and engaged employees are, the less likely they are to steal from their employer.

Removing the unacceptable behaviour

Organisations need to take an attitude of zero tolerance to shrinkage. The moment that an employee – whoever he is – is known or understood to have got away with some form of dishonesty, the word quickly spreads around the organisation. Failure to dismiss someone for one offence normally means that additional or further offences that others carry out are treated in the same way – and if you don't check such behaviour, it quickly becomes an epidemic. So make up your mind that, as well as rewarding good behaviour, you are going to punish bad behaviour (and in the overwhelming majority of cases, when you have proved the behaviour and followed the correct procedures, this means dismissal).

Measuring and rewarding employee performance

Any shrinkage programme, effectively implemented, ought to be able to demonstrate the differences in results before and after you undertake the initiative. Supervisors and managers ought to closely track the performance of their employees, products, and services, and the overall organisation; and where drawing a direct relationship between an improvement because of the new higher standards and what went on before is possible, this should be made clear to everybody.

Taking such an approach also clearly sets, underpins, and reinforces the standards by which all employees ought to behave. Yet some firms still have doubts, or cannot quite get around to do anything about the problem of shrinkage, even though they know it exists. Why is this?

We give the last word to Lawrence King: 'This story is less told because it isn't part of the published accounts, so it isn't an official number. There is no formal calculation for shrinkage. You are not obliged to publish your shrinkage rates. If you had to declare it, or make it known to shareholders, you would do a lot more about it. And if you did publicise it – it is an indication to shareholders of how efficient and effective you are – or not.'

Using Gantts, PERTs, and Other Yardsticks

In some cases, measuring your employees' progress towards achieving a goal doesn't really take much. For example, if the goal is to increase the number of widgets produced from 100 per hour to 125 per hour, a simple count can tell you whether your employees have achieved that goal. 'Sorry Stella, you're still averaging only 120 widgets per hour!' However, if the goal is to fabricate a prototype electric-powered vehicle in six months' time, the job of measuring and monitoring individual performance gets much more complicated and confusing.

Although you may decide to write out all the different milestones and actions (as demonstrated in 'Developing a System for Providing Immediate Performance Feedback', earlier in the chapter), a graphical representation of the project is often a much easier way of understanding complex projects. The following sections explore *Gantts, PERTs,* and other yardsticks that perform this vital service for business people around the world 24 hours a day, 7 days a week.

Stacking up the Gantt or bar chart

Bar charts, also known as *Gantt charts* (named after that famous industrial engineer, Henry L. Gantt), are probably one of the simplest and most common means for illustrating and monitoring project progress. With a quick glance, you can easily see exactly where the project is at any given date and can compare actual progress against planned progress.

The three key elements of bar charts are:

- ✔ **Timescale:** The timeline provides a scale with which you measure progress. You can express the timeline in any units you want: Days, weeks, months, or whatever is most useful for managing the project. In most bar charts, the timeline appears along the horizontal axis.

- ✔ **Actions:** Actions are the individual activities your employees perform to get from one milestone to the next. In a bar chart, each action is listed – usually in chronological order – vertically along the left side of the chart.

- ✔ **Bars:** Now, what would a bar chart be without bars – an 'unbar' chart, perhaps? Bars are the open blocks that you draw on your bar chart to indicate the length of time a particular action is estimated to take. Short bars mean short periods of time; long bars mean long periods of time. What's really neat about bars is that, as an action is completed, you can fill in the bar to provide a quick visual reference of complete and incomplete actions.

Figure 8-1 shows a typical bar chart; in this case, the chart illustrates the actions that lead up to the third milestone in the corporate budgeting example from the 'Developing a System for Providing Immediate Performance Feedback' section.

In the chart, the timeline is along the top of the bar chart as we suggest. In this example, the timeline stretches from April 15 to June 1, with each increment representing one week. The six actions necessary to reach the third milestone are listed vertically along the left side of the bar chart. Finally, you see those neat little bars that are really the heart and soul of the bar chart. Leave the bars unfilled until an action is completed; then you may colour them in if you like.

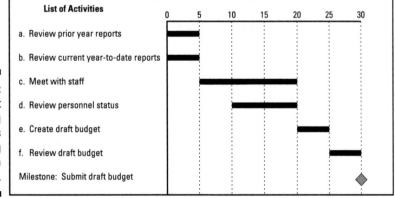

Third Milestone: Submit Draft Budget

Figure 8-1: A bar chart illustrating actions leading up to a milestone.

If you complete all actions according to the bar chart, you reach the third milestone (represented by the diamond in Figure 8-1) on June 1. If some actions take longer to complete than estimated, you may not reach the milestone on time and someone may end up in hot water. Conversely, if some actions take less time than estimated, the milestone can be reached early.

The advantages of the Gantt chart are its simplicity, ease of preparation and use, and low cost. In addition, it is a visual representation of progress available to all. If you send it as an e-mail attachment or put it up on the wall, everyone knows where they stand.

Gantt charts can be used to chart the progress of everything from a simple product modification to the development of the A380 Airbus.

Following flow charts

When the going gets tough, the tough get going – and flowing. Although bar charts are useful for simple projects, they don't illustrate the sequential flow of actions in a project (and therefore aren't as useful for complex projects). On the other hand, *flow charts* do a good job of illustrating this sequential flow. Although flow charts look completely different to bar charts, they also have three key elements:

- ✔ **Actions:** In the case of flow charts, arrows indicate actions. Arrows lead from one event to the next until the project is complete. The length of the arrows doesn't necessarily indicate the duration of an action. The arrows' primary purpose in a flow chart is to illustrate the sequential relationship of actions to one another.

- ✔ **Events:** Events, represented in flow charts by numbered circles, signify the completion of a particular action.

- ✔ **Time:** Time estimates are inserted alongside each action (arrow) in the flow chart. By adding the number of time units along a particular path, you can estimate the total time for the completion of an action.

Figure 8-2 shows a flow chart of the corporate budgeting example illustrated in Figure 8-1. As you can see, the flow chart shows exactly how each action relates to the others. By following the longest path in terms of time, you can determine the *critical path* of the project. This kind of analysis is called the *critical path method (CPM)* and assumes that you can estimate the time to complete individual actions with a high degree of certainty. The *critical path* highlights the actions that determine the soonest – and, more importantly, the latest – that you can complete a project. In this case, the soonest is 30 days; the latest is 35 days.

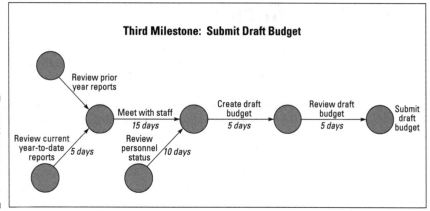

Third Milestone: Submit Draft Budget

Review prior year reports

Meet with staff — 15 days

Create draft budget — 5 days

Review draft budget — 5 days

Submit draft budget

Review current year-to-date reports — 5 days

Review personnel status — 10 days

Figure 8-2:
A flow chart for the corporate budgeting example.

PERT, short for *program evaluation and review technique,* is a variation of the critical path method used when you can't estimate with a high degree of certainty the time required to complete individual actions. Using some very interesting statistical techniques (zzzzz . . .), PERT averages a range of possible times to arrive at an estimate for each action.

Inserting software

Project planning and performance assessment and measurement has become much more straightforward with the availability of project-based software. You key items into a spreadsheet, which makes all the necessary calculations, and get up-to-the-minute data for the sake of a few clicks of the mouse! Microsoft Project, one of the foremost project-planning software packages on the market today, enables you to create and revise project schedules quickly and easily. Setting up a project with Microsoft Project is as easy as 1, 2, 3:

1. **Enter the actions to be completed.**

2. **Enter the sequence of the actions and their dependencies on other actions.**

3. **Enter the resources (people and money) required to complete the action.**

As a project progresses, you can input data such as actual start and completion dates, actual expenditures, and more, to get a realistic picture of where the project is at any time. You can print out these results in the form of tables, charts, or graphs – whatever your preference – and then save them for future reference.

Reading the Results

You establish your goals, you set performance measures, and you obtain pages of data for each of your employees. Now what? Now you determine whether the expected results were achieved, as follows.

- ✔ **Compare results to expectations:** Was the expected goal achieved? Suppose that the goal is to complete the budget by June 1. When was the budget completed? It was completed on May 17 – well ahead of the deadline. Brilliant! The mission was accomplished with time to spare.

- ✔ **Record the results:** Make note of the results – perhaps put them in the files that you maintain for each employee or print them out on your computer and post them in the work area.

- ✔ **Praise, coach, or counsel your employees:** If they did the job right, on time, and within budget, congratulate your employees for a job well done and reward them appropriately: A written note of appreciation, a day off with pay, a formal awards presentation – whatever you decide.

  However, if employees did not achieve the expected results, find out why and what you can do to ensure that they do achieve the expected results the next time. If employees need only additional support or encouragement, coach them for a better performance. You can listen to your employees, refer them to other employees, or provide your own personal examples. If the poor results stem from a more serious short-coming, then retrain, or discipline your employees. (More on this subject in Chapter 15.)

Top five project management Web sites

The following five Web Sites are our favourites for more info on project management:

- ✔ PM Forum: www.pmforum.org/

- ✔ Gantt Chart and Timeline Centre: www.smartdraw.com/resources/centers/gantt/

- ✔ Balanced Scorecard Institute: www.balancedscorecard.org/

- ✔ Association for Project Management: www.apm.org.uk

- ✔ Performance Measurement Association: www.som.cranfield.ac.uk/som/cbp/pma/

Chapter 9

Tackling Performance Appraisals

In This Chapter

▶ Recognising the importance of performance appraisals
▶ Developing performance appraisals
▶ Avoiding mistakes in appraisals
▶ Making appraisals work for you

*T*imely and accurate performance appraisals are an extremely important tool for every business manager or supervisor. So, if performance appraisals are so important to the successful management of employees, why do most managers and supervisors dread doing them, and why do so many employees dread receiving them? According to studies on the topic, an estimated 40 per cent of all workers never receive performance appraisals. And for the 60 per cent of workers who do receive performance appraisals, most of the appraisals are conducted poorly. Very few employees actually receive regular, formal performance appraisals that are thoughtful, complete, and beneficial to the employee – or to the organisation.

Ask any human resources manager whether formal performance appraisals are really necessary and the answer, of course, is a resounding yes! However, if you look a little below the surface, the reality may be something quite different. Although most managers consider performance appraisals a necessary tool in developing their employees, reinforcing good performance, and correcting poor performance, these appraisals are often too little, too late. They often miss the mark as tools for developing employees. If performance appraisals are done poorly, managers are better off not doing them at all – especially if the alternative to appraisals is more frequent coaching.

In this chapter, we consider the benefits of performance appraisals and explore the right and wrong ways to do them.

Appraising Performance: Why it Matters

You can find many good reasons for conducting regular formal performance appraisals with your employees. Formal performance appraisals are just one part of an organisation's system of delegation, goal setting, coaching, motivating, and ongoing informal and formal feedback on employee performance. If you don't believe us, try a few of these positive elements of performance appraisals on for size:

- ✓ **A chance to meet regularly:** In any case, you should be making sure that you know what your employees are doing and being available for support when needed. To do this, you need to meet regularly anyway; and so you have a much better basis for effective regular formal reviews when they happen.

- ✓ **A chance to summarise past performance and establish new performance goals:** All employees want to know whether they're doing a good job. Formal performance appraisals force managers to communicate performance results – both good and bad – to their employees and to set new goals. In many organisations, the annual performance appraisal is the only occasion when supervisors and managers speak to their employees about performance expectations and the results of employee efforts for the preceding appraisal period.

- ✓ **An opportunity for clarification and communication:** You need to continually compare expectations. Try this exercise with your manager. List your ten most important activities. Then ask your manager to list what she considers to be your ten most important activities. Surprise – the chances are that your lists are quite different. On average, business people who do this exercise find that their lists overlap only 40 per cent at best. Performance appraisals help the employer and employee to compare notes and make sure that assignments and priorities are in sync.

- ✓ **A forum for learning goals and career development:** In many organisations, career development takes place as a part of the formal performance appraisal process. Managers and employees are all very busy and often have difficulty setting aside the time to sit down and chart out the steps that they must take to progress in an organisation or career. Although career development discussions should generally take place in a forum separate from the performance appraisal process, combining the activities does afford the opportunity to kill both birds with the same stone . . . or something like that.

- ✓ **A formal documentation to promote advancement or dismissal:** Most employees get plenty of informal performance feedback – at least of the negative kind along the lines of: 'You did what? Are you nuts?' Most informal feedback is verbal and, as such, undocumented. If you're trying to build a case to give your employee a promotion, you can support your case much more easily if you have plenty of written documentation (including formal performance appraisals) to justify your decision. And, if you're coming to the conclusion that you need to dismiss someone for poor performance, then you must have written evidence, including performance appraisals, that you have tried to address this performance before.

So, the preceding list gives very important reasons for conducting regular formal performance appraisals. However, consider this statement: Many companies have paid a lot of money to employees and former employees who have successfully sued them for wrongful or unfair dismissal, or for other biased and prejudicial employment decisions. Imagine how lonely you'd feel on the witness stand in the following scene, a scene that's replayed for real in courts of law and employment tribunals the length and breadth of the country:

Lawyer: So, Manager-on-the-spot, would you please tell the court exactly why you terminated Employee X?

Manager-on-the-spot: Certainly, I'll be glad to. Employee X was a very poor performer – clearly the worst in my department.

Lawyer: During the five years that my client was with your firm, did you ever conduct formal performance appraisals with Employee X?

Manager-on-the-spot: Er . . . well, no. I meant to, but I'm a very busy person. I was never quite able to get around to it.

Lawyer: Manager-on-the-spot, do you mean to say that, in all the time with your firm, Employee X never received a formal performance appraisal? Exactly how was my client supposed to correct the alleged poor performance when you failed to provide Employee X with the feedback needed to do so?

Manager-on-the-spot: Hmmm . . .

Spelling Out the Performance Appraisal Process

Believe it or not, one of the very most important things you can do as a manager is to conduct accurate and timely performance appraisals of your employees. As the saying goes, feedback is the breakfast of champions – make it a regular part of your management diet!

Many managers, however, tend to see the performance appraisal process in very narrow terms: How can I get this thing done as quickly as possible so I can get back to my real job? (Whatever their 'real' job is as managers.) In their haste to get the appraisal done and behind them, many managers merely consider a few examples of recent performance and base their entire appraisal on them. And because few managers give their employees the kind of meaningful, ongoing performance feedback that they need to do their jobs better, the performance appraisal can become a dreaded event – full of surprises and dismay. Or it can be so sugar-coated that it becomes a meaningless exercise in management. Neither scenario is the right way to evaluate your employees.

Have separate discussions for each of the following:

- ✔ Pay rises and bonuses
- ✔ Promotions
- ✔ Career development
- ✔ Ways to improve present performance and develop future performance
- ✔ Poor performance

Of course, in practice you can't possibly keep each of the topics totally separate from the rest. But you can prioritise; and you must spell out to the employee the specific purpose of the present discussion.

The performance appraisal process begins on the day that your employees are hired, continues each and every day that they report to you, and doesn't end until, through transfer, promotion, dismissal, or resignation, they move out of your sphere of responsibility.

The performance appraisal process is much broader than just the formal, written part of it. The following five steps help you encompass the broader scope of the process. Follow them when you evaluate your employees' performance:

1. **Set goals, expectations, and standards – together.**

   Before your employees can achieve your goals, or perform to your expectations, you have to set goals and expectations with them and develop standards to measure their performance. And after you've done all this, you have to communicate the goals and expectations *before* you evaluate your employees – not after. In fact, the performance review really starts on the first day of work. Tell your employees immediately how you evaluate them, show them the forms to be used, and explain the process.

Make sure that job descriptions, tasks, and priorities are clear and unambiguous, and that you and your employees understand and agree to the standards set for them. This is a two-way process. Make sure that employees have a voice in setting their goals and standards and that you have their agreement. Refer to Chapter 7 for more on setting goals.

2. Give continuous and specific feedback.

Catch your employees doing things right – every day of the week – and tell them about it then and there. And if you catch them doing wrong (nobody's perfect!), then let them know about that, too. Feedback is much more effective when you give it regularly and often than when you save it up for a special occasion (which can become victimisation if the feedback is constantly negative). The best formal performance appraisals contain the fewest surprises.

Constantly bombarding your employees with negative feedback has little to do with getting the performance that you want from them and costs you their respect.

3. Prepare a formal, written performance appraisal with your employee.

Every organisation has different requirements for the formal performance appraisal. Some appraisals are simple, one-page forms that require you to tick a few boxes; others are multi-page extravaganzas that require extensive narrative support. The form often varies by organisation, and by the level of the employee being evaluated (the ones you can buy at an office supply store are worthless). Regardless of the requirements of your particular organisation, the formal performance appraisal should be a summary of the goals and expectations for the appraisal period – events that you have discussed previously (and frequently) with your employees. Support your words with examples and make appraisals meaningful to your employees by keeping your discussion relevant to the goals, expectations, and standards that you developed in Step 1.

As a collaborative process, have the employee complete her own performance appraisal. Then compare your (the manager's) comments with the employee's comments; the differences that you find become topics of discussion and mutual goal setting.

4. Meet personally with your employees to discuss the performance appraisal.

Most employees appreciate the personal touch when you give the appraisal. Set aside some quality time to meet with them to discuss their performance appraisal. This doesn't mean five or ten minutes, but at least an hour or maybe more. When you plan performance appraisal meetings, less is definitely not more. Pick a place that's comfortable and free from distractions. Make the meeting positive and upbeat. Even when you have to discuss performance problems, centre your discussions on ways that you and your employees can work together to solve them.

The tone of performance appraisals and discussions can often become defensive as negative elements are raised and the employee starts to feel that she will get a small, or no pay rise. Start with letting the employee share how her job is going, what's working – and what's not – then share your assessment, starting with the positive.

5. **Set new goals, expectations, and standards.**

The performance appraisal meeting gives you and your employee the opportunity to step back from the inevitable daily issues for a moment and take a look at the big picture. You both have an opportunity to review and discuss the things that worked well and the things that, perhaps, didn't work so well. Based on this assessment, you can then set new goals, expectations, and standards for the next review period. The last step of the performance appraisal process becomes the first step, and you start all over again.

The entire process consists of setting goals with your employees, monitoring their performance, coaching them, supporting them, counselling and guiding them, and providing continuous feedback on their performance – both good and bad. If you've been doing these things before you sit down for your annual or semi-annual performance appraisal sessions with your employees, you're going to find reviews a pleasant and positive experience, looking at the past accomplishments, instead of being a disappointment for both you and your employees.

When it comes to conducting performance appraisals, managers have plenty of things to remember. Here are a few more:

- ✔ Communication with employees should be frequent so no surprises occur (OK, *fewer* surprises). Give your employees informal feedback on their performance early and often.

- ✔ The primary focus of performance appraisals should be on going forward – setting new goals, improving future performance – rather than on looking back.

- ✔ Learning and development should always be included as a part of the performance appraisal process (although sometimes a discussion about pay rises can be separate).

- ✔ You need to make performance appraisal a priority yourself – a part of your 'real' job – you are, after all, dependent on the performance of your employees for your own success and effectiveness.

Turning the tables: Upward and 360-degree evaluations

In recent years, a new kind of performance appraisal has emerged. Instead of the typical downward appraisal where managers review their workers' performance, the upward appraisal process stands this convention on its head by requiring workers to evaluate their managers' performance. If you think that getting a performance appraisal from your manager is uncomfortable, you haven't seen anything yet. There's nothing quite like the feeling you get when a group of your employees appraise you, giving you direct and honest feedback about the things you do that make it hard for them to do a good job. Ouch!

However, despite the discomfort that you may feel, the upward appraisal is invaluable – who better to assess your real impact on the organisation than your employees? The system works so well that companies such as Federal Express and others have institutionalised the upward appraisal and made it part of their corporate culture. Recent surveys show that many of the world's top companies are using some form of the upward performance appraisal to assess the performance of their managers.

Also popular is the 360-degree evaluation. The *360-degree evaluation process* is when you're appraised from all sides – superiors, subordinates, colleagues, and anyone from other departments with whom you happen to be working at the time. Levi Strauss & Co, for example, dictates that all employees are evaluated by their supervisors and by their underlings and peers.

The results can be quite a surprise to the lucky manager who is the subject of the appraisal, who may find that other employees see her as less caring and visionary than she thought. A study by Charles Handy many years ago found the same thing – that 70 per cent of managers and supervisors who rated themselves as caring and concerned were rated in turn as autocratic and distant by their employees.

Avoiding Common Traps

Appraisers can easily fall into certain traps in the appraisal process. To avoid making a misstep that may result in getting your foot stuck in one of these traps, keep in mind these common mistakes that appraisers make:

- ✔ **The halo effect:** This happens when an employee is so good in a particular area of their performance that you ignore problems in other areas. For example, you may give your star salesperson (whom your firm desperately needs to ensure continued revenue growth) a high rating (a halo) despite the fact that she refuses to complete and submit paperwork within the required time limits.

✔ **The recency effect:** The opposite of the halo effect, the *recency* effect happens when you allow an instance of poor performance to adversely affect your assessment of an employee's overall performance. For example, your administrative assistant has done a very good job for you in the months preceding her appraisal, but last week she missed a customer's deadline for submission of a proposal to continue with their advertising account. Your firm lost the account and you gave your assistant a scathing performance appraisal as a result.

✔ **Stereotyping:** This occurs when you allow preconceived notions about your employees to dictate how you rate them. For example, you may be convinced that women make better electronic parts assemblers than men do. As a result, your stereotyping automatically gives female employees the benefit of the doubt and higher ratings, while men have to prove themselves before you take them seriously. In extreme cases, such an approach may land you in an employment tribunal or a court of law.

✔ **Comparing:** Often, when you rate two employees at the same time, you're tempted to compare their performances. If one of the employees is a particularly high performer, your other employee may look bad in comparison – despite her individual level of performance. Conversely, if one of the employees is a particularly low performer, the other employee may look really good in comparison. Make your assessment of an individual employee's performance and allow it to stand on its own two feet and not be subject to how good or bad your other employees are.

✔ **Mirroring:** Everyone naturally likes people who are most like themselves. That's why you can easily fall into the trap of rating highly those employees who are most like you (same likes, dislikes, interests, hobbies, and so forth) and rating lowly those employees who are least like you. Although this is great for the employees you favour, the employees you don't favour don't appreciate it. Take some advice: Don't do it.

✔ **Discomfort:** One reason that many managers dread doing performance appraisals is that it forces them to acknowledge the failings of their employees and then talk to their employees about them. Few managers enjoy giving their employees bad news, but employees need to receive the bad news as well as the good (just be ready to duck when you give them the bad news). Otherwise, they don't know where they need to improve. And if they don't know where they need to improve, you can bet they don't improve.

Sorting Out Why Appraisals Go Bad

Appraisals go bad for a variety of reason, including:

✔ They are not done regularly or frequently enough. The Chartered Institute of Personnel and Development recommends that appraisals are done every three months, or every six months as a minimum, if there is to be any effective or positive result.

✔ Appraisals are driven by bureaucratic processes, rather than employee development, career enhancement, or pay rises.

✔ They are imposed by the human resources department, rather than being driven by strategic and operational performance.

✔ Managers or employees lack genuine commitment to appraisals; and this invariably reflects the fact that a lack of genuine commitment exists throughout the organisation.

From our experience, few employee appraisals are done well. Not only do managers write appraisals that lack any meaningful examples and insights, but they also fail to give the main process of the performance appraisal – the discussion – the time and attention that it deserves. Performance appraisal meetings also often become one-way presentations from manager to employee, rather than two-way discussions or conversations. As a result, performance appraisals often fail to have the kind of impact that the managers and supervisors who gave them intended.

Real apprehension can surround the appraisal process from both sides of the equation. Often, managers don't feel adequate to the task, and workers don't get the kind of timely and quality feedback that they need to do the best job possible. In addition, an underlying tension often accompanies the performance appraisal process and comes from the fact that most companies tie money and pay rises to performance appraisals. Appraisals that focus on the pay instead of on the performance, or lack of, are not uncommon.

Some managers practise bad appraisal methods that lead to negative consequences for all concerned – the manager, the employee, and the business:

✔ **Waiting to monitor and give feedback only at scheduled reviews:** Don't be among the many managers who fail to give their employees ongoing performance feedback, waiting for the scheduled review instead. Despite your best intentions and the best efforts of your

Repercussions of bombshells

The following are some real-world examples (though the names have been changed to protect the innocent – and the guilty) of the negative impacts of dropping bombshells:

✔ **Peter Irving:** Peter Irving left university with a first-class degree in production engineering and went to work for one of the United Kingdom's top manufacturing organisations. He quickly worked his way up to the position of deputy general manager, in charge of the production, quality, and delivery of highly specialised medical plastics.

Over this period, his performance was regularly appraised; and he always received glowing reviews. On promotion to deputy general manager, Peter was appraised by the divisional managing director. This happened just once in three years. Peter became frustrated. He applied for promotion within the group of companies, only to be interviewed and then turned down each time.

Finally, he approached the divisional managing director and asked for a performance appraisal. Met with a question as to why he wanted such a thing, Peter relayed his experience of applying for jobs within the company, getting interviews, and being turned down every time. Peter told the director that he needed to know why. The director advised him to smile more.

Peter left the company shortly afterwards. He secured a general manager's position with a direct competitor, and took his client list with him.

✔ **Eileen Whitaker:** Eileen joined Polsons Ltd as divisional sales manager. Located in East Yorkshire, Polsons makes medium- to high-quality clothing under contract to the main British supermarket and department store chains. Eileen had spent all of her working career in Hampshire and Dorset; but when the chance came to join Polsons, she jumped at it and relocated without any hesitation.

Eileen had an excellent first year, doubling turnover in her division, and gaining substantial and very profitable new contracts with smaller regional supermarket chains, as well as maintaining and increasing the volume of business conducted with national department stores and supermarkets.

At the end of her first year, Eileen met with Polsons' managing director for her performance appraisal. The managing director told Eileen that her performance was not up to scratch and that her contract was terminated immediately. Eileen knew the figures, as did everyone else in the company, and pointed them out to the director, who responded, 'Oh yes, I agree with all of that. But the main thing is you're not really one of us.'

Eileen received £250,000 in compensation for her dismissal. Again, she took her client list with her to a direct competitor; and the story quickly got around the supermarket and department store sector, compounding the problem for Polsons.

✔ **Jimmy Robertson:** Jimmy was a top-class professional footballer. He joined one of London's top clubs, and for three years enjoyed regular first-team football. Then the number of his appearances began to decline. He found himself left out of the most important games; in particular, he was not being picked for critical cup or European matches.

Finally, he went to see the club's manager. When pinned down, the manager stated: 'Jimmy, you do not run fast enough. Your pace has dropped.'

For six months, in training, Jimmy ran the fastest sprints of everyone at the club. This did not prevent him being transferred to the team's local rivals at the end of that particular season. Whatever he did, Jimmy was simply not wanted. The manager had lost faith or favour – and so Jimmy left anyway.

employees, assignments can easily go astray. Schedules can stretch, roadblocks can stop progress, and confusion can wrap its ugly tentacles around a project. However, if you haven't set up systems to track the progress of your employees, you may not be aware of any of this until it is too late. So you end up angry and frustrated, and you shout at your employees because of mistakes you should have spotted.

✔ **Dropping bombshells:** A bombshell of negative feedback that comes out of the blue and blind-sides an employee leaves destruction in its wake. If instead of checking up on progress along the way, and coaching and supporting people's efforts, you choose to drop bombshells on people, you destroy the morale of the particular individual being ambushed as well as the morale of everyone else. Other employees quickly realise that, if this can happen to one person, it can happen to them also.

Ambushes clearly take a lot less time to accomplish, and can get the bad manager through the discomfort of doing performance appraisals properly. However, they always store up trouble for the future.

Preparing for the No-Surprises Appraisal

If you're doing your job as a manager, the appraisal holds no surprises for your employees. Follow the lead of the best managers: Keep in touch with your employees and give them continuous feedback on their progress. Then, when you do sit down with them for their formal performance appraisal, the session is a recap of the things that you've already discussed during the appraisal period, instead of an ambush. Keeping up a continuous dialogue lets you use the formal appraisal to focus on the positive things that you and your employees can work on together to get the best possible performance.

Above all, be *prepared* for your appraisals!

Anecdotal evidence

The following stories illustrate and reinforce the need to conduct performance appraisals thoroughly and effectively, the results that accrue from doing so, and the consequences if performance appraisal is not adequate or targeted effectively.

- Arnold Weinstock, former chief executive of GEC, built the electrical conglomerate into the most valuable British organisation in great part on the basis of weekly performance appraisals and reviews with all of his top, senior, and general managers and divisional directors. Often conducted late at night or over the weekend, these performance reviews normally consisted of a one-hour telephone conversation in which Arnold Weinstock would question each top manager closely on the following areas: performance, performance targets, and revenues; reasons for achievement or non-achievement; proposals for the following week; review and commentary on longer-term plans and issues. As one manager said: 'Arnold knew the stuff, and you needed to know it. If you couldn't answer his questions in detail, or if you tried to flannel your way out of things – you didn't last.'

- Mark McCormack, founder and chief executive of sports representation agency IMG until his death in 2004, used to manage-by-walking-about (MBWA) as far as possible. He tried to meet up with every top and senior manager, as well as other employees in the organisation; and anyone he could not meet, he telephoned, just as Arnold Weinstock did. Again, the purpose was to get to the detail of performance and progress, and to hammer out any problems or issues. Mark McCormack stated: 'The reason for this is quite simple. We represent the interests of some of the most famous and high-profile people in the world. If we do a bad job for them, they will simply go elsewhere; and that means we are doing a bad job for us, and for those clients and connections with whom we seek to develop business. Only by attending to performance review in this way, and in this detail, can we hope to keep everybody happy and satisfied.'

- The strategic human resources unit of a large United Kingdom local authority devised a system of merit pay. Merit was decided by a rigorous system of performance appraisal; and anyone meeting the merit criteria received a merit pay award. Cometh the hour, cometh the system – and after working through the performance appraisal exercise with all 53,000 staff employed by the local authority, 30 merit awards were allocated. Of the 30, almost half went to the 14 members of the strategic human resources unit that had dreamed up the system in the first place! If you're determined to introduce merit pay, do at least put the ideas out to full consultation before you go live – it will save you a fortune, and moreover, you'll get a reputation for being completely fair and transparent.

Top five performance appraisal Web sites

The best information on the Web about the topics addressed in this chapter are on these Web sites:

✔ Chartered Institute of Personnel and Development: www.cipd.co.uk/performancemanagement

✔ Advisory, Conciliation and Arbitration Service (ACAS): www.ACAS.org.uk/performanceappraisal

✔ Accenture: www.accenture.com/staffmanagement/performanceappraisalandmeasurement

✔ Introduction to Performance Appraisal: www.performance-appraisal.com/intro.htm

✔ Work911: www.work911.com/performance/

Like interviews, many managers leave their preparation for performance appraisal meetings to the last possible minute – often just before the employee is scheduled to meet with them. 'Oh, no. Cathy is going to be here in five minutes. Now, what did I do with her file? I know it's here somewhere!' The average manager spends about one hour preparing for an employee review covering a whole year of performance.

To avoid this unprofessional and unproductive situation, follow these tips:

✔ Set time aside, make a proper appointment with the employee, and stick to it.

✔ Make a clear statement to the employee: 'The purpose of this performance appraisal is as follows . . .' and stick to it.

Performance appraisal is a year-round job. Whenever you recognise a problem with your employees' performance, mention it to them, make a note of it, and drop it in your employees' files. Similarly, whenever your employees do something great, mention it to them, make a note of it, and drop it in their files. Then, when you're ready to do your employees' periodic performance appraisals, you can pull out their files and have plenty of documentation available on which to base the appraisals. Not only does this practice make the process easier for you, but also it makes the appraisal a lot more meaningful and productive for your employees.

Part IV
Working with (Other) People

'If you want to be part of our management team, you've got to be able to do this.'

In this part . . .

No manager is an island. Managers work with other people – clients, teams, coworkers, and their own managers, to name a few – all the time. In this part, we introduce some key skills for communicating effectively with others, working with teams, managing flexible employees, and navigating the shifting waters of ethics and office politics.

Chapter 10

Effective Communication: Getting Your Message Across

In This Chapter

▶ Talking about communication

▶ Looking at new ways to communicate

▶ Facing barriers to communication

▶ Listening well

▶ Communicating your thoughts in writing

▶ Presenting effectively

*H*ow important is getting your message across to your employees, peers, boss, suppliers, clients, and customers? Very! Your roles as cheerleader, advocate, negotiator, coach, setter of standards, and role model all demand that you are an expert and effective communicator. So commit yourself to becoming an expert and effective communicator – you cannot be a good manager otherwise.

You have more sources of information and more ways to communicate than ever before – and more are on the way. And you need to be an expert performer whichever methods you are using. If you are making a presentation, you need to know and understand in advance what you want people to remember and do – and not do – as a result. If you are sending e-mails, you want people to remember and act on them, not just delete them. If you are participating in a meeting, you want the other participants to respect, value, and, where necessary, act on your contributions. So, the key is to master all of the different communication skills, and be able to apply them when you have to.

This chapter is about communicating with others and, in particular, how you do it.

Understanding Communication: The Cornerstone of Business

Communication is all-important for the growth and survival of today's organisations. How big or how small the organisation is doesn't matter – communication must be the cornerstone of every organisation.

In business, communication takes place in a variety of formats. Table 10-1 shows the order in which the bulk of business communication occurs. However, the formal training most people receive reverses this order, as Table 10-2 illustrates in its listing of formal communication training.

Table 10-1	The Order of Business Communications
Communication format	*Frequency of use*
Listening	Most frequent
Speaking/Presentation	Next most frequent
Writing	Next most frequent
Reading	Least frequent

Table 10-2	Formal Education Provided in Communications
Communication format	*Training provided*
Reading	From the age of 5
Writing	From the age of 5
Speaking/Presentation	Seldom
Listening	Very seldom!

So what we are trained to do bears no relationship to how people truly communicate. Many managers fail because they don't understand this critical point. The occasional speeches you make, the beautifully crafted memos you write, and the many articles on chaos theory that you read don't have any effect on how you really communicate with your employees. You *can* make a difference when you talk to your employees one on one, face to face, day in and day out. Listening to them and really hearing what they have to say are both vital.

The other thing to note is that compared with the spoken word, most other means of communication are relatively ineffective, especially when taken in isolation.

Table 10-3		Channels of Communication	
Communication method	**How information is imparted**	**Result**	**Effect on performance**
Simple centralised	Information flows to central person	Central person can perform task alone	Good performance
Simple decentralised	Information flows all around the network	No one person has all the required information	Grapevine, leading to poor performance and infighting
Complex centralised	Information flows to and from central person	Central person becomes saturated	Poor performance, lobbying, distortion
Complex decentralised	Depends on quality and completeness of information for effective flows all around the network	No one person becomes saturated	Good performance, provided that information is openly available
Hierarchical	Information flows up and down	No one person has all the required information	Poor performance on long/large hierarchies
Briefing	Information flows from briefer to group	Depends on quality of briefer	Depends on quality of briefer
Hourglass	Key figure is at 'neck'	Filtration and limitation	Leads to performance required by the 'neck'
Chains	Information flows along chain	Distortions at links	Poor understanding likely; poor motivation, morale. Slow movement of information.
Cascade	Information cascade (for example, briefing groups)	Dilution at every stage	Loss of quality, leading to poor performance

Table 10-3 shows that the best means of communication are face to face, individually or with small groups. So keep in mind that techniques such as cascades and briefing groups, though they are comfortable for managers and have a neat and tidy look, are not effective means of communication.

Having said all this, it is necessary to recognise the need for formal and written communication at certain times. Documentation is obviously still essential for contracts, invoices, and deliveries; for maintaining staff records; and for noting specific organisational, industry, government, and European Union directives.

The Cutting Edge of Communication and Information Technology

The explosion in information technology has brought with it numerous, often surprising and powerful new ways to communicate. Whether you like them or not, they're here, and they're here to stay. And more are on the way. You can opt to ignore them and be left behind, or you can choose to use these new technologies to your advantage. (See Chapter 19 on ways to harness the power of technology.)

Today's manager no longer needs to be in an office to communicate with clients and colleagues. You can be anywhere – using your mobile phone while at a restaurant or in your car, or logging on to the Internet while in bed in a hotel in the middle of nowhere. All it takes is the right tools.

Taking advantage of e-mail, voice-mail, fax machines, mobile phones, pagers, and overnight air delivery services, business is now a 24-hours-a-day, 7-days-a-week affair. You can leave a message at any time of the day or night at almost any business. If you're a voice-mail user, you can access your date- and time-stamped messages remotely from anywhere in the world that you can make a phone call and reply to them, forward them to colleagues, or save them for future reference.

Additionally, employers know that employees who have such equipment spend more of their personal time doing work. A study of individuals whose company provides them with telecommunications equipment indicates that these individuals work 20 to 25 per cent more hours in their own time (though whether or not this is a good thing for overworked employees is a different question altogether).

Whatever the organisation or situation, you need to be able to communicate effectively. Talk to your staff, colleagues, peers, and superiors. And get in the habit of sending e-mails and other notes that have a purpose – giving information or asking for something to be acted on. Otherwise your people will get into the habit of assuming that you have nothing to convey.

Speed and flexibility

Whatever your choice of communication equipment, the only reason for having it is to make you and your organisation faster, more flexible, more competitive, more effective – and more profitable. If you kit people out with the equipment they need, everyone benefits.

According to the Chartered Management Institute, technological innovation, effectively used, gives any business the edge over less flexible competitors. These advantages arise as the direct result of the ability of flexible firms to harness technology in order to work faster and more responsively.

The following advantages should always accrue from the introduction of effective communication and information technology systems:

- ✔ A business unfettered by bureaucratic red tape and expensive existing information systems can implement new production and service technologies more rapidly and effectively than others.

- ✔ As companies become electronically linked, outsourcing of functions, from accounting to product development, creates many opportunities for highly skilled subcontractors.

- ✔ Electronic bulletin boards and online data services give everyone access to more market data and business opportunities than ever before, allowing them to attack new opportunities quickly.

- ✔ Cheap computer-aided design and manufacturing software, together with flexible working practices, allow anyone to develop new products quickly and effectively, and get them to market much more responsively.

- ✔ Groups of companies are increasingly using information links to form networks and alliances, and engaging in partnerships as much as in direct competition.

- ✔ Mobile computing lets you compete anywhere in the world without the necessity of setting up expensive regional offices.

Use the latest advances in computing and telecommunications technology to make your organisation faster and more flexible. The faster information is distributed and acted on within your organisation, the more competitive and successful your business is likely to be.

Gadgets and gizmos

Organisations and their staff are now potentially swamped with technology. New gadgets and gizmos come on to the market and every manager thinks they have to have them – and all employees fight to own them if they possibly can.

An immediate word of caution: Make sure you're buying any new technology because it makes your business more effective and profitable, and not just as a fashion item or status symbol. Technological wizards are experts at making overtly reasoned and substantive cases for new gadgets, when in fact what they are after is just the latest 'must have'.

Make sure that any upgrade or purchase of new equipment is compatible with what you already have. Otherwise, you may be faced with having to invest in a complete technological refurbishment – and that *will* be expensive.

Any technology still has to deliver the required message to those receiving it in ways the recipients can accept, understand, and act on. A message beautifully presented on-screen, on a Web site, or via a computer link is useless if people don't know where to look for it, or can't access or download it.

Videoconferencing and electronic meetings

Not too many years ago, if you wanted to have a meeting with your design team members in London, production engineers in Nottingham, and sales staff scattered all over the countryside, all of you had to get to a central location for the meeting. Hours of travel and thousands of pounds later, you all gathered in the same place at the same time. Heaven help you if you left something important back at the office!

Once again, technology has saved the day. With a computer, a video camera, and some special software, you can create your very own videoconference – live and in living colour! Phones are OK for conducting business, but sometimes you need to be able to *see* what your client is trying to describe to you.

And sometimes your counterpart needs to visualise what on earth you're trying to say. Thus the miracle of videoconferencing. Which do you prefer, Option A or Option B?

- ✔ **Option A:** 'I just made the changes to the sales figures and printed out a new graph. Now, sales rose 39.5 per cent in 2005 to £45.5 million. Our north-western sales office led the surge. In the first quarter of 2006 we saw a decline to an annualised figure of £39.1 million in sales, primarily due to weak sales out of the south central and north central sales offices that were off target by a combined total of £4.2 million. The second quarter looks a lot better. It looks like we're back on track with an annualised number of £44.7 million. Did you get all that?'

- ✔ **Option B:** 'I just made the changes to the sales figures and printed out a new graph – you should be able to see it now on your computer monitor. Do you have any questions?'

Similarly, you can link together large groups of individuals into *virtual* meetings, where everyone can see and speak to each other together, through videoconferencing. Videoconferencing is rapidly becoming more common as computers and telecommunications systems get more powerful. Use it to set up meetings of employees at different locations – whether across the country or around the world. You can save substantial amounts of both time and money.

Now you need never be stuck on the M25 waiting for the traffic to clear, or endure another night on a lumpy mattress in some nameless town in the middle of nowhere. Unless, of course, that's your idea of fun. Just turn on your computer, fire up the video camera, and meet to your heart's content!

Use technology – don't let it use you. Always ask yourself the best way of conducting this meeting. Sometimes the best way is videoconferencing and *teleconferencing* (the capability to hold meetings using telephone rather than video technology); at other times, you need to get people together face to face.

Badmouthing Bad Communication

Effective communication isn't easy. The next sections talks about the all-too-common problems you may encounter along the road to model communication. However you are communicating – whether face to face, or through the use of technological wizardry – barriers and blockages to effective communication can, and do, occur whether by accident, negligence, or design.

- ✔ **Accident:** With the best will in the world, you may choose the wrong language or medium to get your message across. When you understand this, you simply put it right as quickly as you possibly can. If you keep delivering messages in the wrong way or using the wrong medium, you eventually put people's backs up, however well intentioned you may be.

- ✔ **Negligence:** Barriers and blockages can arise by default, usually as the result of managerial complacency. The organisation and its managers think that things are 'going along pretty well', or 'as well as can be expected', or at least 'not too bad'. Almost invariably, this extends to communication. Poor communication is simply 'one of those things', which leads to managers facing communication problems with indifference or a shrug of the shoulders. If this happens, your peers and colleagues quickly get the message that the organisation does not care for them, what they are doing, or what happens to them.

- ✔ **Design:** Barriers and blockages are intended and created by those within the organisation for their own ends. The huge range of technology available gives ample opportunity for those who need or want to manipulate systems and messages to do so. This is especially the case with bad news – think of the number of times that you have received bad news late on a Friday afternoon, and have then had the whole weekend to mull it over.

Jo Moore, an adviser working at the British Home Office, produced an immediate response to news of the 9/11 bombings in New York that said:

'This is an excellent day to bury bad news.'

While Jo Moore lost her job because of this callous statement, this kind of approach is commonplace in most organisations. So be careful if you try to manipulate information to serve a particular purpose, otherwise your efforts may be counterproductive.

Other barriers and blockages include the following.

- ✔ **Physical distance:** Distance hinders communication simply because you cannot see the other person. You can't see their facial expression, what they're thinking, or how they're receiving what you tell them. Especially if you have bad news to deliver, you should always deliver it face to face.

- ✔ **Psychological distance:** Psychological distance springs from reinforcing the gap between you and those with whom you are communicating through the use of status, rank, job title, dress, and mannerisms. Managers also use psychological distance – not always honestly – to assert their position, as well as to reinforce their ability to get their own way.

✔ **Interest:** People respond to those things that they are interested in. So if you want a response, deliver the message in a way that means it is of interest to the receivers. Especially highlight opportunities that will arise as the result; emphasise the positives; and make sure that people know where they stand and what they have to do as the result of your communication. Otherwise be prepared for supreme indifference!

✔ **Withholding information:** Issuing different information to different individuals and groups on a need-to-know basis sets up barriers. The consequence is that full information is not available to everyone; while on the surface this may appear to be sensible, you need to make sure that you are withholding information from the highest possible motives. Otherwise the impression given is one of the following:

- Contempt for your employees and colleagues, in that they are not capable of understanding all the information available

- An implied lack of capability on the part of employees and colleagues to understand what is being done in their name

- Differences in value placed on different groups of staff, colleagues, and employees – especially those who are not on the 'need to know' list

- Inequality of access – in order to be privy to certain information, you must have reached a certain level or rank within the organisation

- General disrespect – again to those excluded from the 'need to know' list

So unless a personal issue or a trade secret is involved, you should at least start from the position that the more everyone knows, the better life is going to be.

People hate being treated with arrogance and disrespect. If you constantly adopt a superior pose to your employees and colleagues, they lose their respect for you in turn, and for everything that you set out to do.

Poisoning the well of communications

The problems created by communication barriers and blockages are greatly compounded when the organisational context is deemed to be *toxic,* by which we mean that standards, quality of working life, and overall integrity have become greatly compromised. In these situations many communications take the following forms:

- ✔ **Blaming and scapegoating:** Managers find junior employees to carry the can for corporate failings. Accusation, counter-accusation, backbiting, and backstabbing prevail. Individuals may be named and shamed openly; or more insidiously, they may not be named officially, but their names are allowed to leak out through the organisational grapevine.

- ✔ **Departmental feuding:** Departments are actively encouraged to go to war with each other in the always mistaken belief that putting departments at loggerheads promotes improved performance and output.

- ✔ **Meddling:** People or departments meddle outside their legitimate areas of concern or activity; or lobby to be included on projects that are not otherwise within their normal remit. One of the most extreme forms of meddling is where top and powerful individuals promise favoured customers or staff that special activities and deals can be done on their behalf; and so they meddle and interfere in the workloads of others in order to deliver the promised favour.

- ✔ **Keeping secrets:** Information becomes a commodity to be used as a source of influence and as a bargaining chip. Communication is therefore concerned with controlling, editing, filtering, and presenting, rather than disseminating quality information.

Toxic communicators issue toxic communications – whatever they put out is done with thought of their own advantage, rather than the good of the organisation, colleagues, and employees. Some individuals also introduce *toxicity* – gossip and rumour designed to have a particular effect. Toxic communicators misrepresent, lie, and cheat, and manipulate information for their own particular ends.

As a manager, you need to be constantly aware of the aspects of communication that can and do go wrong, and the reasons. Good managers address these problems as soon as they arise, by making sure that everything is brought out into the open and fully debated. Rumours are addressed, and confirmed or squashed. Meddling, dishonesty, and toxicity are dealt with by removing the rewards and advantages that others seek through behaving in these ways.

Hear, Hear! The Art of Listening

The communication equation has two sides. The previous sections discussed the side that most people think about when they hear the word 'communication' – the *doing* side. However, just as important is the other side of the equation – the *listening* side.

You're a busy person. You probably have ten million things on your mind at any given time: the proposal you have to get out before 5 p.m. today; the budget spreadsheets that don't seem to add up; lunch; and, if that isn't enough already, the latest office gossip. With all the distractions, you can easily come over to other people as rude and distant if you're not careful.

When you don't give the person on the other side of your desk your full attention, you short-change both yourself and the other person. Not only do you miss out on getting their message, but your inattention sends its own special message: 'I don't really care what you have to say.' Is that the message you really want to convey? When you listen actively, you increase the likelihood that you understand what the other person is saying. Depending on what you're talking about, understanding can be quite important.

Don't leave listening to chance. Be an active listener. When someone has something to say to you, make a decision to participate in the communication, or to let the other person know that you're busy and have to get back to him later. 'Sorry, I've got to sort this lot out before lunch. Can we get together later this afternoon?' If you decide to communicate, then clear your mind of all its distractions. Forget for a moment the proposal that has to go out in a few hours, the spreadsheets, and that growling in the pit of your stomach. Give the other person your full attention.

Of course, making an effort to give your full attention is easier said than done. How can you focus on the other person and not allow all the people and tasks vying for your attention to distract you? The following tips may help:

- **Express your interest:** One of the best listening techniques is to be interested in what your counterpart has to say. For example, give the person you're talking to your full attention and ask questions that clarify what he has to say. You can say, 'That's really interesting. What brought you to that particular conclusion?' The greatest turn-off to communication is for you to yawn, look around the room aimlessly, or otherwise show that you're not interested in what your colleague is saying. The more interest you show, the more interesting the speaker becomes.

- **Maintain your focus:** People speak at the rate of approximately 150 words per minute. However, people think at approximately 500 words per minute. This gap leaves a lot of room for your mind to wander. Make a point of keeping your mind focused on listening to what the other person has to say. If your mind starts to wander, then rein it back in right away.

✔ **Ask questions:** If something is unclear or doesn't make sense to you, then ask questions to clarify the subject. Not only does this practice keep communication efficient and accurate, but it also demonstrates to the speaker that you're interested in what he has to say. *Reflective listening* – summarising what the speaker has said and repeating it back – is a particularly effective way of ensuring accuracy in communication and demonstrating your interest. For example, you can say, 'So you mean it's your belief that we can sell our excess capacity to other firms?'

✔ **Seek the key points:** Figure out what exactly your counterpart is trying to tell you. Anyone can easily get lost in the forest of details of a conversation and miss seeing the trees as a result. As you listen, make a point of categorising what your speaker has to say into information that is key to the discussion and information that isn't really relevant. If you need to ask questions to help you decide which is which, then don't be shy – ask away!

✔ **Avoid interruptions:** Although asking clarifying questions or employing reflective listening techniques is OK, continually interrupting the speaker or allowing others to do so is not OK. When you're having a conversation with an employee, make him the most important thing in your life at that moment. If someone telephones you, don't answer the phone – that's what voice-mail is for, after all. If someone knocks on your door and asks whether he can interrupt, say no, but that you can talk after you finish your current conversation. If your building is on fire, *then* you may interrupt the speaker.

✔ **Listen with more than your ears:** Communication involves a lot more than the obvious, verbal component. According to communications experts, up to 90 per cent of the communication in a typical conversation is non-verbal. Facial expressions, posture, position of arms and legs, and much more add up to the non-verbal component of communication. Because this is the case, you must use all your senses when you listen, not just your ears.

✔ **Take notes:** Remembering all the details of an important conversation hours, days, or weeks after it took place can be quite difficult. Be sure to take notes when you need to remember something. Jotting down notes can be a terrific aid to listening and remembering what was said. Plus, when you review your notes later, you can take the time to organise what was said and make better sense of it.

By practising the listening habits listed above, you understand the message, and your colleagues appreciate the fact that you consider them important enough to give them your full attention. So listen early and listen often.

Harnessing the Power of the Written Word

At first thought, you may consider that the Information Revolution has made the written word less important. Nothing is farther from the truth. Indeed, instead of making the written word less important, the Information Revolution has merely increased the variety of written media at your beck and call and increased the speed at which the written word travels. Writing well in business is more important than ever – you need to write concisely and with impact.

Regardless of whether you're writing a one-paragraph e-mail or a 100-page report, business writing shares common characteristics. Use the list of writing tips that follows and don't forget to practise these tips every opportunity you get. The more you write, the better you get at it. So write, write – and write again.

- ✔ **Get to the point.** Before you set pen to paper (or fingertip to keyboard), think about what you want to achieve. Determine what information you're trying to convey, and what you want the reader to do as a result. Think about who your audience is and how you can best reach that audience. Get into the habit of saying to yourself – or writing down on a notepad – 'The purpose of this e-mail/report/memo is . . .'

- ✔ **Get organised:** Organise your thoughts before you start to write. Jotting down a few notes or creating a brief outline of your major points may be beneficial. Bounce your ideas off colleagues and business associates or find other ways to refine your thoughts and get an all-important reality check.

- ✔ **Write the way you speak:** Written communication and spoken communication have a lot more in common than many people think. The best writing most closely resembles normal, everyday speech. Writing that is too formal or stilted is less accessible and harder to understand than conversational writing. Although this doesn't mean that you should start using slang like 'gonna' and 'ain't' in your reports and memos, it does mean that you can loosen up.

- ✔ **Make it brief and concise:** Write every word with a purpose. Make your point, support it, and then move on to the next point. Don't, repeat *don't* fill your memos, letters, and other correspondence with needless fluff simply to give them more weight or to make them seem more impressive. If you can make your point in three sentences, don't write three paragraphs or three pages to accomplish the same goal.

✔ **Keep it simple:** Simplicity is a virtue. Avoid the tendency to use a complicated word when a simpler one works. Be alert to the cryptic acronyms and jargon that mean nothing outside of a small circle of industry insiders and replace them with more common terminology whenever possible.

✔ **Write and then rewrite:** Few writers can get their thoughts into writing perfectly on the first try. The best approach is to write your first draft without worrying too much about whether you've completed it perfectly. Next, read through your draft and edit it for content, flow, grammar, and readability. Keep polishing your work until it shines.

✔ **Convey a positive attitude:** No one likes to read negative memos, letters, reports, or other business writing. Instead of conveying the intended points to their intended targets, negative writing often only reflects poorly on its author, and the message gets lost in the noise. Be active, committed, and positive in your writing. Even when you convey bad news, your writing can indicate that a silver lining is inside even the blackest cloud.

If you're interested in developing better writing skills, you can find plenty of books to help. However, Peter still swears by the timeworn 1971-vintage printing of *The Elements of Style,* by William Strunk, Jr. and E. B. White. The book's advice is timeless, the writing direct and compelling. Consider Rule 13:

> ***Omit needless words.*** Vigorous writing is concise. A sentence should contain no unnecessary words, a paragraph no unnecessary sentences, for the same reason that a drawing should have no unnecessary lines and a machine no unnecessary parts. This requires not that the writer make all his sentences short, or that he avoid all detail and treat his subjects only in outline, but that every word tells.

A survey by Office Angels, an employment agency, found that people working in companies and organisations especially hated the following phrases:

✔ Blue-sky thinking

✔ Thinking outside the box

✔ Hitting the ground running

✔ Work smarter, not harder

This type of language has come to be known as 'management speak' – and no manager worthy of the name should use it. Truth to tell, when the phrases are printed as we do here, you can see that they're all pretty meaningless – and meaningless they certainly are to those who have to endure listening to them. So make up your mind never to use them.

Making Presentations

Although many people dread the idea of standing up in front of a group of people, the ability to give oral presentations, speeches, and the like is a key skill for managers. Of course, some managers already know the value of being able to give effective presentations.

Preparing presentations

When you see great speakers or presenters in action, you may think that because of their extraordinary skill, making a presentation takes little preparation on their part. This is like saying that because an Olympic gymnast makes his floor routine look so perfect and so easy, he never has to practise it. What you don't see are the years of almost daily preparation that lead to those 90 seconds of glory.

Preparation and practice are the keys to giving great presentations. The following can help you in preparing your presentations:

✔ **Determine what you want to accomplish:** Briefly outline the goals of your presentation. What exactly do you want to accomplish? Are you trying to convince decision makers that they should give you a bigger budget or extend your deadline to design a product that actually works? Are you seeking to educate your audience or to train employees in a new procedure? Are you presenting awards to employees in a formal ceremony? Each kind of presentation requires a different approach; tailor your approach according to your aim.

Get into the habit of writing down the purpose of the presentation, who your audience is, and the key points you need to make to have the best effect.

Give the audience what they want. If you're presenting to top and senior management, go heavy on facts and figures – they need to know how much what you are proposing is going to cost them.

✔ **Determine how you have to present.** If you have five minutes to make your presentation, then you need to limit yourself to the one or two critical and salient features you need to get across. The longer you have, the greater your opportunity. But beware – if you're speaking for more than 20 minutes, you must be prepared for people's attention to wander. So if you're making a longer presentation, break it into manageable chunks.

Use the time available well. Do not cram too much material into too short a space of time. Deal with the most important issue first. If you only have a short period, then limit the presentation to this issue; if longer is available, you can cover more material.

✔ **Develop the heart of your presentation:** Build an outline of the major points that you want to communicate to your audience. Under each point, note any important supporting sub-points. Don't try to accomplish too much; keep your major points down to no more than a few. Sketch out any visual aids that you need to reinforce and communicate the ideas that you're presenting verbally.

✔ **Write the introduction and conclusion:** After you finish the heart of your presentation, you can decide on your introduction and conclusion. Make the introduction accomplish three goals:

- Tell your audience what they're going to gain from your presentation.

- Tell your audience why the presentation is important to them.

- Get your audience's attention.

The conclusion is just as important, as is the final punctuation – the full stop – of your presentation. Write your conclusion to accomplish three objectives:

- Briefly summarise your key points.

- Refer your listeners back to the introduction.

- Inspire your audience.

✔ **Prepare your notes:** Preparing notes to use as an aid in your presentation is always a good idea. Not only do notes help you find your way when you get lost – helping to build your confidence – but they also ensure that you cover all the topics that you planned to cover. Write brief but specific notes. The idea is for notes to trigger your thoughts on each key point and sub-point, not to be a word-for-word script.

✔ **Practice makes perfect:** After you sketch out your presentation, practise it. Depending on your personal situation, you may be comfortable simply running through your notes a few times the night before the big event. Alternately, you may want to rehearse your presentation in front of a colleague or even a video camera so that you can review it at your leisure. Don't forget: The more presentations you make, the better you get at making them.

Make the most of the time that you have before your presentation – preparation pays off in a big way when the time comes to get up in front of your audience and start your performance.

A picture is worth a thousand words

Studies show that approximately 85 per cent of all information received by the human brain is received visually. Think about that statistic the next time you make a presentation. Although your spoken remarks may convey a lot of valuable information, your audience is likely to remember more of the information when you present it to them visually.

The Nelson/Economy/Pettinger axiom of visual learning is:

> If you don't see it, you can't believe it (and you certainly won't remember it!).

So how does this affect your presentations? Whenever possible, think of ways to present your information visually. The following are just a few of your options:

- Photographs
- Charts
- Displays
- Product samples
- Prototypes
- Role plays
- Graphs
- Maps

Once, Peter was asked to make a presentation to his company's executive team of some very complex financial data, as shown in Figure 10-1.

Peter was able to re-present this data using bar charts. Figure 10-2 shows the vastly improved, and more understandable, version of the same financial information.

Western Group Financials

	Past Year	Current Year
Direct Labour	£19,887,000	£21,896,000
Fringe Benefits	£7,504,000	£8,259,000
Overhead Applied	£9,945,000	£10,938,000
Cost of Money	£13,000	£14,000
Travel	£2,801,000	£1,952,000
Other Direct Cost	£278,000	£356,000
G&A Applied	£4,973,000	£5,475,000
Total	£45,401,000	£48,890,000

Figure 10-1:
Financial
data in
spreadsheet
format.

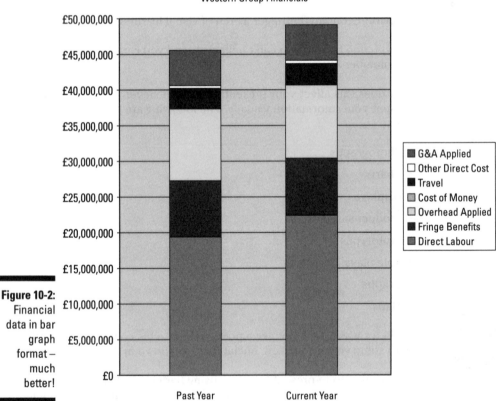

Figure 10-2:
Financial
data in bar
graph
format —
much
better!

The approaches shown in Figure 10-3 are also simple, clear, and effective.

(a) Tabulation

Year	Sales £	Profit £
0000	3430	114
0001	3560	119
0002	4740	240
0003	5862	650
0004	4711	350

(b) bar chart

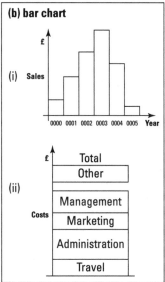

(c) Line graph

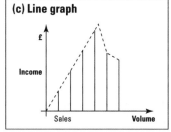

(d) Scatter diagram

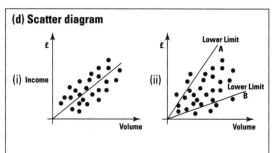

(e) Pie chart

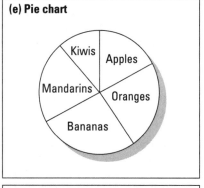

(f) Pictograms

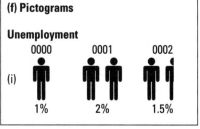

Figure 10-3:
Different
presentation
of data.

Top five communication Web sites

The following Web sites provide excellent information about communicating effectively:

✔ *Business Communication Quarterly* magazine: www.bcq.theabc.org/

✔ Presentations.com: www.presentations.com

✔ BPP Malpas: www.bppmalpas.org.uk/presentations

✔ Cass Business School: www.cass.ac.uk/executivedevelopment

✔ London Business School: www.lbs.ac.uk/executiveprogrammes

Presentation tools, visual aids, and other props serve several purposes. First, they convey your information much more quickly than do your spoken words. Second, people retain visual information longer than other kinds of information. Finally, presentation tools, visual aids, and other such props provide your audience with a welcome break from your oral presentation.

Consider using the following presentation tools and props wherever and whenever possible:

✔ **PowerPoint:** For presentations in front of large groups, computer projections – most often coupling a laptop computer with a high-power liquid crystal display (LCD) projector and the Microsoft PowerPoint software – are the choice of the pros. Not only are presentations crystal clear, but also you can easily fit one or more complete presentations into your laptop computer and carry it around with you anywhere. One danger with computer presentations, however, is that if your computer goes on the blink, or if your destination has no suitable projector to hook your computer to, your presentation is going to be notably absent. Each of us has travelled thousands of miles to make PowerPoint presentations using laptop computers, and at the last minute discovered that clients haven't arranged for LCD projectors in advance. So, be prepared for the fact that anything that can go wrong will go wrong; have a back-up you can use if you have to.

✔ **Flip charts/whiteboards:** If you're presenting to a smaller group – say, up to about 30 people – flip charts and whiteboards at the front of the room are a handy way to present visual information. *Flip charts* are those big pads of paper that hang from an easel. You can set up your whole presentation on the flip charts beforehand and you can scribble notes on them for emphasis as you speak.

Never forget that you're the one doing the presentation, not the flip chart or the whiteboard.

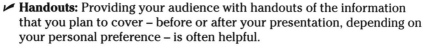

✔ **Handouts:** Providing your audience with handouts of the information that you plan to cover – before or after your presentation, depending on your personal preference – is often helpful.

Never ever fall victim to the practice of providing handouts and then reading from them. Nothing is more boring to an audience than following a presenter's handouts as he reads through pages and pages of text word for word.

When using visual aids, keep a few points in mind if you want to have a happy audience.

✔ **Don't try to jam too much information into each of your aids.** Keep the typescript large, and keep the quantity of words and numbers to a minimum. And use colour to your advantage by emphasising the different points that you want to make by using different shades.

✔ **Have everything ready well in advance of your presentation.** Don't start your presentation by spending five minutes fumbling with setting up your projector or flipping through a disorganised stack of notes. This flustering doesn't impress your audience and it doesn't enhance your self-confidence.

✔ **Check out everything!** Make sure your electronics, sound, lights, and other tools are working before you find out otherwise at a key point in your presentation.

✔ **Don't forget that you're the centre of attention – not your visual aids.** Use visual aids to support your presentation; don't use your presentation to support your visual aids!

Say what needs to be said; write what needs to be written; demonstrate what needs to be demonstrated.

Making your presentation

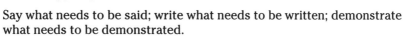

The waiting is over and your audience is gathered, raptly waiting to hear the pearls of wisdom that you're going to fling all about the room. At this point, all your hours of preparation pay off. Follow these steps as you begin your presentation:

✔ **Relax!** What do you have to be nervous about? You're thoroughly prepared for your presentation. Your notes are in order, your visual aids are positioned and ready to go, and your audience is sincerely interested in what you have to say. As you wait for the presentation to start, breathe deeply and stay alert.

✔ **Greet your audience members:** One of the pluses of arriving early is being able to welcome your audience members personally as they arrive for your presentation. Not only does this practice establish an initial level of rapport and interest, but getting a chance to talk to your audience members before you launch into your presentation helps you feel more at ease in front of the group.

✔ **Listen closely to your introduction:** Make sure that the facts are accurate, and listen for comments that you can incorporate into your initial remarks. For example, if the individual who introduces you mentions that not only are you a brilliant manager, but you're also an avid skier, you can work a humorous anecdote about skiing into the beginning of your presentation.

✔ **Wait for your audience's attention:** As a presenter, you must capture the full attention of your audience. One particularly effective technique is to stand in front of your audience and say nothing until everyone's attention is focused on you. Of course, if that doesn't do the trick, you can always resort to the old stand-bys – threats and intimidation!

✔ **Make your presentation:** Start at the beginning, finish when you're done, and have fun with everything in between. This really is your opportunity to shine – make the most of it.

Always begin on time. Never begin late, unless your client or the presentation organiser specifically instructs you to do so. And never overrun, again unless the organiser specifically instructs or requests you to do so.

Chapter 11

Working Together in Teams and Groups

In This Chapter

▶ Flattening the organisation

▶ Empowering employees

▶ Categorising teams

▶ Recognising the advantages of teams

▶ Managing new technology and teams

▶ Making meetings work

*I*n practice, few managers work in isolation, and most have responsibilities for teams and groups of staff. Teams and groups start out as disparate collections of individuals who are gathered together for a purpose, and whose remit is to deliver specific results, resolve problems, address particular issues, and create ways of working that are suitable for the work in hand. A team is two or more people who work together to achieve a common goal.

Teams offer an easy way to tap the knowledge and resources of all employees – not just supervisors and managers – to do the work of the organisation and deliver its goals. This in turn means having teams that produce and deliver products and services, enhance business performance, contribute their own expertise for the greater good, and solve the organisation's problems. A well-structured team draws together employees with different skills and knowledge, often from different functions and levels of the organisation to help find the best way to approach an issue. Smart companies have discovered (and not-so-smart companies are figuring out) that to remain competitive, they can no longer rely solely on management to guide the development of work processes and the accomplishment of organisational goals. The companies need to involve those employees who are closer to the problems and to the organisation's customers as well. Guess who those employees are? The front-line workers!

Perhaps management expert Peter Drucker best answers the question 'Why use teams?' when he considered the importance of ranking knowledge over ego in the modern organisation. According to Drucker, 'No knowledge ranks higher than another; each is judged by its contribution to the common task rather than by any inherent superiority or inferiority. Therefore, the modern organisation cannot be an organisation of boss and subordinate. It must be organised as a team' (*Harvard Business Review*).

This chapter discusses the main kinds of teams and how they work, the impact of computer-based technology on teams, and insights for conducting the best team meetings ever.

Phasing Out the Old Hierarchy

The last couple of decades have seen a fundamental shift in the distribution of power and authority in organisations. Until recently, most organisations were *vertical* – they had many layers of managers and supervisors between top management and front-line workers. The classic model of a vertical organisation is the traditional military organisation. In the old army, privates report to corporals, who report to sergeants, who report to captains, and so on, up to the top general. When a general gives an order, it passes down the line from person to person until it reaches the person who is expected to execute it.

Until relatively recently, large companies such as Ford, British Airways, and British Telecom weren't that different from this rigid, hierarchical model; and this remains a serious problem in some public services. Employing hundreds of thousands of workers, these organisations depended – and in many cases still depend – on legions of supervisors and managers to control the work, the workers who did it, and when and how they did it. (Okay, perhaps today's legions are smaller.) The primary goal of top management was to command and control workers' schedules, assignments, and decision-making processes very closely to ensure that the company met its objectives (and to ensure that workers weren't asleep at their desks!). The result of this kind of organising is, without any exception, that less gets done, more slowly, more expensively, with more errors, for fewer people.

Downsizing organisations

The problems presented by a hierarchical model of organisation are compounded by the fact that, in many cases, supervisors and managers make little or no direct contribution to the production of a company's products or services. Instead of producing things, managers merely manage other managers or supervisors and serve as liaisons between levels, ultimately doing little more than pushing paper from one part of their desk to another. In the model's worst scenario, the levels of supervisors and managers actually impeded their organisations' capability to get tasks done – dramatically adding to the cost of doing business and slowing down the response time of decision making. All those expense account lunches added up. Although this problem was overlooked as the global economy continued to expand in the last half of the 20th century, factors such as the economic slowdown in the late 1980s, and the telecoms and dot-com crashes in the early 2000s, made for quite a wake-up call for those companies with unproductive – or worse, counterproductive – middle management.

John Tusa, former Deputy Director General of the BBC, stated: 'If many large organisations entered the University Boat Race, the cox would be doing all the rowing, while each of the eight crew shouted contrary orders.'

Although downsizing workforces after economic downturns has obvious negative effects on the employees who lose their jobs – and in many cases, their hopes for a comfortable retirement – this dark cloud has a silver lining. In flatter organisations, a new life (and a quicker pace) comes to the following important areas:

- ✔ **Decision making:** Decisions, which may have taken weeks or even months to make in the old, bloated bureaucracy, are made in hours or minutes.

- ✔ **Communicating:** Instead of being intercepted and possibly distorted by middle managers at numerous points along its path, communication now travels a more direct – and much speedier – route from front-line workers to top management and vice versa, or to whomever the person needs to get information from. There's nothing like cutting six layers of management out of an organisation to improve communication!

Also, this transformation from vertical to *horizontal* businesses (organisations with a minimum of levels of management) has a fundamental impact on financial and organisational elements:

- ✔ **Quantifiable benefits to the bottom line:** By cutting out entire layers of management employees, many companies save money by substantially reducing the costs of personnel, facilities, and expense account lunches.

- ✔ **Movement of authority and power:** This move happens from the very top of the organisation down to the front-line employees who interact with customers on a day-to-day basis. With fewer middle managers to interfere, front-line employees naturally have more autonomy and authority.

Moving towards co-operation

More than ever before, businesses worldwide are rewarding employees for co-operating with each other instead of competing against one another. Organisations are no longer measuring employees only by their individual contributions, but also by how effective they are as contributing members of their work teams.

Coupled with this shift of authority is a fundamental change in the way that many businesses structure their work. Of course, most businesses still organise their operations by departments, divisions, and so forth, but smart managers now encourage, rather than discourage, their employees to cross formal organisational lines, and set up teams made up of employees from different departments whose members work together to perform tasks and achieve common goals.

Following are benefits that your organisation can reap from promoting co-operation:

- ✔ **Reducing unproductive competition:** Promoting a co-operative, team-oriented work environment reduces the chance of your employees becoming over-competitive.

  If allowed to continue unabated, over-competitiveness results in the shutdown of communication between employees and, ultimately, reduces organisational effectiveness (as over-competitive employees build and defend private fiefdoms). Besides, over-competition between employees invariably leads to backbiting, in-fighting, and denigration of other people; and it can lead to bullying, victimisation, and harassment.

- ✔ **Sharing knowledge:** Knowledge is power. If you're in the know, you have a clear advantage over someone who has been left in the dark – especially if your finger is on the light switch. In a co-operative work environment, team members work together and thereby share their areas of knowledge and expertise, using it to the best advantage of everyone – they don't defend it or use it as a bargaining chip.

- ✔ **Fostering communication:** Using teams helps to break down the walls between an organisation's departments, divisions, and other formal structures to foster communication between organisational units.

- ✔ **Achieving common goals:** Developing teams with members from various departments encourages workers from all levels and all parts of a company to work together to achieve common goals.

Empowering Your Teams

So if organisational structures are flatter (see the previous section), employees gain more authority and autonomy from top management. The result: Employees are more responsive to customers' needs and resolve problems at the lowest possible level in the organisation. The transfer of power, responsibility, and authority from higher-level to lower-level employees is called *empowerment*.

By empowering workers, managers place the responsibility for decision making with the employees in the best position to make the decision. In the past, many managers felt that *they* were in the best position to make decisions that affected a company's products or customers. How wrong they were. Although they may have been right in some cases, their driving need to control workers and processes at all costs often blinded managers – so much so that control became more important than encouraging employee initiative.

Recognising the value of an empowered workforce

Effective managers know the value of empowering their workers. Not only can employees serve customers better, but also by delegating more responsibility and authority to front-line workers, managers are free to pursue other important tasks that only they can do, such as coaching, 'big-picture' communicating, long-range planning, and production and service scheduling. The result is a much more efficient, more effective organisation all round. For example:

- ✔ Nissan UK runs the most productive car factory in the world, measured in terms of output per member of staff. One of the keys is that the company has given full responsibility and autonomy to the production crews (the teams) for all aspects of each car they produce. In particular, the company refers complaints from distributors and customers directly back to the crew who made the car. No quality assurance hierarchy exists; everything is the responsibility of the particular crew.

- ✔ British Airways' cabin crew staff deliver a top-quality service on long haul flights around the world. When they meet up, each team has only one hour to mould themselves into an effective crew for the particular flight. Crew members are individually rostered, which means that they seldom, if ever, work with the same people more than once. The cohesion required of the crews is founded on extensive training, clear team rules, the authority of the cabin services director, and the total commitment of every member of the team (many of whom have wanted to be cabin crew staff from an early age). Within these rules, every member of the crew is then expected to do whatever is right in the particular set of circumstances to keep the travelling public happy.

Empowerment is also a great morale booster in an organisation. Managers who empower their workers show that they trust them to make decisions that are important to the company's success.

Managing your teams

If you want productive, effective, and profitable groups working in harmony together, then concentrate on the following:

✔ Managing the task, ensuring that everybody knows what the purpose of the group is, and what they are supposed to be contributing to it.

✔ Managing the people, ensuring that you have effective, productive, and positive working relationships between everyone involved, whatever their profession, occupation, or expertise.

✔ Managing communications between everyone involved; and managing communication between different work groups, disciplines, and occupations.

✔ Managing individuals, to ensure that everyone gets the best possible opportunity to make the contribution required.

✔ Clarity of purpose and common aims and objectives, to which everyone has agreed and to which they can contribute.

✔ Group and team spirit, a combination of shared values, together with specific ways of working, a helpful attitude, and a positive atmosphere within the group.

✔ Managing conflict, ensuring that the potential for conflicts within all groups is assessed openly and honestly. You need to pay particular attention to the nature and mix of personalities involved, the nature and mix of expertise and talent involved, and any divergence of objectives between group members, individuals, and the overall objectives of the group.

Finally – finally – do make sure that the style of management and leadership is itself participative, positive, and supportive! No point lies in creating work groups and expecting them to succeed, if the organisation is constantly restraining and restricting the capability of those groups to operate to their full potential.

Identifying the Advantages of Teams

Teams not only have the potential to make better decisions, they can also make faster decisions as well. Because team members are closest to the problems and to one another, fewer delays occur because of the need to communicate with or get approval from others in the organisation.

Teams used to be considered beneficial only for projects of short duration. However, many companies no longer follow this line of thinking. According to Peter Drucker, 'Whereas team design has traditionally been considered applicable only to short-lived, transitory, exceptional task-force assignments, it is equally applicable to some permanent needs, especially to the top-management and innovating tasks' (*Harvard Business Review*). Indeed, the team concept has proved itself to be a workable long-term solution to the needs of many organisations.

Smaller and nimbler

Large organisations often have a hard time competing in the marketplace against smaller, more nimble competitors. Smaller units within a large organisation – such as teams – are better able to compete. The rate and scope of change in the global business environment has led to increased competitive pressure on organisations in almost every business sector, so the importance of speed and responsiveness also increases.

As customers can get products and services faster, their expectations are constantly rising; and so organisations have to be able to meet these expectations. As they can buy products more cheaply as a result of technology improvements or global competition, they expect lower prices as well. And the expectation of quality in relation to price has dramatically increased over the years – especially with consumers' experience in obtaining more advanced electronics and computer technology for progressively lower prices. In short, customer values are changing so that they now want products and services 'any time, any place, any where'.

Innovative and adaptable

Teams can lead to increased innovation. According to then-Harvard economist Robert Reich in the *Harvard Business Review,* 'As individual skills are integrated into a group, the collective capacity to innovate becomes something greater than the sum of its parts.'

Teams are more adaptive to the external environment as it quickly or constantly changes. Thus, a team's size and flexibility give it a distinct advantage over competing organisations structured in a more traditional way. At Xerox and Hewlett-Packard, for example, design, engineering, and manufacturing functions are closely intertwined in the development of new products – dramatically shortening the time from concept to production compared with their previous, more hierarchical structure. Indeed, Hewlett-Packard now only manufactures to order; and this decision is becoming more commonplace in other organisations and industry sectors.

Setting Up and Supporting Your Teams

The first point you need to consider when setting up a team is what kind of team to set up. Three main kinds of teams exist: *formal, informal,* and *self-managed.* Each type of team offers advantages and disadvantages depending on the specific situation, timing, and the organisation's needs.

Whatever kind of team you are setting up, you must have a good mix of characteristics. You need people with creative bursts of energy; people who are going to question everything; and people who are going to do the painstaking bits – the attention to detail, progress chasing and checking, and making sure that everything is done on time. And you need effective team leadership!

Meredith Belbin produced a structure for the composition of effective teams, which is shown in Table 11-1.

Table 11-1	Members of Effective Teams	
Type	*Typical features*	*Positive qualities*
Company Worker	Conservative, dutiful, practicable	Organising ability, practical common sense, hard working
Chair	Calm, self-confident, controlled	A capacity for treating and welcoming all potential contributors on their merits and without prejudice
		A strong sense of objectives

Type	Typical features	Positive qualities
Shaper	Highly strung, outgoing, dynamic	Drive and readiness to challenge inertia, ineffective-ness, complacency, or self-deception
Plant (Questioner)	Individualistic, serious minded, unorthodox	Genius, imagination, intellect, knowledge
Resource Investigator	Extroverted, enthusiastic, curious, communicative	A capacity for contacting people and exploring any-thing new An ability to respond to challenge
Monitor-Evaluator	Sober, unemotional, prudent	Judgement, discretion, hard-headedness
Team Worker	Socially oriented, rather mild, sensitive	An ability to respond to people and to situations, and to promote team spirit
Completer-Finisher	Painstaking, orderly, conscientious, anxious	A capacity to follow through Perfectionism

Source: Belbin (1986)

Belbin's main points are that effective teams and groups have to do all these jobs as required in effective teams and groups; and so someone has to be pre-pared to carry them out. With teams and groups of five or six members only, someone has clearly got to be prepared to carry out more than one role. And a certain amount of discipline and commitment to the particular group needs to exist, requiring members, in many cases, to do things in ways that they are not normally comfortable or familiar with.

All of this applies to any team, whatever its purpose.

Formal teams

A *formal team* is set up for a particular purpose and has specific goals to achieve. These goals can range from developing a new product line, deter-mining the system for processing customer invoices, or planning a company picnic. Types of formal teams include:

✔ **Quality improvement group and work improvement group:** A formal team assembled in order to tackle specific problems and issues relating to product and service innovation and development; specific problems and issues concerning quality, durability, and accessibility; and managing customer complaints.

✔ **Project team:** A team drawn together for a specific purpose, and assembled for the duration of the particular project. Successful and effective project teams are crucial to the success of civil engineering and other engineering projects, the design and installation of information systems, and the development of new products and services.

✔ **Task force:** A formal team assembled on a job and finish basis to address specific problems or issues, very often at strategy or policy level. For example, a task force may be assembled to determine why a particular strategic initiative is not delivering the results intended. Task forces are also a well-known and understood approach to addressing the detail required to implement new strategy and policy initiatives. A task force usually has a deadline for solving the issue and reporting the findings to top and senior management.

✔ **Committee:** A long-term or permanent team created to perform an on-going, specific organisational task. For example, some companies have committees that select employees to receive awards for performance or that make recommendations to management for safety improvements. Although committee membership may change from year to year, the committees continue their work regardless of who belongs to them.

✔ **Command team:** Made up of a manager or supervisor and all the employees who report directly to that person. Such teams are by nature hierarchical and represent the traditional way that managers communicate tasks to workers. Examples of command teams include company sales teams, management teams, and executive teams.

Formal teams are important to most organisations because much of the communication within the company traditionally occurs within the team. News, goals, and information pass from employee to employee via formal teams. And they provide the structure for assigning tasks and soliciting feedback from team members on accomplishments, performance data, and so on.

Informal teams

Informal teams are casual associations of employees that spontaneously develop within an organisation's formal structure. Such teams include groups of employees who eat lunch together every day, form bowling teams, or simply like to hang out together – both during and after work. The membership of informal teams is in a constant state of flux as members come and go and friendships and other associations between employees change over time.

Although informal teams have no specific tasks or goals that management has assigned, they are very important to organisations for the following reasons:

- ✔ Informal teams provide a way for employees to get information outside formal, management-sanctioned communication channels.

- ✔ Informal teams provide a (relatively) safe outlet for employees to let off steam about issues that concern them and to find solutions to problems by discussing them with employees from other parts of the organisation – unimpeded by the walls (actual and metaphorical) of the formal organisation.

For example, a group of women employees at NYNEX Corporation, a large telecommunications firm, created *mentoring circles.* The purpose of these informal teams – developed outside the formal NYNEX organisation – was to fill the void created by a lack of female top-level managers to serve as mentors for other women in the organisation. Organised in groups of 8 to 12 employees, the circles provide the kind of career networking, support, and encouragement that mentors normally offer to their charges.

Ad hoc groups are informal teams of employees assembled to solve a problem with only those who are most likely to contribute invited. For example, you may form an ad hoc team when you select employees from your human resources and accounting departments to solve a problem with the system for tracking and recording pay changes in the company's payroll system. You don't invite participants from shipping to join this informal team, because they probably can't provide meaningful input to the problem.

Self-managed teams

Self-managed teams combine the attributes of both formal and informal teams. Normally established by management, self-managed teams often quickly adopt lives of their own as members take over responsibility for the day-to-day workings of the team. Self-managed teams usually contain from 3 to 30 employees whose job is to meet together to find solutions to common worker problems. Self-managed teams are also known as *high-performance teams, cross-functional teams,* or *super-teams.*

To compress time and gain benefits, an organisation's self-managing teams must be:

- ✔ Made up of people from different parts of the organisation
- ✔ Small because large groups create communication problems

- ✔ Self-managing and empowered to act, because referring decisions back up the line wastes time and often leads to poorer decisions

- ✔ Multifunctional, because that's the best – if not the only – way to keep the actual product and its essential delivery system clearly visible and foremost in everyone's mind

Self-managed teams of workers at Batchelor's Foods in Britain increased productivity by 25 per cent every year for ten years. This was partly driven by investment in production technology; however, that the work teams were able to operate to maximum efficiency and effectiveness was an essential component of the improvement. Teams of six were allowed to divide up the work as they saw fit; and when they additionally became responsible for handling production and output defects, rejects from end of production and packaging functions, and customer complaints, rejection rates fell to negligible levels. And another by-product was that production crew absenteeism fell from 7 per cent to negligible as well!

Otikon, a hearing technology specialist, organises all its staff into self-managed project teams. The additional difference at Otikon is that the company expects staff to find projects on which to work, as well as receiving assignments. Over the past five years, the company has developed revolutionary mainstream hearing technology, using such different sources of information and expertise as the mobile phone industry, television and radio, and the music recording industry. Lars Olind, the managing director, states: 'I want people to do what they do best. I want people to enjoy themselves – to have fun. Only by doing this will we get the best products and work out of them.'

More and more, where management is willing to let go of the reins of absolute authority and turn them over to workers, self-managing teams are rising to the challenge and are making major contributions to the success of their firms. Indeed, the future success of many businesses lies in the successful implementation of self-managed teams.

The real world

Empowerment is a beautiful thing when it flourishes in an organisation. However, real empowerment is still rare. Many false substitutes are out there masquerading as empowerment! Although many managers tell a good story about how they empower their employees, few actually do it. When they are real and not pale imitations, empowered teams typically:

- ✔ Make the most of the decisions that influence team success

- ✔ Choose their leaders

- ✔ Add or remove team members

- ✔ Set their goals and commitments

✔ Define and perform much of their training

✔ Receive rewards as a team

Unfortunately, employee empowerment, for the most part, may be only an illusion. A survey of team members showed that plenty of room for change and improvement in the workings of teams still exists. Survey respondents clearly felt that the areas of intra-group trust, group effectiveness, agenda setting/meeting content, and role and idea conformity can do with some improvement.

A great deal of research has been carried out into what makes effective work groups and teams. Work by, among others, Rosabeth Moss Kanter, Charles Handy, Bob Culver, and Lynda Gratton has found that, in the overwhelming majority of cases, teams and groups are not fully empowered – top management is still making the strategic decisions. The studies all find that you can give much greater autonomy to teams and groups as follows:

✔ **Make your teams empowered, not merely participative:** Instead of just inviting employees to participate in teams, grant team members the authority and power to make independent decisions.

- Allow your teams to make long-range and strategic decisions, not just procedural ones.

- Permit the team to choose the team leaders.

- Allow the team to determine its goals and commitments.

- Make sure that all team members have influence by involving them in the decision-making process.

✔ **Remove the source of conflicts:** Despite their attempts to empower employees, managers are often unwilling to live with the results. Be willing to start up a team, and then be prepared to accept the outcome.

- Recognise and work out personality conflicts.

- Tackle resistance from middle management and other vested interests.

- Work to unify managers' and team members' views.

- Minimise the stress of downsizing and process-improvement tasks.

✔ **Change other significant factors that influence team effectiveness:** Each of these factors indicates that an organisation has not yet brought true empowerment to its employees. You have the power to change this situation. Do it!

- Allow the team to discipline poorly performing members.

- Make peer pressure less important in attaining high team performance.

- Train as many team members as you train managers or team leaders.

Although clear examples of companies where management has truly empowered its teams do exist (they're out there somewhere), team empowerment doesn't just happen. Supervisors and managers must make concerted and ongoing efforts to ensure that authority and autonomy pass from management to teams. You can, too!

New technology and teams

According to a *Fortune* magazine article, the three dominant forces shaping 21st-century organisations are the following:

- ✔ A high-involvement workplace with self-managed teams and other devices for empowering employees.
- ✔ A new emphasis on managing business processes rather than functional departments.
- ✔ The evolution of information technology to the point where knowledge, accountability, and results can be distributed rapidly anywhere in the organisation.

The integrating ingredient of these three dominant forces is information. Information technology and the way information is handled are increasingly becoming the keys to an organisation's success.

But information can be tricky to manage. According to Peter Drucker in *Management: Tasks, Responsibilities, Practices*, 'Information activities present a special organisational problem. Unlike most other result-producing activities, they are not concerned with one stage of the process but with the entire process itself. This means that they have to be both centralised and decentralised.' Fortunately, information technology has overcome this challenge.

In a team environment, *process management information* moves precisely to where the team needs it, unfiltered by a hierarchy. Raw numbers go straight to those who need them in their jobs because front-line workers, such as salespeople and machinists, are trained in how to use that information. By letting information flow to wherever the team needs it, a horizontal self-managed company isn't only possible, it's also inevitable. Information technology-enabled team support systems include e-mail, computer conferencing, and videoconferencing, which co-ordinate geographically, as well as across time zones, more easily than ever before. The development and use of computer software to support teams also is growing. An example is the expanding body of software called *groupware*. Groupware consists of computer programs specifically designed to support collaborative work groups and processes.

As organisations make better use of information technology, they don't need middle managers to make decisions as often. The result? The number of management levels and the number of managers can be dramatically reduced. Jobs, careers, and knowledge shift constantly. Typical management career paths are eliminated, and workers advance by learning more skills, making them more valuable to the organisation.

Those managers who remain need to take on new skills and attitudes to be more like coaches, supporters, and facilitators to front-line employees. Supervisors and managers no longer have the luxury of spending time trying to control the organisation – instead, they change it. Their job is to seek out new customers at the same time as they respond to the latest needs of their established customers. Managers still have considerable authority, but instead of commanding workers, their job is to inspire workers.

Meetings: Putting Teams to Work

So what is a discussion about meetings doing in a chapter on teams? The answer is that *meetings* are the primary forum in which team members conduct business and communicate with one another. And with the proliferation of teams in business, it pays to master the basic skills of meeting management.

The trouble with meetings

Everyone needs to hold meetings – you can't achieve anything in isolation. So the priority is to make sure that the way you structure and conduct your meetings is precise and effective.

People have gone to a great deal of time and trouble to try to find ways to avoid long, tedious and boring meetings – with varying degrees of success. Some companies insist that their meetings are conducted standing up, for speed. Others restrict presentations made at meetings to no more than ten minutes or so. Others don't provide refreshments. The point with these – and many other – approaches is to make sure that you concentrate on the matters in hand, have people understand what they are going to be doing as the result, and move on.

Unfortunately, most meetings are a big waste of time. Meeting experts have determined that approximately 53 per cent of all the time that people spend in meetings – and this means the time that *you* spend in meetings – is unproductive, worthless, and of little consequence. And when you realise that most business people spend at least 25 per cent of their working hours in meetings, with upper management spending more than double that, you can begin to gain an appreciation for the importance of effective meeting skills.

Top five teams Web sites

Wondering where to find the best information on the Web about the topics addressed in this chapter? Well, you've come to the right place! Here are our top five favourites:

✔ Meredith Belbin's team roles: `www.belbin.org.uk/superteams`

✔ Roger Cartwright: `www.rogercartwright.net/teamsandteamleadership` `www.humanresources.about.com/cs/involvementteams/`

✔ Teambuildinginc.com: `www.teambuildinginc.com`

✔ Teams and Teamwork: `www.hq.nasa.gov/office/hqlibrary/ppm/ppm5.htm`

✔ Teamwork: `www.fastcompany.com/online/resources/teamwork.html`

So what's wrong with meetings, anyway? Why do so many meetings go so badly, and why can't you ever seem to do anything about it? In their book *Better Business Meetings* (McGraw-Hill), Bob and Peter list the following reasons:

✔ **Too many meetings take place:** When did you ever say to yourself, 'I haven't been to any meetings lately – and I miss them?' Probably never. Indeed, a manager's eternal lament is something more along the lines of: 'How on earth am I supposed to get any work done when all I ever do is get ordered to meetings?' The problem is not just that too many meetings take place; the problem is that many meetings are unnecessary, unproductive, and a waste of your time.

✔ **Attendees are unprepared:** Some meetings happen prematurely, before a real reason to meet arises. At other times, individuals who haven't prepared themselves or the participants for the topics to be discussed lead the meeting. What often results is a long period where the participants stumble around blindly trying to figure out why the meeting was called in the first place.

✔ **Certain individuals dominate the proceedings:** You find one or two in every crowd. You know, the people who think that they know it all and who make sure that their opinion is heard loudly and often during the course of a meeting. These people may be good for occasional comic relief, if nothing else, but they often intimidate the other participants and stifle their contributions.

✔ **They last too long:** Yes, yes, yes. Make sure a meeting doesn't last longer than it needs to. No less, no more. Despite this fact, most managers let meetings expand to fill the time allotted to them. So rather than let the participants leave after the business at hand is completed, the meeting drags on and on and on.

✔ **The meeting has no focus:** Meeting leadership is not a passive occupation. Many pressures work against keeping meetings on track and on topic, and managers often fail to step up to the challenge. The result is a proliferation of personal agendas, digressions, diversions, off-topic tangents, and worse.

The eight keys to great meetings

Fortunately, you have hope. Although many meetings are a big waste of time, they don't have to be. Your dysfunctional meeting blues have a cure! And good news again: The cure is readily available, inexpensive, and easy to swallow.

✔ **Be prepared:** You need only a little time to prepare for a meeting, and the pay-off is increased meeting effectiveness. Instead of wasting time trying to figure out why you're meeting ('Does anyone know why we're here today?'), your preparation gets results as soon as the meeting starts.

✔ **Have an agenda:** An agenda is your road map, your meeting plan. With an agenda, you and the other participants recognise the meeting goals and know what you're going to discuss. And if you distribute the agenda to participants before the meeting, you multiply its effectiveness many times over because the participants can prepare for the meeting in advance.

✔ **Start on time and end on time (or sooner):** You go to a meeting on time, and the meeting leader, while muttering about an important phone call or visitor, arrives 15 minutes late. Even worse is when the meeting leader ignores the scheduled ending time and lets the meeting go on and on. Respect your participants by starting and ending your meetings on time. You don't want them spending the entire meeting looking at their watches and worrying about how late you're going to keep them!

✔ **Have fewer but better meetings:** Call a meeting only when a meeting is absolutely necessary. And when you call a meeting, make the meeting a good one. Do you really have to meet to discuss a change in your travel reimbursement policy? Can't an e-mail message to all company travellers do just as well? Or how about the problem you've been having with the financial reports? Instead of calling a meeting, maybe a phone call can do the trick. Whenever you're tempted to call a meeting, make sure that you have a good reason for doing so.

✔ **Think inclusion, not exclusion:** Be selective over the people you invite to your meetings – select only as many participants as you need to get the job done. But don't exclude people who may have the best insight into your issues simply because of their rank in the organisation or their lifestyle, appearance, or beliefs.

You never know who in your organisation is going to provide the best ideas, and you only hurt your chances of getting those great ideas by excluding people for non-performance-related reasons.

✔ **Maintain the focus:** Ruthlessly keep your meetings on topic at all times. Although doing everything but talking about the topic at hand can be a lot of fun, you called the meeting for a specific reason in the first place. Stick to the topic, and if you finish the meeting early, participants who want to stick around to talk about other matters don't have to hold the other participants hostage to do so.

✔ **Capture action items:** Make sure that you have a system for capturing, summarising, and assigning action items to individual team members. Flip charts – those big pads of paper that you hang from an easel in front of the group – are great for this purpose.

In addition, make assignments and share out follow-up actions to the appropriate people.

✔ **Get feedback:** Feedback can be a great way to measure the effectiveness of your meetings. Not only can you find out what you did right, but you can also find out what you did wrong and get ideas on how to make your future meetings more effective. Ask the participants to give you their honest and open feedback – verbally or in writing – and then use it. You can never see yourself as others do unless they show you.

Chapter 12

Managing Flexible Workers

- -

In This Chapter

▶ Managing new types of employees

▶ Monitoring remote and off-site working

▶ Managing different work patterns

▶ Looking at the future of telecommuting

- -

*I*n recent years a major shift has occurred in the attitudes of companies, and of those who run them, towards more worker-friendly workplaces and working arrangements. This applies to everyone – full-time and part-time, and regardless of length of service, occupation, or hours worked. Legislation now also requires companies to consider making flexible working available to employees who request it; and any denial of such a request normally has to be on the grounds of operational issues only.

Of course, these patterns of work have been long established in the transport, telecommunications, healthcare, and electricity, gas, and water supply sectors. Commercial considerations, the availability of technology, and changes in working demands have all driven organisations to consider how best to optimise their resources, the ways in which work is carried out, and how, when, and where best to engage their staff. Consequently, today's managers must be much more willing to work with the different requirements of their people than ever before. Whether employees need to drop the children off at school in the morning, work only on certain days of the week, or take time off to care for ill relatives and dependants, managers have to be flexible and willing to accommodate these needs. In return, managers know that with a little consideration they can get – and are entitled to expect – much more from their staff.

These changes in the law and shifts in attitudes (as well as changes in the nature of work, technological advances, and reductions in layers of management in many organisations) have led to flexible staff spending the majority of their working time away from the office; employees managed from a distance; employees who work a variety of patterns: of hours; shifts; starting and finishing times; annualised and compressed hours; nine-day fortnights/fifteen-day months; and employees who *telecommute,* or work from home.

Of course, these changes aren't always easy for managers to get used to. For managers who are accustomed to having their staff close by – ready to respond instantly to the needs of customers and clients – managing flexible workers can be disconcerting.

In this chapter, we consider flexible workers, and how to get the best out of them. We explore strategies for managing those who work away from the office, as well as those who work different shifts; and we look at the future of telecommuting and homeworking.

Making Room for a New Kind of Employee

New kinds of employees are already out there – flexible workers. *Flexible workers* are those who work elsewhere besides the regular and familiar offices of the organisation; and those who have accepted (often having asked for) a variety of alternative working arrangements, including flexi-time, hours to suit, and term-time working agreements, to name but three.

Providing flexible working opportunities is a legal obligation if at all possible for the organisation. Alternative working arrangements can range from something as simple as allowing employees to start and end their working days at times that suit them, all the way through to working full-time from home.

Managing people you don't see very often can be challenging, and you must approach it differently to managing those who work in the same place as you.

Perhaps your employees are always on the road, located at different premises, or even at the other end of the country; or maybe they are working evenings only, or else from home. Regardless of the reason for the separation, distance makes it much harder to identify and enforce standards of behaviour and performance. As a manager, you have to be absolutely certain that that those with non-standard patterns and locations of work are performing to the same levels of output and quality as those in the office.

Preparing to be flexible

Is your organisation ready for flexible working? Are *you* ready for flexible working? The following is a quick and easy checklist for determining if your organisation is ready:

✔ Your company sets and enforces clear output and quality standards.

✔ Potential flexible workers have the equipment they need to work effectively away from the office.

✔ The work can be performed away from the office.

✔ The work can be performed without continuous interaction with other employees.

✔ Potential flexible workers have demonstrated that they can work effectively without constant supervision.

✔ Supervisors can manage and monitor employees by results rather than by direct observation.

✔ Non-standard places of work have been assessed to ensure that they are adequately equipped.

✔ Non-standard places and patterns of work conform to health and safety standards.

If you have several ticks, then your organisation is ready, willing and able to implement alternative working arrangements. If you have many empty boxes, you have your work cut out for you before you can reasonably expect flexible working to be a viable option for your organisation.

Whatever the present state of affairs, you need to be clear about why the organisation has chosen to go down the 'flexible' route – whether to maximise the opportunities of technology, cost cutting, dealing with customers on the other side of the world, or anything else.

You then need to assess the corporate and collective attitude to flexible working and, if necessary, this has to be adjusted so that everyone knows and understands why some people have different patterns of work and demands on their time. You need to be comfortable in establishing specific ways of working within any patterns of flexibility; and this includes references to volumes, quality, and reliability of outputs demanded, as well as absolute attention to deadlines.

In all cases you need to engage the means for establishing collective and individual performance indicators and targets, and to make clear how you are going to monitor and supervise those on non-standard patterns of work.

You also need to make sure that you have carried out a full risk assessment; and this must include reference to: technological integrity and security; staff reliability, security and wellbeing; product, service and output delivery viability; and problem identification and resolution capability.

Anticipating changes to the organisation's culture

When an increasing number of people work flexible patterns, a major concern emerges about what happens to the company's culture and staff performance as more and more people work outside the office and outside regular hours. A company's culture is, after all, mostly defined by the daily interactions of staff. Those who are working outside the mainstream and therefore not totally involved in the everyday office environment may have little or no grounding in the culture, and little identity with other employees or with the organisation's values and goals. It's essential to ensure that everyone's made to feel included, whatever their hours of attendance or locations or patterns of work. Wherever and whenever they work, you need to ensure that you're getting the required levels of output from all of your staff. The good news is that you can take a number of steps to help your flexible workers plug into your company's culture, become team players, and gain a stake in the organisation's goals in the process. Consider the following ideas:

- ✔ Schedule regular meetings that everyone attends, in person if possible; or else by chat room or conference call. Discuss current company events and set aside time for the group to tackle and solve at least one major or pressing problem (more if time permits).

- ✔ Create effective communication vehicles that everyone can be a part of. Make sure that everyone gets to know all of the gossip and also anything that is important, pressing, or urgent.

- ✔ Schedule periodic team-building events for everyone, both flexible and standard workers, to build working relationships and trust.

- ✔ Start a programme of regular and inexpensive group events that draw everyone in together. Going out to lunch, helping local charities, having games afternoons – the possibilities are endless.

As a manager, you need to consider that flexible workers face issues that normal employees don't, including:

- ✔ Flexible workers may find that they are not fairly compensated for using home resources (space, computers, electricity, furniture, and so on) that they contribute to the job.

- ✔ Flexible workers may feel that their privacy is being invaded if management efforts are intrusive. Remember that they are not available 24/7. Respect their working hours and use work phone numbers and e-mail addresses – not the home ones – when you want to communicate.

- ✔ Family pressures may intrude on work duties much more for home-based staff than for those who work in normal offices. You therefore need a specific 'work from home' policy in place so that everyone is clear about where they stand.

Also keep in mind that regular employees may become resentful of what they perceive to be the 'special privileges' given to flexible workers. Ensure that everyone knows and understands why all their colleagues work in particular ways, and what their contribution to overall performance is.

These issues don't mean that you just forget about offering alternative working arrangements; you have to be prepared to make such arrangements by law, after all. But keep these issues in mind, and work to ensure that they don't cause problems for anyone, flexible or standard.

Managing from a Distance

Flexible working is becoming more and more commonplace, and you have to be prepared to offer it if people demand it, or else give sound operational and managerial reasons why you cannot offer it. With the changing nature of work today, managers have to adapt to new circumstances. How can you keep up with an employee's performance when you may not have physical contact with them for weeks or even months at a time? Some of the answers lie in a return to basic human interaction, examples of which are in the following list:

- ✔ **Make time for people.** Nothing beats face-to-face meetings in building lasting trusting relationships. Managing is a people job. You need to take time for people; and you need to make time whenever those on flexible work patterns are available and need to meet.

- ✔ **Increase communication as you increase distance.** The greater the distance, the greater the effort all parties need to make to keep in touch. And although some employees want to be as autonomous as possible, minimising their day-to-day contact with you, others quickly feel neglected, isolated, or ignored if you don't make the effort to keep in touch. So increase communications by telephone, send frequent updates, and schedule regular meetings and visits. Also, encourage your employees to contact you (communication is two way, after all), and go out of your way to provide the same types of communications and meetings with each work shift; or else arrange meetings that everyone can get to – and make sure that they do indeed come!

- ✔ **Use technology; don't let technology use you.** Use technology as an active means of communication, not just for giving out information. Promote the exchange of ideas, encourage questions, and make sure that you always ask for a reply. Have discussion boards and chat rooms, and create bulletin boards to make sure that interaction and exchanges do in fact take place.

Today's managers have to work harder to manage all the different patterns of work and ways of working. If you value strong working relationships and clear communication, you need to ask around to make sure that adequate communication is taking place.

Managing Different Shifts and Patterns of Work

Managing people is hard enough, and the fact that the nature of work and working is changing so dramatically and so quickly makes the task harder still. More and more employers have therefore had to develop additional approaches to organising work, so that work gets done at all hours of the day, and so that staff can be employed on hours that suit them. Managing employees who work different hours and shift patterns is a critical issue.

Consider the following points when making the most of working with all shift patterns and non-standard hours:

- ✔ **Effective induction:** All new employees need to get their bearings, and those on shifts are often at a disadvantage because they are working outside normal hours. Make sure that new employees know what they can expect of the job and the organisation, including rules, procedures, and regulations; and make sure that they get to know everyone and get settled in quickly.

- ✔ **Adequate resources:** Giving your employees what they need to be productive encompasses everything from providing the right equipment to making sure they know where to go to ask questions. It also means having full job training, and this means in the ways of doing the job, as well as what to do.

- ✔ **Continuous communication:** This sounds like a cliché or a mantra, but you can't underestimate the value of communication. Many employees suffer because of poor directions and get the label of being difficult to work with, rather than risk appearing slow to grasp an assignment. So you must constantly check whether people who work shifts and non-standard hours have questions or need help. Make every contact count. Some managers make themselves available at shift changeovers to have contact with two shifts at once.

- ✔ **Inclusive recognition:** Publicly acknowledge everyone, whatever their hours or patterns of work. Recognition and appreciation go a long way towards building loyalty and commitment, and getting that little bit extra out of people when you need it.

- ✔ **Equal treatment:** Treat everyone the way you want them to act. If you want them to have a long-term perspective, treat them with a long-term perspective. Get them involved. Make them part of the team, and make them *feel* part of the team. Treat them with courtesy and respect. You gain the additional benefit of being seen as a good employer to work for, and this is always a draw for new people when you need to recruit them.

Long-distance recognition

Everyone needs recognition for their own well-being; and everyone needs recognition from their manager for a job well done. Just because some people are 'out of sight' does not mean they should be 'out of mind' also. Use the following tips to make sure that your flexible staff feel just as valued and appreciated as everyone else:

✔ Make sure that flexible staff have an opportunity to tell both the leader and also everyone else what they have achieved.

✔ Keep a regular review of the achievements of flexible staff so that you don't forget them and so that they remain integrated with everyone else.

✔ Make sure that flexible staff get the same opportunities for recognition, promotion, progress, and variety of work as everyone else.

✔ Make sure that flexible staff get the same opportunities for parties, dinners, and other celebrations as everyone else.

✔ Make sure that flexible staff get 'thank you' notes when appropriate, exactly the same as everyone else.

You can achieve all this if you make the right effort at the right time. Organise yourself to make the effort and you reap the benefits.

Telecommuting and Homeworking

With the proliferation of personal computers, laptops, and all the software and connections necessary, people can really work anywhere. So the question isn't *can* your employees telecommute and work from home, the question is do you let them?

In an old-style office, employees are often no more than a few feet away from you, their manager. If you need them, you can get hold of them. If they are away from their desk or workstation, then no problem, you can catch them later.

Telecommuting and homeworking change this. You can't get hold of people immediately (and they can't always get hold of you). So communication becomes a series of voice-mail messages, e-mails, and faxes. You come to feel disconnected from your staff; and they may also feel disconnected from you.

However, there are many benefits to gain from both telecommuting and home working. Staff productivity and output can be increased by up to 30 per cent. People don't lose time travelling to and from work. Staff are more satisfied with their jobs. And society benefits from fewer cars on the roads every rush hour.

Top five virtual management Web sites

Here's the best of the Web for the topics discussed in this chapter:

- Chartered Institute of Personnel and Development: www.cipd.co.uk/flexibleworking

- Department of Trade and Industry: www.dti.gov.uk/flexibleworking

- ACAS: www.acas.org.uk

- Chartered Management Institute: www.cmi.org.uk

- Trades Union Congress: www.tuc.org.uk

When he worked normal hours, John Holland, a systems analyst at DigitalCompaq, never saw his children from first thing on Monday morning until Friday night or Saturday morning. When DigitalCompaq allowed John to choose his own hours and location of work, he set up an office at home. This enabled him to save nearly five hours commuting per day. He got more work done, more quickly, and to a higher quality; and the family had their evening meal together every day. John subsequently moved his family from a suburban location near London to a large rural location in northern England, some 300 miles from the office. DigitalCompaq was happy with this because John's output continued to rise, and his loyalty and commitment were assured.

Consider the pros and cons of flexible working. The advantages are:

- Depending only on specific deadlines being met, staff can set their own schedules and hours of work.

- Staff have more time for customers.

- Staff can work when they have to and when they need to; and they can also work when they want to (and this can include Saturday afternoons if they choose).

- Your business saves money by downsizing your facilities and premises as well as on the costs of electricity, heating, and other overheads.

- Staff morale gets a boost.

And the disadvantages are:

- ✔ Monitoring performance is harder.
- ✔ Scheduling meetings and get-togethers is more difficult.
- ✔ You may have to buy your staff the equipment they need to be flexible and telecommute.
- ✔ Employees can become disconnected and alienated from the organisation.
- ✔ Managers have to reorder their own priorities and daily schedules to include specific attention to those on non-standard patterns of work.
- ✔ Managers have to be more precise in setting work and assignments.

Ian Baines works for one of the world's best-known airlines near Heathrow airport. With the agreement of the airline, he now works one day per week at home. On his day at home, Ian starts work at the same time as he normally leaves the house. This enables him to get done in a matter of minutes what otherwise takes many hours, if not days, because of constant interruptions. His staff can get hold of him at home if they need to; and if he does have to go into work for meetings on this day, he travels later, which means that he completes his journey in 20 minutes rather than the two hours it takes during the rush hour. And the arrangement leaves him free to deal with institutional problems and his other responsibilities fully and effectively during the rest of the week.

Chapter 13

Ethics and Office Politics

●●

In This Chapter

▶ Doing what is right

▶ Assessing your political environment

▶ Identifying the real side of communication

▶ Discovering the unwritten rules of your organisation

▶ Defending your personal interests

●●

*E*thics and office politics are very powerful forces in any organisation. *Ethics* is the framework of values that employees use to guide their behaviour. You've seen the devastation that poor ethical standards can lead to – witness the string of business failures attributed to less than sterling ethics in more than a few large, seemingly upstanding businesses. Today, more than ever, managers are expected to model ethical behaviour and to ensure that their employees follow in their footsteps – and at the same time to purge the organisation of employees who refuse to align their own standards with those of their employer.

At its best, *office politics* means the relationships that you develop with your colleagues – both up and down the chain of command – that allow you to get tasks done, to be informed about the latest goings-on in the organisation, and to form a personal network of business associates for support throughout your career. Office politics help to ensure that everyone works in the best interests of their colleagues and the organisation. At its worst, office politics can degenerate into a competition in which employees concentrate their efforts on trying to increase their personal power at the expense of other employees, and of their organisations.

This chapter is about building an ethical organisation, determining the nature and boundaries of your political environment, understanding the unspoken side of office communication, unearthing the unwritten rules of your organisation, and, in the worst-case scenario, becoming adept at defending yourself against political attack.

Doing the Right Thing: Ethics and You

With an endless parade of business scandals regarding overstated revenues, mistaken earnings, and misplaced decimals hitting the daily news, rocking the stock market, and shaking the foundations of the global economic system, you may often wonder whether anyone in charge knows the difference between right and wrong. Or if they know the difference, whether they really care.

Of course, the reality is that many business leaders do know the difference between right and wrong, despite appearances to the contrary. Now more than ever, businesses and the leaders who run them are trying to do the right thing, not just because the right thing is politically correct, but also because it's good for the bottom line.

Defining ethics

Do you know what ethics is? In case you're a bit rusty on the correct response, the long answer is that *ethics* is a set of standards, beliefs and values that guide conduct, behaviour, and activities – in other words, a way of thinking that provides boundaries for action. The short answer is that ethics is simply doing the right thing. Not just talking about doing the right thing, but really doing it!

Although you come to a job with your own sense of ethical values, based on your upbringing, your beliefs and your life experiences, the organisations and leaders for which you work are responsible for setting clear ethical standards for you to operate within.

When you have high ethical standards on the job, you generally exhibit some or all of the following personal qualities and behaviours:

   ✔ Accountability

   ✔ Dedication

   ✔ Fairness

   ✔ Honesty

   ✔ Impartiality

   ✔ Integrity

   ✔ Loyalty

   ✔ Responsibility

Ethical behaviour starts with *you*. As a manager, you're a leader in your organisation, and you set an example – both for other managers, and for the many workers watching your every move. When others see you behaving unethically, you're sending the message loud and clear that ethics doesn't matter. The result? Ethics doesn't matter to them, either.

However, when you behave ethically, others follow your example and behave ethically too. And if you practise ethical conduct, it also reinforces and perhaps improves your own ethical standards. As a manager, you have a responsibility to try to define, live up to, and improve your own set of personal ethics.

Creating a code of ethics

Although most people have a pretty good idea about what kinds of behaviour are ethical and what kinds of behaviour aren't, ethics are to some degree subjective, and a matter of interpretation to the individual employee. One worker may, for example, think that making unlimited personal phone calls from the office is okay, while another worker may consider that to be inappropriate.

Instead of leaving your employees' definition of ethics on the job to chance or their upbringing, you need to spell out clearly in a code of ethics that stealing, sharing trade secrets, sexual harassment, and other unethical behaviour is unacceptable and may be grounds for dismissal.

A *code of ethics* spells out for all employees – from the very top to the very bottom of the organisation – your organisation's ethical expectations, clearly and unambiguously.

A code of ethics isn't a substitute for company policies and procedures; the code complements these guidelines.

Four key areas form the foundation of a good code of ethics:

- ✔ Compliance with internal policies and procedures
- ✔ Compliance with external laws and regulations
- ✔ Standards based on organisational values
- ✔ Standards based on individual values

Any code of ethics must cover rights, responsibilities, authority, and accountability; the work carried out, and the ways in which work is carried out; matters of right and wrong; compliance with the law; and a reflection of social and cultural customs and values. Running through this is a strong vein of honesty and integrity.

Of course, a code of ethics isn't worth the paper it's printed on if it doesn't address some very specific issues, as well as the more generic ones listed previously. The following list highlights some of the areas a code of ethics needs to address:

- ✔ Conflicts of interest, especially those that occur when managers are faced with the choice of courses of action that serve their own interests at the expense of those of the organisation.

- ✔ Gifts and gratuities that can be understood or perceived to be inducements to act in a particular way.

- ✔ Financial issues, including fraud, misuse of company funds, attitudes to expenses and bonuses, and other irregularities.

- ✔ Loyalty and dedication to the organisation; this is a two-way process – you cannot expect loyalty and dedication from your employees if you do not provide loyalty in return.

- ✔ Compliance with the law as it stands; and commitment to deal with employees who break the law in accordance with statutory provisions.

- ✔ Conditions in which hard and effective work can be expected, required, and carried out.

- ✔ Commitment to constant improvement of all aspects of the organisation – products and services; working practices; returns to shareholders; and dealings with all stakeholders.

- ✔ Commitment to avoiding favouritism and victimisation – remember, in cases of victimisation, law courts and tribunals normally hear an allegation provided that it can be substantiated. In recent years, there have been huge settlements in favour of those who have proved or demonstrated victimisation or discrimination – so apart from not being right, it can also be very expensive!

- ✔ Prohibitions against disclosing trade secrets, product and service information, or anything concerning the internal workings of the organisation without specific permission to do so.

- ✔ Expectations of the highest standards of conduct in matters concerning employee health, safety and welfare. Make sure that this extends to anyone visiting the organisation. Expose vandalism, fraud, theft, and dishonesty wherever they are found; and again if you do not, you may be cited as an accessory after the fact if and when such a case comes to light.

- ✔ Commitment to exposing sexual misconduct and harassment wherever it is found – remember that not doing so may render you liable to prosecution.

✔ Commitment to establishing and upholding the principles of equality of treatment for all, regardless of race and ethnic origin, gender, sexual orientation, age, disability, occupation, or length of service. Ensure equality of treatment and opportunity for all in specific organisational matters, especially promotions; recruitment and selection; training and development opportunities; project work and secondments; and other specific organisational issues.

✔ Paying particular attention to how technology is used. Of particular concern here are matters to do with the nature of Web sites accessed (such as pornography, religious and political extremism), and the content of e-mails (especially those that are bullying or abusive). Also, clear collective commitment is required to ensure that personal and financial data, supplier and client records, and confidentiality are maintained.

All of this is underpinned by the ways in which you conduct yourself. So make sure that you set the same standards for yourself in all things that you expect from everyone else. And especially never make promises to anyone that you cannot keep – staff, suppliers, customers and clients, or shareholders.

Citing the Ethics Resource Center's comprehensive code

According to the US-based Ethics Resource Center Web site (www.ethics.org), a comprehensive code of ethics has seven parts. These parts are:

1. **A memorable title:** Examples include PricewaterhouseCooper's 'The Way We Do Business' and the World Bank Group's 'Living Our Values'.

2. **Leadership letter:** A cover letter that briefly outlines the content of the code of ethics and clearly demonstrates commitment from the very top of the organisation to ethical principles of behaviour.

3. **Table of contents.** The main parts within the code, listed by page number.

4. **Introduction-prologue.** Explains why the code is important, the scope of the code, and to whom it applies.

5. **Statement of core values.** The organisation lists and describes its primary values in detail. It is more or less universal for organisations to describe themselves as equal opportunities employers who provide equality of treatment for all regardless of sex, gender, racial and ethnic origin, religion, age, occupation, length of service, or hours worked.

6. **Code provisions.** This part is the meat of the code, the organisation's position on a wide variety of issues including such topics as sexual harassment, privacy, conflicts of interest, gratuities, and so forth.

7. **Information and resources.** Places that employees can go for further information or for specific advice.

With the Freedom of Information Act, anyone can request to know what is being said about them or done in their name, so make sure that you commit yourself to the highest possible standards and values. Additionally, with the 'Whistle-Blower's Charter', if someone exposes wrongdoing at your organisation, you cannot discipline or victimise them as a result. So be good and be careful!

In addition to working within an organisation, a well-crafted code of ethics can be a powerful tool for publicising your company's standards and values to people outside your organisation, including suppliers, clients, customers, investors, potential job applicants, the media, and the public at large. Your code of ethics tells others that you value ethical behaviour and that it guides the way you and your employees do business.

Of course, simply having a code of ethics isn't enough. You and your employees must also live according to the code. Even the world's best code of ethics does you no good if you file it away and never use it. Require your employees to read and sign a copy acknowledging their acceptance of the code, that way everyone knows what you expect of them.

Living ethics

You may have a code of ethics, but if you don't behave ethically in your day-to-day business transactions and relationships, you call into question the purpose of having a code in the first place. Ethical challenges abound in business – some are spelled out in your company's code of ethics, or in its policies and procedures, and some aren't. What, for example, do you do if:

- ✔ One of your favourite employees gives you tickets to a football match?
- ✔ An employee asks you not to discipline her for a moderate breach of company policies?
- ✔ You sold a product to a client that you later found out to be faulty, but your boss wants you to forget about it?
- ✔ Your department's financial results are actually lower than what appears in your boss's presentation to the board of directors?
- ✔ You find out that your star employee actually didn't graduate from university as he claimed in his job application?
- ✔ You know that a product you sell doesn't actually do everything your company claims it does?

You make ethical choices on the job every day, and how you make those choices has an impact on your business and personal world. According to Trainingscape (www.trainingscape.com), you have six keys to making good ethical choices:

E: Evaluate circumstances through the appropriate filters. Filters include culture, laws, policies, circumstances, relationships, politics, perception, emotions, values, bias, prejudice, and religion.

T: Treat people and issues fairly within the established boundaries. And remember that fair doesn't always mean equal.

H: Hesitate before making critical decisions. (Richard calls this 'wait-a-minute'.)

I: Inform those affected of the standard/decision that you have set/made.

C: Create an environment of consistency for yourself and your working group.

S: Seek guidance when you have any doubt. Make sure that the guidance comes from people who are honest and whom you respect.

Evaluating Your Political Environment

How political is your office or workplace? As a manager, having your finger on the political pulse of the organisation is particularly important. Otherwise, the next time you're in a management meeting, you may blurt out, 'Why is it so difficult to get an employment requisition through human resources? You'd think it was their money!' only to find out that the owner's daughter-in-law heads the human resources department.

With just a little bit of advance information and forethought, you can approach this issue much more tactfully. Getting in touch with your political environment can help you be more effective, and it can help your department and your employees have a greater impact within the organisation.

Assessing your organisation's political environment

Asking your colleagues insightful questions is one of the best ways to assess your organisation's political environment. Such questions show you to be the polite, mature, and ambitious employee you are, and the questions are a sure sign of your well-developed political instincts. Give these questions a try:

- ✔ What's the best way to get a special item approved?

- ✔ How can I get a product from the warehouse that my client needs today when I don't have time to do the paperwork?

- ✔ Can I do anything else for you before I go home for the day?

Although asking politically pointed questions gives you an initial indication of the political lie of the land, you can do more to assess the political environment in your organisation. Watch out for the following signs while you're getting a sense of how your organisation really works:

- ✔ **Find out how others who seem to be effective get tasks done.** How much time do they spend preparing before sending through a formal request? Which items do they delegate and to whose subordinates? When you find people who are particularly effective at getting tasks done in your organisation's political environment, emulate them, and apply their methods to your own goals.

- ✔ **Observe how the organisation rewards others for the jobs they do.** Do managers swiftly and enthusiastically give warm and personal rewards in a sincere manner to make it clear what behaviour they consider important? Do they give credit to everyone who helped make a project successful, or is the manager the only one singled out for praise? By observing your company's rewards, you can tell what behaviour your organisation expects of employees. Practise this behaviour.

- ✔ **Observe how the organisation disciplines others and for what.** Do your managers come down hard on employees for relatively small mistakes? Do they criticise employees in public or in front of colleagues? Do they hold everyone accountable for decisions, actions, and mistakes even if someone had no prior involvement? Such behaviour on the part of management indicates that they don't encourage risk taking. If your management doesn't encourage risk taking, make your political style outwardly reserved as you work behind the scenes.

- ✔ **Consider how people behave towards each other, and how appropriate this is.** If for example you are in a staff meeting and someone blurts out, 'That's a stupid idea. Why would we even consider doing such a thing?', this is clearly unacceptable. Make sure that people conduct themselves with respect and professionalism at all times. Rudeness needs to be replaced with: 'That's an interesting possibility. Can we explore the pros and cons of implementing such a possibility?' The degree of mutual respect that you find in your company indicates how you need to act to conform to the expectations of others.

Identifying key players

So now that you've discovered that you work in a political environment (did you really have any doubt?), you need to determine who the key players are. Why? Because these individuals can help make your department more effective and provide positive role models to you and your employees.

Key players are those politically astute individuals who make things happen in an organisation. You can identify them by their tendency to make instant decisions without having to refer people 'upstairs', their use of the latest corporate slang, and their affinity for always speaking up in meetings, if only to ask, 'What's our objective here?'.

Sometimes influential people don't hold influential positions. For example, Jack, as the department head's assistant, may initially appear to be nothing more than a clerk. However, you may find out that Jack is responsible for scheduling all his boss's appointments, setting agendas for department meetings, and vetoing actions on his own authority. Jack is an informal leader in the organisation and, because you can't get to the department head without going through Jack, you know that Jack has much more power in the organisation than his title may indicate. This *Personal Assistant Syndrome* reflects the need to be able to influence those who act as gatekeepers to top and senior managers.

Use the following questions to identify the key players in your organisation:

✔ Which employees do others go to for advice in your organisation?

✔ Which employees do others consider to be indispensable?

✔ Whose office is located closest to those of the organisation's top management and whose are located miles away? Evidence shows that the farther away you work from head office, the less influence you have.

✔ Who are the members of the inner circle? Who eats lunch with top and senior management?

As you work out who the key players in your organisation are, you start to notice that they have different office personalities. Use the following categories to help you figure out how to work with the different personality types of your organisation's key players:

✔ **Movers and shakers:** These individuals usually far exceed the boundaries of their office positions. For example, you may find a mover and shaker who is in charge of purchasing helping to negotiate a merger. Someone in charge of the physical plant may have the power to designate a wing of the building to the group of her choosing. Non-political individuals, on the other hand, tend to be bogged down by responsibilities – such as getting their own work done.

- **Corporate citizens:** These employees are diligent, hardworking, company-loving individuals who seek slow but steady, long-term advancement through dedication and hard work. Corporate citizens are great resources for getting information and advice about the organisation. You can count on them for help and support, especially if your ideas seem to be in the best interest of the organisation.

- **The town gossips:** These employees always seem to know what's going on in the organisation – usually before those individuals who are actually affected by the news know it. Assume that anything you say to a gossip gets back to the person your comment is about. Therefore, always speak well of your bosses and colleagues when you are in the presence of town gossips – unless of course you want to introduce something to the rumour mill.

- **Firefighters:** These individuals relish stepping into a potential problem with great fanfare at the last conceivable moment to save a project, client, deadline, or whatever. Keep a firefighter well informed of your activities so that you aren't the subject of the next 'fire'.

- **The vetoers:** These people have the authority to kill your best ideas and ambitions with a simple comment such as, 'We tried that and it didn't work.' In response to any new ideas that you may have, a vetoer's favourite line is, 'If your idea is so good, then why aren't we already doing it?' The best way to deal with vetoers is to keep them away from you. Try to find other individuals who can get your ideas approved or rework the idea until you hit on an approach that satisfies the vetoer.

- **Techies:** Every organisation has technically competent workers who legitimately have a high value of their own opinions. Experts can take charge of a situation without taking over. Get to know your experts well – you can trust their judgements and opinions.

- **Moaners and whiners:** A few employees are never satisfied with whatever you do for them. Associating with them inevitably leads to a pessimistic outlook, which you cannot easily turn around. Or worse, your boss may think that you're a whiner, too. In addition, pessimistic people tend to get promoted less often than optimists. Be an optimist: Your optimism makes a big difference in your career and in your life.

Redrawing your organisation chart

Your company's organisation chart may be useful for determining who's who in the formal organisation, but it really has no bearing on who's who in the informal political organisation. What you need is the real organisation chart. Figure 13-1 illustrates a typical official organisation chart.

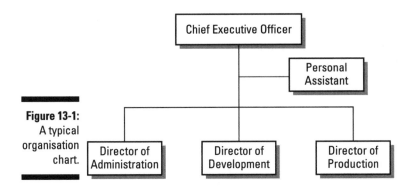

Figure 13-1:
A typical organisation chart.

 Start by finding your organisation's official organisation chart – the one that looks like a big pyramid. Throw it away. Now, from your impressions and observations, start outlining the *real* relationships in your organisation in your mind. (But be careful! You don't always want people to know what you are up to.) Begin with the key players whom you've already identified. Indicate their relative power by level and relationships by approximation. Use the following questions as a guideline:

- ✔ **Whom do these influential people associate with?** Draw the associations on your chart and connect them with solid lines. Also connect friends and relatives, other clear associates, and anyone who you know enjoys particular patronage or favour.

- ✔ **Who makes up the office cliques?** Be sure that all members are connected, because talking to one is like talking to them all.

- ✔ **Who are the office gossips?** Use dotted lines to represent communication without influence and solid lines for communication with influence.

- ✔ **Who's your competition?** Circle those employees that managers are likely to consider for the next promotion that you're up for. Target them for special attention.

- ✔ **Who's left off the chart?** Don't forget about these individuals. The way today's organisations seem to change every other day, someone who is off the chart on Friday may be on the chart on Monday. Always maintain positive relationships with all your colleagues and never burn bridges between you and others within and throughout the company. Otherwise, you may find yourself left off the chart some day.

The result of this exercise is a chart of who really has political power in your organisation and who doesn't. Figure 13-2 shows how the organisation really works. Update your organisation chart as you find out more information about people. Take note of any behaviour that gives away a relationship – such as your boss cutting off a colleague in mid-sentence – and factor this observation into your overall political analysis. Of course, understand that you may be wrong. You can't possibly know the inner power relationships of every department. Sometimes, individuals who seem to have power may have far less of it than people who have discovered how to exhibit their power more quietly.

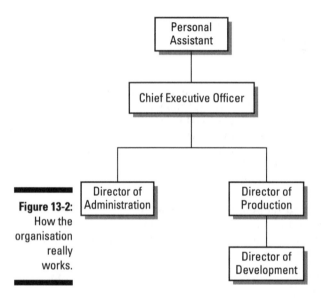

Figure 13-2: How the organisation really works.

Scrutinising Communication: What's Real and What's Not?

One of the best ways to determine how well you fit into an organisation is to see how well you communicate. But deciphering the real meaning of communication in an organisation takes some practise. So how do you determine the real meaning of words in your organisation? The best way of getting to the underlying meanings by observing behaviour, reading between the lines, and, when necessary, knowing how to obtain sensitive information.

Believing actions, not words

One way to decipher the real meaning of communication is to pay close attention to the corresponding behaviour of the communicator. The values and priorities (that is, the ethics) of others tend to come through more clearly in what they do rather than in what they say.

So, for example, if your manager repeatedly says she is trying to get approval for a pay rise for you, look at what actions she has taken towards that end. Did she make a call to her boss or hold a meeting? Did she submit the necessary paperwork or establish a deadline to accomplish this goal? If the answers to these questions are no, or if she is continually 'waiting to hear', the action is probably going nowhere fast. To counter this situation, try to get higher up on your boss's list of priorities by suggesting actions that she can take to get you your pay rise. You may find that you need to do some or all of the footwork yourself. Alternatively, your manager's actions may indicate that your boss is not a power player in the organisation. If that's the case, then make a point to attract the attention of the power players in your organisation who can help you get the pay rise you deserve.

Reading between the lines

In business, don't take the written word at face value. Probe to find out the real reasons behind what is written. For example, a typical notice in a company newsletter announcing the reorganisation of several departments may read like this:

> With the departure of J. R. McNeil, the Marketing Support and Customer Service department will now be a part of the Sales and Administration division under Elizabeth Olsen, acting Divisional Director. The unit will eventually be moved under the direct supervision of the sales director, Tom Hutton.

Such an announcement in the company newsletter may seem to be straightforward on the surface, but if you read between the lines, you may be able to conclude:

> J. R. McNeil, who never did seem to get along with the director of sales, finally did something bad enough to justify getting fired. Tom Hutton apparently made a successful bid with the board of directors to add the area to his empire, probably because his sales were up 30 per cent from last year. Elizabeth Olsen will be appointed as acting divisional director for an interim period to do some of Tom's dirty work by clearing out some of the dead wood. Tom thus starts with a clean slate, 20 per cent lower overheads, and an almost guaranteed increase in profits for his first year in the job. This all fits very nicely with Tom's personal strategy for advancement – both the organisation's and also his own. (*PS: A nice congratulatory call to Tom may be in order.*)

Announcements like these have been written dozens of times by so many people that they appear to be logical and valid when you initially read them. By reading between the lines, however, you can often determine what is really going on. Of course, you have to be careful not to jump to the wrong conclusions. J. R. McNeil may have simply gone on to better opportunities and the company has taken advantage of that event to reorganise. Make sure to validate your conclusions with others in the company to get the real story.

Probing for information

In general, you can get excellent information about your organisation by being a trusted listener to as many people as possible. Show sincere interest in the affairs of others, and they may talk about themselves more openly. After they begin talking, you can shift the topic to work, work problems, and eventually more sensitive topics. Ask encouraging questions and volunteer information as necessary to keep the exchange equitable.

Even after you've developed such trusted relationships, you need to know how to probe to uncover the facts about rumours, decisions, and hidden agendas. Start by adhering to the following guidelines:

- Have at least three ways of obtaining the information.
- Check the information through two sources.
- Promise anonymity whenever possible.
- Generally know the answers to the questions you ask.
- Be casual and non-threatening in your approach.
- Assume that the initial answer is superficial.
- Ask the same question different ways.
- Be receptive to whatever information people give you.

One more thing: If you find yourself in an organisation that is rife with political intrigue, where you're always looking over your shoulder and are worried when the next rumour is going to be about you, seriously consider changing jobs! While every organisation has its share of politics, spending too much time worrying about it is certainly counterproductive, and it can't be good for your wellbeing.

Uncovering the Unwritten Rules of Organisational Politics

Every organisation has rules that are never written down and seldom discussed. Such unwritten rules pertaining to the expectations and behaviour of employees in the organisation can play a major role in your success or failure. Because unwritten rules aren't explicit, you have to piece them together by observation, insightful questioning, or simply through trial and error.

Never underestimate the power of the unwritten rules of organisational politics. In many companies, the unwritten rules carry just as much importance, if not more, than the written rules contained in the company's policy manual.

Be friendly with all

The more individuals you have as friends in an organisation, the better off you are. If you haven't already done so, start cultivating friends in your immediate work group and then extend your efforts to making contacts and developing friendships in other parts of the organisation. The more favourably your colleagues view you, the greater your chances of becoming their manager in the future. Cultivate their support by seeking advice or by offering assistance.

Interpreting the company policy manual

Even when written in black and white, an organisation's policies are rarely what they appear to be. Most policies came about as a directive from the top to solve a particular problem. For example, if the company employs an individual who prefers to wear gaudy jewellery, the individual can be confronted in a two- to three-minute discussion that probably settles the matter. More often, however, managers appoint a task force to develop a dress code and company plan for personal hygiene. Even after the policy is in place, the targeted individual is likely to be oblivious to any perceived problem and may even wholeheartedly endorse the new code 'for all those who need it'; that is, seemingly everyone except the actual target.

You can explain many policies in the same way. Be alert to the following ways in which some employees try to shirk their responsibilities as a result:

✔ Refer to the policy only when it clearly supports exactly what they want to do.

✔ Always assume that a policy that doesn't support what they want is intended for others.

✔ Claim an inability to equitably enforce policies they don't like by citing a rumoured abuse or possible misinterpretation.

✔ When a conflict arises about policy implementation, argue that the policy is too specific (for general application) or too general (for specific circumstances).

✔ Argue that all policies should be considered as flexible guidelines.

The point is that sometimes policies don't work. Your job is to recognise that some policies don't work and to try to change those policies. For example, if you want to give your employees the flexibility to set their own work schedules, but company policy prohibits that, do whatever you can to get management to accept a new policy that accomplishes your goal.

You never know whom you'll report to in the future. As one saying goes, 'Be nice to people on the way up because you may meet them on the way down.' And as an Arabic proverb goes, 'Keep your friends close and hold your enemies closer.'

Build a network by routinely helping new employees who enter your organisation. As they join, be the person who takes them aside to explain how the organisation really works. As the new employees establish themselves and move on to other jobs in other parts of the organisation, you have a well-entrenched network for obtaining information and assistance.

Knowing others throughout the organisation can be invaluable for clarifying rumours, obtaining information, and indirectly feeding information back to others. An astute manager maintains a large number of diverse contacts throughout the organisation, all on friendly terms. The following are excellent ways to enlarge your network:

- ✔ **Walk around:** Those managers who walk the floor tend to be better known than those managers who don't. Return telephone and e-mail messages in person whenever possible. Not only do you have the opportunity for one-on-one communication with the individual who left you the message, but also you can stop by to see everyone else you know along the way.

- ✔ **Get involved:** You need to meet superiors, peers, and colleagues from a wide range of functions, departments, divisions, and locations, and take every opportunity that presents itself to do so. This includes attending meetings, discussion groups, professional gatherings, and problem-solving discussions; and some companies and organisations also have strong sports and social clubs.

- ✔ **Join committees:** Whether the committee forms to address employee security or simply to determine who cleans out the refrigerator in the employee lounge, take part. You get to meet new people in an informal and relaxed setting.

Help others get what they want

A fundamental, unwritten rule of office politics is: Getting what you want is easier when you give others what they want. Win the assistance of others by showing them what they stand to gain by helping you. When a benefit isn't readily apparent, create or allude to one that may occur if they offer to help. Such benefits can include:

- ✔ **A favour returned in kind:** Surely you can provide some kind of favour to your counterparts in exchange for their assistance. Lunch or the temporary secondment of an employee to their department is always a popular option.

✔ **Information:** Don't forget: Information is power. Everyone desperately wants to know the latest and greatest information and gossip in an organisation – and your colleagues are no different. Be the one to give them information if you can.

✔ **Money:** Perhaps you have a little extra money in your equipment budget that you can allocate to someone's project in exchange for that person's help.

✔ **A recommendation:** Top and senior managers trust your judgement. Your willingness to recommend a colleague for promotion to a higher position or for recognition because of their extraordinary performance is a valuable commodity. The right words to the right people can make all the difference to someone's success in an organisation.

We're not suggesting that you do anything unethical or illegal. Don't violate your personal set of ethics or company policy to get ahead. When you provide these kinds of benefits to others in your organisation, make sure that you are within your company's rules and policies. And as a side benefit, you may actually find satisfaction in giving to others.

Don't party at company parties

Social affairs are a serious time for those employees seeking to advance within a company. Social events offer one of the few times when everyone in the company is supposed to be on an equal footing. Don't believe it, though. Although social functions provide managers at the top a chance to show that they're normal people and give employees below a chance to ask questions and laugh at their bosses' jokes, parties are also a time to be extremely cautious.

Beware of whom you talk to and, of course, what you say. Social functions, such as holiday parties and company picnics, aren't the time or the place to sink your career by making some injudicious comment or by making a fool of yourself. Managing most social encounters involves art and skill, especially those encounters that involve colleagues. If you have to attend such functions, then make them work to your advantage. Use these techniques at your next company party:

✔ Use the middle of the room to intercept individuals whom you especially want to speak to. As an alternative strategy for getting their attention, watch the hors d'oeuvres table or the punch bowl. Go for refills when the person you are seeking does so.

✔ Drink orange juice or mineral water. Never ever get drunk on the organisation's premises, in the organisation's time, or at an organisational social function.

✔ Keep discussion loose and light and avoid discussing work topics with anyone other than your boss. Try to move on before the person you're speaking to runs out of topics to discuss and has a blank expression. Don't fawn or brown-nose. These behaviours are more likely to lose respect for you than to gain it.

✔ Leave the social function only after the departure of the highest-ranking company official. If you have to leave before, let that person know why.

Manage your manager

Successful managers know the importance of managing not just their employees, but their manager as well. The idea is to encourage your manager to do what most directly benefits you and your staff. The following tried-and-tested techniques for manager management have evolved through the ages:

✔ **Keep your manager informed of your successes:** 'That last sale puts me over quota for the month.'

✔ **Support your manager in meetings:** 'Gadsby is right on this. We really do have to consider the implications of this change for our customers.'

✔ **Praise your manager publicly:** 'Ms Gadsby is probably the best manager I have ever worked for.'

Although a well-controlled relationship with your manager is important, you need connections to those above your manager too. A key relationship to develop is with your manager's manager – an individual who is likely to have a very big influence on your future career.

Volunteer for an assignment that happens to be one of your manager's boss's pet projects. If you do a good job, the senior boss may well ask you to do another project. If you don't have an opportunity like a pet project, try to find an area of common interest with your manager's boss. Bring up the topic in casual conversation and agree to meet later to discuss it in more detail. But do make sure that you keep your own integrity, though; you don't want to give the impression that you're cavalier with the organisation's ranks, hierarchies, and ways of working.

Move ahead with your mentors

Having a mentor is almost essential for ensuring any long-term success within an organisation. A *mentor* is an individual – usually someone higher up in the organisation – who provides advice and helps to guide your progress. (See Chapter 20 for an in-depth discussion about mentors.) Mentors are necessary because they can offer you important career advice, as well as becoming your advocate to higher levels of the organisation – the levels that you don't have direct access to.

Make sure the person you select as your mentor (or who selects you, as is more often the case) has organisational clout and is vocal about touting your merits. If possible, get the support of several powerful people throughout the organisation. *Sponsorships* (your relationships with your mentors) develop informally over an extended period of time.

Seek out a mentor by finding an occasion to ask for advice. If you find the advice extremely helpful, frequently seek more advice from the same person. Initially, ask for advice related to your work, but as time goes on, you can ask for advice about business in general and your career advancement specifically. Proceed slowly, or your intentions may be suspect. Always display tact and discretion in your approach to your mentor:

- ✔ **The wrong approach:** 'Mr Fairmont, I've been thinking. In the marketing department, a lot of bad rumours have been going around about you and Suzy. I could try to squash some of them if I see something in it for me. You know: You take care of me, and I take care of you. What do you say?'

- ✔ **The right approach:** 'Here's that special report you asked for, Ms Smith. Correlating customer colour preferences with the size of orders in the Eastern region was fascinating. You seem to be one of the most forward-looking people in this organisation.'

Be trustworthy

Similar to having a mentor is being a loyal follower of an exceptional performer within the organisation. Finding good people to trust can be difficult, so if you're trustworthy, you're likely to become a valued associate of a bright peer. As that person rises quickly through the organisation, she can bring you along. However, whenever possible, make sure that you have many connections – when people fall, they fall very quickly and you don't want your protégé taking you with them.

Protecting Yourself

Inevitably, you may find yourself on the receiving end of someone else's political aspirations. Astute managers take precautions to protect themselves – and their employees – against the political manoeuvrings of others. These precautions can also help if your own strategies go wrong. What can you do to protect yourself?

Document for protection

Document the progress of your department's projects and activities, especially when expected changes in plans or temporary setbacks affect your project. Documenting the changes or setbacks gives you an accurate record of your projects' history and ensures that individuals who don't have your best interests at heart don't forget what happened (or inappropriately use what happened against you). The form of the documentation can vary, but the following are most common:

- ✔ Confirmation memos
- ✔ Activity reports
- ✔ Project folders
- ✔ Correspondence files
- ✔ Notes

Don't make promises you can't keep

Avoid making promises or firm commitments for your employees when you don't want to or you can't follow them through. Don't offer a deadline, final price, or guarantee of action or quality unless you're sure you can meet it. When you make promises that you can't fulfil, you risk injuring your own reputation when deliveries are late, or costs are higher than expected. If you find yourself forced to make promises when you aren't certain you can meet them, consider taking one of the following actions:

- ✔ **Hedge:** If you have to make a firm commitment to an action that you're not sure you can meet, hedge your promise as much as possible by building in extra time, staff, money, or some other qualifier.

- ✔ **Extend time estimates:** If you have to make a time commitment that may be unrealistic, extend the estimate (add extra time to what you think you really need) to give yourself room to manoeuvre. If your employees deliver early, they're heroes.

- ✔ **Extend deadlines:** As deadlines approach, bring any problems you or your staff encounter – even the most basic ones – to the attention of the person who requested that you do the project. Keeping people informed prevents them from being surprised if you need to extend your deadlines.

Top five ethics and office politics Web sites

Wondering where to find the best information on the Web about the topics addressed in this chapter? Well, you've come to the right place! Here are our top five favourites:

✔ Business for Social Responsibility: `www.bsr.org`

✔ Ethics Resource Center: `www.ethics.org`

✔ Office Politics: `www.officepolitics.co.uk/frame.html`

✔ Corporate Social Responsibility: `www.csr.org.uk`

✔ Business.com: `www.business.com/directory/human_resources/workforce_management/office_politics`

Be visible

To get the maximum credit for the efforts of you and your staff, be sure to publicise your department's successes. To ensure that credit goes where credit is due, do the following:

✔ **Advertise your department's successes.** Routinely send reports about successfully completed projects and letters of praise for every member of your staff to your manager and to your manager's boss.

✔ **Use surrogates.** Call on your friends in the organisation to help publicise your achievements and those of your employees. Be generous in high-lighting your employees' achievements. If you highlight your own achievements at the expense of your hard-working employees, you appear tactless and boastful – and dishonest.

✔ **Be visible.** Make a name for yourself in the organisation. The best way to do that is to perform at a level that separates you from the rest of the pack. Work harder, work smarter, and respond better to the needs of the organisation and your customers, and you get noticed!

Part V
Tough Times for Tough Managers

'Look, Filligrew, this company has always insisted its employees leave their private lives at home.'

In this part . . .

No one ever said that being a manager is easy. Rewarding? Yes. Easy? No. In this part, we present strategies for managing change in the workplace, disciplining employees easily and effectively, conducting dismissals and layoffs, and taking care of yourself.

Chapter 14

Managing Change at Work

. . . .

In This Chapter

▶ Dealing with crises

▶ Processing change

▶ Helping others through change

▶ Inspiring initiative in others

▶ Moving on with your life

. . . .

*N*othing stays the same, in business or in life. Change is all around us – it always has been, and it always will be. But while many people consider change something to fear and avoid at any cost, the reality is that change brings with it excitement, new opportunities, and growth.

So what does change mean to you as a manager? The world of business is constantly changing, and the pressures on managers to perform are greater than they've ever been before. In addition, most organisations have gone from being bastions of stability and status quo in the stormy seas of change to being agile ships, navigating the fluid and ever-changing waters in which they float. 'Heywood, we have decided to reorganise the division. Starting tomorrow, you're in charge of our new factory in Singapore. I hope you like Chinese food!'

The words *business* and *change* are quickly becoming synonymous. And the more things change, the more everyone in an organisation is affected. This chapter is about managing and thriving on change and about helping your employees find ways to take advantage of change (instead of change taking advantage of them!).

Peter Drucker stated: 'One does not manage change. One leads and directs change.' So *you* have to take the initiative!

Keeping Pace

What's your typical business day like? You get into the office, grab a cup of coffee, and scan your appointment diary. Looks like a light day for meetings – two in the morning and only one in the afternoon. Maybe you can finally get a chance to work on the budget goal you've been meaning to complete for the past few months, plus have some extra time to go for a walk at lunch to unwind. Wouldn't that be nice! Next, you pick up your telephone to check your voice-mail. Of the 25 messages that have come in since you last checked, ten are urgent. When you check your e-mail, you find much the same ratio.

As you begin to think how you can respond to these urgent messages, an employee arrives with a crisis that needs your immediate attention. He tells you that the computer network has broken down, and until someone fixes it, the entire corporate financial system is in meltdown. While you're talking to your employee, your boss calls to tell you to drop everything because he's selected you to write a report for the chief executive that you absolutely have to do by the close of business today.

So much for working on your budget goal. And you can forget that relaxing walk at lunch. This day is turning out to be just another fun day in management!

Choosing between legitimate urgency and crisis management

Urgency has its place in an organisation. The rate of change in the global business environment demands it. The revolutions in computer use, telecommunications systems, and information technology demand it. The necessity to be more responsive to customers than ever before demands it. In these urgent times, companies that provide the best solutions faster than anyone else are the winners. The losers are the companies that wonder what happened as they watch their competitors streak by.

However, an organisation has a real problem when its managers manage by crisis and fall into the trap of reacting to change instead of leading change. When every problem in an organisation becomes a drop-everything-else-you're-doing crisis, the organisation isn't showing signs of responsiveness to its business environment. Instead, the business is showing signs of poor planning and lousy execution. Someone (perhaps a manager?) isn't doing their job.

Recognising and dealing with crises

Sometimes forces beyond your control as a manager cause crises. For example, suppose that a vital customer requests that you submit all project designs by this Friday instead of next Friday. Or perhaps the city sends you a notice that a maintenance crew plans to cut off the power to your plant for three days to perform essential maintenance on switching equipment. Or bad weather cuts off all flights into and out of the United Kingdom for the rest of the week.

On the other hand, many crises occur because someone in your organisation makes a mistake, and now you (the manager) have to fix everything. The following are avoidable crisis situations:

✔ Hoping that the need goes away, a manager avoids making a necessary decision. Surprise! The need didn't go away, and now you have a crisis to deal with.

✔ An employee forgets to relay an important message from your customer, and you're about to lose the account as a result. Another crisis. (See Chapter 15 for details about disciplining employees.)

✔ A colleague decides that informing you about a major change to a manufacturing process isn't important. Because of your experience, you would have quickly seen that the change was likely to lead to quality problems in the finished product. When manufacturing grinds to a halt, you come in after the fact to clean up the mess. One more crisis to add to your list.

You have to be prepared to deal with externally generated crises. You have to be flexible, you have to know your stuff, and you need to know what can go wrong. But your organisation can't afford to become a slave to internally generated crises. Managing by crisis forgoes one of the most important elements in business management. That element is *planning*.

You establish plans and goals for a reason – to make your company as successful as possible. However, if you continually set your plans and goals on the back-burner because of today's crisis, why waste your time making plans in the first place? And where does your organisation go then? (Refer to Chapter 7 for a discussion on the importance of having plans and goals.)

When you, as a manager, allow everything to become a crisis through your own inaction or failure to anticipate change, not only do you sap the energy of your employees, but eventually, they lose the ability to recognise when a real crisis exists. After responding to several manufactured crises, your employees begin to see the crises as routine, and they may not be there for you when you really need them.

Embracing Change

Change happens, and you can't do anything about it. You can try to ignore it, but does that stop change? No, you only blind yourself to what is really happening in your organisation. You can try to stop change, but does that keep change from happening? No, you're only fooling yourself if you think that you can stop change – even for a moment. You can try to insulate yourself and those employees around you from the effects of change, but can you really afford to ignore it? No, to ignore change is to sign a death warrant for your organisation and, quite possibly, for your career.

Unfortunately, from our personal observations, most managers seem to spend their entire careers trying to fight change – trying to predict and control change and its effects on the organisation. But why? Change is what allows organisations to progress, products and services to get better, and people to advance, both personally and in their careers.

 If you're in charge of leading, directing, and managing change, you give yourself the best possible chance of success by breaking down what needs to be done into the following components: change from what, to what, when, where, how, and why.

Identifying the four stages of change

Change is not a picnic. Despite the excitement that change can bring to your working life – and that's both good and bad excitement – you've probably had just about all the change you can handle right about now, thank you. But as change continues, you go through four distinct phases in response:

1. **Deny change.** When change happens, the first response you have (if you're like most people) is immediate denial. 'Whose stupid idea was that? That idea is never going to work here. Don't worry, they'll see their mistake and go back to the old way of doing things!' Operating with this attitude is like an ostrich sticking its head in the sand: If you can't see it, it goes away. You wish!

2. **Resist change.** At some point, you realise that the change isn't just a clerical error; however, this realisation doesn't mean that you have to accept the change lying down! Resistance is a normal response to change – everyone goes through it. The key is not to let your resistance get you stuck. The quicker you accept the change, the better for your organisation and the better for your career.

3. **Explore change.** By now, you know that further resistance is futile and the new way just may have some pluses. 'Well, maybe that change actually does make sense. I can see what opportunities can make the change

work for me instead of against me.' During this stage, you examine both the good and bad that come from the change, and you decide on a strategy for managing the change.

4. **Accept change.** The final stage of change is acceptance. At this point, you have successfully integrated the change into your routine. Now the change that you so vigorously denied and resisted is part of your every-day routine; the change is now the status quo.

At the end of your change responses, you come full circle, and you're ready to face your next change.

When you're asking people to face up to great changes, put it in a personal context. You can ask colleagues to think about changes in their personal lives, such as moving house, getting married/divorced, having children, or changing career. You go through exactly the same cycle when having to face changes within the organisation.

Figuring out if you're fighting change

You may be fighting change and not even know it. Besides watching the number of grey hairs on your head multiply, how can you tell? Look out for these seven deadly warning signs of resistance to change:

- ✔ **You're still using the old rules to play a new game.** Sorry to be the ones to bring you this bad news, but the old game is gone, lost forever. The pressures of global competition have created a brand new game with a brand new set of rules. For example, if you're one of those increasingly rare managers who refuses to find out how to use a computer (don't laugh, they do exist!), you're playing by the old rules. Computer literacy and information proficiency form the new rule. If you're not playing by the new rules, not only is this a warning sign that you're resisting change, but you can bet on being left behind as the rest of your organisation moves along the path to the future.

- ✔ **You're dodging new assignments.** Usually, two basic reasons cause you to avoid new assignments. First, your current job may be overwhelming you and you can't imagine taking on any more duties. If you're in this situation, try to remember that new ways often make your work more efficient or even wipe out many old things that you do. Second, you may simply be uneasy with the unknown, and so you resist change.

Dodging new assignments to resist change is an old game. One very common practice is for those who are resisting change to create present crises, and then fill the whole of their waking lives clearing up the mess – the mess that they themselves have made.

✔ **You're trying to slow things down.** Trying to slow down is a normal reaction for most people. When something new comes along – a new way of doing business, a new assignment, or a new approach to the marketplace – most people tend to want to slow down, to take the time to examine and analyse the facts, and then decide how to react. The problem is that the newer something gets, the slower some people go.

As a manager, you want to remain competitive in the future. You don't have the luxury of slowing down every time something new comes along. From now on, the amount of the new that you have to deal with is going to greatly outweigh the old. Instead of resisting the new by slowing down (and risking making your organisation uncompetitive and obsolete), you need to keep up your pace. How? When you're forced to do more with less, focus on less.

✔ **You're working hard to control the uncontrollable.** Have you ever tried to keep the sun from rising in the morning? Or tried to stop the dark clouds that drop rain, sleet, and snow on your house during a storm? Or tried to stay 29 years old forever? Face it: You just can't control many things in life – you're wasting your time if you try.

Are you resisting change by trying to control the uncontrollable at work? Perhaps you want to try to head off a planned corporate reorganisation, or stop your foreign competitors from having access to your domestic markets, or delay a much larger company acquiring your firm. The world of business is changing all around you, and you can't do anything about it. You have a choice: You can continue to resist change by pretending that you're controlling it (believe us, you can't), or you can concentrate your efforts on working out how to respond to change most effectively in order to ensure that everything works to your advantage.

✔ **You're playing the role of victim.** Oh, woe is me! This response is the ultimate cop-out. Instead of accepting change and finding out how to respond to it (and using it to the advantage of your organisation and yourself), you choose to become a victim of it. Playing the role of victim and hoping that your colleagues feel sorry for you is easy to do. ('Poor Samantha, she's got a brand new crop of upstart competitors to handle. I wonder how she can even bring herself to come to work every morning!')

But today's successful businesses can't afford to waste their time or money employing victims. If you're not giving 100 per cent each day that you go to work, your organisation may well find someone who can.

✔ **You're hoping someone else can make things better for you.** In the old-style hierarchical organisation, top management almost always took responsibility for making the decisions that made things better (or worse) for workers. We have a newsflash: The old-style organisation is changing, and the new-style organisation that is taking its place has empowered every employee to take responsibility for decision making.

Global competition, information systems and technology, and the need for flexibility and responsiveness all require you to make decisions more quickly than ever. In other words, the employees closest to the issues must make the decisions; a manager who is seven layers up from the front line and 3,000 miles away can't do it. You hold the keys to your future. You have the power to make things better for yourself. If you wait until someone else makes things better for you, you're going to be waiting an awfully long time.

✔ **You're absolutely paralysed, like a rabbit in the headlights.** This condition is the ultimate sign of resistance to change and is almost always terminal. Sometimes change seems so overwhelming that the only choice is to give up. When change paralyses you, not only do you fail to respond to change, but also you can no longer perform your current duties. In today's organisation, such resistance is certain death.

Instead of allowing change to paralyse you, become a leader of change. Here are some ideas for how to do this:

- Embrace the change. Become its friend and its biggest cheerleader.

- Be flexible and be responsive to the changes that swirl all around you and through your organisation.

- Be a model to those employees around you who continue to resist change. Show them that they can make change work for them instead of against them.

- Focus on what you can do – not what you can't do.

- Recognise and reward employees who have accepted the change and who have succeeded as a result.

If you notice any of these warning signs of resistance to change – in yourself or in your colleagues – you can do something about it. As long as you're willing to embrace change instead of fighting it, you hold incredible value for your organisation, and you can take advantage of change rather than falling victim to it. Make responsiveness to change your personal mission: Be a leader of change, not a follower of resistance.

Aiding Your Employees through Change

When your organisation finds itself in the midst of change – whether because of fast-moving markets, changing technology, rapidly shifting customer needs, or some other reason – you need to remember that change affects everyone, not just you as a manager. And although some of your employees can cope with change with hardly a hiccup, others may have a very difficult time adjusting to their new environment and the expectations that come along with it. Be on the alert for employees who are resisting or having a hard time dealing with change, and then help them make the transition through the process.

The following tips can help your employees cope with change on the job:

- **Show that you care.** Managers are very busy people, but don't ever be too busy to show your employees that you care – especially when they're having difficulties at work. Take a personal interest in your employees and offer to help them in any way you can.

- **Widely communicate the potential for change.** Nothing is more disconcerting to employees than being surprised by changes that they didn't expect. As much as possible, give your employees a full briefing on potential changes in the business environment, and keep them up to date on the status of the changes as time goes on.

- **Seek feedback.** Let your employees know that you want their feedback and suggestions on how to deal with potential problems resulting from change, or about how to capitalise on any opportunities that may result.

- **Be a good listener.** When your employees are in a stressful situation, they naturally are going to want to talk about it – this part of the process helps them cope with change. Set aside time to chat informally with employees, and encourage them to voice their concerns about the changes that they and the organisation are going through.

- **Don't give false assurances.** Although you don't want to needlessly frighten your employees with tales of impending doom and gloom, you must tell them the truth. Be frank and honest with your employees and treat them like the adults they are.

- **Involve employees.** Involve employees in planning for upcoming changes, and delegate the responsibility and authority for making decisions to them whenever practicable.

- **Look to the future.** Paint a vision for your employees that emphasises the many ways in which the organisation can be a better place as everyone adapts to change and begins to use it to their benefit.

Change can be traumatic for the people who are experiencing it. Stay alert to the impact of change on your employees, and help them work their way through it. Not only will your employees appreciate your support, showing their appreciation with loyalty to you and your organisation, but also morale will improve and your employees will be more productive as a result.

Encouraging Employee Initiative

One of the most effective ways to help employees make it through a change process in one piece is to give them permission to take charge of their own work. You can encourage your employees to take the initiative in coming up with ideas to improve the way they do their work, and then to implement those ideas.

The most successful organisations are the ones that actively encourage employees to take the initiative, and the least successful ones are those organisations that stifle initiative.

So make sure that everyone knows what you are trying to achieve, and then get everyone involved. The following examples illustrate effective and not-so-effective strategies for managing change:

- ✔ **VXR Radio:** VXR Radio, a commercial music station, gave notice that its broadcasting equipment was to be replaced and upgraded. It required all staff to train fully and effectively in the new equipment so that when switch-over day came, there were no glitches or hiccups. One shift manager accordingly scheduled all of her staff on training courses provided by the manufacturers of the new equipment over the three months' lead time. When the changeover came, her people transferred smoothly and effortlessly. They were involved in the new processes right from the start, they were fully familiar with the machinery and they knew how to operate it to broadcast standard.

- ✔ *The Times* **and** *The Sun* **versus** *Financial Times*: After the revolution in newspaper printing in the United Kingdom, many newspapers moved from traditional printing presses and technology in Fleet Street to new premises in Wapping. This led to major conflict at News Corp, the owners of *The Times* and *The Sun* newspapers. For many weeks fighting occurred outside printing establishments, with journalists, managers, and printers victimised, harassed, and beaten up.

  Contrast with this with the experience of the *Financial Times*, whose staff also moved to premises in Wapping the same week without fuss, bother, or conflict. The owners of the *Financial Times* simply told staff what they required, and then left the staff to implement the changes. Top managers provided the resources, information, and reassurances necessary and the organisation achieved the move with full involvement – and no conflict whatsoever.

As a manager, you need to make your employees feel secure enough to take the initiative in their jobs. Not only does this help your employees weather the change that swirls all around them more successfully, but they also create a more effective organisation and provide better service to customers in the process. Ask your employees to take the following suggestions and put them into practice:

- ✔ Look for ways to make improvements to the status quo, and follow through with an action plan.

- ✔ Focus suggestions on areas that have the greatest impact on the organisation.

- ✔ Follow up suggestions with action – and where necessary, implement your own suggestions and recommendations.

> ✔ Use what you are doing to look for areas of improvement throughout the organisation, not just within your department or business unit.
>
> ✔ Don't make frivolous suggestions. They reduce your credibility and distract you from more important areas of improvement.

Making Changes within Yourself

If you've done everything you can to deal with change at work and take control of your business life, but you're still feeling lost, you may be facing a much deeper issue that's not readily apparent on the surface.

When you read a book, do you ever wish that you had written it? When you go to a seminar, do you ever think that you could teach it? Have you ever wondered what owning your own business is like, being your own boss and completely responsible for your company's profits or losses?

If you answered yes to any of these questions, you may not be truly happy until you pursue your dream. Maybe you want to start a new career or move to a new company. Or perhaps you have an opportunity with your current employer to make a job change that can take you to your dream. Maybe you want to go back to university to pursue an advanced degree. Or maybe you just want to take a vacation or a short leave of absence. It may very well be that all the change you need to make is within yourself.

Top five change management Web sites

Check out our top five favourite sites for managing change:

✔ Change Management Resource Library: www.change-management.org

✔ ManagementFirst: www.managementfirst.com/experts/change.htm

✔ Bernard Burnes: www.managingchange.com

✔ Change Management Learning Centre: www.change-management.com

✔ London Business School: www.lbs.ac.uk/leadership/change

Chapter 15

Employee Discipline: Setting Standards and Enforcing Them

In This Chapter

▶ Disciplining your employees

▶ Setting standards

▶ Following the twin tracks of discipline – performance and behaviour

▶ Writing a script

▶ Developing improvement plans

▶ Putting improvement plans into action

*W*ouldn't it be nice if all your employees always carried out their tasks perfectly? Wouldn't it be nice if they all loved the organisation as much as you do? The fact is that your employees do make mistakes, and some of them may exhibit attitudes that are poor. Every organisation has employees (and managers) who exhibit varying degrees of these behaviours, but don't worry too much about it. However, when your employees make repeated, serious mistakes, when they fail to meet their performance goals and standards, or when it seems that they'd rather be working somewhere else (anywhere but where they are now!) and they prove that by ignoring company policies, you have to take action to stop the offending behaviours, immediately and decisively.

When employees aren't performing up to standard, or when they allow a poor attitude to overcome their ability to pull with the rest of the team, these employees cost your organisation more than do the employees who are working at or above standard and pulling their share of the load. Poor performance and poor attitudes directly and negatively affect your work unit's efficiency and effectiveness. Also, if other employees see that you're letting their colleagues get away with poor performance, they have little reason to maintain their own standards. Not only do you create more management headaches, but also the morale and performance of your entire work unit decrease as a result.

In this chapter, you discover the importance of dealing with employee performance issues before they become major problems. You find out why you need to focus on performance and not personality. You also discover and implement a consistent system of discipline that can work for you, regardless of your line of business.

Understanding the Need for Employee Discipline

Employee discipline always has a bad name. Because of the abuses that more than a few over-zealous supervisors and managers have committed, the word *discipline* conjures up visions of crazed management tirades, embarrassing public scoldings, and worse – bullying, victimisation, discrimination, and harassment for many workers.

The reality is that far too many employees confuse the terms *discipline* and *punishment,* considering them to be one and the same. This belief can't be farther from the truth, at least when discipline is done well.

The word *discipline* comes from the Latin *disciplina,* meaning teaching or learning. In organisations, discipline comes from several sources:

- ✔ Within the individual, reflecting their personal, professional, and occupational commitment.
- ✔ Within the work group, reflecting the collective commitment and team spirit that are present.
- ✔ Within the organisation, reflecting the set and established overall standards.

Punishment, on the other hand, is derived from the Latin root *punire,* which itself derives from the Latin word *poena,* or penalty. Interestingly, the English word *pain* also found its beginnings in the Latin *poena.*

The whole point of this little digression is that employee discipline ought to be a positive experience. At least when you do it the right way! Through discipline, you bring small concerns to your employees' attention so that they can take actions to correct them before they become major problems.

The primary goal of discipline isn't to punish your employees; you want to help guide them back to a satisfactory job performance. Of course, sometimes this step isn't possible, and you have no choice but to dismiss employees who can't perform satisfactorily. However, dismissal is the very last resort, and you only use it when all other options are exhausted.

Two main reasons to discipline your employees exist:

- **Performance problems:** All employees must meet goals as part of their jobs. For a receptionist, a goal may be always to answer the telephone on the second ring or sooner. For a sales manager, a goal may be to increase annual sales by 15 per cent. When employees fail to meet their performance goals, you have to administer some form of discipline.

- **Behaviour and misconduct:** Sometimes employees behave in ways that neither you as a manager nor the organisation can accept. For example, if an employee abuses the company sick leave policy, you have a valid reason for disciplining that employee. And you must always discipline employees who sexually harass or threaten other employees.

In practice, discipline ranges from simple verbal exchanges – 'William, your report was a day late. You must submit future reports on time' – to more serious matters, handled formally – 'Sorry, Mahmood, I warned you that I can't tolerate any further insubordination. I'm now treating this as a formal disciplinary matter.' A wide variety of options lies between these two extremes, the use of which depends on the nature of the problem, its severity, and the work history of the employee involved. For example, if the problem is an isolated incident and the employee normally performs well, the discipline you dish out is less severe than if the problem is repeated and persistent.

Always carry out discipline as soon after the relevant incident as possible. As with rewarding employees, your message is much stronger and more relevant when it has the immediacy of a recent event. If too much time lapses between an incident and the discipline that you conduct afterwards, your employee may forget the specifics of the incident. Not only that, but you also send the message that the problem isn't that serious because you didn't bother doing anything about it for so long.

Managers practise effective discipline when they notice performance shortcomings or misconduct before these problems become serious. Effective managers help to guide their employees along the right path. Managers who don't discipline their employees have only themselves to blame when poor performance continues unabated or acts of misconduct escalate and get out of hand. Employees need the active support and guidance of their supervisors and managers to know what the organisation expects of them. Without this guidance, employees sometimes find it difficult to keep on the right path.

Following Procedures

This part of the manager's job is quite simple – you must follow procedures! Statutory provisions and procedures cover all aspects of employee discipline, so before you do anything or tackle anyone, you must commit yourself to following whatever procedures your organisation has in place. Failure to follow your own organisation's procedure normally renders any subsequent dismissal *automatically unfair*, no matter what the employee has actually done.

Disciplinary procedures exist to protect everyone involved – you, the employee, and the organisation – and to ensure that you deal with everything in a fair, even, and impartial way.

Your company probably has its own disciplinary procedures. If it does not, the procedures that the Advisory, Conciliation and Arbitration Service (ACAS) publishes are normally deemed to apply; you must follow these standards or be prepared to give substantial reasons why you did not. If you do not follow the correct procedures, the disciplinary action you take is normally deemed in law to be automatically unfair (and this also applies to dismissal, see Chapter 16).

Your business's disciplinary procedures must meet the following criteria:

- ✔ They must be in writing, stating to whom they apply and how they are to be applied.

- ✔ The organisation must publish and issue them and make them available to all staff.

- ✔ They must consist of a series of warnings, both oral and written.

- ✔ They must give examples of gross misconduct that triggers summary dismissal when proved (see the section 'Dealing with misconduct: The second track', later in this chapter). In addition, your procedures must allow employees to be accompanied and/or represented when they are facing disciplinary matters; and all procedures must allow for an appeals process, even where summary dismissal is the outcome.

Managers and supervisors need to know the disciplinary procedures, what they can and cannot do and when and where to go for help. Your organisation should train and brief all employees in the content of the procedures so that they understand the triggers for disciplinary action for both behaviour and performance issues.

When facing a disciplinary issue, employees are entitled to respond to your statement of the facts and to state their own case. If you are accusing employees of a serious breach of conduct or performance, they are entitled to face their accusers and refute the charges (if they can).

The law requires disciplinary warnings to include a clear statement of what is wrong; what needs to happen now and by when; how, when, where, and by whom progress is to be checked; and any further follow-up action deemed necessary.

Focusing on Performance, Not Personalities

You're a manager (or a manager-to-be). You're not a psychiatrist or a psychologist – even if you feel that you sometimes do nothing but give counselling to your employees. Your job isn't to analyse your workers' personalities or to attempt to understand why your employees act the way they do – no one can read minds about things like attitude. Your job *is* to assess your employees' performance against the standards that you and your employees agree to and to be alert to employees' violations of company policy. If your employees are performing above standard, reward them for their efforts. (Refer to Chapter 5 for more information on rewarding and motivating your employees.) If, on the other hand, they're performing below standard, you need to find out why (possibly a process, motivation, or training problem is out of a particular employee's control) and, if necessary, discipline them.

We're not saying that you shouldn't be compassionate. Sometimes employees' performance suffers because of family problems, financial difficulties, or other pressures unrelated to the job. Although you can give your employees the opportunity to get through their difficulties – you may suggest some time off or a temporary reassignment of duties – they eventually have to return to meeting their performance standards.

If personal problems or other difficulties are overwhelming an employee, you need to encourage her to seek confidential help from professional sources, through your organisation's employee assistance or support programme, occupational health department, or other professional support. It's not your job as a manager to tackle this yourself; it is your job to see that the employee is properly supported.

To be fair, and to be sure that discipline focuses on performance and not on personalities, ensure that all employees fully understand company policies and that you communicate these policies clearly. When your organisation takes on new employees, make sure they get an induction to key company policies. When your human resources representative drops off new employees at your office door, take the time to discuss your department's philosophy and practices. Periodically sit down with your employees to review and update their performance standards.

When you apply discipline, use it consistently and fairly. Always follow procedures. Although you must always discipline your employees as soon as possible after a shortfall in performance or act of misconduct, rushing to judgement before you have all the facts is a mistake. Take time out to investigate where doing so is necessary or desirable; and you must investigate fully when you are dealing with allegations of serious or gross misconduct. When you do confront employees with their misdemeanours, ask a clear question: 'Can you give me an explanation?'

You need to treat all employees exactly the same, regardless of seniority, occupation, length of service, or hours worked. Not to do so simply invites trouble, in the form of action (potentially including legal action) that an employee may take against you, or lobbying from those whom you have treated more harshly.

Identifying the Two Tracks of Discipline

Two key reasons exist for disciplining employees: performance problems and misconduct (see the section 'Understanding the Need for Employee Discipline', earlier in this chapter). The twin-track system of discipline includes one set of discipline options for performance problems and another for misconduct. These tracks reflect the fact that misconduct, usually an employee's wilful act, is a much more serious transgression than a shortfall in performance. Performance problems often aren't the employee's direct fault and you can usually correct them with proper training or motivation.

These two tracks reflect the concept of *progressive discipline*. Progressive discipline means that you always select the least severe step that results in the change in behaviour or performance that you want.

You must have disciplinary procedures, and these must be available to all employees. Disciplinary procedures must state the nature of warnings and sanctions, and how long any warning is to remain on file. Disciplinary procedures are used as the basis of recording the nature of the misdemeanour, the actions taken, and the outcomes.

All warnings must be formally notified to the employee, whatever the eventual outcome. For example, if your employee responds to a verbal warning and improves as a result, then you can move on to your next management challenge. However, if the employee doesn't respond to a verbal warning, you then progress to the next step – reconvening the disciplinary matter with the view to issuing a written warning.

So, as you prepare to discipline your employees, first decide whether you're trying to correct performance-related behaviour or misconduct. Then decide the best way to get your message across. If the transgression is minor – a lack of attention to detail, for example – you may only need to conduct a short conversation. Anything more serious, requiring formal disciplinary action, requires you to notify the employee of that action in writing – (again!) follow the procedures!

Dealing with performance problems: The first track

If you've done your job right, each of your employees has a job description and a set of performance standards. The job description is simply an inventory of all the different duties that accompany a particular position. Performance standards, on the other hand, are the measurements that you and your employees agree to use in assessing your employees' performance. Performance standards form the basis of periodic performance appraisals and reviews.

Although every organisation seems to have its own unique way of conducting performance assessments, employees usually fall into one of three broad categories:

- ✔ Outstanding performance
- ✔ Acceptable performance
- ✔ Unacceptable performance

When it comes to employee discipline, you're primarily concerned with correcting unacceptable performance. You always want to help your good employees become even better employees, but your first concern has to be to identify employees who aren't working up to standard and to correct their performance shortcomings.

Many organisations have procedures to deal with poor performance that are separate from their approaches to bad behaviour and misconduct. Again, whichever is the case in your organisation, you must enforce the procedures fairly and evenly. Again, if you get as far as the formal stages in managing unacceptable performance, you must state your case in writing; allow the employee to respond; allow the employee to be accompanied or represented; and make a clear statement about what is to happen as a result of the particular case.

The following disciplinary actions are listed in order of least to most severe. Don't forget: Use the least severe step that results in the behaviour you want. If that step doesn't do the trick, move down the list to the next step:

- ✔ **Verbal guidance, counselling, and support:** This form of discipline is certainly the most common step that managers take first when they want to correct an employee's performance. A manager verbally counsels a variety of employees many times a day. Verbal counselling can range from a simple, spontaneous correction performed in the corridor ('Jasmine, you need to let me know when our clients call with a service problem') to a more formal, sit-down meeting in your office ('Sam, I am concerned that you don't understand the importance of checking the correct address prior to shipping orders. Let's discuss what steps you're going to take to correct this problem and your plan to implement them').

Some organisations treat this discussion as an informal warning, particularly if the individual has had many instances of verbal guidance and counselling without a visible improvement in performance. You may, or may not, choose to put a file note on the individual's personnel file (not forgetting that the employee has a right to see what's in their file); you ought, in any case, to make a note in your own diary of who you spoke to, and what you spoke about.

✔ **Written counselling:** When employees don't respond favourably to verbal counselling, or when the magnitude of performance problems warrants a different approach, consider written counselling. Written counselling formalises the counselling process by documenting your employees' performance shortcomings in a written memo. The supervisor presents written counselling to an employee in a one-to-one session. After the employee has an opportunity to read the document, you can discuss the employee's plans to improve her performance. This documentation becomes a part of your employee's personnel file.

✔ **Moves and transfers:** If, with the best will in the world, a particular employee is simply not getting the hang of the job, then a move to new duties may be best for all concerned. Consult with the employee and see what she thinks. However, if she is perfectly happy struggling with the job, you nevertheless have to make it clear that this situation can only go on for so long. Put a clear time limit on when the performance has to improve; and make it clear that, if no improvement is forthcoming, the two of you are going to have to sit down and make alternative plans. In all cases, support the employee as much as you can and give her the best possible chance to improve.

✔ **Dismissal:** When all else fails, dismissal is the ultimate form of discipline for employees who are performing unsatisfactorily. As any manager who has fired an employee knows, dismissing employees isn't fun. Consider it as an option only after you exhaust all other avenues.

Perhaps needless to say, in these days of unfair and wrongful dismissal and high levels of compensation, you must document employees' performance shortcomings very well and support them with facts. For further information on the ins and outs of this important form of discipline, see Chapter 16.

Dealing with misconduct: The second track

Misconduct is a wholly different animal from performance problems, so it has its own discipline track. Although both misconduct and performance problems can have negative effects on a company's bottom line, misconduct is usually considered to be much more serious than performance shortcomings because it indicates a problem with your employees' attitudes or ethics. And modifying performance behaviours is a great first step in eventually modifying workers' attitudes or belief systems.

Misconduct covers any aspect of employee behaviour. What constitutes misconduct varies between organisations and occupations, and managers have to make their own judgement on this, within the constraints of the given situation. It is usual to specify:

- ✔ **Serious misconduct,** such as persistent bad timekeeping or frequent absenteeism, which is likely to lead to sanctions and/or dismissal if the employee does not remedy it.

- ✔ **Gross misconduct,** which normally leads to dismissal when proved. Organisations normally have to provide written examples of what constitutes gross misconduct in their disciplinary procedures (see the section 'Following Procedures', earlier in this chapter). The usual examples are bullying, victimisation, discrimination, and harassment; physical and verbal violence and abuse; fraud and theft; and misusing drugs and alcohol.

The discipline that results from misconduct has much more immediate consequences for your employees than does the discipline that results from performance problems. Although performance may take some time to bring up to standard – what with preparing a plan, scheduling additional training, and so forth – misconduct has to stop right now! When you discipline your employees for misconduct, you put them on notice that you don't tolerate their behaviour.

Your organisation's disciplinary procedure must incorporate at least two levels of warning, verbal and written, to meet statutory requirements. Make sure that you adhere to this procedure. The only exceptions are for serious or gross misconduct, in which case you may proceed to a final warning or to dismissal where the case against the employee is proved.

As in the first track, you have a progressive approach from least to most severe. Your choice depends on the nature of the misconduct; and the employee's work record may also influence you (for example, if the employee has had recent warnings for misconduct, you may move on to the second or final warning).

- ✔ **Verbal order:** When you catch employees doing something wrong, you simply speak to them, and tell them that you don't tolerate their behaviour. This has the desired effect in the overwhelming majority of cases. If this does not work and the employee does not change her behaviour, then you are into a formal disciplinary situation, and you need to issue a formal warning.

✔ **First warning:** When an employee's misconduct is minor or a first offence, but she has not responded to verbal orders and directions, the first warning provides the least severe option for putting her on notice that you're aware of the misconduct and determined to do something about it. At each warning, the employee receives a written confirmation of her warning, together with what happens next if her behaviour or conduct does not improve. In many cases where the verbal order didn't work, a first warning is all that the situation requires.

✔ **Second warning:** Unfortunately, not all your employees get the message when you give them a first warning. Also, the magnitude of the offence may require that you skip the first warning and proceed directly to the second or even final warning – this applies especially to persistent breaches of health and safety guidelines, or disrespectful conduct that falls immediately short of outright harassment. All written warnings signal to your employee that you're serious and that you're documenting her behaviour for her personnel file.

✔ **Final warning:** Where, despite all your best efforts, behaviour and conduct are not improving, you proceed to a final warning. The final warning states clearly that if behaviour and conduct do not improve, dismissal is your next option. Make it clear in the final warning who will review the employee's conduct and behaviour, when, and where, and make sure that you stick to this timetable.

✔ **Suspension:** Where serious allegations are made against an individual, it is usual to suspend them from work while you conduct an investigation. Suspension should normally be on full pay; the employee is after all innocent until proved guilty. If you do suspend someone without pay, you must have substantial reasons for doing so and be prepared to give those reasons in writing.

✔ **Dismissal:** In particularly serious cases of misconduct, dismissal may be your first choice in disciplining a worker. This rule is particularly true for extreme violations of safety rules, theft, gross insubordination, and other gross misconduct. Dismissal may also be the result of repeated misconduct that less severe discipline steps don't correct. See Chapter 16 for more information about dismissing employees.

Disciplining Employees: A Suite in Five Parts

One right way and many wrong ways to discipline employees exist. Forget the many wrong ways for now and focus on the right way. Whatever the disciplinary situation you are facing, follow your organisation's procedures and document everything.

Structure your approach around the five steps outlined in the following sections. By following these steps, you can be sure that your employees understand what the problem is, why it exists, and what they need to do to correct its.

Describing the unacceptable behaviour

Make clear exactly what your employee is doing that is unacceptable. When describing unwanted behaviour to an employee, make sure that you're excruciatingly specific. Don't make vague statements such as 'You have a bad attitude,' or 'You make a lot of mistakes' or 'I don't like your work habits'.

Always relate unacceptable behaviour to specific performance standards that the employee hasn't met or to specific policies that the employee has broken. Specify exactly what the employee did wrong and when the behaviour occurred. And don't forget to focus on the behaviour and not on the individual.

Following are some examples of describing behaviour for you to consider:

- ✔ Your performance last week was below the acceptable standard of 250 units per week.
- ✔ You failed the drug test you took on Monday.
- ✔ The last three analyses you submitted to me contained numerous mathematical errors.
- ✔ You have been late to work three out of four days this week.

Expressing the impact to the work unit

When an employee engages in unacceptable behaviour – whether her work doesn't meet the organisation's standards or she engages in misconduct – the behaviour typically affects the work unit negatively. When an employee is consistently late to work, for example, you may have to have someone else to cover that employee's position until the offender finally turns up. Doing so takes your other employee away from the work that she should be doing, reducing the efficiency and effectiveness of the work unit. And if an employee engages in sexual harassment, if you don't immediately do something about it, you are in fact tolerating it, which can lead to legal action being taken against you as an employer.

Continuing with the examples that we use in the preceding section, following are the next steps in your discipline script:

- ✔ Because of your below-standard performance, the work unit didn't meet its overall targets for the week.
- ✔ This specifically breaks our drug-free workplace policy.
- ✔ Because of these errors, I now have to take extra time to check your work before I can forward it onwards.
- ✔ Because of your lateness, I had to pull Helen from her position to cover yours.

Specifying the required changes

Telling your employee that she did something wrong does little good if you don't also tell that employee what she needs to do to correct the behaviour. As a part of your discipline script, tell your employee the exact actions that you want her to adopt. Tell the employee that her behaviour must be in accordance with an established performance standard or company policy.

Following are some examples of the third part of your discipline script:

- ✔ You must bring your performance up to the standard of 250 units per week or better immediately.
- ✔ You are required to set an appointment with the company's employee assistance programme for drug rehabilitation.
- ✔ I expect your work to be error free before you submit it to me for approval.
- ✔ I expect you to be in your seat, ready to work, at 9 a.m. every morning.

Outlining the consequences

Of course, if the unacceptable behaviour continues, you need to have a discussion with the employee about the consequences. Make sure that you get your message across clearly and unequivocally and that your employee understands it.

Here are some possibilities for the fourth part of your script:

- ✔ If you can't meet the standard, I'll send you for further training to improve your skills.
- ✔ If you refuse to undergo drug rehabilitation, you are incapable of working effectively, and this may eventually lead to your dismissal.

✔ If the accuracy of your work doesn't improve immediately, I'll have to issue a written note to be placed on your employee file.

✔ If you're late again, I will request that the general manager convene a formal disciplinary hearing in your case.

Providing emotional support

Give your employee an emotional boost by expressing your support for her efforts. Make this support sincere and heartfelt – you do after all want your employee to improve, don't you?

Work to build a strong foundation of positive aspects and trust that you can draw on when dealing with the negatives:

✔ You have, after all, worked here for a very long time.

✔ You've never been in any trouble before.

✔ You usually show a great commitment to everything that you do.

And finally, accentuate the positive:

✔ But let's try to avoid that – I know you can do better!

✔ I really want this to work out, so let's find you the help you need.

✔ Can I do anything to help you overcome this situation?

✔ We can avoid that situation – I'm counting on you to turn this around!

Putting it all together

After you develop the five parts of your discipline script, put them together into a unified statement that you deliver to your wayward employees. Although you undoubtedly discuss the surrounding issues in some detail when you meet, make the script the heart of your discipline session.

The five parts of the script work together to produce the final product as follows:

✔ Your performance last week was below our standard of 250 units per week. Because of your below-standard performance, the work unit didn't meet its overall targets for the week. You must bring your performance up to the standard of 250 units per week or better immediately. If you can't meet the standard, I'll send you for further training to improve your skills. But let's try to avoid that – I know you can do better!

✔ You failed the drug test you took on Monday. This specifically breaks our drug-free workplace policy. You are required to make an appointment with the company's employee assistance programme for drug rehabilitation. If you refuse to undergo drug rehabilitation, you are incapable of working effectively, and this may eventually lead to your dismissal. I really want this to work out, so let's find you the help you need.

✔ The last three analyses you have submitted to me contained numerous mathematical errors. Because of these errors, I now have to take extra time to check your work much more thoroughly before I can forward it onwards. I expect your work to be error free before you submit it to me for approval. If the accuracy of your work doesn't improve immediately, I'll have to issue a written note to be placed on your employee file. Can I do anything to help you avoid that outcome?

✔ You have been late to work three out of four days this week. Because of your lateness, I had to pull Helen from her position to cover yours. I expect you to be in your seat, ready to work, at 9 a.m. every morning. If we should be aware of any special circumstances, please say so now. Otherwise, if you're late again, I will request that the general manager convene a formal disciplinary hearing in your case. We can avoid that situation – I'm counting on you to turn this around!

Making a Plan for Improvement

Managers love plans – plans for completing projects on time, plans for meeting the organisation's financial goals in five years, and plans to develop more plans. In the case of employee discipline, one more plan exists. The *performance improvement plan* is a crucial part of the discipline process because it sets definite steps for the employee to undertake to improve performance within a fixed period.

If your employee's performance transgressions are minor and you're giving only verbal counselling and guidance, working up a performance plan is probably overkill. Also, because employees must correct most instances of misconduct right now or else face the consequences, performance improvement plans generally aren't appropriate for correcting employee misconduct. However, if your employee's poor performance is habitual and you've started the disciplinary procedure, a performance plan is definitely what the doctor ordered.

A performance improvement plan consists of the following three parts:

✔ **Goal statement:** The goal statement provides clear direction to your employees about what it takes to achieve a satisfactory improvement. The goal statement, which is tied directly to your employee's performance standards, may be something along the lines of 'Completes all her assignments on or before agreed deadlines' or 'Is at his station ready to work at exactly 9 a.m. every day.'

✔ **Schedule for attainment:** What good is a plan without a schedule? Not having a schedule is like eating an ice-cream cone without the ice cream or like watching television with the sound turned off. Every good plan needs a definite completion date, with fixed milestones along the way if the plan for goal attainment is complex.

✔ **Required resources/training:** The performance improvement plan must also contain a summary of any additional resources or training that can be brought to bear to help employees bring their performance up to scratch.

Figure 15-1 shows a sample performance improvement plan for a worker who makes repeated errors in typed correspondence.

Performance Improvement Plan

Jack Smith

Goal statement:

★ Complete all drafts of typed correspondence with two or fewer mistakes per document.

Schedule for attainment:

★ Jack must meet the above goal within three months after the date of this plan.

Required resources/training:

★ Jack will be enrolled in the company refresher course in typing and reviewing correspondence. This training must be successfully completed no later than two months after the date of this plan.

Figure 15-1: A sample performance improvement plan.

Implementing the Improvement Plan

After you put performance improvement plans in place, your job is to ensure that they don't just gather dust on your employees' shelves. Follow up with your employees to make sure that they're acting on their plans and making progress towards the goals you both agreed to. Yes, following up on improvement plans takes time, but that time is well spent. Besides, if you can't find the time to check your employees' progress on their improvement plans, don't be surprised if they can't find the time to work on them.

Check that your employees are following through with the goal statements you agreed to, that they're keeping to their schedules, and that they're receiving the training and other resources you agreed to provide. If not, you need to emphasise the importance of the improvement plans with your employees and work with them to figure out why they haven't implemented them as agreed.

Top five discipline Web sites

Wondering where to find the best information on the Web about the topics addressed in this chapter? Well, you've come to the right place! Here are our top five favourites:

- Croner: `www.croner.com/discipline`

- Trades Union Congress: `www.tuc.org.uk//performance`

- Employee Discipline: Building Blocks for Success: `www.shrm.org/consultants/library/HRM0502.pdf`

- Advisory, Conciliation and Arbitration Service (ACAS): `www.acas.org.uk/disciplinary procedures/procedures/discipline`

- Sanyo UK (A model of concise disciplinary (and other) staff management procedures): `www.palgrave.com/rpettinger/sanyostaff handbook`

To assist your employees in implementing their improvement plans, schedule regular progress reporting meetings with them on a daily, weekly, or monthly basis. More extensive improvement plans necessitate more frequent follow-up. Progress meetings serve two functions.

- They provide you with the information you need to assess your employees' progress towards meeting their plans.

- They demonstrate to your employees, clearly and unequivocally, that their progress is important to you. If you demonstrate that the plans are important to you, your employees can make the plans a priority in their busy schedules.

Set up performance improvement plans with your employees and stick with them. One of the most difficult challenges of management is dealing with a poor performer who improves when under scrutiny and then lapses again. Stick with your plan. If an employee can't maintain the necessary performance standards, then you may want to consider whether she is really suited for continued employment with your organisation.

Chapter 16

Resignations, Dismissals, and Redundancies

In This Chapter

▶ Understanding the various kinds of dismissal

▶ Taking necessary precautions before dismissing an employee

▶ Firing employees: A step-by-step approach

▶ Deciding at what time to dismiss employees

*B*eing a manager is a tough job. And of all the tough jobs that managers have to do, firing employees has to be the absolute toughest. No matter how many times you fire someone, dismissing an employee is never a pleasant thing to do.

The mechanics of what you have to do before you dismiss an employee – setting goals, gathering data, assessing performance, carrying out discipline, and completing the paperwork – aren't so tough. The tough part is all the emotional baggage that goes along with firing someone, especially someone you've worked with for a while and have shared good and bad times with. However, no matter how difficult it is, telling an employee that you no longer need his services is sometimes your only option.

This chapter deals with the reasons employees are dismissed and why they resign, the different kinds of dismissals, and exactly how you can carry them out. You discover the difference between a redundancy and a dismissal, as well as the importance of following procedures and having documentation to support your actions.

Accepting Resignations

Employees have many reasons to resign from their jobs. You may find the thought that anyone voluntarily chooses to leave your particular brand of workers' paradise hard to believe, but leave they do, and for all kinds of reasons. Sometimes employees find better promotional or pay opportunities with another firm. Sometimes employees find themselves in dead-end work situations or leave because of personality conflicts with their manager or other employees. Sometimes employees leave because of emotional stress, family needs, alcohol dependency, or other personal reasons. Following are the main ways employees leave voluntarily:

- ✔ **Resignation:** Resignation occurs when an employee decides to leave his position with your firm with no prodding or suggestion to do so from you. Unfortunately, the best employees always seem to be the ones who resign. Although you can't force someone to stay with your organisation forever (nor would you want to), you can make sure that people aren't leaving because your organisation isn't adequately addressing problems. A certain department experiencing a high turnover of staff, for example, is a warning sign that work conditions are too stressful, or that you may have a bad manager or supervisor in the position. Conducting exit interviews with leavers can be a particularly useful tool for uncovering problems that you need to address. Don't let employees leave without first asking them why they decided to resign, and what the organisation can do better.

- ✔ **Resignation (encouraged):** An encouraged resignation occurs when you suggest to an employee that he leave his job. Such resignations are often used as face-saving measures for employees who you are about to fire. Instead of sacking them, you can offer them the opportunity to resign. This approach can help to dampen the hurt of being fired, plus it keeps a potentially damaging incident off the employee's record. Be careful that you do this in such a way as to avoid a *constructive dismissal* (when you conduct yourself in such a way that the only course of action open to a reasonable person is to resign and leave), otherwise you'll find yourself in front of an employment tribunal. You normally only encourage people to resign when both you and they are prepared to sign a compromise agreement in which both parties agree that this is the final solution to the matter in hand.

- ✔ **Retirement:** Retirement happens when employees reach the end of their career and decide to leave finally and forever. Occasionally, organisations working to cut costs quickly offer certain employees early retirement, extending the benefits of regular retirement to those who are willing to retire from the company before they have reached the normal age to do so. Retirement is generally a happy time for all involved, marked with celebrations and tokens of the organisation's affection and gratitude (such as a plaque, a gold watch, or a very nice lunch).

Dealing with Dismissals

Dismissals are rarely as easy to deal with as resignations. Dismissals are seldom pleasant experiences – for manager or employee – and this ultimate sanction against an employee is a last resort.

Dismissals come in two types:

- ✔ **Redundancies and lay-offs:** Redundancies and lay-offs occur when an organisation decides to dismiss a certain number of employees for financial reasons. For example, your company loses several key contracts and the revenue that you projected was coming with them. In order to stay afloat, your firm may have no choice but to reduce payroll costs through lay-offs.

    Every company has its own policy for determining the order of lay-offs. In some organisations, the last employee hired is the first to go. In others, employee performance determines lay-offs. Most organisations give first refusal to laid-off employees for new jobs if and when the company's financial health improves.

- ✔ **Dismissal:** An organisation fires employees when these people have no hope of improving their performance, when their job descriptions need to evolve and the people in the jobs aren't able to evolve along with them, or when the employee commits an act of misconduct that is so serious that dismissal is the only choice.

Making employees redundant

Call it what you like, a reduction in workforce, downsizing, rightsizing, re-engineering, or whatever. The causes and results are still the same. Your organisation needs to reorganise its operations, or cut the payroll and related personnel and facilities costs, and some of your employees need to go.

Although understandably traumatic for those employees involved, redundancies and lay-offs are different from dismissals because the employees losing their jobs generally have done nothing wrong. They're usually good employees who follow the rules. They're productive and do their jobs. They're loyal and dedicated workers. They may even be your friends. The real blame usually lies with external factors, such as changes in markets, mergers and acquisitions, and pressures of a more competitive global marketplace; where internal factors do exist they occur normally as the result of organisational or managerial ineptitude.

Always instigate a recruitment freeze during periods of likely and possible redundancies and lay-offs; and if the organisation has vacancies, offer these positions to employees at risk of redundancy before looking elsewhere.

When it becomes apparent that redundancies and lay-offs are inevitable, you must decide how many employees are affected, who they are, and when the redundancies and lay-offs are to take place. You then need to notify and consult with everyone – those who are affected; those who may be affected; and those who aren't affected as well. Make clear the extent of the problems, and notify people that the course of action you are taking is the only way out. You must use formal channels of communication to notify all employees and their representatives, including any trade unions that your organisation recognises.

Give as much notice of redundancy as possible. You have to follow statutory limits – up to 90 days' notice where more than 20 people are being laid off – but common sense in any case dictates getting the matter out into the open as soon as possible. Once redundancies and lay-offs have been discussed at boardroom level, you may as well broadcast them anyway – this type of information always gets out quickly!

The key is getting through what is after all an organisational and business crisis without having to resort to compulsory redundancies. This is not always possible by any means, but you should try to achieve it if you possibly can.

Then follow your business's redundancy and lay-off procedure. The organisation should have codes of practice in its redundancy procedure that specify the position of and processes for:

- ✔ **Early retirement,** in which an individual is allowed to retire before they would normally do so.

- ✔ **Voluntary redundancy,** in which an individual seeks and accepts severance from the organisation on redundancy terms.

- ✔ **Compulsory redundancy,** in which the individual has to accept severance on redundancy terms.

- ✔ **Redeployment and/or transfer,** in which the individual is assigned to another job which they are capable and willing to do in another department or location.

You must make clear the basis on which selection for compulsory redundancies is made. You must not discriminate on grounds of race or religion; sex or gender; pregnancy; disability; or membership/non-membership of a trade union. Keep any recognised trade unions informed and involved of the situation regarding redundancies.

Most organisations opt for 'last in, first out' (LIFO); if you do not follow this, you must specify otherwise by job title, grade, location of work, and so forth. You must always give substantial reasons in writing for selecting particular employees for redundancy.

When you have done all these, then proceed as follows.

1. **Prepare a final list of employees to be laid off.**

    After you turn the organisation upside down to find potential savings, you need to prepare a list of employees to be laid off. Write the list in rank order in the event of a change that may allow you to remove employees from the list. Consider your employees' experience and how long they've been with the organisation if you possibly can. This reinforces the need to make clear who is to be laid off on a basis that you can substantiate for business reasons. And be careful not to discriminate.

2. **Notify affected employees.** By now, many employees are probably paralysed with the fear that they're being made redundant. As soon as you finish developing the lay-off list – updating it to account for employees who may already have found new jobs on their own – notify the affected employees. Private, one-to-one meetings are the best way to handle notification of redundancy.

3. **Provide outplacement services to redundant employees.** If time and money permit, provide outplacement and counselling support to the employees you are laying off. Your organisation can provide training in subjects, such as CV and application writing, financial planning, interviewing, and networking, and allow the employees to use company-owned computers, fax machines, and telephones in their job searches. If you can help your employees by providing job leads or contacts, by all means do so.

4. **Make the redundancies.** Conduct one-to-one redundancy meetings with employees to finalise arrangements and complete redundancy paperwork. Explain the redundancy package, continuation of benefits, and any other company-sponsored redundancy programmes as appropriate. Collect keys, identification badges, and any company-owned equipment and property. Escort (you can do this personally, or have a security guard or human resources representative fill the role) your newly redundant, former employees off the premises and wish them well.

5. **Rally the survivors.** Rally your remaining employees together in an all-hands meeting to let them know that, now that the lay-offs are complete, the firm is back on the road to good financial health. Tell the team that, to avoid future lay-offs, you have to pull together to overcome this immediate downturn in the business cycle.

Processing the types of dismissal

You must have procedures for dismissals and redundancies – and you must follow them. Any dismissal that the employee affected challenges in an employment tribunal is automatically found to be unfair if you don't follow the correct procedures.

Dismissal may be fair, unfair, wrongful, or constructive.

✔ **Fair:** You may dismiss anyone, at any time, for negligence and incompetence; breach of the criminal law – fraud, theft, vandalism, violence, or dishonesty; bullying, victimisation, discrimination, or harassment; other gross misconduct, examples of which ought to be itemised in the organisation's procedures; and some other substantial reason, a catch-all description because you cannot possibly specify every single set of circumstances when you may legitimately dismiss an employee. However, for a dismissal to be fair, you must have evidence of the misconduct, and you must be able to produce this at the point at which dismissal is a possibility or likelihood. You must confront the employee with the evidence, and allow him the time and opportunity to respond. You must take account of any mitigating circumstances that the employee produces. Additionally, you must allow the employee to be represented and/or accompanied at any hearing that may lead to dismissal. You must also allow an appeal. All of this needs to be itemised in the organisation's procedures; again, minimum standards along these lines are available from the Advisory, Conciliation and Arbitration Service, and these are normally deemed to apply unless you can give a good reason why not.

- ✔ **Unfair:** Dismissal is normally automatically unfair if you breach procedures as outlined in the preceding point; or if you dismiss anyone on grounds of sex/gender, race, religion, age, membership of a trade union, refusal to join a trade union, pregnancy, parenthood, or the fact that they have a conviction that is *spent,* meaning the person has served their sentence and the matter is now expunged from their record.

  This applies regardless of job or occupation, length of service, or hours worked. Even if the person has just started working for you, you may not dismiss them on any of the above grounds.

  If you nevertheless dismiss someone on any of these grounds, the dismissal is normally found to be automatically unfair and the penalties for unfair dismissal get steeper each year.

- ✔ **Wrongful:** Dismissal is wrongful if you take actions that breach the employment contract; for example, if you remove the equipment that employees need to do their job, or turn them out of their office making it impossible for them to do their job properly.

- ✔ **Constructive:** Dismissal is constructive if the actions you take against an employee mean that the only course open to that employee is to leave the organisation. When this occurs, the individual normally takes you to tribunal and seeks to prove or demonstrate their case. Constructive dismissal can include such things as encouraging bullying, victimisation, discrimination, or harassment; doing nothing about bullying, victimisation, discrimination, or harassment when it is brought to your attention; or other forms of discrimination about which you do nothing. It can also include giving people tasks that are impossible to perform; failing to deliver rewards and bonuses that you promised or indicated; and even making their working lives such a misery that *anyone* would want to leave.

Many employers go to a great deal of time and trouble to get some form of legal basis for what is otherwise a wrongful or unfair dismissal. For all the well-documented and high-profile cases (such as the bullying of female staff in City of London finance houses, or staff from ethnic minorities in several of the UK's police forces), some organisations and managers still try it on! Managers dig up every slight incident that may conceivably have occurred concerning a particular employee in the dim and distant past, and then present this as damning evidence of the employee's wrongdoing, negligence, or incompetence – anything, in fact, rather than accepting their own organisational and managerial shortcomings. Tribunals and courts do not normally entertain this approach. If you have evidence for dismissal, document it, produce it, operate according to procedures – and then you have nothing to worry about.

Gathering good reasons for firing

As long as you aren't discriminating against your employees, and as long as you follow procedures when you dismiss them, you still have quite a lot of discretion in getting rid of workers. People generally agree, however, on certain behaviours that warrant dismissal. Such behaviours include:

- ✔ **Verbal abuse of others:** Verbal abuse includes swearing, repeated verbal harassment, malicious insults, and other similar behaviour. Your employees have the right to do their jobs in a workplace free of verbal abuse. And verbal abuse of customers and other business associates is just plain bad for business. (Keep in mind, if you don't take action by quickly firing a repeat offender, you put yourself and your company at risk of grievances by those employees being harassed.)

- ✔ **Incompetence:** Despite your continued efforts to train them, some employees just aren't cut out for their jobs. If you have tried to help them and they still can't perform their duties at an acceptable level of competence, parting ways is clearly in the best interest of both the employee and the firm.

- ✔ **Repeated, unexcused lateness:** You depend on your employees to get their jobs done as scheduled. Not only does lateness jeopardise the ability of your employees to complete their tasks on time, but it also sets a very bad example for your other employees who are punctual. If certain employees continue to be late to work after you warn them that you won't tolerate this behaviour, you have clear grounds for dismissal.

- ✔ **Insubordination:** Insubordination – both *repeated insubordination* (where a minor offence occurs repeatedly) and *gross insubordination* (a single major offence) – is normally grounds for dismissal as gross misconduct. Although supervisors commonly encourage their employees to question why a decision is made, after the decision is made, the employees must carry it out. If they're unwilling to follow your direction, the basic employer – employee relationship breaks down, and you don't have to tolerate it.

- ✔ **Physical violence:** Most companies take employee-initiated physical violence and threats of violence very seriously. Employees have the right to do their jobs in a safe workplace; employers have the duty to provide a safe workplace. Physical violence jeopardises your employees' safety and distracts them from doing their jobs. Never let an employee think that you don't take a physical threat seriously – the best way to communicate that is to call the police immediately. The workplace is no place for violence or threats of violence.

✔ **Theft:** Theft of company property or of the property of colleagues, employees, or clients cannot be tolerated. Most companies that catch employees engaging in this nasty little practice dismiss them immediately and without warning. If you decide to dismiss an employee for theft, and you have concrete proof that the employee carried out the crime, you can do so knowing that you're on firm legal ground.

✔ **Intoxication at work:** Although being drunk or under the influence of drugs on the job is sufficient grounds for immediate dismissal, many companies nowadays offer their employees the option of undergoing rehabilitation with an employee assistance programme or enrolling with an organisation such as Alcoholics Anonymous. In many cases, employees can rehabilitate themselves and return to regular service.

✔ **Falsification of records:** Falsification of records is illegal; and is therefore never tolerated. This category includes providing fraudulent information during the recruitment process (universities the employee did not attend, qualifications the employee does not possess, inaccurate information about previous jobs, and so on) and producing other fraudulent information during the course of employment (fake expense reports, falsified timecards, cheating at professional or internal career path examinations, and so on).

Some of these behaviours are considered gross or serious misconduct that merit immediate dismissal with no verbal or written warning and no second chance. If you can prove that such behaviour took place or witness it, you can dismiss the employee(s) involved immediately, according to your organisation's established procedures.

Easing into Dismissal

One of the hardest tasks any manager ever has to do is to fire an employee. Dismissing an employee isn't a pleasant way to spend an afternoon. Most managers prefer doing most anything else. ('John, maybe we should go for a quick swim in the shark tank.') Although the reasons for dismissing employees are clear cut and relatively easy for managers to use as a basis for a dismissal, having that basis doesn't make the task any easier.

The next sections point out reasons you may want to dither over dismissals, then talk about exhausting alternatives.

Trying to avoid the inevitable

Your job as a manager offers plenty of examples to prove that you can't avoid the inevitable. Nevertheless, when it comes to dismissing employees, you may join the legions of managers who use one or more or the following reasons to put off having that difficult discussion:

- ✔ **Fear of the unknown:** Dismissing an employee can be a frightening prospect, especially if you're getting ready to do it for the first time. Is your employee going to cry? Have a heart attack or stroke? Get mad? Beat you up? Don't worry, most managers get worried about a first-time dismissal. If you're in that particular boat, read up on the firing process before you do it. Reading about the firing process can help provide you with both logical and emotional support. (Unfortunately, the last time never seems to come around until you retire.)

- ✔ **Emotional involvement:** Considering that you spend between a quarter and a third of your waking hours at work, becoming friends with some of your employees is natural. Doing so is fine until you have to discipline or dismiss one or more of your friends. Letting any employee go is tough enough, much less an employee with whom you have developed a personal, as well as professional, relationship.

- ✔ **Fear of a negative reflection on you:** If you have to dismiss one of your employees, what are you saying about yourself as a manager? In the case of a lay-off, is it your fault that the organisation didn't attain its goals? If you're firing an employee, did you make the wrong choice when you decided to hire that person? Many managers opt to put up with performance problems in their employees rather than draw attention to their own shortcomings, whether real or perceived.

- ✔ **Possibility of legal action:** The fear of legal action is often enough to stop the most strident of companies and their managers in their tracks. This reinforces the point that you have to have grounds for dismissal, and that you must follow the dismissal procedures.

- ✔ **Discomfort:** Many managers are reluctant to fire employees because 'they don't quite like to' or 'it's not very nice'. So they fail to tackle the problem (in which case it gets a lot worse), or they do nothing until a crisis has already broken.

Rodney Ledward was a gynaecologist who during the course of his career botched hundreds of operations, which caused untold lasting and sometimes permanent damage to many of his patients. When the case finally came to light, it quickly became apparent that Rodney Ledward's history of malpractice was widely known. However, his managers had been reluctant to tackle him because he was known to have a strident and unpleasant personality, and so tackling him would have been unpleasant!

You can, of course, hope that the problem just goes away – but don't hold your breath! Problem employees never just go away.

Few managers end up regretting firing a wayward employee too soon – far more regret not taking action more quickly when the writing is on the wall.

Working up to dismissal

Can you dismiss an employee humanely? We like to think so. If you focus on being fair and professional, you have a good chance of minimising the negative impact while making the best of a situation that's not working. Here are some guidelines that can help you make this difficult transition a little easier before getting to dismissal:

- **Give the employee the benefit of the doubt.** You need to be sure that you're giving the employee a fair chance to succeed – not necessarily an endless number of chances, but a fair chance. This idea is especially important when the employee is new. You can say something like: 'I don't know how you've been managed in the past, but I want to make it clear what we expect of you in this position so that we can agree on some mutual goals for your job.' Summarise your expectations in writing and set up a timeframe for reviewing progress on the employee's goals. Ask the employee to come to you if he has questions or needs help in meeting the expectations, and acknowledge when the employee has done some good work. Don't expect your employees to know what you want without open, two-way communication.

- **Make it clear when employees aren't meeting your expectations.** You have a much easier time dealing with problems when they're small than when they become huge. Bring up your concerns and the reasons for them being concerns. You can use a disclaimer, such as 'I know you're capable of improving in this area of your job', but you also at some point need to be clear that if improvement isn't forthcoming, the employee may lose the job. Document these discussions for clarity, reinforcement, and to provide evidence if you need it later that you have made an honest attempt to manage the employee fairly.

- **Exhaust alternative approaches to dismissal.** Some managers find it useful to try one or more attempts to get through to an employee who isn't performing well. You can discuss other opportunities that may better match the employee's abilities, for example. Or you can offer the employee a 'career day': 'Tom, I want you to take a career day tomorrow. Take the day off and don't come to work. I'm still going to pay you, but I want you to go to the beach, a museum, your kid's school, or even just watch television all day – and simply focus on one question: 'Is this job really what you want to be doing with your life right now?' Come back and give me your answer, and if you do really want to stay in your position, we have to talk about what needs to change in order for you to keep your job and not have to leave.'

✔ **Relate performance to pay.** 'Jane, we have some mutually agreed goals, but I haven't seen you actually change your behaviour or achieve any of the results we discussed. I don't like surprises, and I'm sure you don't either. So I want to make it clear that your next performance review is in a few months and if you haven't shown substantial improvement in your performance, you won't be getting a salary increase.' Typically in this approach, the person quickly falls in line or ends up leaving of her own accord – either way, you have solved your problem.

✔ **Extend probationary and trial periods.** 'Ronan, you seem dead keen on this job, but your performance is not yet up to scratch. We very much want to keep you on. However, we must extend your probationary period for a further three months, just to make sure that you really are fitting in.' Again, when you take this approach the person quickly falls into line or ends up leaving of his own accord. And if you have specified a further trial period, then make sure that you review the person's performance when the period finishes.

If you've tried and tried all of these approaches, and you still see no improvement, then you have no choice but to dismiss. That being the case, act quickly. The sooner you deal with the situation the better – for the employee, for you, and for the work group. You have to move from hoping your employees improve to looking at the evidence to see whether they are, in fact, improving. Remember, sometimes the biggest incentive you can offer your work group is to get rid of people who aren't performing, thereby sending a clear message to everyone else that the group can't afford to have anyone who isn't pulling their weight. In reality, the reaction from other employees – who often know more about a colleague's performance than anyone else in the organisation can ever hope to – is 'What took you so long?' Even during a dismissal you can still be gracious: 'I thought things would work out, but they haven't and you're going to have to leave.'

Heeding the Warning Before You Fire an Employee

Firing an employee is unpleasant enough without being dragged through the courts on a charge of unfair or wrongful dismissal. The problem is that, although most organisations have clear procedures for disciplining employees, some managers ignore these procedures in the heat of the moment. Seemingly a manager's minor oversight can lead to major monetary damages awards in favour of former employees.

Before you fire an employee for any reason, make sure that you can meet the following criteria and, where necessary, defend your position. Take our word for it: You'll be glad you did!

- ✔ **Procedures:** Use your procedures, follow them to the letter, and demonstrate – in writing – that you did so.

- ✔ **Documentation:** Remember the rule: Document, document, and then document some more. If you're firing an employee because of performance shortcomings, you better have the performance data to back up your assertions. If you're firing an employee for stealing, you better have proof that this employee is the thief. You can never have too much documentation. This rule is always true when you take employee relations actions, but particularly when you dismiss an employee.

- ✔ **Fair warning:** Make sure that you spell out performance standards clearly to employees in advance. Explain company policies and practices along with your expectations. Give your employees fair warning of the consequences of continued performance problems. The law is quite clear: Dismissing an employee without warning, especially for performance-related behaviour, is generally considered unfair. However, certain kinds of employee misconduct, including physical violence, theft, and fraud, are grounds for dismissal without warning.

- ✔ **Response time:** You must give your employees enough time to rectify their performance shortcomings. The amount of time considered reasonable to improve performance depends on the nature of the problem to be addressed. For example, if the problem is lateness, you can expect the employee to correct the behaviour immediately. However, if the employee is to improve performance on a complex and lengthy project, demonstrating improvement may take weeks or months.

- ✔ **Fairness and reasonableness:** Your company's policies and practices should be reasonable. The performance standards you set with your employees should be achievable by the average worker, and penalties should match the severity of the offence. Put yourself in your employees' shoes. If you were being dismissed, would you consider the grounds for dismissal to be reasonable? Be honest!

- ✔ **Avenues for appeal:** Offer employees ways to appeal your decision to higher-level management. Again, the law requires that avenues exist for dismissed employees to present their cases to higher management. Sometimes a direct supervisor is too close to the problem or too emotionally involved, which can cause errors in judgement that someone who is not personally involved in the situation can see easily.

Firing an Employee Fairly in Three Steps

Although your job is to point out your employees' shortcomings and help your employees perform to the standard you require, the employees are ultimately responsible for their performance and behaviour. When you arrive at the last disciplinary step prior to firing your employees, letting them know that the responsibility and choice are theirs and theirs alone is important;

you can't do this critical step for them. Your employees improve their performance or leave. And if they decide to leave, have your employee express his choice in writing!

Assuming that the employee has made his choice, and that choice is to continue the misconduct or below-standard performance, the choice is then yours. And your choice is to dismiss before the employee does any more damage to your organisation.

Keep three key goals in mind when firing employees:

- ✔ **Follow procedures.** You don't want to be lumbered with a high-level compensation case for firing someone who deserved that action, simply because you did not follow procedures.

- ✔ **Provide a clear explanation for the firing.** According to legal experts, many employees claim for unfair dismissal simply in hopes of discovering the real reason they were fired.

- ✔ **Seek to minimise resentment against your company and yourself by taking action to maintain your employee's dignity throughout the dismissal process.** The world is a dangerous enough place without incurring the wrath of potentially unstable former employees.

Fire an employee in a meeting in your office or other private location. Make the meeting concise and to the point; set aside 20 to 30 minutes for the meeting. Dismissal meetings aren't intended to be discussions or debates. Your job is to inform your employee that he is being fired. This meeting isn't going to be fun, but keep in mind that you're taking the best course of action for all concerned. One more thing: Have a witness with you when you dismiss an employee – especially when the person being dismissed is of a different gender. Ideally, bring someone along from human resources who can step in with a discussion of the administrative details of the dismissal, such as turning in keys and equipment, continuing benefits, severance pay, and so forth. In addition, make sure the employee has the option of having a colleague or representative with him.

In this context, these are the three steps for firing an employee:

- ✔ **Tell the employee that you are dismissing him.** State simply and unequivocally that you've made the decision to fire him. Don't use euphemisms – 'We're letting you go'; 'We're allowing you to spend more time with your family' – this is degrading and demeaning, to the employee and also to you. Dismiss the employee face to face – however uncomfortable it is, it is what you are paid for. Be sure to note that you considered all relevant evidence, that you reviewed the decision and all levels of your organisation's management agreed to it, and that the decision is final. If you did your homework and used a system of progressive discipline (refer to Chapter 15) in an attempt to correct your employee's behaviour, the announcement should come as no surprise. Of course, no matter the circumstances, a firing shakes anyone to the core.

✔ **Explain exactly why you are dismissing the employee.** If the firing is the result of misconduct, cite the policy that the employee broke and exactly what he did to break it. If the firing is due to a failure to meet performance standards, remind the employee of past attempts to correct his performance and the subsequent incidents that led to your decision to fire him. Stick to the facts. Confirm the facts in writing – and the stated and written reasons *must* be the same, otherwise the dismissal is normally considered unfair.

✔ **Announce the effective date of the dismissal and provide details on the dismissal process.** A firing is normally effective on the day that you conduct your dismissal meeting. Keeping a fired employee around is awkward for both you and your employee and you should avoid this situation at all costs. If you're offering a severance package or other dismissal benefits, explain them to your employee as well as how he can make arrangements for gathering personal effects from his office. Go through the dismissal paperwork with the employee and explain how you will pay any remaining wages due, including any notice period to which they're entitled.

Dismissal can be quite traumatic for the employee on the receiving end of the news. Expect the unexpected. Although one employee may quickly become an emotional wreck, another may become belligerent and verbally abusive. To help defuse these situations, consider applying the following techniques:

✔ **Empathise with your employee.** Don't try to sweeten the pill, but be understanding of your employee's situation. The news you have just delivered is among the worst news that anyone can get. If your employee becomes emotional or cries, don't try to stop him – hand him a tissue and carry on with the discussion.

✔ **Be matter-of-fact and firm.** Even if your employee becomes angry, you must maintain a calm, businesslike demeanour throughout the dismissal meeting. Don't lead your employee to believe that he is participating in a negotiating session or that he can do something to change your mind. Be firm in your insistence that the decision is final and not subject to change.

✔ **Keep the meeting on track.** Although letting your employee vent his feelings is appropriate, don't allow the employee to steer the meeting from the main goal of informing him about the dismissal. If the employee becomes abusive, inform the employee that you will end the meeting immediately if he can't maintain control.

You may find it helpful to prepare a *dismissal script* to read during the dismissal meeting. A script is beneficial because it helps to ensure that you don't forget to mention an important piece of information, and it provides instant documentation for your employee's personnel file (which you should retain). Practise the script before you go into the dismissal meeting.

Here is a sample dismissal script for an employee with continuing performance problems:

> 'Bronwyn, we've decided that today is your last day of employment with the firm. The reason for this decision is that you can't maintain the performance standards that we agreed to when we hired you last year. As you know, we have discussed your failure to meet standards on many occasions over the past year. Specifically, the disciplinary hearing that we had on 5 October notified you that you had one month to bring your performance up to standard or we may dismiss you. You didn't achieve this goal, and I therefore have no other choice but to terminate your employment, with immediate effect. Ali from personnel is here to discuss your final pay and benefits and to collect your office keys and voice-mail password.'

Determining the Best Time to Dismiss

Any manager probably has his own idea of what day of the week and time of the day to dismiss employees. Monday dismissals are the way to go because of A, B, and C. Or Friday dismissals are best because of X, Y, and Z. And is it better to carry out a dismissal as the first task in the morning, or should you wait until the close of business?

We think that dismissing an employee as soon as you decide you have to do so, regardless of the day of the week, makes the most sense. Once you've decided that an employee needs to go, every additional day is a drain on the organisation – and on yourself.

So what time is the best to dismiss someone? The best approach is when his colleagues aren't there to witness the dismissal, prior to starting work or at the end of the day. The idea is to minimise the embarrassment for the dismissed employee.

If you dismiss an employee earlier in the day, he has to face his colleagues and explain why his is packing up his belongings and why the security guard is preparing to escort him off the premises. Your intent isn't to punish or embarrass your employee – you want to make the dismissal process as painless and humane as possible. Allow an employee to save face by scheduling the dismissal meeting at a time when you can avoid public display.

Never be afraid to take advice from an employment lawyer, especially where there might be questions over the probability, likelihood or potential for discrimination or harassment. In these cases, compensation is uncapped, and you need to know precisely where you stand if the case goes wrong.

Top five dismissal Web sites

Wondering where to find the best information on the Web about the topics addressed in this chapter? Well, you've come to the right place! Here are our top five favourites:

- Confederation of British Industry: `www.cbi.org.uk/employeerelations`

- Trades Union Congress: `www.tuc.org.uk/employeerelations`

- Advisory, Conciliation and Arbitration Service (ACAS): `www.acas.org.uk/disciplineanddismissal`

- Institute of Directors: `www.instituteofdirectors.com/employeerelations`

- Croner: `www.croner.com/dismissal`

Chapter 17

Managing Me: Taking Care of No. 1

In This Chapter

▶ Balancing work and personal time

▶ Working too hard and too long

▶ Identifying stress

▶ Managing stress before it manages you

As the old saying goes, everything in moderation. Unfortunately, with regard to work, many people (both managers and workers alike!) don't find much moderation – you're in overdrive from the moment you arrive early in the morning until you go home, often late at night. Nothing's wrong with getting caught up in your work, but when work begins to intrude into your personal life and affect your health, a bit too far and a bit too often, then you have a problem.

No matter how high up in the organisation you are, or how important your job is, or how much you're getting paid, you have to take care of yourself first. You have to be your No. 1 priority. When you take care of yourself, you're in top form, and you're a more valuable asset to your organisation, your customers, and your employees. And you also have a much better chance of surviving to retirement and having an opportunity to enjoy the fruits of all your hard work. Doesn't that sound nice?

Weighing the Work–Life Dilemma

Balancing your time on the job and your time away from the job can be a very difficult proposition. Everyone has to make money but at the same time, everyone has a life outside of work. You have friends, family, clubs, hobbies, sports, and any number of other ways to keep busy. Sometimes you want the change of perspective and frame of mind that just taking a few minutes to watch a sunset or walk on the beach can give you.

You normally work long hours and accept them as a part of today's workplace. At an average of about 1,850 hours per annum (and rising) workers in the United Kingdom put in more hours than anyone else in the European Union; and they put in nearly as many hours as workers in the United States (who average nearly 2,000 hours a year).

And yet working long hours doesn't always translate to better productivity. Years ago, British Telecom admitted that it rewarded its managerial staff for long hours at work rather than output (though this has since changed). And in 2005, journalist Will Hutton produced 'The Productivity Report', which compared the working hours and output of workers in the United States, United Kingdom, Germany, and France. French workers, who worked the fewest hours, had the highest output per hour worked – 25 per cent higher than productivity per hour in the United Kingdom. Second was Germany, 13 per cent higher than the United Kingdom; and then the United States, 8 per cent higher than the United Kingdom. So the key really is to use your time at work productively; after a certain length of time, while attendance undoubtedly goes up, productivity falls. And more and more attendance eventually wears you out, causing your productivity to fall still further.

Reaping the benefits of a balanced work life and personal life

Finding a suitable balance between your work life and your personal life is one of the most important steps you can take. Employees whose work and personal lives are in balance are happier, healthier, more productive, and a lot easier to live with. In addition, they provide better customer service. But when employees allow their jobs to take over their lives, the results can be devastating.

Who benefits when your work life and personal life are balanced, when you're happy with the relationship between the time and effort that you put into your work, relative to the rest of your life and the others in it, and the other things you want to be doing? You do, and your company, your partner, family, and loved ones benefit, as well. Here's how:

- ✔ You have improved self-esteem and health, are happier, and feel more valued by your employer.
- ✔ You have more control over your working life.
- ✔ You are more motivated, more efficient, and more effective.
- ✔ Your relationship with your manager improves.
- ✔ You're less likely to be absent from work.
- ✔ Your organisation becomes an employer of choice.
- ✔ Your organisation keeps its employees for longer.

Making the case for a more flexible workplace

So you have pressures from both the legal side, in which employees can ask for flexible working arrangements, as well as from specific groups of workers, to adopt a more flexible approach. Nevertheless, in many cases, top management still remain to be convinced of the benefits of such an approach; and so in many cases, it is down to you as a manager to ensure a more favourable work/life balance for everybody. You therefore have to develop a business case for creating a flexible workplace, clearly spelling out the benefits to your organisation of making the changes. Suggest that the organisation first makes the change as an experiment or pilot programme for flexible working that can be implemented permanently if it is successful. As you move through the process, consider the impact of alternative work arrangements on your customers (in many cases, flexible work schedules can actually directly benefit your customers by extending the hours of service available to them), as well as on meetings and other continuing activities.

The following list shows the steps to take:

- ✔ **Identify core business needs:** Determine whether your organisation truly needs to adopt alternative work arrangements. Identify the core needs of your business, and then determine what kinds of alternative work arrangements may be appropriate. Consult with management (and with recognised trade unions and staff representatives if you have them) to determine what kinds of arrangements may be acceptable, and what kinds aren't. Survey employees to find out what they think. Quantify for the organisation both the benefits and the costs of making the desired change. Present your findings and your specific ideas to management for approval.

- ✔ **Develop policies and procedures:** For alternative work arrangements to be successful – and to ensure that you treat all employees fairly – develop and implement clear and complete policies and procedures before you roll out any new programme. Don't reinvent the wheel. By doing a search on the Internet, you can find plenty of policies that you can model yours after. (See our 'Top five work/life Web sites' at the end of the chapter for a start.)

- ✔ **Have a trial period:** When making a significant change, first run a pilot programme before you finalise your arrangements. Communicate your new policies widely, and make sure that your employees understand them. Invite employees to participate, and then start your programme. After a month or two, gather results and evaluate them.

- ✔ **Go live:** Make changes to your programme as determined by the evaluation of the trial period, then create your final policies and procedures. Inaugurate your new programme with much fanfare and celebration. You're on your way!

Managing balance

As a manager, not only do you have to watch out for yourself, you also have to keep a close eye on your employees to ensure that they aren't showing the symptoms of overwork and burn out (long hours, declining performance, domestic upheaval – and even alcohol and drug misuse). Although managers have always had certain tools available to help their employees balance work and personal time – hiring them on a part-time basis or granting employees an unexpected day off with pay, for example – a number of new tools are in most managers' toolboxes for accomplishing the same goal:

- ✔ **Flexitime:** Allowing employees to set their own work start and end times within a band of time approved by management

- ✔ **Compressed working week:** Working a full-time, 40-hour-a-week schedule in fewer than five workdays each week (for example, four 10-hour days a week); or, as with many nurses, working three 12.5 hour shifts per week only

- ✔ **Shift swapping:** Allowing employees to swap shifts as desired among themselves

- ✔ **Self-rostering:** Allowing employees to sign up for their own work schedules each week or month

- ✔ **Job sharing:** Sharing a full-time job with another employee, with each person usually working 20 hours a week

- ✔ **Telecommuting:** Working from home or from a remote office, sometimes a day or two a week, sometimes on a full-time basis

You increasingly need to take a proactive approach to all this, too, because workers have a legal right to ask for flexible schedules; and in most cases, you have to be able to prove or demonstrate why you can't allow this, if you intend to refuse their request (refer to Chapter 12 for more about flexible working).

Avoiding Becoming a Workaholic

When overwork becomes more than an occasional event and you often push everything that isn't related to your job out of the picture, then you have a classic case of *workaholism*. And workaholism isn't good. Not only can workaholism lead you to neglect your family and social life, but it can actually make you less productive and less efficient. Although you may think you're getting more done with all the extra time you put into your job, the chances are that you're actually getting less done.

So how can you tell whether or not you're a workaholic? Check yourself again the following warning signs of workaholism:

- ✔ When you go to parties, you talk mostly about work.

- ✔ You dream about work.

- ✔ You seldom take a day off work or go on holiday.

- ✔ On the rare days that you do take a holiday, you take work with you, regularly call in to check your voice-mail messages, and always check your e-mails.

✔ You work more than 45 hours a week.

✔ You eat lunch at your desk, or skip lunch altogether, because you don't have time for lunch.

✔ You're absolutely convinced that you're not a workaholic, even though you exhibit some or all of the preceding symptoms.

Do others tell you that you're a workaholic? Are your relationships outside of work suffering, and do you have a hard time relaxing and having fun? If so, you can follow these steps to cure yourself of this obsessive addiction to work, including:

✔ Work fewer hours. Commit to a 40-hour-a-week schedule and stick to it.

✔ Clearly separate your work life from your personal life. Leave your work at the office when you go home every day.

✔ Spend time with friends and family.

✔ Slow down!

✔ Take holidays (and don't bring your work with you or check in with the office before your holiday is over).

✔ Set up a regular exercise schedule and stick to it!

✔ Take time for lunch, and get outside the office as often as possible to eat it.

Make the time now to take positive steps to cure yourself of your work addiction. You can do it if you try. We guarantee that you can be a changed person if you simply let go. Go ahead: What do you have to lose (besides an aggravated ulcer or two)?

Knowing the Symptoms of Stress

Stress at work is a highly emotional, subjective, and contentious issue. On the one hand, the British Health and Safety Executive produces data stating that up to 50 million working days are lost each year in the United Kingdom because of stress. On the other, many organisations and managers still consider that anyone who complains of stress has no character, courage, backbone, or commitment to the organisation. And in between you often find great difficulty in quantifying or getting to grips with what stress at a particular workplace actually is – one person's stress is another's challenge.

The first aspect to recognise is that some amount of workplace pressure is inevitable. You may be doing a great job yourself, but you have to work with others who see things differently, who have different priorities, and who have their own preferred ways of operating. The presence of change and differences in individual working styles, aspirations, and approaches, as well as differing workplace priorities, all cause pressure. And the stress you bring with you from your domestic and personal life multiplies the stress in your work life. Are you struggling with the mortgage? Do you have rows at home about the fact that you never seem to be able to get to the kids' school plays?

So how do you know whether you're stressed out? Use the list of stress indicators in Table 17-1 to identify the extent of stress in your business and personal lives. Tick the Yes, I Have It! column if you feel that particular stress. Because your business and personal lives affect each other, determining and dealing with the sources of stress is important.

Table 17-1	Symptoms of Stress
The symptom	*Yes, I have it!*
Aggression	
Hostility	
Headaches	
Indigestion	
Sleep disorders	
Defensiveness	
Poor judgement	
Nervousness	
High blood pressure	
Ulcers	
Fatigue	
Anxiety	
Depression	
Memory loss	
Inability to concentrate	
Mood swings	

Any one of these symptoms can indicate a stress problem, but the more symptoms you have, the greater the damage being done to your mind and body.

If you experience more than a couple of these symptoms, take a serious look at what creates the stress in your life. Do something about stress before it's too late!

Fortunately, you can figure out how to manage your stress. Although you can't always prevent stress from entering your life, you can take definite steps to reduce the negative effects. Discover how to take control of stress so that it doesn't take control of you. You can start with the next section.

Managing Your Stress

Organisations must deal with stress because, when employees allow stress to overcome them, they lose their effectiveness. And when employees lose their effectiveness, the organisation loses its edge.

Most stress management training focuses on treating the symptoms of stress and not on curing the root causes within the organisation. We see a problem with this approach. The training programmes teach workers relaxation techniques to decrease their level of stress, but they don't force top management to make better and faster decisions. The training shows employees how to reinforce and develop their own self-esteem, use their own time better, and be more productive; but it doesn't address the root causes of the problem – bad decision making, faulty or inadequate equipment, and, above all, staff shortages.

You can't wait for someone else to do something to reduce your stress. Find out how to manage stress yourself. Fortunately, managing stress isn't as hard as you may think. Effective stress management boils down to this: Change the things that you can change and accept the things that you can't change – and know the difference between the two.

Changing the things you can

You can take several steps right now to change your work environment and decrease your stress. If these steps sound familiar, you've probably thought about doing them before, but you just couldn't seem to get around to it. Well, now is the time. Don't delay and put it off until tomorrow. The life you save may be your own!

  ✔ **Get healthy:** You know that doing regular, vigorous exercise is one of the best things you can do for yourself. Not only do you make your mind and your body stronger, but you also work off tons of frustration and stress. And when you're under stress, your body quickly becomes depleted of certain vitamins and minerals. Determine to stick to a healthy diet – whether you are working long hours, or spending a lot of time away from home, you have no reason for not being able to eat well and exercise properly.

✔ **Have fun:** If you're not having fun, why bother? Remember, you're going to spend up to a third of your adult life at work. Of course, you need the money, and you need the psychological satisfaction that doing a good job brings with it, but don't ever take work so seriously that you can't have fun with your job and your colleagues.

Someday, when you retire, do you want people to remember you as the manager who kept an eye on the company's cash flow, or do you want them to remember you as the manager who affected your employees' lives and made their jobs more rewarding in the process?

✔ **Find out how to say no:** Remember the old saying: 'You can please some of the people some of the time, but you can't please all the people all the time.' Recognise that you can't do everything for everyone. And if you do try to do everything, the result is that nothing gets done well. When you already have a full plate of work to do and someone tries to give you more, say no.

✔ **Relax:** Relaxation is an extremely important part of any programme of stress management. When you relax, you give your brain a break, and you provide yourself with a necessary opportunity to recharge your batteries before going back into overdrive.

You may not have taken a break for a while, so you may be a little rusty at it. When you take a break to relax, make a real break from your routine. Get up from your desk and go somewhere where you can remove yourself from the day-to-day business at hand.

✔ **Manage your schedule:** If you don't manage your own schedule, it quickly finds a way to manage you. Get a personal planner, desk calendar – anything that enables you to take charge of your working schedule, and take charge of the meetings that you attend and the appointments you keep.

If someone invites you to a meeting, don't automatically agree to go. Find out the topic of the meeting and your expected role. If you don't think that the meeting is worth your time to attend, don't! Send someone else if necessary. When you're pursuing your goals and priorities, keeping the goals and priorities of others from intruding can be incredibly difficult. Steadfastly refuse to let someone else's crisis become yours!

✔ **Streamline:** Why make your job harder than it has to be? As a manager, you're in the perfect position to be on the lookout for ways to improve your organisation's work processes and systems. Be brutal in reviewing everything your department does and remove unnecessary steps.

Simplify, shorten, and condense. Fewer steps in a process translates into your workforce expending less effort, fewer problems, fewer things going wrong, more things going well, and, ultimately, less stress for you to endure.

✔ **Look for silver linings:** Be an optimist. Look for the good in everything you do and everyone you meet. You may be amazed by how much better you feel about your job, your colleagues, and yourself. And you may be just as amazed by how much better your colleagues feel about you when they can depend on you to lift their spirits. Be an ambassador of optimism. You decrease your own stress and the stress of those employees around you, too.

Accepting the things that you can't change

You just can't change certain things, no matter how hard you try. Instead of changing the unchangeable, you end up stressed, defeated, or ill. And such an outcome isn't good in anyone's book. When you can't change the unchangeable, you have one choice left: Change yourself:

✔ **Surrender:** Stop fighting change. To continue the fight simply causes your stress level to increase – along with your blood pressure and the number of bottles of antacid that it takes to quell the fire in your stomach. Surrender to change; become one with it. Instead of trying to row against the swift currents of change, let go and drift with them.

Understand that you can use change to your advantage. After you stop fighting change, you can concentrate on making change work for you and for your organisation (refer to Chapter 14 for more on change).

✔ **Don't take change personally:** Change doesn't affect just you. Everyone has to deal with change and the effects of change on the working environment. But the question is not how everyone else responds to change; the question is how *you* respond to change. Do you retreat into your shell? Do you get frustrated and angry? Or do you take charge? You need to be fully aware of when you're reacting like this, and the reasons why – and you need to be honest enough to know when your reactions are due to pressures and stresses at work.

✔ **Adjust your attitude:** Losing perspective is easy to do. After you've worked at a job for a few years, you can begin to get delusions of grandeur. 'How would this place survive without me?' Before long, you become resentful when people don't give your opinion the widespread respect you feel it deserves, and you begin to dislike performing the mundane tasks that are a part of your job.

As you get hot under the collar about your current status, remember that many people are only two or three months' salary away from bankruptcy. How long could you survive if you lost your job? And don't be so sure that your organisation will never have lay-offs or redundancies. Who do you think the organisation would let go first: Employees who willingly do whatever they can to get the job done or employees who think that they're above all that? If you picked the former, you may be due for a nasty surprise. Adjust your own attitude before someone adjusts it for you!

✔ **Don't be a victim:** Whatever happens, use the changing circumstances to the advantage of yourself, your colleagues, your work, and your organisation. Victims become angry, frustrated, and resentful – and this increases, rather than reduces, stress. Refuse to be a victim of change and instead become its biggest fan. And if you really can't stand the changes your organisation is making, then find another company.

✔ **Control your anger:** Getting mad when your job doesn't go your way may be expressive, but showing anger isn't a productive use of your time and energy. Being angry about something you can do nothing to change saps your energy and distracts you from accomplishing the tasks that you can do something about.

What do you do when you get stuck in rush-hour traffic? Do you stew and fume? Does your blood pressure go up as your face gets redder and redder? Does your anger help you go any faster or get you home any sooner? No! Instead of wasting time trying to change the unchangeable, catch up on some phone calls, relax to some new tunes, or listen to a book on tape. Exchange your anger for a productive activity, or the anger may eat you alive.

Henry George runs his own building services company, and his 'patch' is the M62 corridor in Merseyside, Greater Manchester, Lancashire, Yorkshire, and Humberside. Henry regularly gets held up in traffic jams, and some of these have been really serious – one kept him on the motorway for over eight hours. This particular jam led to extensive coverage on Radio 4 and the radio station invited people to ring in with their nightmares. This they did in their hundreds! All except Henry – who phoned in to say: 'I've been stuck here for many hours, that is true. But it is a lovely day. I have plenty to do; and because I can't go anywhere at the moment, I am getting on with it. I have my phone, my laptop, and my sandwiches and a flask of coffee. And so far, I have accomplished all of the tasks that would have otherwise had to wait until the weekend.'

✔ **Don't worry about details or trivia:** Much of what happens during the course of a normal business day is small stuff – filling out forms, pulling messages off your voice-mail system, poking at a few buttons on your computer keyboard. The big stuff can be few and far between. Something like 80 per cent of your time is spent getting 20 per cent of your results. The point is: Most of what you do is small stuff, so don't worry about it. If you're going to worry, at least save it for something that's really important!

Trying out some specific stress-reduction exercises

While you're changing the things you can change and accepting the things you can't change, you can use specific exercises to reduce your stress. These exercises are great because you can do them anywhere – at the office, at home, or in your car on the way to work. In addition, the exercises are effective on any kind of stress, whatever the source. The next time you feel your stomach tying itself into knots and your blood pressure starting to rise, give these exercises a try:

- **Breath control:** In. Out. In. Out. That's it. Take a deep breath. Hold it; don't let go. Now, exhale slowly. Feel the stress leave your body as you let go of your breath. Controlled breathing can have a calming effect.

  When you feel stressed, give this ancient yoga breathing exercise a try: Breathe in through one nostril for a count of one while placing a finger against the side of your nose to close your other nostril. Hold the breath for eight counts and then exhale through your other nostril for four counts. Then reverse the procedure starting with your other nostril and repeat the exercise for a total of four complete cycles. Not only will it calm you down; but if you do the exercise properly, you can't be doing anything else!

- **Positive affirmations:** Every negative has a positive. Instead of thinking, 'This is going to take absolutely hours', think, 'This is exactly what the customer wants.' Instead of thinking, 'Oh no! Here we go again,' think, 'I did a good job last time round, so I'm going to do a good job this time as well.' Be positive. The more positive your life, the less stress you experience. (Plus you're a lot more fun to be around than those moaners and whiners you have to work with.)

- **Progressive relaxation:** Progressive relaxation starts with you – and you can do it anywhere. Relax in your chair or, even better, lie down in a darkened room. Starting with your feet, concentrate on tensing up your muscles for several counts, and then let the muscles in your feet relax. Next, move to your calves. Tense your calf muscles for several counts and then let them relax. Keep moving up the rest of your body until you get to the top of your head. Finally, tense all your muscles at once, and then relax. The result is a general release of tension and increased relaxation. It also helps blood circulation, and keeps your muscles both active and relaxed. More seriously, airline companies have adopted a form of progressive relaxation, which they recommend to passengers as a way of helping to avoid deep vein thrombosis on long flights.

- **Daydreaming:** Imagination is a very powerful tool. No matter where you are, you can take a holiday anywhere you want, any time you want. When the crowd at your door is five deep, your phone is ringing off the hook, everyone has a problem instead of a solution, and your blood pressure is erupting like Krakatoa, daydreaming is definitely in order.

Close your door, switch on the answerphone, turn down your lights, kick your ergonomic chair back into its full relax mode, and let your mind drift away. Picture yourself in a boat on a river with the sun shining and the birds chirping. Take yourself far away from the challenges of the day. You can then drift back when you're ready.

✔ **Laugh:** Don't take your job so seriously that you lose your sense of humour. Having fun with your job and with your colleagues is an important way to reduce stress on the job. Not only does a good laugh provide you with a great way to release stress, it also reminds you that life is more than work. And it is!

If you've done everything you can to reduce stress, have become a leader of change, and have taken control of your business life, but you're still stressed out, you may have to face the fact that you have much deeper issues to contend with. If this is the case, be strong enough to seek help, and change your job or your way of life. Because, if the job and the work are truly that bad, they're not worth it.

Top five work/life Web sites

Wondering where to find the best information on the Web about balancing your work and personal life? Well, you've come to the right place! Here are our top five favourites:

✔ Work & Family Connection: `www.workfamily.com`

✔ Workoptions.com: `www.workoptions.com/articles.htm`

✔ Xanthis Ltd: `www.xanthis.ltd.uk`

✔ Health and Safety Executive (HSE): `www.hse.gov.uk/stress`

✔ Dr Steve McKeown: `www.stevemckeown.net`

Part VI
Tools and Techniques for Managing

'Look, Mr Brinkley, you don't fool me —
you don't have a proper accountant in
this company do you?'

In this part . . .

Although you don't have to be a technical wizard to be a manager, you can benefit from keeping abreast of some of the key tools and technologies that drive today's business. In this part, we consider the basics of accounting and budgeting and how to harness the power of technology. We also talk about how to develop employee skills and about some of the most recent management trends.

Chapter 18

Budgeting and Accounting

. . . .

In This Chapter

▶ Creating your budget

▶ Applying professional budget tricks

▶ Understanding accounting basics

▶ Interpreting financial statements

▶ Other ways of looking at money

. . . .

*A*s a manager, you need to understand the basics of budgeting and accounting. When your colleagues start throwing around terms such as *staff budget, cash flow, profit and loss statement,* and *balance sheet,* don't you want to do more than simply nod your head and respond with a blank stare? Here's some good news: You don't need an MBA to grasp these basics.

In this chapter, we cover the importance of budgeting in an organisation, as well as putting together a budget by using some of the professional tricks of the budget trade. We then introduce the survival basics of accounting.

Exploring the Wonderful World of Budgets

A *budget* is an itemised forecast of an individual's or company's income and expenses expected for some period in the future. Budgets provide the baseline of expected performance against which managers measure actual performance. Accounting systems generate reports to compare expected performance against actual performance to provide financial information on an organisation's financial status. With this information, managers with budget responsibility act as physicians to assess the current financial health of their businesses.

When you receive the latest accounting report, it says that sales are too low compared to budget. What does that mean? As a responsible manager (this means you!), you need to work out why. Maybe your sales force is having problems getting the product delivered to your customers quickly. Or per-haps your competition developed a new thingamajig that is taking sales away from your product. Whatever the problem is, you can't know if you don't understand the basics of budgeting.

Because business is changing all the time (find out all about change in Chapter 14), you may wonder why you bother having a budget. Without a long-term plan and goals, your organisation lacks focus and wastes resources as employees wander aimlessly about. A budget isn't just an educated guess that reflects your long-term plans and allows you to act on them, it's a per-sonal commitment to making a designated future happen. The best budgets are flexible, allowing for changes in different key assumptions, such as income results. Of course, planning becomes more difficult as the world changes all around you, but plan you must.

Winston Churchill said: 'When circumstances change, so do I.' This must be your attitude to budgeting – changes in circumstances simply do not allow you to stick rigidly to a single course of action.

Budgets also fulfil another important purpose: They provide a baseline against which you can measure your progress towards your goals. For exam-ple, if you're 50 per cent of the way through your financial year but have actu-ally spent 75 per cent of your budgeted operating funds, then you have an immediate indication that a potential problem exists if you don't see any sig-nificant change in your expenditure. You've under-budgeted your expenses for the year, or you're overspending. Whenever budgeted performance and actual performance disagree, or are in *variance,* the job of the responsible manager is to ask why, and then to put right any problems that he finds.

Depending on your organisation's size, the budgeting process may be quite simple or very complex. Regardless of your organisation's size, you ought to budget for everything. Following are examples of budget areas that just about every organisation needs:

- ✔ **Sales budget:** The sales budget is an estimate of the total number of products or services that the organisation will sell in a given period. Determine the total turnover by multiplying the number of units by the price per unit.

- ✔ **Staff budget:** Staff budgets consist of the number and name of all the various positions in a company along with the salary or wages budgeted for each position.

- ✔ **Production budget:** The production budget takes the sales budget and its estimate of quantities of units to be sold and translates those figures into the cost of labour, material, and other expenses required to produce those units.

✔ **Administration and overheads budget:** Administration and overheads budgets contain all the different expenses that a department may incur during the normal course of operations. You budget for things like travel, training, office supplies, and so forth as expenses.

✔ **Capital budget:** This budget is a manager's plan to acquire *fixed assets* (anything your organisation owns that has a long useful life), such as furniture, computers, facilities, physical plant, and so forth to support the operations of a business.

Whether you're responsible for budgeting as a part of your managerial duties or not, you need to have a basic understanding of the process your business goes through to account for the money it makes and the money it spends.

Making a Budget

You have a right and a wrong way to do a budget. The wrong way is simply to make a photocopy of the last budget and submit it as your new budget. Some people simply add a bit here and there, and then hand the slightly revised budget in, hoping it's good enough.

The right way is to gather information from as many sources as possible, review and check the information for accuracy, and then use your good judgement to guess what the future may bring. A budget is a *forecast* – a commitment to the future – and is only as good as the data that goes into it and the good judgement that you bring to the process.

Review the basic steps in putting together a budget:

1. **Closely review your budgeting documents and instructions.**

   Take a close look at the budgeting documents you're working with and read any instructions your accounting staff provides with them. Although your organisation may have done something the same way for years, you never know when that procedure may change.

2. **Meet with staff.**

   When you're starting the budget process, meet with your staff members to solicit their input. In some cases, you need the specific input of your employees to forecast accurately. For example, you may need to know how many trips your sales people plan to make next year and where they plan to go. In other cases, you can simply ask for employee suggestions. One employee may ask you to include a pay increase in the next budget. Another may inform you that the current phone system is no longer adequate to meet the needs of employees and customers and that you should budget for a new one. Whichever the case, your staff can provide you with very useful and important budget information.

3. Gather data.

Pull out copies of previous budgets and accounting reports and then compare budgeted figures to actual figures. Work out whether you overspent or underspent and by how much. If no historical data is available, find other sources of information that can help guide the development of figures for your budget.

Determine how much business you plan to bring in during the next budget period, and what it will cost to bring it in. Consider whether you need to hire more people, lease new facilities, or buy equipment or supplies. Furthermore, consider the possibility of large increases or decreases in sales or expenses and what effect they would have on your budget.

4. Apply your judgement.

Hard data and cold facts are very important in the budgeting process; they provide an unbiased, unemotional source of information on which to base your decisions. However, data and facts aren't everything – not by a long shot. Budgeting is part science and part art. Take the data and facts and then apply your own judgement to determine the most likely outcomes.

When you're new to management, you have little experience on which to draw, so you have a natural tendency to rely more heavily on data. However, as you become more accomplished in management and budgeting, your personal experience and judgement come to the fore.

5. Produce a draft.

Depending on how your organisation does business, either fill out your budget forms and send them to your budget people for processing, or enter them in the budget model yourself. The result is a budget draft that you can review and modify before you finalise it. Don't worry if the draft is rough or is missing information. You have a chance to fill in the gaps soon enough.

6. Check results and redraft as necessary.

Check over your draft budget and see whether it still makes sense to you. Are you missing any anticipated sources of revenue or expenses? Are the numbers realistic? Do they make sense in a historical perspective? Are they too high or too low? Will you be able to support them when you present them to upper management? The fun part of budgeting is playing with your numbers and trying out different scenarios and what-ifs. When you're satisfied with the results, sign off on your budget and turn it in. Congratulations! You did it!

The accuracy of your budget hinges on two main factors: the quality of the data you use to develop your budget and the quality of the judgement you apply to the data you're working with. Although judgement is something that comes with experience, the quality of the data you use depends on where you get it. You can use three basic approaches to develop the data for building a budget:

✔ **Build it from scratch.** In the absence of historical data, when you're starting up a new business unit, or when you just want a fresh view, you want to develop your budgets based strictly on current estimates. In this process, widely known as *zero-based budgeting,* you build your budget from scratch, determining the people, facilities, travel, advertising, and other resources that you require to support it. You then cost out each need, and the budget is complete. Perhaps not too surprisingly, the answer that comes out of building a budget from scratch is often quite different from one that results from using historical data. Funny how that works; and funny, too, how many errors and omissions building from scratch can show in some cases.

✔ **Use historical figures.** One of the easiest ways to develop data for your budget is to use the actual results from the preceding budget period. Although the past is not always an indication of the future – especially when an organisation is undergoing significant change – using historical data can be very helpful in relatively stable organisations and you may have an interest in seeing which numbers have gone up and which have gone down.

✔ **Use the combination approach.** Many managers do both. They use a combination of zero-based budgeting and historical figures for determining which data to include in their budgets. To use this approach, gather historical data and compare the figures to the best estimates of what you think performing a particular function costs. You then adjust historical data up or down, depending on your view of reality.

Budgeting and the Real World

In any organisation, a certain amount of mystery and intrigue – some call it smoke and mirrors – hovers around budgets and the budgeting process. Indeed, whether your organisation is a one-person operation or the central government, you can use many tricks of the budget trade to ensure that you get all the resources you need and desire. *Note:* In these days of big-business scandals and shenanigans, we definitely aren't suggesting that you do anything illegal, immoral, or unethical. The tricks we suggest in this section are quite legal, and they're time-honoured techniques for budgeting that all kinds of organisations around the world use every day.

As a manager, finding out how the budget game is played is definitely in your interest. Generally, the goal of the budget game is to build in enough extra money to actually be able to get the job done. In the worst case, you have enough resources available to protect your employees and vital functions when the business goes sour. In the best case, you have money left over after you pay all your necessary expenses. You can turn the money back into the accounts department with much fanfare and accept the accolades from the powers that be for your expert resource management skills, or you can apply the money to the purchase of some equipment or other department needs. Of course, if you work for the government or for many large commercial corporations, your goal is to spend every penny of your budgeted amount so that your budget doesn't decrease in the following year.

The make-or-buy decision

One of the most common decisions that a business makes is whether to make – that is, build or perform with in-house staff – or buy in goods and services that are necessary for the operation of the business. For example, say that you need a security guard for your reception area to ensure the safety of your clients. Do you take on someone new as an employee, or does contracting with a company that specialises in providing security services make more sense?

When you consider such a make-or-buy decision, the first point to think about is the cost of each alternative to your firm. Say that in Case A, you hire your security guard as a full-time employee for £6.00 an hour. In Case B, a security services firm provides a guard for £8.00 an hour. On the surface, hiring a security guard as an employee seems to make the most sense. If the guard works 2,000 hours a year, then in Case A you spend £12,000 a year for your guard and in Case B you spend £16,000 a year. By employing the guard yourself, you stand to save £4,000 a year. Right?

Maybe not. See why.

Case A: Hire in-house security guard

Hourly pay rate	£6.00
Fringe benefits rate (pension, employer's health care) @ 35%	£2.10
Overheads rate (including NI, holiday cover, accommodation) @ 50%	£3.00
Total effective pay rate	**£11.10**
Hours per year	× 2,000
Total annual staff cost	**£22,200**

Annual liability insurance increase	£4,000
Uniforms/cleaning	£1,000
Miscellaneous equipment	£500
Total annual cost	**£27,700**

Case B: Contract with security firm

Hourly pay rate	£8.00
Total effective pay rate	**£8.00**
Hours per year	× 2,000
Total annual cost	**£16,000**

Surprise, surprise. Instead of saving £4,000 per year by hiring an in-house security guard, you're actually going to spend almost £12,000 more each year because more costs are involved in hiring an in-house employee than just his hourly pay. You have to add all the fringe benefits, national insurance, any pension contributions, and more, plus the employee's share of overheads – facilities, electricity, air-conditioning, and so forth – to the basic wage rate to get a true picture of the cost of the employee to your organisation. Furthermore, you need to purchase additional liability insurance, uniforms, uniform cleaning, and any other additional equipment.

On the other hand, when you contract with a security services firm, the firm bears the cost of fringe benefits, overheads, insurance, uniforms, and equipment. You simply pay the hourly fee and forget it. Furthermore, if the guard isn't any good, you just make a phone call, and a replacement is sent immediately. No messy dismissals or potential tribunal cases to worry about.

Now, which deal do you think is the better one? On the face of it, no contest; contracting with the security organisation makes more sense. However, you have to remember that you lose control over the quality of service provided; the guard is not your employee, but the contractor's; and the security firm may have nobody who is any better to send to you if this one does not work out.

Second – and this applies to all sorts of out-sourcing – you may find that the contracting organisation no longer wishes to do business with you at some time in the future; or else it goes broke. In both cases, you face having to find a new contracting organisation or take on your own employee in any case. Also, you may prefer simply to have everyone who works on your premises as an employee, and so you accept the increased cost in return for better overall control.

You can play the budget game up front, when you develop the budget, or during the course of the budget period. The following sections tell you how to develop a solid budget.

Producing real budgets

This section lists some of the games that the pros play when they develop budgets. Again, these are not immoral or unethical, they're simply what's necessary to survive and prosper in the real world. Although these techniques are most appropriate for new or unstable departments or projects, you can use them when developing any budget. We may be exaggerating just a bit on some of these points, but most of them have a very clear ring of truth.

- ✔ **Do some selective padding.** Simple, but effective. The idea is to pad your anticipated expenses so that your budget targets are easy to achieve. You end up looking like a hero when you come in under your budget, plus you get some extra money to play with at the end of the year. This situation is known as win–win. Do be careful though – most senior managers have worked their way up and know how the game is played. If you go really over the top, they'll think that you're pulling their leg, and will reject your budget accordingly!

- ✔ **Tie your budget request to your organisation's values.** This is the 'Everything in the organisation is rosy' approach to budgeting. If you want to beef up your budget in a particular area, just pick one of your organisation's values – for example quality – and tie your request to it. When your boss asks you to justify why you have tripled your office furniture budget, just tell him that your employees can't do quality work without large, hand-crafted walnut desks.

- ✔ **Create more requests than you need, and give them up as you have to.** You don't want to appear unreasonable in your budget demands – don't forget, you're a team player! When you draft your budget, build in items that are of relatively low priority to you overall. When your boss puts on the pressure to reduce your budget (and bosses always do), give up the things you didn't really care so much about anyway. Doing so ensures that you get to keep the items that you really do want.

✔ **Shift the timeframe.** Insist that the budget items are an investment in the company's future. The secret is to tie these investments to a big payoff down the road. 'If we double our staff budget, we'll be able to attract the talent that we need to expand our operations.'

✔ **Be prepared.** The best defence is a good offence. Know your budget numbers cold and be ready to justify each budget item in intimate detail. Don't rely on someone else to prepare for you – this can be your finest hour as a manager. Be a star and go for it!

Staying on budget

After your new department or project starts up, you need to monitor your budget closely to make sure that you don't exceed it. If your actual expenditure starts to exceed your budget, you need to take quick and decisive action. Following are some of the ways that experienced managers make sure that they stay on budget:

✔ **Freeze non-essentials.** Some expenses, such as staff, overheads, and electricity, are essential to an operation or project and you can't stop them without jeopardising the organisation's performance. Others, such as purchasing new carpeting, upgrading computer monitors, or travelling first-class, are discretionary and you can postpone them without jeopardising performance. Freezing non-essential items of expenditure is the quickest and least painful way to get your actual expenditure back in line with your budgeted expenditure.

✔ **Freeze recruitment.** Although you may have budgeted for new staff, you can save money by imposing a recruitment freeze. Not only do you save on the cost of hourly pay or salaries, but you also save on the costs of fringe benefits, staff accommodation, and overheads expenses. And because you aren't tinkering with your current employees' pay or perks, generally everyone is happy with your decision. Of course, you may need to fill some critical positions in your organisation, budget problem notwithstanding. You can determine which positions you have to fill if they become vacant, and which jobs other employees can cover.

✔ **Postpone products, services, and projects.** The development and production phases of new products and projects can burn up a lot of money. By postponing the start-up and implementation of these new products and projects, you can get your budget back on track. Sometimes it only takes a few weeks or months to make a difference.

✔ **Delay payments to suppliers.** Instead of paying right on time, you can delay your payments over a longer period. If you're going to go down this route, you're generally best off working this out with your suppliers in advance (that is, if you want them to continue to be your suppliers in the future).

Delaying payments to suppliers used to be a manager's favourite for improving cash flow. Of course, you do have to balance your decision to delay payments against the supplier's ability to remain in business without being paid! Otherwise you may find next time that you've got no supplies – because you've got no supplier!

✔ **Hammer suppliers.** If you are in a powerful position and take a large volume from a particular supplier, you can use this to drive the price down. Again however, you do have to balance such a decision against the supplier's capability and willingness to continue to do business with you on this basis. And if suppliers find outlets that are prepared to do business with them on more favourable terms, they may refuse to do business with you.

✔ **Freeze wages and perks.** These kinds of savings directly affect your employees, and we can guarantee that they aren't going to like that at all. Most employees are used to regular wage and salary increases. Although increases aren't as generous as they were a decade ago, employees still consider them to be essential. However, if you have made cuts and still need to cut more, then you really don't have any choice but to freeze your employees' wages, salaries, and other things such as overtime and bonuses at their current levels.

✔ **Lay off employees and close facilities.** You are in business to make money, not to lose money. When sales aren't sufficient to support your expenses – even after enacting cost-savings measures such as the ones in this list – you must take drastic action. Action doesn't get much more drastic than laying off employees and closing facilities. However, if your budget is as far off as it must be if you reach this point, then cut you have to. Refer to Chapter 16 for more information on conducting employee lay-offs and redundancies.

Understanding the Basics of Accounting

The accounting system that takes up gigabytes of storage space on your company's network server depends on a few very basic assumptions. These assumptions determine how every pound and penny that flows into and out of your organisation is assigned, reported, and analysed.

Some managers believe that they can get by with little or no knowledge of accounting and finance. This attitude is a mistake. As a manager, you must be just as familiar with these accounting basics as are the employees who work in your accounting department. Not only does this knowledge help to ensure that you understand and control your organisation's financial destiny, but also if you're in command of the financial side of your business as well as the technical side, then you're also much more likely to survive the next round of corporate lay-offs.

Working out the accounting equation

Daily events affect every business's financial position. A manager spends cash to buy a stapler and is reimbursed out of the petty cash fund. The company uses its overdraft facility to pay supplier invoices. Customers pay bills and those payments are deposited. Employees receive their salaries. Each of these *financial transactions* and many more has its place in the accounting equation.

The accounting equation states that an organisation's *assets* are equal to its *liabilities* plus its *share capital*. The accounting equation looks like this:

Assets = Liabilities + Share Capital

This simple equation drives the very complex system of accounting used to track every financial transaction in a business, provide reports to managers for decision making, and provide financial results to owners, shareholders, lenders, the taxation authorities, and other stakeholders.

So what exactly does each part of the accounting equation represent? Take a look at each part and what it comprises.

Assets

Assets are generally considered to be anything of value – primarily financial and economic resources – that a company owns. The most common forms of assets in a business include the following:

- ✔ **Cash:** This asset encompasses money in all its forms, including cash, other accounts, money market funds, and marketable securities, such as stocks and bonds. Every business likes to have lots of cash.

- ✔ **Accounts receivable (or debtors):** This asset represents the money that customers who buy goods and services on credit owe to your company. For example, if your business sells a box of CD-ROMS to another business and then bills the other business for the sale instead of demanding immediate payment in cash, this obligation becomes an account receivable until your customer pays it. Accounts receivable are nice to have unless the companies or individuals that owe you money run away, close down, or decide to delay their payments for six months.

- ✔ **Stock:** Stock is the value of merchandise held by your business for sale, the finished goods that you have manufactured but have not yet sold, as well as the raw materials and work in progress that are part of the manufacture of finished goods. Stock usually becomes cash or an account receivable when your organisation sells it. Stock that sits around on a shelf forever isn't the best way to tie up your company's assets. Keeping your stock moving all the time is much better, because you are generating sales.

✔ **Prepaid expenses:** Prepaid expenses represent goods and services that your firm has already paid for but not yet used. For example, your company may pay its annual liability insurance premium at the beginning of the year, before the insurance policy actually goes into effect. If your organisation cancels the policy during the course of the year, then the insurance company refunds part of the premium to your business.

✔ **Equipment:** Equipment is the property – machinery, desks, computers, phones, and similar items – your organisation buys to carry out its operations. For example, if your company sells computer supplies to individuals and other businesses, you need to purchase shelves on which to store your goods, fork-lifts to move it around, and phone systems on which to take orders from your customers. As equipment ages, it loses value. You account for this loss through *depreciation*, which spreads the original cost of a piece of equipment across its entire useful lifetime. When in doubt, depreciate.

✔ **Property:** Property includes the land, buildings, and facilities that your organisation owns or controls. Examples include office buildings, manufacturing plants, warehouses, sales offices, mills, farms, and other forms of property.

Assets are divided into two major types: *current assets* and *fixed assets*.

✔ **Current assets** can be converted into cash, normally within one year. Such assets are considered to be *liquid.* In the preceding list of assets, cash, accounts receivable, stock, and prepaid expenses are considered current assets. Liquid assets are useful to have around in case you ever get into difficulties; however, you do need to remember that, once people know that you are in difficulties, the prices that you are able to charge when trying to raise cash tend to go down.

✔ **Fixed assets** require more than one year to convert to cash. In the preceding list of assets, equipment and property are classified as fixed assets. If your business gets into trouble and you need cash, fixed assets probably won't do you much good unless you can use them as collateral for a loan.

Liabilities

Liabilities are generally considered to be debts that you owe to others – individuals, other businesses, banks, and so on – outside the company. In essence, liabilities are the claims that outside individuals and organisations have against a business's assets.

The most common forms of business liabilities include the following:

- ✔ **Accounts payable (or creditors):** Accounts payable are the obligations that your company owes to the individuals and organisations from which it purchases goods and services. For example, when you visit your local office supply store to buy a couple of pencils and bill the purchase to your company's account, this obligation becomes an account payable. If you need to, you can negotiate delayed payments with suppliers in times of need, but you do need to be careful not to jeopardise your credit rating or business confidence.

- ✔ **Short-term loans:** Short-term loans are loans made to your organisation by individuals, financial institutions, or other organisations that you are due to pay back within one year. If, for example, your firm takes a 90-day loan to increase its inventory of CD-ROMS to satisfy a rapid increase in customer demand, this is considered a short-term loan.

- ✔ **Expenses:** Expenses are those items that your company incurs and has to pay regardless of the volumes of business conducted. Examples include payroll, sick leave due to employees, taxes payable, and interest due to lenders.

- ✔ **Bonds and debentures:** Some large companies issue bonds and debentures to raise money to finance expansion or achieve other goals. Bonds and debentures represent the money that a company owes to the individuals and organisations that purchase the bonds and debentures as an investment on which there is a fixed and assured rate of return.

- ✔ **Mortgages:** When organisations purchase property, they often do so by incurring long-term loans known as *mortgages*. Mortgages differ from standard loans in that they're usually secured on the property that the mortgage finances. For example, if your company defaults in its payments on the mortgage used to purchase your office building, ownership of the office building reverts to the entity that originally issued the mortgage, usually a bank or investment group.

Like assets, liabilities are also divided into two major types: *current liabilities* and *long-term liabilities*.

- ✔ **Current liabilities** are repayable within one year. In the preceding list of liabilities, accounts payable, short-term loans, and accrued expenses are considered current liabilities.

- ✔ **Long-term liabilities** are repayable in a period greater than one year. In the preceding list of liabilities, bonds and debentures and mortgages are classified as long-term liabilities.

Share capital

All businesses have owners. In some cases, the owners are a few individuals who founded the company. In other cases, the owners are the many thousands of individuals who buy the company's stock through public offerings. *Share capital* is the shareholders' possession of the assets of a business after all liabilities have been paid. *Shareholders' liabilities* – their responsibilities if the business goes bankrupt – are limited to the face value of the shares themselves.

Retained earnings

Retained earnings are the profits left over from conducting business once shareholders have received their dividends. *Dividends* are what's paid out to those who put their money into shares in the company – their reward for their investment and risk. Retained earnings are then used to reinvest in the business, new product and service development, financing new ventures, and developing and expanding into new markets.

Knowing double-entry bookkeeping

Double-entry bookkeeping is the standard method of recording financial transactions that forms the basis of modern business accounting. Invented in 1494 by Luca Pacioli, a bored Franciscan monk (he must have been really bored to invent accounting!), double-entry bookkeeping recognises that every financial transaction results in a record of a *receipt* (also known as an asset) and a record of an *expense* (also known as a liability).

Consider this example: Your company buys £1,000 worth of CD-ROMs from a manufacturer to resell to your customers. Because your company has established an account with the disk manufacturer, the manufacturer bills you for the £1,000 instead of demanding immediate cash payment. Here's the double-entry version of the accounting equation illustrating the £1,000 purchase of CD-ROMs now in stock:

Assets	=	*Liabilities*	+	*Share capital*
£1,000	=	£1,000	+	£0
(Stock)		(Accounts payable)		

In this example, assets (stock) increase by £1,000, the cost of purchasing the CD-ROMs to stock your shelves. At the same time, liabilities (accounts payable) also increase by £1,000. This increase represents the debt you owe to your supplier of CD-ROMs. In this way, the accounting equation always stays balanced.

Identifying the Most Common Types of Financial Statements

An accounting system is nice to have, but the system is worthless unless it can produce data that is useful to managers, employees, lenders, suppliers, owners, investors, and other individuals and firms that have a financial stake in your business. And believe us, a lot of people have a financial interest in your business.

All financial statements are nothing more than reports, intended for distribution to individuals outside the accounting department, that summarise the amounts of money contained in selected accounts or groups of accounts at a selected point or period. Each type of financial statement has a unique value to those people who use it, and different individuals may use some or all of an organisation's financial statements during the normal course of business. The following sections review the financial statements that you're most likely to encounter during your career as a manager.

The balance sheet

The *balance sheet* is a report that illustrates the value of a company's assets, liabilities, and share capital – the company's financial position on a specific date. Think of it as a snapshot of the business. Although it can be prepared at any time, a balance sheet is usually prepared at the end of an accounting period, usually a year, quarter, or month.

Figure 18-1 shows a typical balance sheet.

As you can see, the balance sheet provides values for every major component of the three parts of the accounting equation. By reviewing each item's value in the balance sheet, managers can identify potential problems and then take action to solve them.

The profit and loss account

Assets and liabilities are all very nice, thank you, but many people really want to see the bottom line. Did the company make money or lose money? In other words, what was its profit or loss? This job belongs to the *profit and loss account* (sometimes called the profit and loss statement).

	January 31, 2007
ASSETS	
CURRENT ASSETS	
Cash and cash equivalents	£458,000
Assets and liabilities	£11,759,000
Stock	£154,000
Prepaid expenses and other current assets	£283,000
Refundable income taxes	£165,000
TOTAL CURRENT ASSETS	£12,819,000
EQUIPMENT AND FURNITURE	
Equipment	£4,746,000
Furniture, fixtures, and improvements	£583,000
	£5,329,000
Allowance for depreciation and amortisation	£(2,760,000)
	£2,569,000
COMPUTER SOFTWARE COSTS, NET	£3,199,000
NET DEPOSITS AND OTHER	£260,000
	£18,847,000
LIABILITIES AND SHAREHOLDERS' EQUITY	
CURRENT LIABILITIES	
Loans payable to bank	£1,155,000
Accounts payable	£2,701,000
Accrued compensation and benefits	£2,065,000
Income taxes payable	£0
Deferred income taxes	£990,000
Current portion of long-term debt	£665,000
TOTAL CURRENT LIABILITIES	£18,847,000
LONG-TERM DEBT, less current portion	£864,000
DEFERRED RENT EXPENSE	£504,000
DEFERRED INCOME TAXES	£932,000
STOCKHOLDERS' EQUITY	
Common stock	£76,000
Additional paid-in capital	£803,000
Retained earnings	£8,092,000
	£8,971,000
	£18,847,000

Figure 18-1:
A typical balance sheet.

A profit and loss account adds all the sources of a company's revenues and then subtracts all the sources of its expenses to determine its net income or net loss for a particular period of time. Whereas a balance sheet is a snapshot of an organisation's financial status, a profit and loss account is more like a movie; the various roles are explained in the following sections.

Figure 18-2 illustrates a simple profit and loss account.

Turnover

Turnover is the value received by a company through the sale of goods, services, and other sources such as interest, rent, royalties, and so forth. To arrive at net sales, total sales of goods and services are offset by returns; and also by *allowances* such as discounts, special offers, and other product- and service-based promotions (for example, handing out the products free in the streets, or giving discounts for booking online).

Expenses

Expenses are all the costs of doing business. For accounting purposes, expenses are divided into two major classifications:

- ✔ **Cost of goods sold:** For a firm that retails or wholesales merchandise to individuals or other companies, this figure represents the cost of purchasing merchandise or stock. By subtracting the cost of goods sold from revenue, you end up with the company's *gross profit.*

- ✔ **Operating expenses or overheads:** Operating expenses or overheads are all the other costs of doing business not already part of the cost of goods sold. Operating expenses or overheads are usually further subdivided into *selling expenses,* which include marketing, advertising, product promotion, and the costs of operating stores, and *general and administrative expenses,* which are the actual administrative costs of running the business. General and administrative costs typically include salaries, accounting, data processing, and purchasing; and the cost of corporate facilities including rent, rates, heating, lighting, water, telecommunications and transport.

Net profit or loss

The difference between revenues and expenses (after adjustment for interest income or expense and payment of taxes) is a company's net profit or net loss. Also commonly known as a company's *bottom line,* net profit or loss is the cash you have on hand after you've paid all the bills, and it's the figure that everyone wants to know when they are assessing the firm's financial health. Many corporate executives and managers have found themselves on the street when their companies' bottom lines dipped too far into the loss side of the equation.

		Twelve months ended
		January 31, 2007
TURNOVER		
Gross sales	£58,248,000	
Less: Returns	£1,089,000	
Net Sales		£57,159,000
COST OF GOODS SOLD		
Beginning stock	£4,874,000	
Purchases	£38,453,000	
Less: Purchase discounts	£1,583,000	
Net purchases	£36,867,000	
Cost of good available for sale	£41,741,000	
Less: Ending stock	£6,887,000	
Cost of Goods Sold		£34,854,000
GROSS PROFIT		£22,305,000
OPERATING EXPENSES		
Total selling expenses	£8,456,000	
Total general expenses	£1,845,000	
Total operating expenses		£10,301,000
Operating income		£12,004,000
Other income and expenses		
Interest expense (income)	£360,000	
Total other income and expenses		£10,301,000
Income before taxes		£11,644,000
Less: Income taxes		£3,952,000
Net income		£7,692,000
Average number of shares		3,500,000
Net income		£2.20

Figure 18-2:
A simple profit and loss account.

The cash-flow statement

The cash-flow statement shows the movement of cash into and out of a business. It doesn't take an Einstein to realise that when more cash is moving out of a business than is moving into the business for a prolonged period, the business may be in big trouble. Without cash to pay employees' salaries, suppliers' invoices, loan payments, and so forth, operations quickly cease to exist.

Cash-flow statements come in several varieties:

- The **simple cash-flow statement** arranges all items into one of two categories: cash inflows and cash outflows.

- The **operating cash-flow statement** limits analysis of cash flows to only those items having to do with the operations of a business, and not its financing.

- The **priority cash-flow statement** classifies cash inflows and outflows by specific groupings chosen by the manager or other individual who requests preparation of the statement.

Analysing Business Health

If you don't know exactly what you're looking for, analysing a company's financial records can be quite a daunting task. Fortunately, over many years, expert business financial analysts have developed ways to assess the performance and financial health and wellbeing of an organisation quickly.

Using financial ratios

By comparing the ratios of certain key financial indicators to established standards and to other firms in the same industries, interested parties can assess how well a business is doing. The key ratios are:

- **Current ratio:** This ratio is the capability of a company to pay its current liabilities out of its current assets. A ratio of 2 or more is generally considered good. Consider this example:

Current ratio	=	*Current assets*	÷	*Current liabilities*
	=	£100 million	÷	£25 million
	=	4.00		

✔ **Quick ratio:** The quick ratio (also known as the *acid-test* ratio) is the same as the current ratio with the exception that stock is subtracted from current assets. This ratio provides a much more rigorous test of a firm's capability to pay its current liabilities quickly than does the current ratio, because stock can't be liquidated as rapidly as other current assets. A ratio of 1 or better is acceptable. Do note, however, that large organisations in practice tend to extend their overdraft facilities or limit dividends to shareholders if they need to, rather than selling off assets that they wish to keep for the longer term. The acid test is however critical in analysing the cash flow and performance of small and medium-sized organisations.

Quick ratio = *(Current assets – inventory)* ÷ *Current liabilities*

= (£100 million – £10 million)   ÷   £25 million

= £90 million   ÷   £25 million

= 3.60

✔ **Debtors turnover ratio:** This ratio indicates the average time it takes for a firm to convert its accounts receivable into cash. A higher ratio indicates that customers are paying their bills quickly, which is good. A lower ratio reflects slow collections and a possible problem that management needs to address, which is bad. Your boss isn't going to like it.

Debtors turnover ratio = *Net sales* ÷ *Accounts receivable*

= £50 million   ÷   £5 million

= 10.00

You can gain one more interesting piece of information quickly from the debtors turnover ratio. By dividing 365 days by the debtors turnover ratio, you get the average number of days that it takes your firm to turn over its debtors, which is commonly known as the *average collection period.* The shorter the average collection period, the better the organisation's situation is, and the better your job security is.

Average collection period = *365 days ÷ Debtors turnover ratio*

= 365 days ÷ 10.00

= 36.5 days

✔ **Debt-to-equity ratio:** This ratio measures the extent to which the organisation depends on loans from outside creditors versus resources provided by shareholders and other owners. A ratio in excess of 1 is generally considered unfavourable, because it indicates that the firm may have difficulty repaying its debts.

The debt to equity ratio indicates the *capital gearing* of the firm. People expect to see as much of the equity as possible in the form of share capital, because there is then little risk of the creditors calling in their loans. So the higher the volume of debt in relation to equity, the higher the *gearing* (or volatility) of the organisation; and when that gearing shows no signs of coming down, stock markets and other backers and interested parties begin to lose confidence in the organisation.

Debt-to-equity ratio	=	*Total liabilities*	÷	*Share capital*
	=	£50 million	÷	£150 million
	=	0.33 or 33 per cent		

✔ **Return on investment:** Often known by its abbreviation, *ROI,* return on investment measures the capability of a company to earn profits for its owners. Don't forget: Profit is good and loss is bad. Because owners – shareholders and other investors – prefer to make money on their investments, they like an organisation's ROI to be as high as possible.

Return on investment	=	*Net income*	÷	*Share capital*
	=	£50 million	÷	£150 million
	=	0.33 or 33 per cent		

Using other measures

As a manager, you must be able to do the following calculations, and know and understand what they mean for your company, your business, and your own department or domain. These calculations enable you to be very precise about where the resources for which you're responsible are used and consumed. They provide the basis for assessing the effectiveness of particular activities, and they enable you to measure and assess financial performance and give information that your company can review as often as necessary or desired.

✔ **Income/Expenditure/Profit/Loss: Per employee; per product or service; per product or service cluster; per location; per outlet.** This information helps to ensure that everyone knows where money is being made and lost, and by whom.

- **For the employees:** Take the number of employees and divide the total turnover by this figure so that you know how much turnover is produced on average per employee.

- **For the products and services:** Divide total sales by the number of outlets you have, so that you can see average sales per outlet. You can also identify the relationship between sales of one product or service and others.

Top five accounting Web sites

If you want to find out more about accounting (and, hey, who wouldn't?), here are our top five Web sites:

✔ *Business Finance* magazine: www.businessfinancemag.com

✔ Institute of Chartered Accountants: www.ica.org.uk

✔ Association of Certified and Chartered Accountants: www.acca.org.uk

✔ *AccountingWEB*: www.accountingweb.co.uk

✔ Accounting Conventions: www.dti.gov.uk/accountingconventionsandaccountingpractices

You can then develop this further in your own ways, so that the data works for you in your situation. For example:

✔ Percentage of payroll spent on front-line staff; administrative staff; corporate staff; head office.

✔ Products and services that attract peoples' attention in the first place; products and services that sell; and the products and services that make money. For example, car companies use top-of-the-range models to attract; they then sell largest volumes of lower to mid-range models; and they make their money through finance plans, service guarantees, add-ons, and guaranteed insurance arrangements.

Chapter 19

Harnessing the Power of Technology

In This Chapter

▶ Using technology to help you

▶ Understanding the pros and cons of technology

▶ Going for efficiency and productivity

▶ Putting technology to use

▶ Developing a technology plan

*L*ike everything else in life, technology has its good and bad points. With computers, for example, managers and workers alike have more ways to waste time than ever before. When all you could do with a keyboard was type, you couldn't get any manager anywhere near one – they used to have secretaries to do that kind of stuff. Now, call it a computer, add e-mail and the Internet, and you can't get managers away from it. Some research shows that managers spend up to five hours of their working day on the computer; and when you add the average of three hours a day in meetings, this does not leave very much time for the real work to be done. And do you really need to spend half an hour typing, editing, spellchecking, and colour printing a gorgeous, 64-shades-of-grey memo when a handwritten note or quick phone call works just as well? You may automatically assume that your employees are more productive simply because they have computers at their fingertips, but are you (and your organisation) really getting the most out of this innovative and expensive technology?

So in this chapter, we explain how to harness *information technology* – technology used to create, store, exchange, and use information in its various forms. We examine the technology edge, and consider how technology can help or hinder an organisation. We look at how technology can improve efficiency and productivity, and how to get the most out of technology. Finally, we describe how to create a technology plan.

Using Technology to Your Advantage

You can easily get the impression that information technology is taking over the world. Certainly, computers and telecommunications technology are ever more important. CEOs, top and senior managers all use computers and mobile phones exactly the same as everyone else, because they too (some would say above all) need to be able to be instantly flexible and responsive when required. Overall, information technology can give you and your business tremendous advantages and, as a manager, you must capitalise on them – before your competition does.

Information and telecommunications technology are only as good as the people who use them. So whatever technology you implement, make sure that your staff know and understand how they're supposed to use their equipment; and especially, make sure that they understand where the boundaries lie – what they are *not* allowed to use the technology for (such as booking holidays in the firm's time, and downloading from controversial or obscene Web sites).

First, understand the technology and what it can do for you, your organisation, and your staff. You need to take the decision whether you are going to let technology use you, or use it yourself for more effective, productive, and high-quality work.

The following sections outline four basic considerations for putting modern technology to work for you.

Know your business

Before you can design and implement an effective information technology strategy for your business, you have to completely understand how your business works – what work is done, who's doing it, and what resources they need to get their work done.

One way to know your business is to approach it as an outsider. Pretend you're a customer and look at how your company's people and systems handle you. Do the same with your competitors to see how their people and systems handle you. Compare the differences and the similarities to determine how you can improve your own organisation as a result of what you've discovered.

Create a technology-competitive advantage

Few managers understand how technology can become a competitive advantage for their businesses. Although they may have vague notions of potential efficiency gains or increased productivity, they're clueless when dealing with specifics.

Information technology can create real and dramatic competitive advantages over other businesses in your markets, specifically by:

- ✔ Using the Internet as a marketing tool, as a part of your corporate and institutional presentation and image building (refer to Chapter 9). The Internet can enhance and develop the image and presentation that you want for all of your marketing activities, as well as being a vehicle for sales.

- ✔ Make sure that the messages you put out on the Internet are the same or complementary to those put out elsewhere.

- ✔ Using the Internet as an additional marketing, sales, customer, and client liaison vehicle.

- ✔ Using the Internet to discover potential (and we stress *potential*) staff, suppliers, customers, and product and service outlets.

- ✔ Linking everyone in the company with each other, and with key suppliers, distributors, outlets, customers, and clients.

- ✔ Providing up-to-the-minute information on pricing, products, and services.

Any Web site that you develop must be kept up to date. If it is to be fully effective and complementary to the full range of your business activities, you must have it checked once a week; some organisations do this once a day, and the best have staff dedicated to changing the Web site as soon as anything occurs that requires a change.

Develop a plan

If you're serious about using information technology to full advantage, you must have a plan for its implementation. You can find details about creating a technology plan later in this chapter (see the section 'Planning and Implementation'), but the following are several points to remember in the planning process:

- ✔ **Don't buy technology just because it's the latest and greatest thing.** Everybody loves gadgets – and everybody loves the latest gadget above all. However, just because an item is new doesn't mean that it's right for your business. Be sure that whatever technology you include in your plan makes sense for your business.

- ✔ **Plan for the right period of time.** Different kinds of businesses require different *planning horizons*, the time periods covered by their plans. If you're in a highly volatile market – wireless communications, for example – then your planning horizon may be only six months or so ahead. If you're in a stable market – say, a grocery chain – your planning horizon may extend three to five years into the future.

✔ **Make the planning process a team effort.** You're not the only one who's going to be affected by all this new technology that you bring into your company. Keep customers and suppliers informed of any changes that affect them; and above all, involve your staff – they are the people, after all, who are going to be using the new technology.

✔ **Weigh up the costs of upgrading your old system versus moving to a new system.** Every system eventually comes to the end of its useful life. So you have to choose whether to patch up what you have or replace it altogether. And you need to approach that decision from the point of view of how long the system is likely to remain useful into the future, whether you're patching it up or replacing it.

Get some help

If you're a fan of technology and expert in it, that's great – but beware! Don't get drawn down the line of being blinded by technology for its own sake; always keep in mind the use to which you are going to put it, and how people less expert and enthusiastic than you are going to use it. Involve everyone, and if necessary, engage a technician or technology consultant to advise on the process. If you do bring in a consultant, again make sure that you involve the staff affected in making the changes.

Evaluating the Benefits and Drawbacks of Technology

Think for a moment about the incredible progress of information technology just in your lifetime. Can you believe that three decades ago, the personal computer had yet to be introduced commercially? Word processing used to mean a typewriter and a lot of correction fluid or sheets of messy carbon paper, but computers have revolutionised the way in which business people can manipulate text, graphics, and other elements in their reports and other documents. Mobile phones, fax machines, the Internet, and other business technology essentials are all fairly recent innovations.

So how can technology help your business? Information technology can have a positive impact in two very important ways:

✔ **By automating processes:** Not too many years ago, most business processes were manual. For example, your organisation's accounting and payroll departments most likely did their calculations entirely by hand, using only calculators to assist them. What used to take hours, days, or weeks can now be accomplished in minutes. Other commonly automated processes are stock tracking, customer service, call analysis, and purchasing.

✔ **By automating personal management functions:** Managers now need to have their diaries and personal planners on computer for ready access. While this doesn't replace wallcharts (which are essential for everyone to see in public anyway), managers do increasingly need to have their own personal data with them at all times. Managers are additionally finding that they can use their own computers to keep track of projects, get product and service performance data for themselves, contact employees by e-mail and mobile phone, and surf the Internet for data that they need to know.

Before you run off and automate or upgrade everything, keep this piece of information in mind: If your present system is inefficient or ineffective, simply upgrading the existing system won't necessarily make your system perform any better. In fact, upgrading it can make your system perform worse than the manual version. Whatever you do, review and evaluate all processes in detail. Cut out any unnecessary steps as you go along, and make sure that your system is designed for the future and not the past. And if that sounds a time-consuming process, it is time well spent.

Just as information technology can help a business, it can also hinder it. Here are a few examples of the negative side of information technology:

✔ Widespread worker abuse of Internet access has reduced worker productivity by 10 to 15 per cent. Forrester Research, an American think tank, estimates that 20 per cent of employee time on the Internet at work doesn't involve their jobs; other studies in the United Kingdom by the Chartered Management Institute, put the figure as high as 30 per cent of time.

✔ Hackers have sent periodic waves of computer viruses and malicious attacks through the business world, leaving billions of pounds of damage and lost productivity in their wake.

✔ E-mail messages can be unclear and confusing, forcing workers to waste time clarifying the intention or covering themselves in case of problems.

✔ Employees are forced to wade through an ever-growing quantity of spam and junk e-mail messages.

✔ The slick, animated, and sound-laden computer-based full-colour presentations so common today often tend to drown out the message you're trying to get across. People lose sight of what they are supposed to absorb, do, or act on as the result of the presentation.

So you have to take the bad with the good with information technology. But don't take the bad lying down. You know the problems and difficulties – so recognise them at the outset, and take active steps to prevent them occurring. You can do this by:

- ✔ **Staying abreast of the latest information technology innovations and news.** Although you don't need to become an expert on how to install a network server or configure your voice-mail system, you do need to become conversant in the technology behind your business systems.

- ✔ **Hiring experts.** Although you must have a general knowledge of information technology, plan to hire experts to advise you on the specifics. Always seek expert advice in the design and implementation of critical information technology-based systems.

- ✔ **Managing by walking around.** Make a habit of dropping in on employees, wherever they're located, and observe how they use your organisation's information technology. Ask them for their opinions and suggestions for improvement. Research and implement changes as soon as you discover a need.

One point is certain: Everyone is lumbered with the present state of technology, and the great speed at which it develops. You therefore have to know and understand what technology can do for you; and also to become quickly aware of what any new innovations or inventions can do for you.

Improving Efficiency and Productivity

In recent years, British industry has shifted from primary manufacturing and engineering activities to domination by the service sector. The service sector – whether public services, commerce, financial services, leisure, travel, tourism, or retail – depends on the speed and quality of information and data processing to maintain, secure, and develop competitive advantage.

The idea that businesspeople who manage information best have a competitive advantage in the marketplace seems obvious enough. The sooner you receive information, the sooner you can act on it. The more effectively you handle information, the easier you can access that information when and where you need it. The more efficiently and effectively you deal with information, the fewer expenses you incur for managing and maintaining your information.

Managers often cite the preceding reasons, and others like them, as justification for spending obscenely huge amounts of corporate resources to buy computers, install e-mail and voice-mail systems, and train employees to use them. Unfortunately, for years researchers found no evidence to prove that office automation resulted in measurable productivity gains. This led many to label the phenomenon the 'productivity paradox', meaning that technology that is supposed to make a job easier, quicker, to a higher standard, and with fewer errors actually results in fewer results delivered, less quickly. The problem is now that work is done at the speed at which the machine goes, rather than the speed at which the individual works.

Author Eliyahu Goldratt defined information as 'the answer to a question'. Many information systems are great at providing data, but not so hot at providing information (at least within this definition). As a managers you should first spend a lot of time identifying the questions that need an answer, discovering who needs the answer (customer, supplier, employee, management), determining how fast they need the answer (now, within one minute, one hour, one day), and working out how frequently they need the answer (daily, weekly, monthly). When the answers to these questions become clear, you have a rational basis to evaluate alternate technologies based on how well they meet the criteria needed. Lots of technology seems to be designed to provide an immediate answer to a question that you only need to ask once a month.

PC versus Apple

The question of what hardware and software to buy and install is always a key question. The original debate used to centre around whether to install Windows-based personal computers (PCs) or buy Apple computers, which looked better, were easier to use, and allegedly produced better work when operated by those who knew what they were doing. Additionally, those in the know used to cite the mere adequacy, rather than excellence, of Microsoft software as a reason for looking elsewhere. Presently, with the greatly increased range of technology available, the debate, to the unwary, is even more complex.

It all again beggars the questions: What do you want the technology to do for you? How is it to be integrated into the rest of the organisation and its work? What about the staff who are going to use the technology?

The answers to these questions must be your guide. The technology itself – both hardware and software – is of no consequence; what does matter is its use and value to the organisation. This and no other is the basis for choosing your PC, Apple/iMac, or anything else. They are working tools, not fashion items or 'must haves'.

And be in no doubt that information technology projects can, and do, overrun on cost and installation times, and then underperform when it comes to usage and value, particularly if you are driven by the technology itself rather than the answers to the questions given earlier. The public sector, commerce and industry alike are riddled with major technology projects that have been under-designed, under-costed, and under-evaluated. The UK's National Health Service national database was costed originally at £440 million; to date, it has cost £2.7 billion and is still not fully functional. And this situation can happen to anyone, at any level. So be careful, and don't get sidetracked by arguments around the brand and cachet of the technology itself, especially when this is driven by fashion and fad rather than value.

The key to effective planning and implementation of information technology systems is knowing and understanding what they are supposed to do for you. You also need to know and understand the full environment and context in which they are to be implemented, and, above all, the results that they are to deliver for you. For example:

- Ryanair and easyJet have transformed the entire air travel sector of Western and Central Europe. They cut out the costs of employing travel agents to make bookings, requiring people to book online or, at a high premium, through their own call centres. However, the online booking facility is not an end in itself, it is underpinned by the major cost and price advantages that each of the companies delivers, relative to the competition and alternatives from European flag-carrier airlines. And when Michael O'Leary, the CEO of Ryanair, was asked whether by getting customers to book online he was eliminating those who did not have computer access, he simply replied: 'We are the largest volume carrier in Europe; and we carry more passengers than British Airways.'

- Honda UK at Swindon has a fully automated supply-side process. As parts are removed from the shelves to go on to the production lines, they are automatically deducted from the stock levels; and when the stock level reaches a particular point, a request to suppliers is automatically generated. The supply side contract means that suppliers must dispatch within two hours, and Honda must receive their requirements within four hours.

Other companies have taken an enlightened view of 'the technology in its environment' to great effect. For example:

- Semco, a Brazilian manufacturing company and global iconic organisation, cancelled one computerised accounting and billing system because it did the job more slowly than clerks working with calculators.

- Mobile communications retailer Carphone Warehouse forbids its staff to send e-mails to each other unless, and until, they have first talked face to face, or unless the particular member of staff is not on the premises for some reason. This is because the company takes the view that far more gets done far more quickly when people talk to each other, than when they write to each other.

So merely installing computers and other information technology does not automatically lead to gains in employee efficiency or product and service performance. As a manager, you must take the time to analyse and evaluate the environment in which the work has to be done. To be fully effective, the technology must integrate fully with the aims and objectives of the business, the ways in which it delivers products and services, and the capabilities and qualities of the staff doing the work.

Getting the Most Out of Information Technology

The personal computer shifted the power of computing away from huge mainframes and onto the desks of individual users. Now, computer networks are bringing about a new revolution in business. Although the personal computer is a self-sufficient island of information, when you link these islands together in a network, individual computers have the added benefit of sharing with every computer on the network. So you have a huge potential to tap into. Nevertheless, make sure that you concentrate especially on the following:

- ✔ **Networks improve communication:** Computer networks allow anyone in an organisation who is connected to the network to communicate with anyone else quickly and easily. With the click of a button, you can send messages to individuals or groups of employees. You can send replies just as easily. Furthermore, employees on computer networks can access financial, marketing, and product information needed to do their jobs from throughout the organisation.

- ✔ **Networks save time and money:** In business, time is money. The faster you can get something done, the more tasks you can complete during the course of your business day. E-mail allows you to create messages, memos, and other internal communications, to attach work files, and then to transmit them instantaneously to as many colleagues as you want. And these colleagues can be located across the room or around the world – and they all get the same message at the same time.

- ✔ **Networks improve understanding of markets, products and services:** Information communicated via computer networks is timely, direct, and standardised. Everyone gets the same message and so everyone can have the same understanding of the company's vision and values; and especially of its products, services, and markets, and the ways in which these are performing. All staff therefore ought to have a much clearer understanding than was previously possible of just how products and services are delivered, and what the markets need, want, and demand.

- ✔ **Networks improve and underpin staff cohesion:** Because everybody has the same access to information, and receives the same messages in an unfiltered way, there is a much greater potential for mutual cohesion and commitment, provided that networks are used to support the organisation's core values and staff management practices. However, problems always occur if you deliver different messages to different groups of staff – and this information and these differences will become very much more apparent more quickly as the result of the presence of information technology, simply because so many people have access to so much more information. Be very careful to set yourself high standards and transparency in your approach.

Getting inta the intranet

The logical extension of networks is the creation of corporate and organisational intranets. *Intranets* are internal e-mail and Web-based information management and information exchange systems and most organisations now have them. The key question is the use that you put an intranet to, and how you allow access to it.

You can use an intranet in many different ways – for example to push out information, to speed-up product and service delivery processes and functions, or to reinforce and support communication and co-ordination between departments, divisions, functions, and locations. Managers are being pushed (in many cases, very unwillingly) towards a much greater openness of information and communications, and a much greater all-round awareness of everything that is going on within the organisation. A main driver of this is the sheer volume of information and speed of access that intranets allow. Information gets around the organisation even more quickly than before – and lack of information gets around it as well. If you don't know something, you now have a much greater range of other people to ask. Make sure that the information provided is complete, open, and transparent whenever possible.

One or two words of warning, however: You should never allow people to use the intranet or any organisational network for personal gain or advantage; and do make sure that you keep genuinely confidential information (commercial and staff related) private, by having an effective password system that protects everyone where required.

So your first step towards getting the most out of information technology is to commit yourself to concentrating on each of these areas. Of course, additional functional requirements exist for everyone connected. However, using networks to underpin culture, values, product and service knowledge, and staff awareness reinforces the very foundations of the organisation.

Planning and Implementation

When it comes to the fast-changing area of technology, having a *technology plan* – a plan for acquiring and deploying information technology – is a must. Many businesses buy bits and pieces of computer hardware, software, and other technology without considering the technology that they already have in place, and without looking very far into the future. Then, when they try to hook everything together, they're surprised that their thrown-together system doesn't work.

Managers who take the time to develop and implement a technology plan don't have this problem, and aren't forced to spend far more money and time fixing systems problems. Follow these steps for a smooth process:

1. **Create the plan.** As manager, you have the vision and purpose – what the technology is supposed to deliver, how, when, where, and to whom. However, in order to give this vision life, you have to be able to present it in ways that your colleagues and staff can understand, so get them involved. Without doubt, they will be able to see potential that you have not thought of; and they will also be able to see any glitches or problems; it is they, after all, who are going to be implementing and using the technology in the pursuit of your grand vision.

2. **Screen and select suppliers.** Go out yourself to actual and potential suppliers. Once you have debated your requirements with your staff and created a technology plan, take the plan with you. Show potential suppliers what you want, and ask them if they can deliver it. And if they say 'No, we cannot deliver this; but we can deliver something that is much better', listen to them, evaluate their response, and take the issue back to your organisation for debate with your colleagues – or else walk away. If a supplier says 'No, we cannot deliver this; we will deliver what we always deliver regardless of customer requirements' – then just walk away.

3. **Implement the plan.** So everyone has agreed the technology plan and you have chosen your supplier. Now comes the tricky part – implementation. Be in absolutely no doubt that glitches, delays, overruns, and teething troubles are going to occur – everyone has these, and you're no different. At the implementation phase build in as much slack and leeway as necessary to allow for these problems to arise and for you to resolve them.

4. **Monitor performance.** And so finally your system is up and running. Congratulations all round! However, this is crunch time to determine whether the system is really going to deliver what you planned. Keep in mind that, especially in the early stages, glitches and teething troubles with the system are going to happen. So make sure that you have a tight and high-quality service level agreement with your supplier, committing it to coming in and fixing any problems as soon as they arise or become apparent. Make sure that your supplier has staff who are fully trained in your system; if not, then call the supplier to account for this. And if (hypothetically of course!) the system does not deliver what you and your colleagues expected, then you have a serious problem, but one that you have to face; otherwise you find yourself in the position of all the large corporations and public service bodies that have tried to make the unworkable work.

 'Everything takes twice as long as you think, and costs twice as much.' While this is never an excuse for organisational slackness or waste of resources, it does underpin the point that nothing ever goes completely according to schedule.

Top five information technology Web sites

You can find loads of IT info on the Web, but these sites are the cream of the crop:

✔ *Wired* magazine: www.wired.com

✔ *Computerworld*: www.computerworld. com

✔ IBM: www.ibm.com

✔ Accenture: www.accenture.com

✔ *InternetWorld*: www.internetworld. com

Technology is a strategic expense; and all organisations and managers need to see technology projects as investments on which there are demonstrable and quantifiable returns. Make sure that whatever you do is guided by the business, product, service, and market drivers of the organisation, and the goals, results, and targets that the organisation expects you to deliver as a manager. Use this as your guiding principle when planning and implementing technology projects, and you get much less wrong than those who do not take the time and trouble to prepare fully.

Chapter 20

Developing and Mentoring Employees

. . . .

In This Chapter

▶ Understanding the importance of developing employees

▶ Building career development plans

▶ Grasping the mentoring process

▶ Developing employees despite downsizing

. . . .

Time for a quick look in the mirror. What kind of manager are you? Do you take on new employees and then just let them go on their merry way? Or do you stay actively involved in the progress and development of your employees, helping to guide them along the way? If you're a manager-to-be, do you know what having a mentor is like, someone who takes a personal interest in your career development? Mentoring is vitally important because as well as needing to make your own mistakes (and you will!) you also need someone to guide you, act as a sounding board, strengthen and test your determination, and indicate areas where you could improve.

Employee development is the process by which you make everyone (including yourself) better at their jobs and improve their willingness to carry them out to the best of their abilities. Employee development is also concerned with the development of skills, knowledge, attitudes, and behaviour; building experience and achievements into expertise. Employee development concentrates on the key areas of workplace development, professional and occupational priorities, and personal choices, so that everyone benefits, and so that individuals take an active responsibility for their own future.

The best employee development is continuous and requires that you support and encourage your employees' initiative. Recognise, however, that all development is self-development; you can really only develop yourself. You can't force your employees to develop. They have to want to develop themselves. You can, however, help set an environment that makes it more likely that they want to develop, grow, and succeed.

Explaining How Employee Development Helps

Development boils down to one important point: As a manager, you're in the best position to provide your employees with the support they need to advance in your organisation. Not only can you provide them with the time and money required for training, but also you can provide them with unique on-the-job learning opportunities and assignments, mentoring, team participation, and more. Besides, someone has got to be there to take your place when you get promoted. Employee development involves a lot more than just going to a training class or two. In fact, approximately 90 per cent of development occurs on the job.

Training, learning, and development are all different aspects of the same process:

- ✔ **Training** is the most straightforward – you tell people how to do something that is either more or less standard; or you take a step-by-step approach to something more complex.

- ✔ **Learning** requires you to create the conditions, environment, and context – and employee confidence – in which development is most effective.

- ✔ **Development** is what goes on with everyone in all aspects of their lives, including work. From a manager's point of view, you should see employee development as a combination of personal, professional, occupational, and career advancement and enhancement; and the improvements of knowledge, attitudes, behaviour, and experience, as well as skills and expertise.

Now, in case you don't have any inkling whatsoever why developing your employees is a good idea, the following list provides the full justification:

- ✔ **Development assures that your employees have the knowledge they need.** Have you ever wondered why your employees continue to mess up assignments that you know they can perform? Have you ever actually seen your employees perform the assignments in question? Believe it or not, your employees may not know how to do those assignments. So you need to equip them with the skills and knowledge to do the job, and to train them to use any technology required. You also need to foster the attitudes and understanding necessary to ensure that they do everything to the best of their ability.

For example, say you give a pile of figures to your assistant and tell him you want them organised and added up within an hour. However, instead of presenting you with a nice, neat computer spreadsheet, your employee gives you a confusing mess. No, your employee isn't necessarily incompetent; your employee may not know how to put together a spreadsheet on his computer. The solution may be as simple as walking; through your approach to completing the assignment with your employee and then having him give it a try.

✔ **Employees who work effectively are better employees.** Simply put, effective employees are better employees. If you can help your employees to develop and begin to work more effectively – and doubtless you can – why wouldn't you? No one in your organisation knows everything he needs to know. Find out what your employees don't know about their jobs and then make plans with them about how and when they can find out what they need to know. As your employees achieve their development goals, they get better and better all the time, and your organisation reaps the benefits in greater employee efficiency and effectiveness – and you too get better and better as the result.

✔ **Someone has to be prepared to step into your shoes.** Do you ever plan to take a holiday? Or get a promotion? How are you going to go anywhere or do anything outside of the office if you don't help to prepare your employees to take on the higher-level duties that are part of your job? We all know managers who are so worried about what's going on at the office that they call in several times a day even when they're on holiday. Whether they're in the Seychelles, Venice, or at the top of Mount Snowdon, they spend more time worrying about the office than they do enjoying themselves.

The reason that many managers don't have to call their offices when they're on holiday is because they make it a point to help develop their employees to take over when they're gone. You can do the same thing, too; the future of your organisation depends on it. Really.

✔ **Your employee wins, and so does your organisation.** When you allocate funds and time to employee development, your employees win by gaining higher-level skills and new ways of viewing the world; and your organisation wins because of increased employee motivation and improved work skills. When you spend money for employee development, you actually double the effect of your investment because of this dual effect. Almost better than a trip to Las Vegas! And most important, you prepare your employees to fill the roles into which your organisation needs them to move in the future.

✔ **Your employees are worth your time and money.** New employees cost a lot of money to recruit and train. Not only do you have to consider the investment in financial terms, but also you and the rest of your staff have to make an investment in time.

And it makes no sense to anyone if you let otherwise good and committed staff go for the want of giving them proper opportunities for development. You incur the expense and disruption of having to attract, recruit, and select new staff anyway; and you have then to create an induction programme to get the new starter as familiar, confident, and productive as quickly as possible. So concentrate on doing what you can for those you already employ; and make sure that if they have ambitions, you go as far as you possibly can to fulfil them. You will always lose staff, of course, but you want to keep these losses to a minimum if you can.

When employees see that you have their best interests at heart, they're likely to want to work for you and learn from you. As a result, your organisation attracts talented people. Invest in your employees now, or waste your time and money finding replacements later. The choice is yours.

✔ **The challenge stimulates your employees.** Face it: Not every employee is fortunate enough to have the kind of exciting, jet-setting, make-it-happen job that you have. For this reason, some employees occasionally become bored, lackadaisical, and otherwise indisposed. Why? Employees constantly need new challenges and new goals to maintain interest in their jobs. And if you don't challenge your employees, you're guaranteed to end up with an unmotivated, low-achievement workforce or employees who jump at offers from employers who will challenge them. Which option do you prefer?

✔ **Capability and willingness.** Employee development is not an end in itself. You must take on the kind of employees who are seeking opportunities in the first place. All employee development therefore becomes a partnership, a relationship between employee aspirations, and organisations' and their managers' commitment to match and fulfil those employee aspirations wherever possible. And if those who are less motivated see their colleagues getting on, this may fire them up anyway. So make sure that everyone is enthusiastic and committed, whether they intend to stand for promotion; or they simply want to get better at what they're already doing; or they need to acquire new skills and new technologies because their profession or occupation demands it.

Working in the factory: Not what it used to be

Many jobs that people with a relatively low level of education used to carry out have been transformed out of all recognition. For example, the factories in the United States and Western Europe that Japanese car and electrical goods companies established during the 1970s revolutionised both factory work and manufacturing.

Companies such as Sharp, Sony, Nissan, and Toyota set out to change their reputation for producing cheap, low-quality, and often shoddy goods. In the new locations, they paid above the market and industry rate in return for what they called conformity and commitment. These

Japanese companies spent millions training production staff to be fully skilled and totally flexible, able to do any job demanded, both before and after the production lines were switched on.

The results transformed manufacturing; and ruined British car and electrical goods companies in many cases. Employee development – a demonstrable commitment to staff and their future – drove everything the Japanese companies did. As employee capabilities increased, their enthusiasm, ambition, and aspirations also increased, which multiplied the beneficial effect.

Creating Career Development Plans

The career development plan is the heart and soul of your efforts to develop your employees. Unfortunately, many managers don't take the time to create development plans with their employees, instead trusting that when a need arises, they can find training to accommodate that need. This kind of reactive thinking ensures that you're always playing catch up to the challenges that your organisation faces.

Why wait for the future to arrive before you prepare to deal with it? Are you really so busy that you can't spend a little of your precious time planting the seeds that your organisation can harvest years from now? No! Although you do have to take care of the seemingly endless crises that arise in the here and now, you also have to prepare yourself and your employees to meet the challenges of the future. To do otherwise is an incredibly short-sighted and ineffective way to run your organisation.

All career development plans must contain at minimum the following key elements:

✔ **Specific learning goals:** When you meet with an employee to discuss his development plans, you identify specific learning goals. Learning goals are simply goals that mean an employee has a firm aim during their development, such as: 'By the end of August, Steve will have learned to use the network to a professional level, and will be able to train others in its operations'.

And don't forget: Each and every employee in your organisation benefits from having learning goals. Don't leave anyone out!

For example, say that your employee's career path starts at the position of junior buyer and works up to manager of purchasing. The key learning goals for this employee may be learning the stocks and supplies; training how to plan for stock replacement; spreadsheet analyses; and introduction to management.

✔ **Resources required to achieve the designated learning goals:** After you identify your employee's learning objectives, you have to decide how he may reach them. Development resources include a wide variety of opportunities that support the development of your employees. Your employee may require secondments and projects, job shadowing, *stretch assignments* (assignments that aren't too easy or too hard, and involve some learning and discomfort), formal training, and more. Outsiders or internal trainers can conduct formal training, or the employee may benefit from a self-guided series of learning modules. If the training requires funding or other resources, identify those resources and make efforts to obtain them.

✔ **Employee responsibilities and resources:** Career development is the joint responsibility of an employee and his manager. A business can and does pay for things, but so can employees (as any employee who has paid out of his own pocket to get a university degree can testify). A good career development plan should include what the employee is doing in his own time.

✔ **Required date of completion for each learning goal:** Plans are no good without a way to schedule the milestones of goal accomplishment and progress. Each learning goal has to have a corresponding date of completion. Don't select dates that are so close that they're difficult or unduly onerous to achieve, or so far into the future that they lose their immediacy and effect. The best schedules for learning goals allow employees the flexibility to get their daily tasks done while keeping ahead of the changes in the business environment that necessitate the employees' development in the first place.

✔ **Standards for measuring the accomplishment of learning goals:** For every goal, you must have a way to measure its completion. Normally, the manager assesses whether the employees actually use the new skills they've been taught. Whatever the individual case, make sure that the standards you use to measure the completion of a learning goal are clear and attainable and that both you and your employees are in full agreement with them.

The career development plan of a junior buyer may look like the one shown in Figure 20-1.

Career Development Plan

Skill goals:

* Become expert in stock-replacement techniques and schedules.

* Become effective in spreadsheet analysis.

Learning goal:

* Learn the basics of management and supervision.

Plan:

* Shadow supervisor in daily work for one half-day per week, starting immediately.

* Attend quarterly supervisor's update seminar on the first Wednesday of January, April, July, and October. (No cost: in-house.)

* Secondment to stock-control centre: the first two weeks of May, 2007.

* Successfully complete fast-track certificate in management no later than 31 July, 2007 (£1,800, plus travel costs).

* Continue self-funded accounting certificate programme at local higher education college. (To be completed successfully by 31 March, 2008).

Measures:

Stock control. Test by supervisor in April 2007 on the following elements: ability to describe the stock control system; ability to assess the stock control system for strengths and weaknesses; ability to state where improvements need to be made, or to state why no improvements are required.

Spreadsheet analysis. Test by supervisor in May 2007 on the following elements: data entry; data evaluation and explanation; data manipulation; data presentation in the context of management reports.

Management as a learning goal. Review at supervisions/appraisals for: communication skills, such as contribution to meetings and operational understanding; from 2007 onwards to be given tasks to be assigned to others, and to act as coach and mentor to members of the work group.

Figure 20-1:
A sample career development plan.

This career development plan contains all of the necessary elements outlined in the preceding list. A career development plan doesn't have to be complicated to be effective. In fact, when it comes to employee development plans, simpler is definitely better. Of course, the exact format you decide on isn't so important. The most important point is that you do career development plans, and that you and the employees stick to them!

Helping Employees to Develop

Employee development takes the deliberate and continuous efforts of employees with the support of their managers. If employees or managers lose heart, commitment, or faith, then employees don't develop, and the organisation suffers the consequences of not having the employees it needs to meet the challenges it faces. This outcome definitely isn't good. As a manager, you want your organisation to be ready for the future, not always trying to catch up with it.

The employee's role is to identify the areas where development can help to make them better and more productive workers and then to relay this information to their manager. After further development opportunities are identified, the manager and employee work together to schedule and implement them.

As a manager, your role is to be alert to the development needs of your employees and to keep an eye out for potential development opportunities. Managers in smaller organisations may have the assignment of determining where the organisation will be in the next few years. Armed with that information, you're responsible for finding ways to ensure that employees are available to meet the needs of the future organisation. Your job is then to provide the resources and support required to develop employees so that they're able to fulfil the organisation's needs.

To develop your employees to meet the coming challenges within your organisation, follow these steps:

1. **Meet with each employee about their career.**

   Meet with individuals to discuss where you see them in the organisation and also to find out where in the organisation they want to go.

   This effort has to be a joint one! Having elaborate plans for an employee to rise up the company ladder in sales management isn't going to do you any good if your employee hates the idea of leaving actual sales to become a manager of other salespeople.

2. **Discuss your employee's strengths and weaknesses.**

   Have a frank discussion regarding the employee's strengths and areas for development. Your main goal here is to identify the areas that the employee is interested in and good at – that is, strengths that your employees can develop to allow their continued progress in the organisation and to meet the future challenges that your business faces. Focus the majority of your development efforts and resources on these opportunities.

   Spend time developing strengths as well as improving weaknesses. Improving and enhancing a skill that your employee finds easy and enjoyable is more valuable for you and your organisation than forcing the employee to be merely adequate at things others excel in. However, everyone needs to be proficient in essential tasks, even if they don't like them.

3. **Assess where the employee is now.**

   Determine the current state of your employee's skills and talents. Doing an assessment provides you with an overall road map to guide your development efforts.

4. **Create a career development plan.**

   A *career development plan* is an agreement between you and your employee that spells out exactly what formal support (tuition, time off, travel expenses, and so on) they may receive to develop their skills, and when they may receive it. Career development plans have review and evaluation points, assessments of progress, and agreements on the next step (refer to Figure 20-1).

5. **Follow through on your agreements, and make sure that the employee follows through on his.**

   Don't break the development plan agreement. Make sure that you provide the support that you agreed to provide. Make sure that your employee upholds his end of the bargain, too! Check on his progress regularly. If he misses schedules because of other priorities, reassign his work as necessary to ensure that he has time to focus on his career development plans.

So when is the best time to sit down with your employees to discuss career planning and development? The sooner the better! Unfortunately, many organisations closely tie career discussions to annual employee performance appraisals. On the plus side, doing so ensures that a discussion about career development happens at least once a year; on the minus side, development discussions become more of an afterthought than the central focus of the meeting. Not only because of that limitation, but also with the current rapid changes in competitive markets and technology, once a year just isn't enough to keep up. Planning for career development only once a year is like watering a plant only once a year.

The top ten ways to develop employees

The basics for developing employees are

1. Provide employees with opportunities to learn and grow.

2. Be a mentor to an employee.

3. Let an employee fill in for you in staff meetings.

4. Give employees secondment and project work opportunities.

5. Allow employees to pursue and develop any ideas they have.

6. Provide employees with a choice of assignments.

7. Send your employee to a seminar on a new topic.

8. Take an employee along with you when you call on customers.

9. Introduce your employees to top managers in your organisation and arrange to have them perform special assignments for senior people.

10. Allow an employee to shadow you during your workday.

Conducting a career development discussion twice a year with each of your employees isn't too often. Quarterly is even better; and a brief chat once a month is best of all. And make sure that you commit to this – it represents time, money, and effort well spent! Include a brief assessment in each discussion of the employee's development needs. Ask your employee what he can do to fulfil these needs. If he requires additional support, determine what form of support the employee needs and when you should schedule the support. Adjust career development plans and redirect resources as necessary.

Finding a Mentor, Being a Mentor

When you're an inexperienced employee working your way up an organisation's hierarchy, having someone with more experience to help guide you along the way is invaluable. Someone who's already seen what it takes to get to the top can advise you about the things that you must do and the things that you shouldn't do as you work your way up. This someone is called a *mentor*.

A mentor is most typically an individual elsewhere or higher up in the organisation who isn't your boss. A manager's job is clearly to coach and help guide employees. Although managers certainly can act as mentors for their own employees, mentors most often act as confidential advisers and sounding boards for their chosen employees and therefore aren't typically in the employee's direct chain of command. Anyone can be a mentor; but doing so takes both capability and commitment. You can be a mentor to staff within your department, but if you do this, beware of accusations of patronage or favouritism.

The day that a mentor finds you and takes you under his wing is a day for you to celebrate because not everyone is lucky enough to find a mentor. And don't forget that someday you may be in a position to be a mentor to someone else. When that day comes, don't be so caught up in your busy business life that you neglect to reach out and help someone else find his way up the organisation.

Mentors provide definite benefits to the employees they mentor, and they further benefit the organisation by providing necessary guidance to employees who may not otherwise get such help. Mentors are a real benefit, both to your employees and to your organisation, because they can

- **Explain how the organisation really works.** Mentors are a great way to find out what's really going on in an organisation. You've probably noticed that a big difference exists between what's formally announced to employees and what really goes on in the organisation, particularly within the ranks of upper management. Your mentor probably has detailed knowledge behind the formal announcements, and he can convey that knowledge to you (at least, the knowledge that isn't confidential) without your having to find it out the hard way.

- **Lead by example.** By watching how your mentor gets tasks done in the organisation, you can discover a lot. Your mentor has probably seen everything before, and he can help you discover the most effective and efficient ways to get things done. Why reinvent the wheel or get beaten up by the powers that be when you don't have to?

- **Provide growth experiences.** A mentor can help guide you to activities above and beyond your formal career development plans that are helpful to your growth as an employee. For example, though your official career development plan doesn't identify a specific activity, your mentor may strongly suggest that you join a group, such as Toastmasters, to improve your public-speaking skills. Your mentor makes this suggestion because he knows that public-speaking skills are very important to your future career growth.

- **Provide career guidance and discussion.** Your mentor has probably seen more than a few employees and careers come and go over the years. He knows which career paths in your organisation are dead ends and which offer the most rapid advancement. This knowledge can be incredibly important to your future as you make career choices within an organisation. The advice your mentor gives you can be invaluable.

The mentoring process often happens when a more experienced employee takes a professional interest in a new or inexperienced employee. Employees can also initiate the mentoring process by engaging the interest of potential mentors while seeking advice or working on projects together. However, recognising the potential benefits for the development of their employees, many organisations have formalised the mentoring process and made it available to a wider range of employees than the old, informal process ever could. If a formal mentoring programme isn't already in place in your organisation, why don't you recommend starting one?

Balancing Development and Downsizing

You've seen the stories: a thousand employees laid off at Barclays Bank, thousands more employees laid off at Vauxhall Motors, and even more thousands laid off in the National Health Service. Most companies aren't immune when the economy downturns. Maybe your organisation has felt the sharp knife of re-engineering, downsizing, or reductions. If so, you may ask, 'Isn't employee development too difficult to perform when everything is changing so fast around me? My employees may not even have careers next year, much less the need to plan for developing them.'

Actually, nothing can be further from the truth. Although businesses are going through rapid change, employee development is more important than ever. As departments are combined, dissolved, or reorganised, employees have to be ready to take on new roles, duties that they may never have performed before. In some cases, employees may have to compete internally for positions or sell themselves to other departments to ensure that they retain their employment with the organisation. In this time of great uncertainty, many employees feel that they may have lost control of their careers and even their lives.

Career planning and development provide employees in organisations undergoing rapid change with the tools that they need to regain control of their careers. The following list tells what some of the largest and most high-profile companies have done to help get their employees through redundancies and reorganisations.

  ✔ British Airways has undergone major reorganisations over the past decade in pursuit of reducing staff costs and managerial and administrative overheads. All staff at risk of redundancy are offered opportunities for retraining and redeployment; and they are in a 'staff pool' for a period of up to 12 months before the organisation finally releases them. During this period they have access, within reason, to any training and development that may enhance their future employment prospects.

✔ When MG cars at Ryton, Coventry, closed in 2004, the firm offered staff retraining and re-education opportunities as an integral part of the severance package. The company also promised that, should the factory open under a different ownership, ex-MG employees would be given preference when seeking employment.

✔ Computer giant IBM overhauled the career plans of thousands of employees who transitioned from staff positions to sales positions as a result of a massive corporate reorganisation.

✔ Most famous of all, Mitsubishi, a Japanese manufacturing corporation, transformed itself from producing aircraft and ships into a major car manufacturer without any job losses whatsoever. Staff were simply told what was going to happen, and then retrained as car workers. This was effected through a £42 million investment in training, technology, and re-equipment.

Despite the obvious negative effects of downsizing on employee morale and trust, times of change provide managers with a unique opportunity to shape the future of their organisations. For many managers, this is the first time that they have such an opportunity to help remake the organisation. And each of the stories in the preceding list shows that there are alternatives to simply laying people off.

Employee development is more important than ever as employees are called on to take on new and often more responsible roles in your organisation. Your employees need your support now. Make sure that you're there to provide it. This help just may be one of the most valuable gifts that you can give to your employees.

Top five mentoring and development Web sites

The following Web sites provide the best information on the Web about the topics addressed in this chapter:

✔ Your Big Picture: www.yourbig picture.net

✔ Business Mentoring Scotland: www. businessmentoringscotland.org

✔ SBA Classroom: Business Mentoring Course: www.sba.gov/classroom/ bizmentoring.html

✔ Chartered Management Institute: www.cmi. org.uk/mentoringandcoaching

✔ Chartered Institute of Personnel and Development: www.cipd.co.uk/ employeedevelopment

Chapter 21

Keeping Track of Management Trends

In This Chapter

▶ Getting back to basics

▶ Starting a learning organisation

▶ Tearing down the hierarchy

▶ Opening up the books

▶ Using Six Sigma to improve quality

The graveyard of management innovation is littered with the wreckage of countless systems that were once hot, and now aren't. Zero defects, one-minute management, quality circles, and total quality management all had their time in the sun, and now all have been pushed onto the back shelf. Every management trend has its own unique life cycle, usually short and expensive, especially for those who slavishly follow them.

The fact is, most trends have value. Unfortunately, few organisations actually make the fundamental process and structural changes required to truly transform the organisation. After the programme's novelty wears off – often only a few short weeks or months after its introduction – the organisation goes back to business as usual. But even the most fleeting management fad has the potential to leave some benefit and to effect positive change within organisations. The secret is to look beyond the fads (some of them do have value) and see what their real contribution is in the never-ending search for success.

In this chapter, we consider some management trends, including the return to basics, the learning organisation, the flat organisation, open-book management, and Six Sigma. Many of the most successful and profitable organisations concentrate hardest on the first of these fads and fashions – going back to basics, concentrating on the core of delivering performance, achieving this through staff, and underpinning everything with professional and effective management – and dip into the others only when they believe that is the concept that can make an active contribution to performance and profitability.

Beginning with the Basics

Clearly, all kinds of new opportunities exist in every industry. But, at the same time, this creates all kinds of new obstacles for managers and for their employees. How, for example, can a manager best direct an employee when they may not even have physical contact with each other for weeks or months at a time?

Answers to questions like this one have led many managers to step out of 'the fast-paced, business-at-the-speed-of-light environment and return to the basics of managing people. These basics include:

- ✔ **Making time for people.** You have no substitute for face-to-face time when it comes to building trusting relationships. Managing is a people job, and you need to take time for your people. (Refer to Chapter 12 for ways to improve communication with your employees.)

- ✔ **Embracing change.** You recognise the fact of change, and the effects it has on your employees. If you don't keep employees well informed, they are going to wonder what's going on. So use the fact and inevitability of change to develop face-to-face working relationships, improve communication, and boost the quality of information available.

- ✔ **Increasing communication as you increase distance.** The greater the distance between manager and employee, the greater the effort both parties have to make to keep in touch. But, you can't depend on your employees to take the initiative to keep in touch; you have to keep the channels of communication flowing freely and often. (See Chapter 12 for ways to manage faraway employees.)

- ✔ **Using technology (and not letting it use you).** Technology can obviously be a great benefit, but don't let technology use you. Instead, use technology as a way to beef up your communication with employees, not just as a way to distribute data. Reinforce this policy with regular e-mail and mobile phone contact. (Refer to Chapter 19 for ways to use technology effectively.)

- ✔ **Setting performance targets.** Wherever your employees work and however often you see them (or not), make sure that they stay focused and committed to the achievements and outputs required. Specify timescales and deadlines; and reinforce this with regular contact through every means available.

- ✔ **Sharing results.** Keep your employees constantly informed of progress; and ensure that everybody knows when particular results have been achieved. Make sure that people know and understand that when results have not been achieved, there are going to be other things to do. Again, you can deliver this kind of news more easily when you make sure communication and contact are as effective as possible.

So managers have to work hard to be available to others. If you value strong working relationships and clear communication (we're assuming you do!), you need to return to basics, spending more and higher-quality time with your employees rather than less.

All this has led to the increasing professionalisation of management – an understanding that, whoever they manage and in whatever industry or sector, managers have to be good and expert in each of the areas listed. Indeed, some say we have reached the point where, if you are not taking a professional attitude and are not committed to being expert and proficient in each skill area, maybe management is not right for you.

Creating a Learning Organisation

A *learning organisation* is an organisation skilled at creating, acquiring, and transferring knowledge and at modifying its original assumptions, purposes, and behaviour to reflect new knowledge and insights. Ever since Peter Senge's ground-breaking book *The Fifth Discipline* was published in 1990, the question of how to create and lead organisations in which continuous learning occurs has been at the top of many managers' lists of management techniques to consider.

The problem with the old way of doing business is that organisations are built on the premise that the world is predictable. If you can just build a model that is large and complex enough, you can anticipate any eventuality. This particular view has a problem: The world isn't predictable. The global world of business is chaotic – what's true today is washed away tomorrow as the next wave of change hits. The only constant in today's organisations is change.

The learning organisation is designed around the assumption that organisations are going through rapid change and that managers should expect the unexpected. Indeed, managers who work for learning organisations welcome unexpected events that occur within the organisation, because they consider them to be opportunities, not problems. Instead of static organisations that are strictly hierarchical, learning organisations are flexible. This structure makes managers able to lead change instead of merely reacting to change.

How do you go about designing a learning organisation? Several characteristics are particularly important as you consider turning your organisation into a learning organisation. The more of each characteristic that your organisation exhibits, the closer it is to being a true learning organisation, one that thrives in times of rapid change.

> ✔ **Encourage objectivity.** Over the course of our careers, we've seen managers make many organisational decisions simply to please someone with power, influence, or an incredible ego. Managers made such subjective decisions not through a reasoned consideration of the facts, but

through emotion. As a manager, you must encourage objectivity in your employees and colleagues and practise objectivity in your own decision making.

✔ **Seek openness.** For an organisation to grow, employees have to be willing to tell each other the truth. To make this openness possible, you must create safe environments for your employees to say what is on their minds and to tell you any bad news without fear of retribution. Drive fear out of the organisation if you want to build a learning organisation.

✔ **Facilitate teamwork.** Deploying employee teams is a very important part in the development of learning organisations. When an organisation relies on individuals to respond to changes, it is at the mercy of individual responses (and especially resistance); however, when an organisation relies on teams to respond to change, it can mobilise many more employees much more quickly. And this can mean the difference between life and death in the ever-changing global business environment.

✔ **Create useful tools.** Managers in learning organisations need tools that enable employees to obtain the information that they need to do their jobs quickly and easily. Computer networks, for example, have to be set up with access for all employees, and they have to provide the kinds of financial and other data that decision makers need. The best tools are those that get the right information to the right people at the right time.

✔ **Consider the behaviour you're rewarding.** Remember the phrase 'You get what you reward.' What actions are you rewarding, and what behaviours are you getting in return? If you want to build a learning organisation, reward the behaviours that help you create a learning organisation. Stop rewarding behaviours that are inconsistent with this objective, such as subjectivity and individualism. The sooner you accomplish this mission, the better.

Making a Flat Organisation

A growing trend exists today to flatten organisations by removing layers of management. When businesses flatten their organisations, they widen the span of control (the number of people directly supervised) of the remaining managers, and push authority farther down the chain of command.

Fewer layers of management, and increased decision making and participation by non-management workers, typically results in:

✔ Less bureaucracy

✔ Faster decision making

✔ Improved ability to react to changing markets

✔ Increased reliance on self-managing teams

✔ More empowered and happier employees

✔ More satisfied and happier customers

✔ Reduced costs

✔ Increased profits

Instead of focusing on the structures and maintenance of hierarchy – departments, titles, and so on – flat organisations

✔ Focus on their customers, both internal and external

✔ Encourage all employees to become directly responsive to customer needs

✔ Promote decision making by those employees closer to customers

✔ Eliminate bottlenecks in the flow of information

✔ Support open sharing of information

As more and more organisations turn away from the restrictive culture that is a natural by-product of hierarchy, the flat organisation is becoming an obvious choice – and the best opportunity to capitalise on fast-changing markets.

Unlocking Open-Book Management

In spite of everything, many managers still think of strategy, accounts, financial performance, profits, losses, and turnover as issues of concern only to a select few in the organisation, though the reality is that they are important to everyone who actually works in the organisation. Managers may use this approach as a way to solidify power at the top of organisations, and to prevent everyone else from providing their own input and suggesting improvements to vital financial processes.

Apart from anything else, legal changes driven by both the British government and the European Union mean that companies and their managers have to change this attitude. Employees have statutory rights to know and be told what is being done in their name. They are entitled to know and be told if the company is planning to change its strategy, implement lay-offs and redundancies, revolutionise its technology, or change working practices. Trade unions – if the organisation recognises them – are entitled to be consulted on a wide range of matters, as are all employees through a consultative body or forum.

Much of the open-book approach originally had its roots in what came briefly to be known as the 'new realism'. The 'new realism' was another fad that required employee representatives, including trade unions and organisations to co-operate rather than confront each other.

The first serious and strategic attempts to implement open-book management were introduced for sound business reasons by Japanese companies when they first set up in the United Kingdom. For example, Sanyo UK at Lowestoft in Norfolk established a joint consultative committee at which all its staff, including the recognised trade union, were consulted and kept constantly informed and updated on the following:

- ✔ Productivity and output figures
- ✔ Defects and complaints
- ✔ Profitability, both overall, and also in relation to particular products
- ✔ Staffing levels and output requirements
- ✔ Training and development requirements
- ✔ Working practices, including full flexibility of working and occupation

Both Sanyo and other companies make sure that their staff are fully trained in the financial aspects of the organisation, and know and understand what productivity and output figures mean both to them individually and to everyone else involved.

The result is that employees see a mutual commitment and responsibility on the part of the company and its managers. Employee involvement in all aspects of the organisation and its operations is that much greater, and employees are required to participate in decision making and establishing performance targets, rather than being merely encouraged to do so.

The best organisations underpin open-book management with a single-status approach, meaning that any information goes to all staff, rather than merely to selected groups.

It is also very profitable to open the books up to everyone. Employees have an active stake in the company's performance and understand the direct connection between their own performance and organisational profitability. In some cases this relationship is also underpinned and reinforced through profit-sharing schemes and performance bonuses tied directly to company performance.

Understanding Six Sigma

If any area of management is particularly subject to trends, it's the area of quality. One in a long line of such trends is Six Sigma, a quality-improvement system originated at electronics manufacturer Motorola some two decades ago, which has gained thousands of dedicated adherents over the past few years.

Six Sigma is the name given to what is in effect a rigorous organisation and collective development and training programme that gives managers highly specialised measurement and statistical analysis tools. The six areas of involvement are detailed below. Collectively, each of the areas requires the use of the tools to reduce defects in products and processes, while cutting business costs (and improving customer satisfaction, of course). Corporate fans include such business giants as British Telecom, Citicorp, Johnson & Johnson, and British Airways; and some public-sector bodies also use the approach, including police forces, healthcare trusts, education authorities, and universities.

Six key concepts are at the heart of Six Sigma:

- ✔ **Quality.** The evaluation of products and services is *quality critical*. This means a focus on the attributes most important to the customer; and the concept that quality is in the eye of the customer, not the producer or deliverer.

- ✔ **Defect.** Failing to deliver what the customer wants; this includes failing to meet deadlines and volumes, as well as product or service defects.

- ✔ **Process capability.** What your process can deliver; and what it cannot deliver.

- ✔ **Variation.** What the customer sees and feels, relating the quality and volume of service a customer receives to what they understand and believe other customers get.

- ✔ **Stable operations.** Ensuring consistent, predictable processes to improve what the customer sees and feels; this has to happen across the whole of the organisation.

- ✔ **Design.** Designing processes, products, and services to meet customer needs and wants; relating product and service delivery to process capability; and relating both to staff training, expertise, capability, and willingness.

Top five management trend Web sites

Wondering where to find the best information on the Web about the topics addressed in this chapter? Well, you've come to the right place! Here are our top five favourites:

- ✔ Tom Peters: www.tompeters.com

- ✔ Balanced Scorecard Institute: www.thebalancedscorecard.org

- ✔ *Business 2.0* magazine: www.business2.com

- ✔ Bain & Company: www.bain.com/bainweb/expertise/tools/overview.asp

- ✔ *Management Today* magazine: www.managementtoday.com

According to Dr Mikel Harry, originator of this management trend, application of Six Sigma principles can result in the following:

- Improved customer satisfaction
- Reductions in the times that it takes to get products and services to their outlets and to the customers and clients
- Reductions in the times that it takes to get new products and services developed from scratch
- Greater prospects of new products and services becoming genuinely commercial opportunities
- Increased productivity
- Improved capacity and output
- Reduced total defects
- Increased product reliability
- Decreased times during which work is in progress; speedier and more cost-effective production processes
- Improved process flow, which means that the priority is to ensure that the flows of components and information are co-ordinated with each other

As with everything, the key is commitment. Six Sigma or any other programme only works if it is:

- Related to product and service performance, customer needs and wants, and organisational processes and capability to deliver
- At the core of management and staff training programmes
- A corporate priority, resourced and supported at the top of the organisation
- Given time to work
- Not relinquished as soon as the next fad comes along

Part VII
The Part of Tens

'I think you're finding the transition from worker to manager rather difficult, Bolsover.'

In this part . . .

These short chapters are packed with quick ideas that can help you to become a better manager. Dip into them whenever you have a spare moment for advice at your fingertips.

Chapter 22

Ten Common Management Mistakes

In This Chapter

▶ Failing to accept change as part of the job

▶ Not setting clear goals

▶ Neglecting to make time to communicate with employees

▶ Avoiding delegating responsibility

▶ Failing to remember what's really important

Managers make mistakes. Mistakes are nature's way of showing you that you're developing. Thomas Edison once said that it takes 10,000 mistakes to find an answer. One of the greatest lessons anyone in any management position can discover is to acknowledge that they made a mistake – and then put it right. Of course, you don't want serial bunglers in charge of your organisation; nobody does. But far too often you come across managers who have guessed at what they think they should do, and then gone on to spend vast quantities of organisational resources trying to make the impossible work. This is a waste of everyone's time, effort, and energy, and it can become very expensive.

This chapter lists ten traps that new and experienced managers alike can fall victim to.

Not Making the Transition from Worker to Manager

When you're a worker, you have a job and you do it. Although your job probably requires you to join a team or to work closely with other employees, you're ultimately responsible only for yourself. Did you attain your goals? Did you get to work on time? Was your work done correctly? When you become a manager, everything changes. Suddenly, you are responsible for the results of a group of people, not just for yourself. Did your employees attain their goals? Are your employees highly motivated? Did your employees do their work correctly?

Becoming a manager requires the development of a whole new set of business skills – people skills. Some of the most talented employees from a technical perspective become the worst managers because they fail to make the transition from worker to manager.

Not Setting Clear Goals and Expectations

Do the words *rudderless ship* mean anything to you? They should. Effective performance starts with clear goals. If you don't set goals with your employees, your organisation often has no direction and your employees have few challenges. Therefore, your employees have little motivation to do anything but show up for work and collect their payslips.

Your employees' goals begin with a vision of where you and they want to be in the future. Meet with your employees to develop realistic, attainable goals that guide them in their efforts to achieve the organisation's vision. Don't leave your employees in the dark. Help them to help you, and your organisation, by setting goals and then by working with them to achieve those goals. (Chapter 7 addresses this issue.)

Failing to Delegate

Some surveys rank 'inability to delegate' as the No. 1 reason managers fail. Despite the continuous efforts of many managers to prove otherwise, you can't do everything by yourself. And even if you can, doing everything by yourself isn't the most effective use of your time or talent as a manager. You may very well be the best statistician in the world, but when you become the manager of a team of statisticians, your job changes. Your job is no longer to perform statistical analyses, but to manage and develop a group of employees.

When you delegate work to employees, you multiply the amount of work that you can do. A project that seems overwhelming on the surface is suddenly quite manageable when you divide it up among 12 different employees. Furthermore, when you delegate work to employees, you also create opportunities to develop their work and leadership skills. Whenever you take on a new assignment or work on a continuing job, ask yourself whether one of your employees can do it instead (and if the answer is yes, then delegate it!).

Failing to Communicate

In many organisations, most employees don't have a clue about what's going on. Information is power, and some managers use information – in particular, the control of information – to ensure that they're the most knowledgeable and therefore the most valuable individuals in an organisation. Some managers shy away from social situations and naturally avoid communicating with their employees, especially when the communication is negative in some way. Others are just too busy. They simply don't make the effort to communicate information to their employees on a regular basis, letting other, more pressing business take precedence by selectively 'forgetting' to tell their employees what they need to know.

The health of today's organisations, especially during times of change depends on the widespread dissemination of information throughout an organisation and the communication that enables this dissemination to happen. Managers must empower employees with information so that employees can make the best decisions at the lowest possible level in the organisation, quickly and without the approval of those higher up. This takes time and energy, but is a much better use of organisational resources. (Chapter 10 talks about communication.)

Not Making Time for Employees

To some of your employees, you're a resource. To others, you're a trusted associate. Still others may consider you to be a teacher or mentor, while others see you as a coach or parent. However your employees view you, they have one thing in common: All your employees need your time and guidance during the course of their careers. Managing is a people job – you need to make time for your people. Some workers may need your time more than others do. You must assess your employees' individual needs and address them.

Although some of your employees may be highly experienced and require little supervision, others may need almost continual attention when they're new to a job or task. When an employee needs to talk, make sure that you're available. Put your work aside for a moment, ignore your phone, and give your employee your undivided attention. Not only do you show your employees that they are important, but when you focus on them, you also listen to what they have to say. (Tips and pointers on making time for employees are in Chapter 8.)

Not Recognising Employee Achievements

In these days of constant change, downsizing, and increased uncertainty, finding ways to recognise your employees for the good work they do is more important than ever. The biggest misconception is that managers don't want to recognise employees. Most managers do agree that rewarding employees is important; they just aren't sure how to do so and don't take the time or effort to recognise their employees.

Although pay rises, bonuses, and promotions have decreased in many organisations as primary motivators, you can take many steps that take little time to accomplish, are easy to implement, and cost little or no money. In fact, the most effective reward – personal and written recognition from one's manager – doesn't cost anything. Don't be so busy that you can't take a minute or two to recognise your employees' achievements. Your employees' morale, performance, and loyalty will surely improve as a result. (We cover evaluating and rewarding employees in Chapter 9.)

Failing to Develop

Most managers are accustomed to success, and they initially spent a lot of time on self-development to make that success happen. Many were plucked from the ranks of workers and promoted into positions as managers for this very reason. Often, however, they catch a dreaded disease – *hardening of the attitudes* – after they become managers, and they only want things done their way.

Successful managers find the best ways to get tasks done and accomplish their goals, and then they develop processes and policies to institutionalise these effective approaches to doing business. This method is great as long as the organisation's business environment doesn't change. However, when the business environment does change, if the manager doesn't adjust – that is, doesn't *develop* – the organisation suffers as a result.

This situation can be particularly difficult for a manager who has found success by doing business a certain way. The model of manager as a solid rock that stands up to the storm is no longer valid. Today, managers have to be ready to change the way they do business as their environments change around them. They have to constantly develop, experiment, and try new methods. If managers don't adapt, they are doomed to extinction – or at least irrelevance.

Resisting Change

If you think that you can stop change, you're fooling yourself. You may as well try standing in the path of a hurricane to make it change its course. Good luck! The sooner you realise that the world – your world – includes changes, whether you like it or not, the better. Then you can concentrate your efforts on taking actions that make a positive difference in your business life. You must discover how to adapt to change and use it to your advantage rather than fighting it.

Instead of reacting to changes after the fact, proactively anticipate the changes that are coming your way and make plans to address them before they hit your organisation. Ignoring the need to change doesn't make that need go away. The best managers are positive and forward-looking. (Chapter 14 talks about managing change.)

Going for the Quick Fix over the Lasting Solution

Every manager loves to solve problems and fix the parts of his organisation that are broken. The constant challenge of the new and unexpected attracts many people to management in the first place. Unfortunately, in their zeal to fix problems quickly, many managers neglect to take the time necessary to seek out long-term solutions to their organisation's problems.

If you diagnose cancer, you have to perform major surgery; however, many managers, when faced with serious problems, still do their best to treat them with the equivalent of a sticking plaster. So if you've got problems, find out what caused them and treat them on their own merits. After you find the cause of the problem, you can develop real solutions that have lasting effects. Anything less isn't really solving the problem; you're merely treating the symptoms.

Taking It All Too Seriously

Of course, work is serious, and you have got to be good at it, and concentrate on the things that are important. You carry the weight of staff, shareholder, customer, and supplier expectations on your shoulders and that is often a very heavy burden, especially in times of difficulty.

But keep everything in perspective. Whatever the state of your business, you need to maintain a sunny and positive attitude, and make sure that this spreads to everyone else around you. Nobody wants to work for a misery – or worse still a bully – so don't be one! Being positive and upbeat also makes your life much more straightforward, in that you find it a lot easier to set and maintain standards. People come to you much more readily with things that need to be tackled; and so more gets done, more quickly all round.

And when you finally leave, what do you want people to remember you for? Achievements, of course, but what else? That you made everyone's life unbearable? Or that you delivered everything positively and with a good heart? So, be good at your job – and enjoy it!

Chapter 23

The Ten Best Ways to Recognise Employees

In This Chapter

▶ Praise and recognition

▶ Recognition and money

*A*re you giving your employees the recognition they deserve? We certainly hope so! Why? Because recognising your employees for doing a good job is one of the best ways to keep them motivated and engaged in their work. Recognising workers is about managing people and getting the best out of them. To do this, you have to respect them as people, value them as colleagues, and treat them with integrity, honesty, and openness at all times. And one part of this treatment (some say the biggest part) is to make sure that all your employees know when they have done a good job.

Above all, don't be the misery who says: 'If my people don't hear from me, they know they are doing a good job. But I soon get on to them if they make mistakes!' What a way to spend your working life!

And little or none of this is about money. Of course, money is important – everyone needs it, and it is nice to receive bonuses. But everything has a time and a place. And remember, you can't buy loyalty, trust, and respect, you have to earn them.

You don't have to spend a lot of time or money to show your employees how you feel about them and their work. Use the recognition strategies in this chapter to create the best motivating work environment in which every employee feels valued, trusted, and respected. And if you really want to find out how to recognise and reward employees, then Bob's book, *1001 Ways to Reward Employees*, lists vast numbers of real-life positive rewards, most of which cost little or nothing, but which enhance motivation, morale, trust, and respect out of all recognition.

Support and Involvement

Your employees need information and support in order to do their jobs. Give them what they need when they need it to do their best work. And if they make a mistake in the process, support them and help them to develop as a result of that mistake. You can expect mistakes in any job, but how you handle mistakes when they occur can be critical to building trust, knowledge, and performance. All employees want their manager's support after making a mistake.

Furthermore, involve your employees when you're making key decisions – especially when those decisions affect your employees and their work. You can also involve employees by, when possible, asking them for their opinions and ideas. Doing so further shows that you respect and trust them – and that they actually have ideas worth sharing.

Personal Praise

Nearly 60 per cent of employees state that they never get a simple 'thank you' from their manager for doing a good job. This is common and universal across all sectors and occupations. A 'thank you' is one of the top motivators, and one of the most neglected.

Taking the time to thank employees personally shows them that no matter how busy you are and no matter what else you have to do, nothing is more important to you than them. By thanking them, you're saying that your employees are more important than everything else in your work life. Isn't that why employees are called 'the organisation's greatest asset'?

Remember to make your praise as timely, as sincere, and as specific as possible to have the greatest impact. Actively seek employees out when you have something to commend them for and don't be shy about acknowledging them in front of others – management, peers, or even customers.

Autonomy and Authority

Employees want, and need, to have the space to perform their work the way they see fit. No one likes a supervisor or manager always hovering over their shoulder, micromanaging their every move, reminding them of the exact way everything should be done, and making corrections every time they make a slight deviation. Guess what? Your employees actually may come up with a better way to do the task than your way if you give them a chance.

Tell employees what you want done, provide them with the necessary training and resources, and then leave them to it. When you give them what they need, you increase the likelihood that they will perform to, or even beyond, your expectations.

Flexible Working Hours

Another great, no-cost way to reward your employees is to give them flexibility in their working hours, which includes when they start work and when they finish, the ability to leave work early when they need to, and time off. Because most of them are trying to balance multiple priorities on both the work and home fronts, time is very important. As such, flexibility and time off from work have become increasingly valuable commodities. The law also, in many cases, requires organisation to offer flexible working hours; and if you deny employees' requests for a flexible approach outright, what does that say about your attitude to the law?

People want to spend more time with their families and friends and less time in the office. Of course, with downsizing and re-engineering, employees have more work to do, not less. Giving your employees flexible working hours can help them keep fresh and focused while on the job.

Training and Development

Guaranteed employment may be gone for everybody, but guaranteed employability is still very much alive in today's job market. As a result, employees are increasingly interested in developing new skills where they work. They can enhance their abilities and the value they offer the organisation. Remember, too, that most employee development happens on the job, not in the classroom. New work challenges and responsibilities and the chance to represent one's manager or group are ways to develop, grow, and master new skills.

Giving your employees new opportunities to perform is very motivating. You aren't going to motivate your employees by building a fire under them. Instead, find ways to build a fire within them to make work a place where they want and are able to do their best as they develop and grow. Talking with employees about their long-term hopes and career plans is also important. You develop a strong and mutual bond and trust with each employee. If you know where someone wants to be in five years' time, you can think about aspects of their current job and circumstances that can help them prepare for the future. Don't deny ambition – foster and nurture it.

Your Time

Employees need to take time to get to know their managers; and managers ought to spend time getting to know their employees. This strengthens the mutual bonds of trust, respect, and loyalty.

Having access to one's manager is a big motivator. Access is different from being located physically near where your manager works. Access and accessibility have less to do with physical proximity than with a manager's responsiveness in taking employees' questions and concerns seriously and in getting information, resources, or assistance back to employees in a timely manner. Above all, if you have anything to tell people, tell them. And if you can't do this face to face, then use e-mail, voice-mail, a mobile phone – anything to ensure that your employees know what they need and have to know. And if your people have questions that you can't answer, make sure that you get the answers for them and then get back to them. It is a mark of the trust and value that you place on your employees; and as we have said elsewhere, if you don't tell them, they find it out from someone else anyway. So do it!

Written Praise

People love to receive written praise as a form of recognition. Whether it comes in the form of letters of praise added to their personnel file, a written note of thanks from their manager or peers, or a simple 'thank you' card, written praise has a sense of permanence about it. The glow can last for quite some time; and whenever anybody remembers to bring the matter up, the employee gets a nice warm glow! Written praise also has a multiplier effect as employees refer to previous written thanks time and time again, perhaps posting a note at their desk or creating a 'victory file' specifically for that purpose. They also may decide to show the written information to their families, friends, and colleagues.

Electronic Praise

Similar to written praise, electronic praise enables you to produce positive communication as it occurs in your daily work. Use communication technologies not just to process information, but also to connect with others and to commend them when they've done good work. In an Internet survey that Bob conducted, some 28 per cent of employees report that they view having positive e-mail messages forwarded to them as 'extremely important' and 65 per cent see being copied in on positive e-mail messages as 'extremely or very important'. And it is sheer bad manners, when someone has written in about one of your employees in glowing terms, not to make sure that the employee knows about this also. Reinforce the praise with an e-mail copied to your own manager, which works wonders.

Also don't forget the use of voice-mail and texting as ways of making sure that people know that their achievements are being recognised.

Public Praise

Everyone likes recognition for a good job well done, and in many cases, this includes being publicly recognised. So when employees merit public praise and recognition, make sure that you praise them. Send copies of positive letters and thanks for jobs well done to everyone involved; or if customers and suppliers want to thank your staff in person, then bring them in and let them do it. David Sullivan of Sullivan Development Services used to produce champagne and a buffet for all his staff each time the company received written thanks for a good job. That way, everyone in the organisation knew that their work was important and valued. Taking time at the beginning or end of department or company-wide meetings to thank performers or allowing employees to acknowledge one another at group meetings can also be very effective. Using the company newsletter to post positive information, name top performers, or thank project teams are a few other possibilities that can work well to make people feel important and special when they've achieved.

And So to Money

Of all the areas of recognising employees, recognition and money are the hardest to get right – and the easiest to foul up. If managers give out financial rewards for a job well done, these must apply to everyone involved, and everyone involved must be able to achieve them. If what you are rewarding was genuinely an individual effort, fair enough, reward the individual. But so few people work in complete, genuine isolation or on their own initiative that this is in fact most unlikely. Do be aware that if you don't reward everyone involved, then you can cause deep resentment among those whose efforts you haven't recognised – exactly the opposite of what you intended. For example:

- ✔ Excellent sales people require excellent administrators and appointments secretaries to ensure that their performance levels stay high, and yet those who work in support of sales teams often don't get the bonuses paid to the sales staff themselves.

- ✔ Excellent market traders, commodity, and stockbrokers require an effective back office to ensure that their trades reach maximum value, and yet the back-office staff rarely share in the sometimes huge bonuses paid to the traders.

If you're not careful, failure to recognise everyone involved can cause divisions and damage morale – exactly the opposite of what you intended. When this is clear in your mind, you have then the full range of monetary rewards available. You can use honoraria (voluntary fees) and one-off payments if you need to, or, if the situation demands, you can use bonuses, and percentage rises to ensure that the payments are fully institutionalised. Many organisations use monetary rewards in return for employee suggestions. Some employees prefer to be paid on commission, because they perceive that they are then being rewarded for their own direct efforts.

Many managers additionally make use of incentives like theatre tickets, holiday vouchers, seasonal hampers, and restaurant meals as further ways of providing recognition.

Chapter 24

Ten (Plus Two) Classic Business Books You Need to Know About

. . . .

In This Chapter

▶ Finding traditional business tomes

▶ Locating useful managing books

. . . .

An incredible variety of business books are available for you to read and to buy. Becoming bewildered by all the choices is easy, and sorting out which books are of the greatest benefit to managers is difficult.

So you have to start somewhere. And in the list that follows, we've already done the hard work for you. Every manager should buy and read these classic business and management books before reading any others (except this one of course!).

In Search of Excellence

In Search of Excellence by Thomas J. Peters and Robert H. Waterman (Harper & Row, 1982) is the book that transformed the whole approach to management thinking and practice, above all by bringing real managers, in real companies, out into the open. A bestseller that J. K. Rowling of Harry Potter fame would be proud of, *In Search of Excellence* held the mirror up to 63 companies and evaluated the characteristics that ought to be present in top-performing organisations, and those characteristics that were in fact present in the organisations studied. Surprise, surprise – everything was there! Bias for action, closeness to customer, attention to product and service quality, strength and expertise of leadership – each was present in the excellent companies, and has to be a management priority if the company or organisation is to succeed.

Some may argue that the book is now dated; and others cite the downturn in the performance of many of the companies studied as evidence that the work of Peters and Waterman was not flawless. Well, nothing ever is – and this applies, above all, to business and management books! But read *In Search of Excellence* anyway – it brought management out into the open, and the principles (if not all the examples) still hold good for the most part.

Managing for Results

In Managing for Results (Harper & Row, 1964) – a real classic in the field of management and written by the greatest management writer of them all – Peter F. Drucker takes the development of his management theories a step further by showing readers what they must do to create an organisation that prospers and grows. Drucker encourages readers to focus on opportunities in their organisations rather than on problems. The book suggests that managers take a hard look at an organisation's strengths and weaknesses to develop effective plans and strategies. Drucker also states that managers have to be competent across the whole field of management, as well as expert in their own particular area; and especially, this expertise must cover strategic capability and staff and human resource management.

The Human Side of Enterprise

The first wake-up call for managers everywhere, this book proclaims that (big surprise) people play a major role in the success of any business. *The Human Side of Enterprise* by Douglas McGregor (McGraw-Hill, 1960) produced the birth of Theory X and its negative assumptions of human behaviour ('People are lazy') and Theory Y, which focuses on the positive assumptions of human behaviour ('People want to do a good job'). McGregor argues that relying on authority as the primary means of control in industry leads to 'resistance, restriction of output, indifference to organisational objectives, the refusal to accept responsibility, and results in inadequate motivation for human growth and development.' The book remains relevant reading for managers today, many of whom still haven't a clue why employees are so important.

The Peter Principle

The Peter Principle by Dr Laurence Peter and Raymond Hull (Morrow, 1969) says that in a hierarchy, every employee tends to rise to his level of incompetence. This book is an amusing look at how hierarchies work in organisations and what managers can do to ensure that they don't assign employees to tasks beyond their capabilities. A must!

Competitive Strategy

This book by Michael E. Porter (Free Press, 1980) concentrates on the need for clarity of purpose; and this clarity of purpose is founded in a core, generic, or foundation strategy. The concept is really quite simple – if you do not have clarity of purpose, you cannot expect others to understand what you are delivering, or on what basis.

The core foundation or generic position needs to concentrate on securing cost leadership or cost advantage, or it must concentrate on securing brand leadership and quality advantage, based on differentiation. If securing cost leadership or differentiation and brand advantage is not possible, then you tend to lose out to those organisations that do have one or other of these positions. Securing brand leadership and brand advantage means that you can charge premium prices for your products and services, provided that the benefits delivered through differentiation are those that are of value to the customers. Securing cost leadership or cost advantage means that you have a much greater flexibility in the prices that you can charge; and especially, the cost leader has the greatest strength in withstanding price wars. If you do not have one of these positions, you must have something else that is of value to the customer, for example, convenience, location, or else the confidence of those who operate closely with you in the particular sector, and who need your products, services, or expertise.

Finally, strategy has to have a focus, concentrating on mass markets, or on narrow, specialist, and precisely defined niches that are capable of supporting viable levels of business.

Competitive Strategy is a major piece of work of the highest substance and order. It is essential reading for anyone serious about developing their knowledge and expertise.

The One Minute Manager

Written in a unique parable format, *The One Minute Manager* by Kenneth Blanchard and Spencer Johnson (Morrow, 1982) became an instant business classic. Even today, it is a perennial resident on most business bestseller lists. *The One Minute Manager* teaches readers three very simple but important management skills (One Minute Goal Setting, One Minute Praisings, and One Minute Reprimands), and it does so in an entertaining but informative way. A true classic.

Management Stripped Bare

This book is a cheerful debunking of fads and fashions, management speak, and the actions (or inactions) taken by managers to avoid facing the real issues that directly affect the success and viability of their organisations. The core message of *Management Stripped Bare* by Jo Owen (Kogan Page, 2002) is very clear: Until those in management positions stop talking about 'hitting the ground running' and 'thinking outside the box', and start clarifying their own purpose and developing real expertise in delivering it, organisations will continue to underperform. A really good, informative, substantial, and entertaining read!

In Search of European Excellence

Robert Heller was the first British management guru, and was responsible, many years ago, for founding what is now the Chartered Management Institute as well as the business magazine *Management Today* (another management must-read!).

Written nearly 20 years after Peters and Waterman's book (see earlier in this chapter), *In Search of European Excellence* (Harper Collins, 1998) concentrates on the experiences of some of the largest and best known British and European multinational corporations, companies, and public service bodies. The currency of many of the lessons from Peters and Waterman – clarity of purpose, strength and expertise of leadership, product and service quality, flexibility, and responsiveness – are still found to hold good. Heller draws particular attention to the shortcomings in performance and confidence in companies and organisations where, for whatever reason, these principles and practices no longer apply, or have been allowed to slide.

The book is full of examples from companies and organisations that everyone is very familiar with. The book is substantial and informative, as well as entertaining, and so is another must!

The Fifth Discipline: The Art and Practice of the Learning Organisation

This book by Peter Senge (Century, 1990) started the use of the concept of the learning organisation, which is still going strong in many businesses. It encourages organisations to apply systems thinking, seeing interrelationships instead of just isolated events, incidents, and problems. Senge argues that organisations should make learning a continuous process rather than treat it as a series of distinct, unrelated events. He claims that everyone in an organisation has a responsibility to help create a learning organisation, with top managers playing a crucial role in the process. He also encourages organisations to realise the importance of reflection, as well as action, in business. ('Yes, but who's going to help the customer?' – only someone who has first discovered how to do it properly).

Understanding Organisations

The most famous and foremost of all British management thinkers, Charles B. Handy started his career as a corporate executive at what is now oil company Royal Dutch/Shell, before moving into the world of business schools and management teaching and development.

Understanding Organisations (Penguin, 1996) carries a comprehensive, clear, and concise coverage of every aspect of how people behave in organisations, and what managers therefore need to know, understand, and be able to apply. This includes the tricky areas of roles, character, attitudes, and values, as well as the mainstream of leadership, motivation, groups, and conflict. The book is full of useful examples of how theories of behaviour are applied in practice, and even with a subject that is not necessarily easily accessible to all, it is again a very entertaining read.

Body and Soul: The Body Shop Story

Body and Soul by Anita Roddick (Ebury Press, 1992) tells the story of the founding, development, and subsequent globalisation of British natural cosmetics company The Body Shop. The sheer energy and enthusiasm of the company's founder Anita Roddick, her husband Gordon, and everyone else involved comes shining through on every page.

Body and Soul tells of the clear set of guiding principles and strong ethical base on which the company was created, and the commitment to all stakeholders – especially suppliers in developing countries – that has subsequently been so critical to the company's success. The book also concentrates on the crucial aspects of product and service quality, branding and differentiation, and especially the images of cosmetics and the portrayal of the women who use them.

The Body Shop was founded in the early 1970s, during economic downturns both in the United Kingdom and elsewhere, so the last thing that anyone needed was a new brand of cosmetics. Nevertheless, The Body Shop succeeded and grew. Roddick and her husband founded the company to be distinctive and different from the rest of the cosmetics industry, and in spite of the external pressures and customs of the industry, it succeeded.

So read this book as a guide to the sheer energy, commitment, and enthusiasm you require in order to succeed, and to the fun and adventures that you can have doing it. And read it also in the knowledge and context that in 2006 The Body Shop was sold to L'Oréal – one of those 'other' cosmetics companies.

Maverick!

If Drucker is the greatest authority on management, then *Maverick* by Ricardo Semler (Century, 1992) is the greatest story. Ricardo Semler tells of how he transformed his family firm, a company making commercial white goods and pumps, from one that was in his own words 'moribund, into a company that thrives, chiefly by refusing to squander our greatest asset – the talents of our people.'

The story takes place not in Europe or the United States, but in Brazil. And so Semler achieved everything he did within the ever so slightly difficult confines of an inflation rate of 3,000 per cent (or 10 per cent per day), and a failure rate in the Brazilian capital goods sector of one in three.

Otherwise, everything is in this organisation – fully flexible working, self-managing teams, motivation and commitment, concentration on product and service quality. And it is all underpinned by open-books, full access to information, and a profit-sharing scheme in which 23 per cent of retained profits are given over to the staff. The company has a hierarchy of two levels only, and everyone has full and universal access to managers, including the top managers and Semler himself. *Maverick* is required reading at many business schools – and it is an absolute must for anyone who aspires to manage anything, anywhere.

Index

• A •

Accenture (Web site), 153, 320
acceptance of things you can't
    change, 281–282
accounting
  assets, 296–297
  business health, analysing, 304–307
  double-entry bookkeeping, 299
  financial statements, 300–304
  liabilities, 297–298
  overview, 295–296
  retained earnings, 299
  share capital, 299
  Web sites for, 307
Accounting Conventions (Web site), 307
AccountingWEB (Web site), 307
achievements of employees, not
    recognizing, 348
action, inspiring, 49–50
activity trap, 121
ad hoc groups, 189
advertising used for finding candidates, 67
Advisory, Conciliation and Arbitration
    Service (Web site), 45, 77, 153, 204,
    256, 272
appraisals and goal setting (Web site), 124
asking employees what they want, 83–87
assessments
  in coaching and development, 99
  office politics, assessments of your
    organisation's, 213–214
assets, 296–297
Association for Project Management
    (Web site), 140
Association of Certified and Chartered
    Accountants (Web site), 307
attainable goals, 113
attitude of employee, manager's
    part in, 95–96

authority
  for employees working on delegated
    tasks, taking back, 42
  in job, 84
  as recognition of employees, 352–353
autonomy
  in job, 84
  as recognition of employees, 352–353
  teams and groups, given to, 190–192

• B •

Bain & Company (Web site), 341
balance sheet, 300
Balanced Scorecard Institute (Web site),
    140, 341
basics of managing, 336–337
Batchelor's Foods, 190
behaviours, 219
Belbin, Meredith (management expert),
    186–187
benefits
  authority in job, 84
  autonomy in job, 84
  choice of assignment, 83
  flexible working hours, 83
  learning opportunities, 83
  overview, 83–85
  public praise, 83–84
  time off, 83
  time with manager, 84
  verbal praise, 83–84
  written praise, 83–84
Berdahl, James (Business Incentives), 52
Bernard Burnes (Web site), 240
best style of management, 12–13
Better Business Meetings (Nelson &
    Pettinger), 194
Billot, Hugh (Sheerness Steel), 132–133
Bing, Stanley (*Fortune* magazine), 53

biscuit motivation, 81–83

blaming, 166

Blanchard, Kenneth (*The One Minute Manager*), 360

Blittle, Lonnie (Nissan Motor Manufacturing Corporation USA), 52

Body and Soul (Roddick), 361–362

The Body Shop, 112, 361–362

Bolles, Richard Nelson (*What Colour Is Your Parachute?*), 68

BPP Malpas (Web site), 176

Branson, Richard (Virgin Group), 50

British Airways, 183–184

budgets

  combination approach used to create, 291

  creating, 289–291

  historical figures used to create, 291

  make-or-buy decision, 292–293

  overview, 287–289

  producing realistic, 293–294

  staying on budget, 294–295

  zero-based budgeting, 291

Business Communication Quarterly (Web site), 176

business environment, changes in, 15–17

Business Finance magazine (Web site), 307

Business for Social Responsibility (Web site), 227

business health

  analysing, 304–307

  calculations to determine, 306–307

  financial ratios used to analyse, 304–306

Business Mentoring Scotland (Web site), 333

Business 2.0 (Web site), 341

Business.com (Web site), 227

• C •

cash-flow statement, 304

Cass Business School (Web site), 176

change management

  crisis management, avoiding, 232–233

  employee initiative, encouraging, 238–240

  fighting change, determining if you are, 235–237

  helping your employees deal with change, 237–238

  overview, 231–232

  stages of change, 234–235

  urgency in, 232

  Web sites for, 240

  yourself, making changes within, 240

Change Management Learning Centre (Web site), 240

Change Management Resource Library (Web site), 240

change, resisting, 349

Chartered Institute of Personnel and Development (Web site), 28, 45, 77, 96, 153, 204, 333

Chartered Management Institute (Web site), 28, 106, 204, 333

choice of assignment, 83

Churchill, Winston (prime minister), 49

coaching and development. *See also* employee development

  assessments, 99

  encouragement, 98

  environment for success, creating, 99

  feedback, 99

  goals, setting, 98

  guidelines for, 103–104

  inspiration, 99

  overview, 98–99

  show-and-tell method of teaching, 100–101

  sports coaching metaphors for success in business, 101–102

  successes, making turning points into big, 102

  support, 98

  teamwork, 99

  techniques of, 104–106

  turning points, confronting, 102–104

  Web sites for, 106

The Coaching and Mentoring Network (Web site), 106

code of ethics, 209–212

collaborative leadership, 56–58

Colman's Foods, 56

combination approach used to create budgets, 291

command team, 188

commitment and support, obtaining, 87

committee, 188

communication

  accident, problems due to, 164

  departmental feuding, 166

  design, problems due to, 164

failing to communicate, 347
information technology's effect on, 160–163
interest, problems due to lack of, 165
leadership, 50–51
listening, 166–168
meddling, 166
methods of communication, 159–160
negligence, problems due to, 164
as new function of management, 24–25
office politics, 218–220
overview, 158–160
physical distance, problems due to, 164
presentations, 171–178
problems in, 163–166
psychological distance, problems due to, 164
scapegoating, 166
secrets, keeping, 166
team, of your goals to your, 117–119
toxic communications, 165–166
withholding information, problems due to, 165
written communications, 169–170
company policy manual, 221
competitive advantage, information technology as, 310–311
Competitive Strategy (Porter), 359
compulsory redundancy, 260
Computerworld (Web site), 320
Confederation of British Industry (Web site), 96, 272
confidence as trait of leaders, 54
confidential circumstances, avoid delegating tasks with, 43
constructive dismissal, 262
co-operation, benefits of, 182
Corporate Social Responsibility (Web site), 227
counselling and support for employees working on tasks you have delegated, 42
counselling, avoid delegating tasks with, 41
crisis management, avoiding, 232–233
critical path method (CPM), 138
Croner (Web site), 256, 272
cross-functional teams, 189–190
culture of company with virtual management, 200–201

• D •

The Daily Telegraph (Web site), 77
De Haan, Sydney (Saga), 91
decisiveness as trait of leaders, 55
defining the job, 64
delegation
always delegate, tasks to, 39–40
authority for employees working on tasks you have delegated, taking back, 42
avoid delegation, tasks to, 41–43
confidential circumstances, avoid delegating tasks with, 43
counselling and support for employees working on tasks you have delegated, 42
counselling, avoid delegating tasks with, 41
crisis with, averting, 42
of detailed work, 39
discipline, avoid delegating tasks with, 41
failing to delegate, 346
formalised tracking system of tasks you have delegated, 42
of future duties, 40
of information gathering, 39
long-term vision and goals, avoid delegating tasks with, 41
monitoring of tasks you have delegated, 42, 43–45
myths about, 32–36
overview, 30–32
performance appraisals, avoid delegating tasks with, 41
personal assignments, avoid delegating tasks with, 43
personal follow-up of tasks you have delegated, 42
politically sensitive situations, avoid delegating tasks with, 42
positive performance feedback of employees, avoid delegating tasks with, 41
progress reports of tasks you have delegated, 42
reassigning activities for employees working on tasks you have delegated, 42
of repeat assignments, 39–40
sampling of employees' work of tasks you have delegated, 42

delegation *(continued)*
  sensitive circumstances, avoid delegating
    tasks with, 43
  steps for, 37–38
  of surrogate roles, 40
  trusting your employees, 37
  Web sites for, 45
  what to delegate, 38–43
departmental feuding, 166
design, communication problems
  due to, 164
desired behaviours, creating programmes
  based on, 134–135
detailed work, delegation of, 39
develop, failing to, 348
development for employees. *See* employee
  development
DigitalCompaq, 204
discipline. *See also* dismissals
  avoid delegating tasks with, 41
  consequences of continuing
    unacceptable behaviour,
    outlining the, 252–253
  describing the unacceptable
    behaviour, 251
  emotional support, providing, 253
  final warning, 250
  first warning, 250
  for misconduct, 248–250
  moves and transfers, 248
  overview, 242–243
  performance, focusing on, 245–246
  performance improvement plan, 254–256
  for performance problems, 247–248
  personality, not focusing on, 245–246
  procedures for, following, 243–244
  progressive discipline, 246
  punishment compared, 242
  reasons for, 243
  required changes to unacceptable
    behaviour, specifying, 252
  script for, 250–254
  second warning, 250
  steps for, 250–254
  suspension, 250
  verbal guidance, counselling, and
    support, 247–248
  verbal order, 249
  Web sites for, 256

work unit, expressing the impact of the
  unacceptable behaviour to, 251–252
written counselling, 248
dismissals
  alternatives to, 266–267
  avoiding having to fire an employee,
    excuses for, 265–266
  compulsory redundancy, 260
  constructive dismissal, 262
  as disciplinary measure, 248, 250
  early retirement, 260
  fair dismissal, 261–262
  falsification of records as reason for, 264
  gathering good reasons for firing an
    employee, 263–264
  incompetence as reason for, 263
  insubordination as reason for, 263
  intoxication at work as reason for, 264
  lateness as reason for, 263
  overview, 258–259
  physical violence as reason for, 263–264
  procedures to follow before initiating,
    267–268
  redeployment/transfer, 260
  redundancies and lay-offs, 259–261
  script for, 270–271
  steps for, 268–271
  theft as reason for, 264
  time for, determining best, 271
  transitioning to, 266–267
  types of, 261–263
  unfair dismissal, 262
  verbal abuse of others as reason for, 263
  voluntary redundancy, 260
  Web sites for, 272
  wrongful dismissal, 262
documentation, protecting yourself, 226
double-entry bookkeeping, 299
downsizing
  employee development, balancing,
    332–333
  overview, 180–181
Dr Steve McKeown (Web site), 284
Drucker, Peter F.
  management expert, 130, 180
  Management: Tasks, Responsibilities,
    Practices, 93, 192
  Managing for Results, 358
Dutton Engineering, 56

• E •

early retirement, 260
Economy, Peter (*Leadership Ensemble: Lessons in Collaborative Management from the World's Only Conductorless Orchestra*), 56–57
efficiency, improving, 314–316
electronic praise as recognition of employees, 354–355
The Elements of Style (Strunk & White), 170
emotional support, providing, 253
employee development. *See also* coaching and development
  downsizing, balancing, 332–333
  in factory work, 325
  mentoring, 330–332
  overview, 321–324
  planning for, 325–328
  reasons for, 322–324
  steps for, 328–330
  Web sites for, 333
Employee Discipline: Building Blocks for Success (Web site), 256
employment agencies used for finding candidates, 66
empowerment, 17–18, 22–23, 183–185
encouraged resignation, 258
encouragement, 98
entitlements, when bonuses and incentives become, 92–93
environment for success, creating, 99
equipment for information technology and communication, buying, 162
ethics
  choices, making ethical, 212–213
  code of ethics, creating, 209–212
  defining, 208–209
  overview, 208–209
  Web sites for, 227
Ethics Resource Center (Web site), 211, 227
evaluating your candidates
  notes, reviewing your, 73
  overview, 72
  references, checking, 72–73
  second interviews, conducting, 74–75
  third interviews, conducting, 74–75

examples, using managers from your past as, 25–26
Executive Coaching at the Institute of Directors (Web site), 106
exercises for stress-reduction, 283–284
expectations, not setting clear, 346
expenses, 302
experience as quality in candidate, 63
expert help for information technology, 312

• F •

factory work, 325
fair dismissal, 261–262
falsification of records as reason for dismissal, 264
feedback, 99
The Fifth Discipline: The Art and Practice of the Learning Organisation (Senge), 361
final warning, 250
financial ratios, 304–306
financial statements
  balance sheet, 300
  cash-flow statement, 304
  expenses, 302
  net profit or loss, 302
  overview, 300
  profit and loss account, 300–303
  turnover, 302
Financial Times (Web site), 77
finding candidates, 65–67
first warning, 250
flat organisation, creating, 338–339
Fletcher, Duncan (coach), 101
flexibility due to information technology and communication, 161–162
flexible workers. *See* virtual management
flexible working hours, 83, 353
flexible workplace, creating, 275
flip charts, 176
flow charts, 138–139
formal teams, 187–188
formalised tracking system of tasks you have delegated, 42
friendliness, 221–222
future duties, delegation of, 40

• G •

Gantt Chart and Timeline Centre
　　(Web site), 140
Gantt charts, 136–138
General Electric, 27
goal statement, 254
goals
　　attainable goals, 113
　　communicating your goals to your team,
　　　117–119
　　measurable goals, 113
　　not setting clear, 346
　　overview, 109–112
　　power used to achieve, 122–124
　　prioritizing, 119–122
　　reasons for setting, 111–112
　　relevant goals, 113–114
　　setting, 98, 115–116
　　SMART goals, 113–115
　　specific goals, 113
　　time-bound goals, 114
　　Web sites for, 124
good attitude as quality in candidate, 63
groups. *See* teams and groups
groupware, 192

• H •

halo effect, 147
handouts, 177
Handy, Charles B. (*Understanding
　　Organisations*), 361
hard working as quality in candidate, 62
Harry, Mikel (Six Sigma), 342
Harvester, 56
Hauptfuhrer, Robert (Oryx Energy), 51
Health and Safety Executive (HSE)
　　(Web site), 284
helping others
　　change, helping your employees deal
　　　with, 237–238
　　office politics of, 222–223
high-performance teams, 189–190
historical figures used to create budgets, 291
Holland, John (DigitalCompaq), 204
homeworking, 203–204
horizontal business organisation, 181

Hull, Raymond (*The Peter Principle*), 359
The Human Side of Enterprise
　　(McGregor), 358

• I •

IBM (Web site), 320
In Search of European Excellence (Peters &
　　Waterman), 360
In Search of Excellence (Peters &
　　Waterman), 357–358
incompetence as reason for dismissal, 263
informal teams, 188–189
information technology
　　advantages of, 161–162, 312–313
　　as competitive advantage, 310–311
　　disadvantages of, 313
　　efficiency, improving, 314–316
　　equipment, buying, 162
　　expert help for, 312
　　flexibility due to, 161–162
　　implementing, 318–320
　　intranets, 318
　　knowing your business to use technology
　　　to your advantage, 310
　　networks, 317–318
　　overview, 160–161, 310
　　plan for, 318–320
　　plan for implementation of, 311–312
　　problems, steps to prevent, 314
　　productivity, improving, 314–316
　　speed due to, 161–162
　　teams and groups, as force shaping,
　　　192–193
　　videoconferencing, 162–163
　　virtual meetings, 162–163
　　Web sites for, 320
initiative
　　encouraging employee, 238–240
　　as quality in candidate, 63
inspiration, 99
Institute of Chartered Accountants
　　(Web site), 307
Institute of Directors (Web site), 58, 272
insubordination as reason for dismissal, 263
integrity as trait of leaders, 54–55
interest, communication problems due to
　　lack of, 165
Internet used for finding candidates, 67

InternetWorld (Web site), 320
interviewing candidates
  checklist for, 69–70
  note taking while, 70
  preparation for, 67
  questions not to ask when, 70–71
  questions to ask when, 68–69
  steps for, 72
intoxication at work as reason for
      dismissal, 264
intranets, 318
Introduction to Performance Appraisal
      (Web site), 153
intuition needed when ranking
      candidates, 76–77
involvement as recognition of
      employees, 352

• *J* •

job description, 64
Johnson, Spencer (*The One Minute
      Manager*), 360
J.P. Morgan Chase, 56
Judge Institute, University of Cambridge
      (Web site), 58

• *K* •

key players, identifying, 215–216
King, Lawrence (ORIS Group), 134
knowledge power, 123
Kovac, Frederick (Goodyear Tire and
      Rubber Company), 17

• *L* •

lateness as reason for dismissal, 263
leadership
  action, inspiring, 49–50
  collaborative leadership, 56–58
  communication, 50–51
  confidence as trait of leaders, 54
  decisiveness as trait of leaders, 55
  facilitation of employees goals, 51–52
  integrity as trait of leaders, 54–55
  management compared, 48–49
  optimism as trait of leaders, 53–54

overview, 47–48
  support for employees, 51–52
  talk the talk, 53
  traits of leaders, 52–54
  walk the walk, 53
  Web sites for, 58
*Leadership Ensemble: Lessons in Collab-
      orative Management from the World's
      Only Conductorless Orchestra*
      (Economy), 56–57
Learning and Skills Council
      (Web site), 28, 124
learning opportunities, 83
learning organisation, creating, 337–338
Lewis, Ken (Dutton Engineering), 56
liabilities, 297–298
listening, 166–168
London Business School (Web site),
      28, 176, 240
long-term vision and goals, avoid
      delegating tasks with, 41

• *M* •

macho management, 11–12
make-or-buy decision, 292–293
management
  business environment, changes in, 15–17
  empowering employees, 17–18
  examples, using managers from your past
      as, 25–26
  overview, 15
  steps for, 27–28
  trust in employees, 18–19
  Web sites for, 28
Management Stripped Bare (Owen), 360
*Management: Tasks, Responsibilities,
      Practices* (Drucker), 93, 192
Management Today (Web site), 58, 341
ManagementFirst (Web site), 28, 240
manager management, 224
Managing for Results (Drucker), 358
Managing the Flexible Workforce
      (Pettinger), 95
Marks, Michael (Marks and Spencer), 50
MARS system, 128–131
Maverick (Semler), 362
McCormack, Mark (IMG), 152
McGovern, Phil (Panasonic UK), 23

McGregor, Douglas (*The Human Side of Enterprise*), 358
McKnight, William (3M), 23
measurable goals, 113
measuring and rewarding employee performance, 135–136
meddling, 166
Meek, Catherine (Meek and Associates), 52
meetings
  great meetings, keys to having, 195–196
  overview, 193
  problems, 193–195
mentoring, 224–225, 330–332
mentoring circles, 189
Meredith Belbin's team roles (Web site), 194
micromanagers, 29
Microsoft Project, 139
mirroring, 148
misconduct, discipline for, 248–250
mistakes
  achievements of employees, not recognizing, 348
  change, resisting, 349
  communicate, failing to, 347
  delegate, failing to, 346
  develop, failing to, 348
  goals and expectations, not setting clear, 346
  overview, 345
  in performance appraisals, avoiding, 147–148
  perspective, not keeping things in, 349–350
  quick fix, looking for, 349
  time for employees, not making, 347
  transition from worker to manager, not making the, 345–346
monetary rewards
  alternatives to, 93–95
  entitlements, when bonuses and incentives become, 92–93
  overview, 92
  as recognition of employees, 355–356
monitoring of tasks you have delegated, 42, 43–45
motivation
  asking employees what they want, 83–87
  benefits, 83–85

cash rewards, 92–95
commitment and support, obtaining, 87
effectiveness of rewards system, monitoring, 87
guidelines for system of, 87
manager's part in attitude of employee, 95–96
negative consequences, 79–80
organisational goals, linking rewards to, 87
parameters and mechanics of rewards system, defining, 87
performance-based measures, 88–89
positive accomplishments, focusing on, 89–90
positive consequences, 79–80
positive reinforcement, 80–83, 89–90
praise, guidelines for, 89
small accomplishments, rewarding, 91–92
supportive environment, creating, 85–86
Web sites for, 96
what to reward, deciding, 87–89
Motorola, 112
moves and transfers, 248
myGoals (Web site), 124

• N •

National Health Service (NHS), 118
negative consequences, 79–80
negligence, communication problems due to, 164
Nelson, Bob
  Better Business Meetings, 194
  1001 Rewards & Recognition Fieldbook, 95
  1001 Ways to Energize Employees, 95
  1001 Ways to Reward Employees, 49, 50, 52, 95, 351
net profit or loss, 302
networks, 317–318
new functions of management, 21–25
Nieman, Andrea (Rolm Corporation), 51
Nissan UK, 183
non-standard hours, 202–203
Nordstrom, 18–19
note taking while interviewing candidates, 70

• O •

objectiveness needed when ranking candidates, 75–76
office politics
assessment of your organisation's, 213–214
behaviours, 219
communication, 218–220
company policy manual, 221
friendliness, 221–222
helping others, 222–223
information, obtaining, 220
key players, identifying, 215–216
manager management, 224
mentors, 224–225
organisation chart, redrawing your, 216–218
overview, 213
protecting yourself, 225–227
social functions, 223–224
trustworthiness, 225
unwritten rules of, uncovering the, 220–225
Web sites for, 227
written communication, reading between the lines of, 219–220
Office Politics (Web site), 227
O'Leary, Michael (Ryanair), 49
The One Minute Manager (Blanchard & Johnson), 360
1001 Rewards & Recognition Fieldbook (Nelson), 95
1001 Ways to Energize Employees (Nelson), 95
1001 Ways to Reward Employees (Nelson), 49, 50, 52, 95, 351
open-book management, 339–340
optimism as trait of leaders, 53–54
organisation chart, redrawing your, 216–218
organisational goals, linking rewards to, 87
Orpheus Chamber Orchestra, 56–58
Owen, Jo (*Management Stripped Bare*), 360

• P •

participative management, 12
People Management and Development (Web site), 106

performance
focusing on, 245–246
problems, discipline for, 247–248
performance appraisals
advantages of, 142–143
bad appraisal methods, 149–151
comparing, 148
delegating tasks with, avoid, 41
discomfort, 148
halo effect, 147
how it works, 143–146
mirroring, 148
mistakes in, avoiding, 147–148
overview, 141–143
preparation for, 151–153
recency effect, 148
steps for, 144–146
stereotyping, 148
360-degree evaluations, 147
Web sites for, 153
performance improvement plan
goal statement, 254
implementation of, 255–256
overview, 254–255
required resources/training, 255
schedule for attainment, 255
Performance Measurement Association (Web site), 140
performance-based measures, 88–89
personal assignments, avoid delegating tasks with, 43
personal follow-up of tasks you have delegated, 42
personal goal setting (Web site), 124
personal power, 123
personal praise as recognition of employees, 352
personal referrals used for finding candidates, 66
personality, not focusing on, 245–246
perspective, not keeping things in, 349–350
PERT (program evaluation and review technique), 139
Peter, Laurence (*The Peter Principle*), 359
The Peter Principle (Peter & Hull), 359
Peters, Thomas J.
In Search of European Excellence, 360
In Search of Excellence, 357–358

Petersen, Donald (Ford Motor Company), 51
Pettinger, Richard
 Better Business Meetings, 194
 Managing the Flexible Workforce, 95
physical distance
 communication problems due to, 164
 managing from, 201
physical violence as reason for dismissal,
 263–264
PM Forum (Web site), 140
Poling, Harold A. (Ford Motor Company), 50
politically sensitive situations, avoid
 delegating tasks with, 42
Porter, Michael E. (*Competitive Strategy*), 359
position power, 123
positive accomplishments,
 focusing on, 89–90
positive consequences, 79–80
positive feedback used to encourage
 performance, 127
positive reinforcement
 biscuit motivation, 81–83
 overview, 80–81, 89–90
 rewards, 81–83
power of goal setting (Web site), 124
power used to achieve goals, 122–124
PowerPoint presentations, 176
praise, guidelines for, 89
preparation
 for interviewing candidates, 67
 for performance appraisals, 151–153
 for presentations, 171–173
 for virtual management, 198–199
presentations
 communications, 171–178
 flip charts, 176
 handouts, 177
 overview, 171
 PowerPoint presentations, 176
 preparation for, 171–173
 steps for, 177–178
 visual aids, 173–177
 Web sites for, 176
 whiteboards, 176
Presentations (Web site), 176
presenteeism, 121
Pret a Manger, 120
prioritizing goals, 119–122
process management information, 192

professional associations used for finding
 candidates, 66
profit and loss account, 300–303
program evaluation and review technique
 (PERT), 139
progress reports of tasks you have
 delegated, 42
progressive discipline, 246
project management
 critical path method (CPM), 138
 flow charts, 138–139
 Gantt charts, 136–138
 MARS system for, 128–131
 Microsoft Project, 139
 overview, 125–128
 PERT (program evaluation and review
  technique), 139
 positive feedback used to encourage
  performance, 127
 results, reading, 140
 Sheerness Steel (example), 131–133
 shrinkage, reducing, 134–136
 software, 139
 system for, developing, 128–131
 Web sites for, 140
project team, 188
promises, keeping your, 226
protecting yourself
 documentation, 226
 office politics, 225–227
 overview, 225
 promises, keeping your, 226
 visibility, 227
psychological distance, communication
 problems due to, 164
public praise, 83–84, 355
punishment compared to discipline, 242

qualities important in candidates,
 list of, 62–63
quality improvement group, 188
questions
 to ask when interviewing
  candidates, 68–69
 not to ask when interviewing
  candidates, 70–71
quick fixes, 13–15, 349

• R •

Ramsey, Alf (coach), 101
ranking candidates
  intuition needed when, 76–77
  objectiveness needed when, 75–76
  overview, 75
reassigning activities for employees working
    on tasks you have delegated, 42
recency effect, 148
recognition of employees
  with authority, 352–353
  with autonomy, 352–353
  with electronic praise, 354–355
  flexible workers, 203
  with flexible working hours, 353
  with involvement, 352
  with monetary rewards, 355–356
  overview, 351
  with personal praise, 352
  with public praise, 355
  with support, 352
  with training and development, 353
  with written praise, 354
  with your time, 354
recruitment and selection
  advertising used for finding candidates, 67
  within the company, finding candidates, 66
  defining the job, 64
  employment agencies used for finding
      candidates, 66
  evaluating your candidates, 72–75
  experience as quality in candidate, 63
  finding candidates, 65–67
  good attitude as quality in candidate, 63
  hard working as quality in candidate, 62
  initiative as quality in candidate, 63
  Internet used for finding candidates, 67
  interviewing candidates, 67–72
  job description, 64
  overview, 61–64
  personal referrals used for finding
      candidates, 66
  professional associations used for finding
      candidates, 66
  qualities important in candidates, list of,
      62–63
  ranking candidates, 75–77
  responsible as quality in candidate, 63

  smart as quality in candidate, 63
  stable as quality in candidate, 63
  team player as quality in candidate, 63
  temporary agencies used for finding
      candidates, 66
  waiting for the right candidate, 77–78
  Web sites for, 77
redeployment/transfer, 260
redundancies and lay-offs, 259–261
references, checking, 72–73
relationship power, 123
relationships (interaction between
    milestones and actions), 129–130
relevant goals, 113–114
repeat assignments, delegation of, 39–40
required resources/training, 255
resignations, accepting, 257–258
responsible as quality in candidate, 63
retained earnings, 299
retirement, 258
rewards, 81–83
Roddick, Anita
  Body and Soul, 361–362
  The Body Shop, 49, 112
Roger Cartwright (Web site), 194

• S •

Saga, 91
sampling of employees' work of tasks you
    have delegated, 42
Sanyo UK (Web site), 256
SBA Classroom: Business Mentoring
    Course (Web site), 333
scapegoating, 166
script
  for discipline, 250–254
  for dismissals, 270–271
second interviews, conducting, 74–75
second warning, 250
secrets, keeping, 166
selecting employees. *See* recruitment and
    selection
self-managed teams, 189–190
Semler, Ricardo (*Maverick*), 362
Senge, Peter (*The Fifth Discipline: The Art
    and Practice of the Learning
    Organisation*), 361

sensitive circumstances, avoid delegating tasks with, 43

share capital, 299

Sheerness Steel (example), 131–133

shift work, 202–203

show-and-tell method of teaching, 100–101

shrinkage
  desired behaviours, creating programmes based on, 134–135
  measuring and rewarding employee performance, 135–136
  overview, 134
  reducing, 134–136
  unacceptable behaviour, removing, 135

Six Sigma, 340–342

small accomplishments, rewarding, 91–92

smart as quality in candidate, 63

SMART goals, 113–115

social functions, 223–224

software for project management, 139

specific goals, 113

speed due to information technology and communication, 161–162

sports coaching metaphors for success in business, 101–102

stable as quality in candidate, 63

stages of change, 234–235

staying on budget, 294–295

stereotyping, 148

stress
  acceptance of things you can't change, 281–282
  changes you can make to decrease, 279–281
  exercises for stress-reduction, 283–284
  managing your, 279–284
  overview, 277–278
  symptoms of, 277–279

Strunk, William, Jr. (*The Elements of Style*), 170

styles of management
  best style of management, 12–13
  macho management, 11–12
  overview, 10–11
  participative management, 12
  Theory X management, 11–12
  Theory Y management, 12

successes, making turning points into big, 102

Sugar, Alan (Amstrad), 104

super-teams, 189–190

support
  for employees, 51–52
  overview, 23–24, 98
  as recognition of employees, 352
  for teams and groups, 186–193

supportive environment, creating, 85–86

surrogate roles, delegation of, 40

suspension, 250

Swatch, 112

• T •

talk the talk, 53

task force, 188

task power, 123

team player as quality in candidate, 63

Teambuildinginc (Web site), 194

teams and groups
  ad hoc groups, 189
  advantages of, 185–186
  autonomy given to, 190–192
  command team, 188
  committee, 188
  co-operation, benefits of, 182
  cross-functional teams, 189–190
  downsizing organisations, 180–181
  empowerment, 183–185
  formal teams, 187–188
  groupware, 192
  high-performance teams, 189–190
  horizontal business organisation, 181
  informal teams, 188–189
  information technology as force shaping, 192–193
  management of, 184–185
  meetings, 193–196
  mentoring circles, 189
  overview, 179–180
  process management information, 192
  project team, 188
  quality improvement group, 188
  self-managed teams, 189–190
  setting up, 186–193
  super-teams, 189–190

supporting, 186–193
task force, 188
Web sites for, 194
work improvement group, 188
Teams and Teamwork (Web site), 194
teamwork, 99
Teamwork (Web site), 194
telecommuting, 203–204
Templeton College, Oxford (Web site), 96
temporary agencies used for finding
      candidates, 66
Tesco (Web site), 96
theft as reason for dismissal, 264
Theory X management, 11–12
Theory Y management, 12
third interviews, conducting, 74–75
360-degree evaluations, 147
time
   for dismissals, determining best, 271
   for employees, not making, 347
   with manager, 84
   recognition of employees with your, 354
time off, 83
time-bound goals, 114
The Times (Web site), 77
Tom Peters (Web site), 341
toxic communications, 165–166
Trades Union Congress (Web site), 45, 96,
      204, 256, 272
training and development as recognition of
      employees, 353
traits of leaders, 52–54
transfers, 248
transition from worker to manager, not
      making the, 345–346
transitioning to dismissals, 266–267
trends in management
   basics of managing, 336–337
   flat organisation, creating, 338–339
   learning organisation, creating, 337–338
   open-book management, 339–340
   Six Sigma, 340–342
   Web sites for, 341
trusting your employees, 18–19, 37
trustworthiness, 225
turning points, confronting, 102–104
turnover, 302

unacceptable behaviour
   consequences of continuing, 252–253
   describing, 251
   removing, 135
   required changes to unacceptable
      behaviour, specifying, 252
Understanding Organisations (Handy), 361
unfair dismissal, 262
unwritten rules of office politics,
      uncovering the, 220–225
urgency in change management, 232

• *V* •

Venables, Terry (coach), 101
verbal abuse of others as reason for
      dismissal, 263
verbal guidance, counselling, and support,
      247–248
verbal order, 249
verbal praise, 83–84
videoconferencing, 162–163
virtual management
   advantages of, 204
   culture of company, 200–201
   disadvantages of, 205
   distance, managing from, 201
   homeworking, 203–204
   non-standard hours, 202–203
   overview, 198
   preparation for, 198–199
   recognition for, 203
   shift work, 202–203
   telecommuting, 203–204
   Web sites for, 204
virtual meetings, 162–163
visibility, protecting yourself, 227
visual aids, 173–177
voluntary redundancy, 260

• *W* •

Wafic Said Business School, University of
      Oxford (Web site), 58
waiting for the right candidate, 77–78
walk the walk, 53

Waterman, Robert H.
　In Search of European Excellence, 360
　In Search of Excellence, 357–358
Web sites
　for accounting, 307
　for change management, 240
　for coaching and development, 106
　for delegation, 45
　for discipline, 256
　for dismissals, 272
　for employee development, 333
　for ethics, 227
　for goals, 124
　for information technology, 320
　for leadership, 58
　for motivation, 96
　for office politics, 227
　for presentations, 176
　for project management, 140
　for recruitment and selection, 77
　for teams and groups, 194
　for trends in management, 341
　for virtual management, 204
　for work/life balance, 284
Weinstock, Arnold (GEC), 152
Welch, Jack (General Electric), 27
What Colour Is Your Parachute? (Bolles), 68
White, E.B. (*The Elements of Style*), 170
whiteboards, 176
Wired magazine (Web site), 320
Wise Women Network, 45
withholding information, communication
　problems due to, 165
within the company, finding candidates, 66

Woodward, Clive (coach), 101
Work & Family Connection (Web site), 284
work improvement group, 188
work unit, expressing the impact of the
　unacceptable behaviour to, 251–252
workaholic, avoid becoming, 276–277
work/life balance
　benefits of maintaining, 274
　flexible workplace, creating, 275
　overview, 273–274
　stress, managing your, 279–284
　stress, symptoms of, 277–279
　tools for managing, 275–276
　Web sites for, 284
　workaholic, avoid becoming, 276–277
Work911 (Web site), 153
Workoptions (Web site), 284
written communication, 169–170, 219–220
written praise, 83–84, 354
wrongful dismissal, 262

Xanthis Ltd (Web site), 284

Your Big Picture (Web site), 106, 333
yourself, making changes within, 240

• Z •

zero-based budgeting, 291

FOR DUMMIES®

Do Anything. Just Add Dummies

HOME

UK editions

0-7645-7027-7

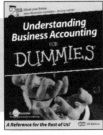

0-470-02921-8

0-7645-7054-4

PERSONAL FINANCE

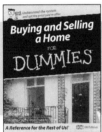

0-7645-7023-4

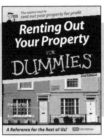

0-470-02860-2

0-7645-7039-0

BUSINESS

0-7645-7018-8

0-7645-7025-0

0-7645-7026-9

Answering Tough Interview
Questions For Dummies
(0-470-01903-4)

Arthritis For Dummies
(0-470-02582-4)

Being the Best Man
For Dummies
(0-470-02657-X)

British History
For Dummies
(0-470-03536-6)

Building Confidence
For Dummies
(0-470-01669-8)

Buying a Home on a Budget
For Dummies
(0-7645-7035-8)

Buying a Property in Eastern
Europe For Dummies
(0-7645-7047-1)

Children's Health
For Dummies
(0-470-02735-5)

Cognitive Behavioural Therapy
For Dummies
(0-470-01838-0)

CVs For Dummies
(0-7645-7017-X)

Diabetes For Dummies
(0-7645-7019-6)

Divorce For Dummies
(0-7645-7030-7)

eBay.co.uk For Dummies
(0-7645-7059-5)

European History
For Dummies
(0-7645-7060-9)

Gardening For Dummies
(0-470-01843-7)

Genealogy Online
For Dummies
(0-7645-7061-7)

Golf For Dummies
(0-470-01811-9)

Hypnotherapy For Dummies
(0-470-01930-1)

Irish History For Dummies
(0-7645-7040-4)

Marketing For Dummies
(0-7645-7056-0)

Neuro-linguistic Programming
For Dummies
(0-7645-7028-5)

Nutrition For Dummies
(0-7645-7058-7)

Parenting For Dummies
(0-470-02714-2)

Pregnancy For Dummies
(0-7645-7042-0)

Retiring Wealthy For Dummies
(0-470-02632-4)

Rugby Union For Dummies
(0-470-03537-4)

Small Business Employment
Law For Dummies
(0-7645-7052-8)

Starting a Business on
eBay.co.uk For Dummies
(0-470-02666-9)

Su Doku For Dummies
(0-470-01892-5)

The GL Diet For Dummies
(0-470-02753-3)

Thyroid For Dummies
(0-470-03172-7)

UK Law and Your Rights
For Dummies
(0-470-02796-7)

Wills, Probate and Inheritance
Tax For Dummies
(0-7645-7055-2)

Winning on Betfair
For Dummies
(0-470-02856-4)

FOR DUMMIES®

Do Anything. Just Add Dummies

HOBBIES

0-7645-5232-5

0-7645-6847-7

0-7645-5476-X

Also available:

Art For Dummies
(0-7645-5104-3)

Aromatherapy For Dummies
(0-7645-5171-X)

Bridge For Dummies
(0-471-92426-1)

Card Games For Dummies
(0-7645-9910-0)

Chess For Dummies
(0-7645-8404-9)

Improving Your Memory
For Dummies
(0-7645-5435-2)

Massage For Dummies
(0-7645-5172-8)

Meditation For Dummies
(0-471-77774-9)

Photography For Dummies
(0-7645-4116-1)

Quilting For Dummies
(0-7645-9799-X)

EDUCATION

0-7645-7206-7

0-7645-5581-2

0-7645-5422-0

Also available:

Algebra For Dummies
(0-7645-5325-9)

Algebra II For Dummies
(0-471-77581-9)

Astronomy For Dummies
(0-7645-8465-0)

Buddhism For Dummies
(0-7645-5359-3)

Calculus For Dummies
(0-7645-2498-4)

Forensics For Dummies
(0-7645-5580-4)

Islam For Dummies
(0-7645-5503-0)

Philosophy For Dummies
(0-7645-5153-1)

Religion For Dummies
(0-7645-5264-3)

Trigonometry For Dummies
(0-7645-6903-1)

PETS

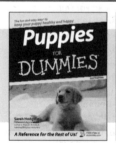

0-470-03717-2

0-7645-8418-9

0-7645-5275-9

Also available:

Labrador Retrievers
For Dummies
(0-7645-5281-3)

Aquariums For Dummies
(0-7645-5156-6)

Birds For Dummies
(0-7645-5139-6)

Dogs For Dummies
(0-7645-5274-0)

Ferrets For Dummies
(0-7645-5259-7)

Golden Retrievers
For Dummies
(0-7645-5267-8)

Horses For Dummies
(0-7645-9797-3)

Jack Russell Terriers
For Dummies
(0-7645-5268-6)

Puppies Raising & Training
Diary For Dummies
(0-7645-0876-8)

Available wherever books are sold. For more information or to order direct go to www.wiley.com or call 0800 243407 (Non UK call +44 1243 843296)

HERITAGE VISITOR ATTRACTIONS

The Editors (Anna Leask and Ian Yeoman)
dedicate this book respectively to
'Malcolm'
and
'My Father'